Jean J. Jusserand

Shakespeare in France under the Ancien Regime

Jean J. Jusserand

Shakespeare in France under the Ancien Regime

ISBN/EAN: 9783743314092

Manufactured in Europe, USA, Canada, Australia, Japa

Cover: Foto ©ninafisch / pixelio.de

Manufactured and distributed by brebook publishing software
(www.brebook.com)

Jean J. Jusserand

Shakespeare in France under the Ancien Regime

SHAKESPEARE IN FRANCE

UNDER THE ANCIEN REGIME

BY

J. J. JUSSERAND

London
T. FISHER UNWIN
PATERNOSTER SQUARE
MDCCCXCIX

TABLE OF CONTENTS

CHAPTER I

EARLY DAYS

PAGE

I. ANCIENT LITERARY RELATIONS BETWEEN FRANCE AND ENGLAND.—Praise of Chaucer by Eustache Deschamps—Opportunities for the two countries to know each other: wars, alliances, voyages, embassies, exiles, religious proscriptions — English students and learned men at the University of Paris—In France, only the *Latin* works of English authors are known and admired—Frenchmen in England—Printers: Barbier, Pynson—Guide-books and travelling notes: Paradin, Perlin, &c. ; appalling accounts of the state of the country—Character of the inhabitants; they are changeful and ferocious—Journeys of illustrious men of letters: Ronsard, Grévin, Brantôme, Du Bartas; Brantôme attends a *Mask*   1

II. DIFFERENT RESULTS OF THESE RELATIONS IN THE TWO COUNTRIES.—French literature known and imitated in London: Skelton, Barclay, Wyatt, Surrey, Spenser—French fashions at the English Court   18

English literature unknown in France—The Anglo-French grammars and dictionaries are for English use: Barclay, Palsgrave, Elyot, Saint-Lien and his dialogues, Cotgrave and Howell—Meurier's school at Antwerp—Elementary methods for merchants—Panurge's English....   20

In France, however, the importance of foreign languages is recognized: opinions of Montaigne, Ronsard, &c. ; but only Italian and Spanish are studied—Henri Estienne—

Du Bartas, Sir Philip Sidney, and James VI.—This ignorance is not caused by national animosities; the great enemy of France in those times is the Spaniard—Ever since the Conquest there exists a traditional belief that all men of note in England speak Latin or French: Morus, Camdenus, Seldenus, &c.—English protests, Starkey 24

III. FOREIGN INFLUENCES ON THE FRENCH STAGE IN THE TIME OF SHAKESPEARE.—They are solely Italian and Spanish—Starting point of dramatic art in France and England—Authorised critics in both countries are in favour of rules: Sackville, Bacon, Jonson—French classical tragedies translated into English—Classical plays at the Court of Elizabeth 32

Literature of the Valois period; Rabelais and Ronsard—Examples of survival on the stage of mediæval "gothism"—The same subjects treated in Paris and London: Roméo, César, Antoine, Pandoste ("Winter's Tale")—National history turned into dramas—Opinion of Ronsard and of La Fresnaye—Tragedies by Bounin, Chantelouve, Claude Billard, Montchrestien, &c.—Rules and liberties: Jodelle, Garnier, Grévin 35

English players in Paris—They perform at the Hôtel de Bourgogne, 1598—Clowneries and music—English comedians in Germany—At Fontainebleau, they play a bloody tragedy before Henri IV. and his son—Great impression produced on the Dauphin 50

An understanding would seem to be possible: Sidney at the Louvre at the same time as Ronsard; Sackville and Ben Jonson in Paris—Their English works remain unknown—Buchanan's Latin plays alone are familiar to French men of letters 57

CHAPTER II

THE TIME OF LOUIS QUATORZE

I. FRENCH INDEPENDENTS.—Diverging tendencies of the two dramatic arts—A group of French independents, under Louis XIII., continues, however, to resemble the

TABLE OF CONTENTS

                                                                           PAGE

English dramatists, but without knowing them—Hardy, Schélandre, Cyrano, Rotrou—Scene-shiftings and "simultaneous scenery"—Scenery of "Pandoste" ("Winter's Tale") at the Hôtel de Bourgogne—Opinion of Sidney—Influence of the Spanish drama—Lope de Vega—Dramatic ideal of Schélandre, Ogier, d'Urfé, La Calprenède, Puget de la Serre—The use of messengers blamed, praise of prose and blank verse, historical dramas, bloody sights — Shakespearean audacities, Cyrano — Shakespearean fancies, Rotrou, Quinault   62

II. TRIUMPH OF THE REGULARS.—Vagabonds disappear—Their spirit survives in secondary *genres*—The nation longs for regularity in government and in art—Richelieu. Chapelain, Mairet—"Sophonisbe," 1634—Corneille and rules : he follows them because the nation wants them—Shakespeare and his "lack of arte"; he perseveres because he has the public with him—Irregulars derided on the French stage ; the "Visionnaires," 1637—D'Aubignac's theories ; his practice ; the "Pucelle d'Orléans"   83

Increasing exigencies—Racine and Molière blamed for too much independence — The literary ideal of the seventeenth century ; Boileau and La Bruyère—Dignity, nobleness, and austerity of that ideal — Port-Royal ; Bossuet—Dictionary of the Academy and selection of words   102

III. FRENCH RELATIONS WITH ENGLAND BEFORE THE RESTORATION.—English continues to be ignored in France ; all the favour is for Italian and Spanish : Corneille, Racine, Madame de Sévigné—Corneille and England — Racine's notes on England — Boileau and foreign literatures—French, the universal language. ... 115

First translations from English ; Hall's "Characters"; Bacon's "Essays" ; Sidney's "Arcadia" — Translators' quarrels—Disdain of ambassadors for the English tongue—The "Journal des Savants" secures an interpreter, 1665. 120

Political and social relations—French literary men in London : Boisrobert, Voiture—Horror caused by the institution of the Commonwealth : ode by Boileau—Saint-Amant in London and his satire on England : his opinion on the English drama, on English actors, on Ben Jonson; on plays, interludes, masks, bloody dramas, 1644 —Coulon's guide-book, 1654 123

IV. RELATIONS WITH ENGLAND AFTER THE RESTORATION.—Cavalier poets in France; Frenchmen of mark at the Court of Charles II.—Louis XIV. asks for information about English literary and learned men—La Fontaine dreams of a journey to England—Saint Evremond and Waller 130

Guide-books and travelling notes; appreciations more detailed and less severe—Thomas Corneille and his "Dictionnaire Universel"—Sorbières and his "Relation" —The country, the women, the gladiators; singular nature of the institutions and inhabitants—Beauty and "ferocity" of the women—Le Pays' impressions—Influence of the "soil"—Football and "coacres"—Letters of Muralt; guide-books by Misson, Beeverel, Moreau de Brasey; dialogues by Miège; remarks of G. L. Lesage; impressions of Chappuzeau—The English language— Coffee-houses and theatres—The stage free in London, encumbered with benches in Paris 136

The two dramatic arts—Shakespeare remodelled in London; Racine disdained; Corneille and Molière transformed—Saint-Evremond ignores Shakespeare, but knows Jonson—Sorbières carries back to France the Duchess of Newcastle's plays—Muralt and Moreau de Brasey mention Shakespeare (but their works are only published in the eighteenth century) 158

V. ENGLAND BETTER KNOWN: FIRST IDEA OF SHAKESPEARE. — Histories of England: Vanel, Rosemond, Larrey—Translations from English; Rycaut and the "Bajazet" of Racine — Addison's "Spectator" in French, 1714—Literary periodicals take more notice of England—First English play adapted for the French stage: Otway's "Venice Preserved" turned into a "Manlius" by La Fosse, 1698—The "Femme poussée à bout," taken from Vanbrugh, 1700 165

Shakespeare crosses the sea—A copy of his works in Louis XIV.'s library; another in Fouquet's—Opinion of the king's librarian on Shakespeare—Shakespeare's name

printed for the first time in a French book, 1685-86—
Judgment of Boyer 170
Apogee and decline of the classic drama in France ... 178

CHAPTER III

THE EIGHTEENTH CENTURY—PART I

1715-1750

I. TOWARDS ANGLOMANIA.—Increasing attention given to English letters—Matthew Prior in Paris—French Review solely devoted to English works, 1717—Various Reviews and translations—The Englishman on the stage; French and English characters, Boissy, 1727—Marivaux and the "Spectateur François"; his "Ile de la Raison," 1727 ... 180
Destouches chargé d'affaires in London—Influence of England on Destouches' plays—Abbé Prévost in London; his descriptions of England; he learns the language on account of Mrs. Oldfield—His judgment on the English drama and on Shakespeare—The celebrated Figg—English manners, "mylords" and men of the people—Rudeness of the people—La Condamine's experience—The "Pour et Contre" of Prévost, 1733 188
Voltaire in London, 1726-29—His impressions on landing—His opinion on the English language—He knows Pope, Swift, and all the worldly and literary society—He sees "Julius Cæsar" performed—His "Lettres sur les Anglais;" irony and paradoxes—Satire on the ideas accepted in France—Importance of literary art in his eyes: that is his real religion—Judgment on English dramatic art and on Shakespeare—The Gardens of Marly—Great stir caused by the "Lettres"—Protestations raised by them—Grévin *versus* Shakespeare 200
II. THE KNOWLEDGE OF SHAKESPEARE SPREADS.—Opinion of Montesquieu—Historical dictionaries—Essays and criticisms by Abbé Prévost, Louis Riccoboni, Abbé Le Blanc: the magic of Shakespeare's style—Opinion of Louis Racine 214

First attempt to translate Shakespeare's works, La Place, 1745—His "Discours sur le Théâtre Anglois"—Success of the undertaking 220

III. INFLUENCE OF SHAKESPEARE AND OF THE ENGLISH DRAMA ON THE FRENCH STAGE.—Survival of the spirit of liberty—The opera, its scope, scenic effects, and changes of place—Concessions made formerly by Abbé d'Aubignac, Thomas Corneille, Boileau—An opera by Boileau and Racine—Perrault's "Parallèle"—The liberal programme: emancipation of the vocabulary—Protests of La Motte-Houdard against verse, narratives, confidants, and rules 224

Dramatists follow theorists from afar—They seek for novelty, but without departing from rules which the public always demands—Crébillon, the unities, the horrible—Crébillon head of a school of art; visit of Mercier—Same situation on the comic stage: novelty and respect for rules—La Chaussée and the "Comédie larmoyante"—Imitation of English domestic dramas—Addison imitated by Destouches 232

IV. VOLTAIRE'S INNOVATIONS.—His love for dramatic art—Tragedy an affair of State; it helps to improve morals—Audacity and activity of Voltaire in every branch of human knowledge—His timidity as soon as it is a question of dramatic art—He feels that reforms are necessary; but he wants them to be very moderate—He pronounces in favour of rules, against prose and blank verse 241

He would like to augment the number of speakers—Unfortunate attempts to show death by poison on the stage, 1724—Scenic effect and change of place in the same town, "Brutus"—A play without love: "La Mort de César"—A transparent coulisse—Direct influence of Shakespeare: "Zaïre" and "Othello"; "Eryphile," "Sémiramis," and "Hamlet"—The stage freed of benches in 1759—Ghosts on the stage, 1732, 1748 ... 247

Various experiments—Gresset risks the murder of a villain on the stage, 1740—President Hénault imitates Shakespeare's historical dramas; his "François II." in prose—Diffusion of English ideas: "l'Anglicisme nous gagne," 1750 264

CHAPTER IV

THE EIGHTEENTH CENTURY—PART II

1750 TO THE REVOLUTION

I. ANGLOMANIA AND FRANCOMANIA.—" Anglicism "—
Good society learns English — English fashions and
novels ; "thé à l'anglaise," "matinée à l'anglaise," everything " à l'anglaise "—French fashions in London ... 270
    Reviews and gazettes " Britanniques "—Guide-books
and notes on journeys to England—Sentimental and
philosophical travellers : sketches and vignettes ... 275
    Favour enjoyed by English literary men in Paris—
Walpole and Madame du Deffand ; Chesterfield and
Madame de Tencin ; Gibbon and Voltaire ; Sterne and
Diderot ; Hume and the Duchesse de La Vallière—
Enthusiasm for Garrick ; his visits to France—Scene
from " Macbeth " acted in dumb show—Relations of
Garrick with Collé, Marmontel, Madame Necker,
Beaumarchais, de Belloy, Clairon, Ducis, &c.—His
great influence 284
    Parallel influence of French ideas in London—Respect
for Boileau's doctrines—Pope ; Blair's Rhetoric—The
old English drama remodelled and attenuated—Shakespeare severely judged by Chesterfield, Hume, and
Gibbon—Garrick covers his nudity ; he raises a Greek
temple to him 296
    Sensibility, tears, brotherhood : Rousseau—Pastoral
emotions—The old austerity is blunted—The word
" Monsieur "—Nature—Opinions of Voltaire, Madame
Victoire, Lieutenant Bonaparte 302

II. RESULTS OF THESE TENDENCIES ON THE FRENCH
STAGE.—Costumes and declamation : Clairon, Le Kain,
Talma—Dramatic methods : Alliance of Thalia and
Melpomene—Continuation of tearful comedy—Tragedies
in prose—" Bourgeois " heroes—The "serious *genre*,"
the "serious drama," "the sombre drama" : Diderot,
Sedaine, Saurin, Beaumarchais, Baculard, Mercier—
Increasing sombreness of the French stage—Theory of
the " sombre "—Going beyond Hercules' columns—

Resemblances and differences of taste in the two countries—Popularity of Young and of Ossian in France—Misinterpretations by Hogarth and Gravelot 311

Protestations: war is inevitable—Make-believe war—Abbé Le Blanc; his caricature of Racinian-Shakespearean dramas—Cubières and his "Manie des drames sombres"—Cubières' sombre dramas 329

III. WAR ABOUT SHAKESPEARE.—Real war, its causes: the Jubilee; the translation by Le Tourneur and others, dedicated to the King, 1776—Preface to the translation—Growing fame of Shakespeare; articles in reviews, in the "Encyclopédie," in critical literary works: Diderot, the Chevalier de Jaucourt, Marmontel, Mercier 354

Growing irritation of Voltaire—Letters and essays concerning Shakespeare—Preliminary skirmishes: Mrs. Montagu "la Shakespearienne," Horace Walpole ... 369

War in due form—Officers, soldiers, deserters—Voltaire's letters to d'Argental and d'Alembert—First letter to the Academy, read by d'Alembert, August 25, 1776—Its great effect—Gille-Shakespeare—Fear of an offensive return of the enemy—Anxious correspondence between "Bertrand" and "Raton" 370

Second campaign, 1778—Voltaire's return to Paris, his triumph, his classical "Irène"—New letter to the Academy—Plan for a new dictionary and for the emancipation of the French language—Liberty everywhere except on the tragic stage 391

IV. RESULTS OF THE WAR.—Continued success of Le Tourneur—Replies to Voltaire—Mrs. Montagu, Baretti, Rutledge, Mercier—The question of patriotism: Mercier, Chastellux... 397

V. SHAKESPEARE ON THE FRENCH STAGE.—Great precautions still required—Survival of classical tastes—Desforges' Latin; Lemierre's arrow 405

Attempt to reduce Shakespearean dramas to the three unities — Drawing-room performances: Chastellux's "Roméo" with a happy ending; the Marquise de Gléon—Spectacles dans un fauteuil: Douin's "Othello," and Butini's — A Shakespearean comedy, by Collot d'Herbois 407

A continuous effort made by Ducis—His character, his poetical methods—He adds to the "sombre" of the English drama, but reduces Shakespeare to the unities—Narratives, confidants, &c.—The "mœurs fluettes" and persistent susceptibilities—"Hamlet," "Romeo," "Lear," "Othello," &c., on the stage—The interpretation: Brizard, Molé, Madame Vestris, Talma 414

VI. THE PERIOD OF THE REVOLUTION.— Persistent timidities—Dramas of Mercier and Marie-Joseph Chénier—The ancient régime survives for tragedy—Judgment of Châteaubriand: Shakespeare as obscure and misshapen as a Gothic cathedral, 1801-2—Judgment of Fiévée, Palissot, Madame de Stael—Legouvé—Pantomimes and ballets drawn from Shakespeare... 438

EPILOGUE

Continuation of classical methods under the Restoration—Romantic and classic writers—Shakespeare hissed, 1822—Stendhal's demands—Poets, painters, and critics—Hugo, Delacroix, Sainte-Beuve, Guizot—The romantic period according to Gautier 449

Shakespeare played in Paris in English, 1827-28—Great success and influence of these performances—Hugo, Dumas, Berlioz—Articles by Charles Magnin and the Duc de Broglie— Preface of "Cromwell" — Dumas' "Hamlet"—Opinion of Flaubert—Shakespearean personages and dramas vulgarised in France: adaptations, drawings, music 454

Conclusion — Final result of these literary wars: "Attila-Shakespeare" has enslaved no one, but has helped the romantic movement and the emancipation of 1830—The French dramatic muse has become more fecund than ever before—The movement of 1830, on which Shakespeare had a marked influence, has given fresh vitality to the French stage 464

INDEX 471

EXPLANATORY LIST OF ILLUSTRATIONS

PAGE

1.—Brizard, the comedian, as King Lear in the adaptation by Ducis of Shakespeare's play, painted by Madame Guiard, a member of the French Royal Academy of Painting, engraved by J. J. Avril .... *Frontispiece*

2.—Part of the *Theatres' Corner* in Southwark, from the large plate by the Dutch engraver Claes Jan Visscher, born 1580 (Bryan), showing "the Globe" and the "Bear Garden" (on another part of the plate, more to the west, is shown "the Swan"). The plate is accompanied with a Description of London in Latin and in French, " A Amsterdam imprimé chez Judocus Hondius, 1620." Reductions of that plate were published in Paris for French use, with some of the inscriptions in French : " Profil de la ville de Londre cappitalle du Royaume d'Angleterre." One of those adaptations was the work of the celebrated Aveline, time of Louis XIV. 37

3.—The meeting of Doraste and Faunia (Florizel
and Perdita in " Winter's Tale ") from a late
French adaptation of Greene's " Pandosto "
(the original made use of by Shakespeare) :
" Histoire tragique de Pandolphe," Paris,
1722, illustrated. Cf. " English Novel in
the Time of Shakespeare," p. 178 ... 41

4.—The Great Hall at Fontainebleau, built
under Charles IX., called afterwards the
" Salle de la Belle Cheminée," on account
of a beautiful chimney carved by Jaquet,
alias Grenoble, during the reign of Henri
IV. (sculptures representing, *e.g.*, the battle
of Ivry). As it was the largest hall in
the palace it was used for pageants and ceremonies,
such as the one here represented by
Abraham Bosse : " Disposition a la séance
tenue à Fontainebleau à la création de Messieurs
les Chevaliers, faite le 14me May,
1633." Plays were sometimes performed
there, and a regular stage was erected in it in
the same year, 1633. The Hall was after
that called " Salle de la Comédie." The
remains of the chimney were scattered (some
are now in the Louvre) though much more
worthy of perfect preservation, wrote Abbé
Guilbert dolefully, than the " légères beautés
d'un vil théâtre, écueil trop ordinaire de la
chasteté et de l'innocence, qui y apprennent
toujours l'art funeste d'y faire un inévitable
naufrage." The hall was entirely repainted
and regilt, and new boxes were added, in 1725,

by Claude Audran. It suffered severely in a
fire in 1856; and it stands now as ruinous
and desolate as it used formerly to be brilliant
and full of "légères beautés." Only the four
walls with their plain outside decoration and
the double external staircase remain.... 53

5.—The mansions for the performance of a
mystery; from the MS. of the Valenciennes
Passion, 1547, preserved in the National
Library, Paris, MS., Fr. 12,536. The large
folding miniature at the beginning of the
volume, and here reproduced, is inscribed:
"Le teatre ou hourdement pourtraict comme
il estoit quant fut jouee le mistere de la
Passion." A name is ascribed to each
mansion: Paradis, Nazareth, Le Temple,
Hierusalem, l'enfer (Hell, with guns), &c.
The MS. is illustrated throughout; Salomé
does not tumble as she used to during the
Middle Ages; far from being mediæval, her
dancing rather recalls modern ballets, fol. 136 63

6.—"Thebes written in great letters upon an
olde doore" (Philip Sidney).—"Babilonia"
in the fresco of Benozzo Gozzoli at the
Camp Santo of Pisa, representing the building
of the Tower of Babel, second half of fifteenth
century 67

7.—Scenery for the performance of "Pandoste ou
la Princesse Malheureuse" ("Winter's Tale"),
at the Hôtel de Bourgogne, 1631, first day.
The play, by Puget de la Serre, was divided
into two "journees," each having five acts.

      We possess the original sketch drawn by the scene-shifter of the hôtel, and from which the scenery for each day was painted; preserved in the valuable album of the "machiniste," Laurent Mahélot (MS., Fr. 24,330 in the National Library, Paris); this album contains also sketches for plays by Rotrou, Mairet, Hardy, &c.; and in a later hand, notes and lists of movables for the performance of plays by Corneille, Racine, Molière....   71

8 —"Pandoste ou la Princesse Malheureuse," 2^d day, from the same MS. as the above. The scenery represents the house of the peasants who brought up "Faunia" (Perdita), the palaces of Pandoste (Leontes) and of Agatocles (Polixenes), and the wood where Doraste (Florizel) met Faunia   75

9.—The performance of a comedy at the "Hôtel de Bourgogne" (the only permanent playhouse in Paris up to 1629) showing the latest embellishments introduced there in the days of Abraham Bosse, the author of the plate (time of Louis XIII.). The inscription below runs :—

> "Que ce théâtre est magnifique !
> Que ces acteurs sont inventifs !
> Et qu'ils ont de préservatifs
> Contre l'humeur mélancolique !" &c.

      The comedians on the stage are the typical *farceurs* of the period : Turlupin who acts the robber, Gros Guillaume "troussé comme un joueur de paume," Gaultier Garguille, with his mask, and then, right and left, staring at each other, a French "seigneur," and a Spanish braggadocio. Notice, on each side, the balustrades already shown in Mahélot's drawing for the second day of "Pandoste." The chandeliers alluded to by Perrault (*see* below, p. 88) hung in front of the curtain and were lowered during the *entractes*; then candle-snuffers performed their duty; *see* the engraving by Coypel of Moliere's playhouse, below, No. 20   85

10.—The third act of "Mirame," a tragedy written by Desmarets de Saint Sorlin and Cardinal de Richelieu, performed with great splendour on the stage of Richelieu's palace in 1639. The original edition, "Mirame," Paris, 1641, fol., has a plate for each act, by Stephen Della Bella. As the unity of place is observed the landscape is the same in all the plates. We are supposed to be in Bithynia, though the actors are dressed in Louis XIII. costumes : " La scene est dans le jardin du palais royal d'Heracle, regardant sur la mer"   89

11.—" Le soir," King Louis XIII. at the play, with Queen Anne of Austria, their son the future Louis XIV., Gaston d'Orleans, and a dog. The theatre represented seems to be the famous one built by Richelieu in his palace at Paris, though the royal arms are displayed above the stage, whereas the arms

of the cardinal had in reality been sculptured
there. But, except for that, the general similitude is striking ; compare the aperture of the
stage in No. 10 above.

In the companion plate, " Le Matin," King
Louis XIII. is seen walking in his gardens 93

12.—An Italian Theatre of the time of Shakespeare. The *Teatro Olimpico* of Vicenza, built
from the drawings of Palladio, after 1580.
Many other theatres were erected in Italy, at the
same period, also in imitation of the theatres
of the ancients ; the best known being the
one at Parma (1618); the least known, but
scarcely less curious, the little theatre built
by Scamozzi in the tourist-ignored town of
Sabbionetta, sixteenth century. The drawing
of Scamozzi with his receipt for "trenta doble
d'oro di Spagna " is to be seen in the museum
at Vicenza 99

13.—A dress for the country, time of Louis XIV.,
" Dame allant à la campagne," by Le Pautre ;
the lady is dressed in lace and embroidery ;
the " country " is a park with cut trees and
stone balustrades 109

14.—The members of the French Academy addressing Louis XIV. on the occasion of the
issue of the first vol. of their Dictionary,
1694. Frontispiece of the dedicatory epistle
to the King. " I. B. Corneille inv. ; I. Mariette
sc." (Jean Baptiste Corneille, painter and
engraver 1649-95 ; Jean Mariette, engraver
and publisher, 1660-1742) 113

15.—"Madame la Duchesse de Bouillon" (Marie-Anne Mancini), niece of Cardinal Mazarin, and one of the admired of La Fontaine. "A Paris, chez J. Mariette, aux Colonnes d'Hercule." La Fontaine wanted to come to England with her in 1687 133
16.—" Coacres et coacresse dans leurs assemblées," a meeting of Quakers, from Misson's "Mémoires et observations faites par un voyageur en Angleterre," La Haye, 1698, 12° 141
17.—"Montague House, now the British Museum" (before its reconstruction) from a plate dated 1813, "Ackerman's Repository of Arts" 145
18.—French officers smoking their pipes; engraved by Abraham Bosse, after Saint Igny, time of Louis XIII. Lines underneath :—

"Quand nous sommes remplis d'humeur melancolique,
La vapeur du tabac ravive nos esprits," &c.

Coffee-houses were not at first so numerous and well frequented in Paris as in London; most travellers notice the difference. In the eighteenth century, however, those places increased immensely in number and importance, and the French capital had nothing to envy the English one in this respect. Mercier writes : "On compte six à sept cents cafés ; c'est le refuge ordinaire des oisifs et l'asyle des indigens. . . . Dans quelques uns de ces cafés on tient bureau académique ; on y juge les auteurs, les pièces de théâtre . . . et les poètes qui vont débuter y font ordinairement plus de bruit, ainsi que ceux qui, chassés de la carrière par les sifflets, deviennent ordinairement satiriques ; car le plus impitoyable des critiques est toujours un auteur sifflé." "Tableau de Paris," 1782, i. p. 227

19.—How men of quality, in the time of Louis XIV., stood on the stage and listened, when so disposed, to a play : " Homme de qualité sur le théâtre de l'opéra.—Saint Jean delin., 1687." They stood if they liked, but they had stools and could sit if they preferred ; they had the same privilege at the comedy as at the opera ...   .

20.—Molière's play-house, as represented by Coypel in his "Suite d'Estampes," to illustrate Molière's comedies, 1726. The one here reproduced (in part) serves as a frontispiece to the edition ; it shows the standing pit, the chandeliers lowered to the level of the boards, as they used to be during the intervals of the acts, and, through a raised corner of the curtain, the gentlemen allowed to have seats on the stage ...   .

21.—The death of Cato ; frontispiece of " Caton, tragédie par M. Addison ; chez Jacob Tonson, à la tête de Shakespeare." Addison's " Cato " translated by Boyer, 1713 ; plate by Du Guernier ...   .

22.—Abbé Prévost, the author of " Manon Lescaut," " aumônier de S. A. S. Mgr. le

Prince de Conti, dessiné à Paris d'après nature, et gravé à Berlin par G. F. Schmidt, graveur du roy, en 1745" 189

23.—" Mrs. Oldfield, the celebrated comedian.—Richardson pinxit—Edward Fisher fecit " ... 193

24.—James Figg, the pugilist and swordsman (described by Abbé Prévost), painted by I. Ellys, engraved by I. Faber. Inscription below :—

"The mighty combatant, the first in fame,
The lasting glory of his native Thame,
Rash and unthinking men ! at length be wise,
Consult your safety and resign the prize,
Nor tempt superior force, but timely fly
The vigour of his arm, the quickness of his eye."

Figg died in 1734 197

25.—Voltaire at twenty-four (1718), engraved by P. A. Tardieu, after Largillière 201

26.—A French view of Greenwich, by Rigaud, 1736, who also engraved plates representing St. James's Park, Hampton Court, &c. His enthusiasm for Greenwich seems to have equalled Voltaire's own ; the plate bears the inscription: " Veue de Greenwich dessiné à côté de l'observatoire, au haut de la colline. De cet endroit on aperçoit de tous les côtés de Greenwich un vaste et délicieux païs et la ville de Londres dans l'éloignement avec le cours de la Tamise, chargée d'une quantité étonante de vaisseaux de toutes grandeurs et de toutes les parties du monde, ce qui fait un aspect admirable.—Paris, chez l'auteur "... 205

LIST OF ILLUSTRATIONS

PAGE

27.—The cut trees of Marly—" Vue générale et en perspective du Jardin, Pavillon, Berceaux ... du château de Marly. Fait par Aveline" 211

28.—" Armide," an opera by Quinault, music by Lully; frontispiece by Berain, engraved by Dolivar, 1686, showing the destruction of the palace of Armide as represented at the Opera 227

29.—" L'auteur siflé." A late eighteenth or early nineteenth century coloured print 233

30.—Mlle. Clairon's visit to Ferney, an unsigned engraving, but the undoubted work of Huber. In their mutual emotion and admiration, Clairon and Voltaire both fell on their knees, worshipping each other's genius. Voltaire, it seems, worshipped longer than he wanted, on account of the difficulty he had in rising. Huber had taken upon himself to preserve for posterity " the countless laughable incidents which happened every other day in that strange Ferney" (Desnoiresterres, " Iconographie Voltairienne," 1879, p. 49). Neither the remonstrances nor the irritation of Voltaire could ever stop Huber, who was always present at Ferney, as a sort of familiar demon, with an ever ready pencil 239

31.—" Les petits Comédiens," by Gravelot, showing how men of quality were seated on the stage, in the eighteenth century; they are seen talking, taking refreshments, &c. This was one of the most famous shows of the

Boulevards ; the actors were children. They were visited by Goldoni : " Ce sont des enfants qui accompagnent si adroitement avec leurs gestes la voix des hommes et des femmes qui chantent dans la coulisse que l'on a cru d'abord et que l'on a parié que c'étaient les enfants eux-mêmes qui chantaient." "Mémoires," 1787, iii., p. 145. As the play is going on, the chandeliers are raised ; compare plate No. 20 253

32.—A performance of Voltaire's tragedy of "Sémiramis," after the removal of the benches for gentlemen, which used to encumber the stage ; drawn by Gravelot, engraved by Massard. On the right, the tomb of Ninus, with Sémiramis dying. *Arzace :—*

"Quelle victime, ô ciel, a donc frappé ma rage ? "

" Œuvres complètes de Voltaire," Genève, 1768 261

33.—Voltaire as a tragic actor, a plate satirizing Voltaire's classical performances : " Le héros de Ferney au théâtre de Châtelaine—T. O. ft., 1772." Below, these lame lines :—

"Ne prétens pas à trop, tu ne scaurais qu'écrire,
  Tes vers forcent mes pleurs, mais tes gestes me font rire."

Voltaire had a temporary theatre, made of planks, erected at Châtelaine, near Ferney,

LIST OF ILLUSTRATIONS

beyond the limits of the Geneva canton; he used it during the period when he did not dare openly to infringe the Genevan decrees forbidding theatrical representations ... 285

34.—Garrick; his portrait by C. N. Cochin, the son (1715-90) 289

35.—Shakespeare, his marble statue bequeathed by Garrick to the British Museum, the work (1758) of Louis François Roubillac of Lyons, a pupil of Coustou. This was the second statue raised to Shakespeare; the first was the one in Westminster Abbey (1741) the work of Scheemakers, a Fleming. The third (according to M. Sidney Lee's list) was an adaptation of the two former. The fourth was the work of M. Ward, an American; the fifth was again due to a Frenchman, M. Paul Fournier, and has lately been erected in Paris. The sixth—the first one due to an English chisel—was inaugurated in 1888 at Stratford, and is the work of Lord Ronald Gower. (A plaster model of it was exhibited in the Paris salon of 1881) 303

36.—The "Shepherds' Refuge," one of the usual ornaments of a "parc à l'anglaise," in the park of Count d'Albon, Prince of Yvetot, at Franconville; second half of the eighteenth century. Le Prieur, "Tableau pittoresque de la vallée de Montmorency," first edition: "Tempé et Paris," 1784, 8°, 2nd., 1788 ... 307

37.—Theatrical declamation, by Eisen; "de Ghendt sc.," illustrating a passage in "La

Déclamation théâtrale, poème," by Dorat, 1766 :—

"Ne va point imiter ces sorcières obscures
Qui n'ont rien d'infernal si ce n'est la figure."

Dorat knew " Macbeth," Makbet, as he calls it, very well, and seems to allude here to the three weird sisters with whom the lady represented by Eisen has as little in common as the poet could wish 313

38.—" L'Avare, The Miser," of Molière, an engraving by Van der Gucht after Hogarth in "The Works of Molière, French and English," London, 1739, 10 vols., 12º, vol. ii. This edition has French and English illustrations by Hogarth, Hambleton, Boucher, &c. The differences in style are striking, as Boucher exaggerates the elegance of his originals, and Hambleton their coarseness; Boucher's Scapin looks a much more distinguished person than Hambleton's Valère (in " The School for Husbands," vol. iii.). The scene here represented is the last in the comedy of " L'Avare," when Anselme and Valère discover that they are father and son, while Harpagon puts out one of the two candles 323

39.—Hamlet. " Hayman inv.—Gravelot sc.," from the Oxford edition of Shakespeare's works, 1744, 6 vols. 4º. Hayman seems merely to have supplied the subjects; Gravelot treated them in his own ultra-French style. Another series of illustrations for Shakespeare was provided by Gravelot (who was then staying in England and had Gainsborough for his pupil), and adorned Theobald's edition of the plays, London, 1757, 7 vols., 12º. In this case Gravelot supplied the drawings, but much of his characteristic elegance disappeared under the hand of Van der Gucht the engraver.... 327

40.—" La tendre humanité," the milk of human kindness. Count d'Albon, Prince of Yvetot, had instituted distributions of soup to the poor in his castle at Franconville; the interest elicited by " l'humanité " was so great in the second half of the eighteenth century that the humane deed of Count d'Albon was made the subject of an engraving : "Étude d'après nature représentant un pauvre venant chercher la soupe chez M. le Comte d'Albon à Franconville," 1784, reproduced in " Tableau pittoresque de la vallée de Montmorency," by Le Prieur 331

41.—The chevalier Michel de Cubières de Palmezeaux, 1785, engraved by the famous diplomatist and engraver, Vivant Denon, another familiar demon of Voltaire's, and the author of several funny plates representing the patriarch at home. The plates had an immense success with everybody except Voltaire 341

42.—"Caverne d'Young," a favourite subject with

landscape gardeners of the second half of the eighteenth century. The one here represented figured among the ornaments of the " parc à l'anglaise" of Count d'Albon, at Franconville in the Montmorency valley. " Passers-by," says Le Prieur in his description of the park, " stop with a shudder before a cave whose dark and frightful appearance proclaims the name of him to whom it was dedicated. The inscription fits the place and recalls the character of the man on account of whom it was made : 'Caverne d'Young'" 351

43.—Le Tourneur (Pierre Félicien), principal author of the first complete translation of Shakespeare's plays in French. " A. Pujas del. ad vivum, 1787.—Ch. L. Lingée, sculp., 1788" 355

44.—The statue of Voltaire by Pigalle, now preserved in the library of the Institute, Paris. The inscription runs : " A Monsieur de Voltaire, par les gens de lettres ses compatriotes et ses contemporains, 1776." It was begun at Ferney in June, 1770 ; Pigalle modelled the head from the original ; the rest from an old soldier who sat to him in Paris (so we read in the " Correspondance Littéraire de Grimm et Diderot," ed. Tourneux, ix., 285.) The man was in any case well chosen, as the remarkable way in which Voltaire's skeleton accorded with the statue was noticed by M. Berthelot when the tomb was opened in 1897 363

	PAGE
45.—Silly "Gille," one of the familiar characters of the "Théâtre de la foire"; time of Voltaire	371
46.—A view of the English Vauxhall drawn by Canaletto during his stay in England, engraved by Müller, 1751 : "Vue du temple de Comus dans les Jardins de Vauxhall." The boxes where people had their dinners were adorned with pictures by Hayman (the same who illustrated Shakespeare in conjunction with Gravelot), and by Hogarth ...	377
47.—The French Vauxhall, "Vue du Vauxhall de la foire Saint Germain, 1772"	381
48.—Voltaire, the year before his death : "Le vieux malade de Fernex tel qu'on l'a vu en Septembre, 1777;" drawn from life, four months before he left Ferney for his last journey to Paris	385
49.—The crowning of Voltaire in his box by Brizard the comedian and by "Belle-et-Bonne" (the pet name of the Marquise de Villette) on the night of "Irène"; to the right, fat Madame Denis, Voltaire's niece; from a contemporary plate inscribed : "Anecdote de l'homme unique à tout âge." The plate shows the sort of railings which divided the pit from the orchestra. Observe, in the corner of the pit, one of the grenadiers (with a cocked hat, his bayonet visible) who were posted there to maintain order. "Le théâtre," said Mercier, "semble une prison gardée à vue," "Tableau de Paris," chap.	

743. Voltaire's box was in reality on the left, as seen in the following plate 389
50.—The crowning of Voltaire's bust, in his presence, at the French Comedy, after the performance of "Irène," March 30, 1778, from a drawing by Moreau the younger, who was present, and who began his sketch on the same night 393
51.—Sébastien Mercier ; a caricature. (A number were published in his day ; in another plate he is represented as an ass covering antique statues with filth, and trampling the works of Racine under his hoofs). This one is inscribed : "Érostrate moderne écrivant sur les arts" 401
52.—Madame Riccoboni (Marie Jeanne Laboras de Mézières), "Bovinet sc." 410
53.—"Mr. Garrick in 'Hamlet,' Act I., sc. iv.," from his portrait by B. Wilson, engraved by J. Mac Ardell 417
54.—Mlle. Fleury as Ophelia, "rôle d'Orfélie dans Hamlet," the "Hamlet" of Ducis. She is represented delivering the line—

"Tu cours venger ton père, et moi sauver le mien."

(She is the daughter of Claudius in the play as adapted by Ducis). From "Costumes et annales des grands théâtres de Paris, ouvrage périodique," by M. de Charnois, 1786, 4 vols., vol. ii., No. xxiii. 421
55.—Ducis writing "Léar," engraved by J. J.

Avril from the painting by Madame Guiard "de l'Académie royale de peinture" ... 427

56.—Miss Smithson (afterwards Madame Berlioz) as Ophelia, by A. de Valmont; "Le Théâtre Anglais à Paris, Mlle. Smithson, rôle d'Offelia dans Hamlet" 457

57.—The players' scene in "Hamlet," one of sixteen lithographs by Eugène Delacroix, illustrating Hamlet; this one, dated 1835. "Votre Majesté et nous avons la conscience libre; cela ne nous touche en rien..." Compare same subject, engraved by Gravelot, above, No. 38 461

SHAKESPEARE IN FRANCE

UNDER THE ANCIEN RÉGIME

CHAPTER I

EARLY DAYS

IN 1645 Jean Blaeu published the fourth part of the "Théâtre du Monde," a magnificent work in folio, printed in Amsterdam, in which all countries and towns are described. Stratford-on-Avon, where the great English dramatist was born, and in whose old mossy church he now sleeps, is not overlooked; the following lines are devoted to it :—

"The Avone . . . passes against Stratford, a rather agreeable little trading place, but which owes all its glory to two of its nurslings : to wit, John de Stratford, Archbishop of Canterbury, who built a temple there, and Hugh de Clopton, judge at London, who threw across the Avone, at great cost, a bridge of fourteen arches."

That is all. Of Shakespeare not a word ; he evidently did not deserve, according to the author of the " Théâtre du Monde," to be counted amongst those nurslings whom a town may be proud of. Stratford had produced an archbishop and a judge ; that was enough for her glory.

A hundred and twenty years later, in 1765, appeared the fifteenth volume of the famous " Encyclopédie." There, too, an article was devoted to Stratford-on-Avon. The article was written by the Chevalier de Jaucourt, and we read in it :—

" Not long ago was still shown in that town the house in which Shakespeare (William) had died in 1616 ; it was even regarded as one of the curiosities of the place ; the inhabitants regretted its destruction, so jealously they glory in the birth of that sublime genius, the greatest known in dramatic poetry."

The article is five columns long, and is entirely dedicated to Shakespeare. The change is striking enough. Shakespeare, so little known that his name did not even come to mind when Stratford was spoken of, is now a "sublime genius, the greatest known in dramatic poetry." The causes of that change, the varying events which brought it about, the quarrels which attended it, and in which the most illustrious men of letters in France and England took part, are well worthy of attention.[1] Their history is intimately

[1] The question, in at least some of its aspects, has been studied before in such works as the book by Lacroix on the " Influence de Shakespeare sur le Théâtre Français," Brussels, 1856 (very meritorious for its time), and the articles by Rathery on the "Relations entre la France et l'Angleterre" (" Revue Contemporaine," 1855). See also the important work devoted by M. Texte

connected with that of French literary tastes and ideals—tastes and ideals sometimes accepted, sometimes contested, but never ignored in Europe from the age of St. Louis to our own.

I.

When old Deschamps wrote, five centuries ago, in the middle of the Hundred Years' War, his graceful and now famous compliment to that "great translator," Geoffrey Chaucer, he had no idea he was performing an unprecedented and peerless deed, a deed that was to remain for centuries unique of its kind. His praise, it is true, was of a limited sort; Chaucer was for him "of worldly loves god in England," only because he had translated the "Romaunt of the Rose." The English poet sang, perhaps, of Troilus; he told, maybe, tales on the road to Canterbury; Deschamps never heard of that; no one did in France; no other French poet spoke of any other English poet for ages. When the Renaissance came, Chaucer was totally ignored in France, and Deschamps himself was scarcely better known.

Yet, the connection and intercourse between the two nations was never interrupted; in peace and in war they remained constantly in touch. The kings of France had Scotch auxiliaries who swore "by Saint Treignan" and spoke Scottish; English students

to "J. J. Rousseau et le cosmopolitisme littéraire," Paris, 1895. Part of the present work appeared in "Cosmopolis," 1896-97; chapter i. was published in a condensed shape (and under a title not of my own choosing) in the "Nineteenth Century," 1898.

elbowed French students at the Paris University; the sovereigns accredited to each other poets and authors of fame as ambassadors. Charles VII. of France was represented by Alain Chartier in Scotland; Charles VIII. by the humanist, Robert Gaguin in England, the said Gaguin falling into a mad quarrel with the rash laureate of the early Tudors. Skelton aimed wild invectives at him, but allotted to him none the less a crown of laurel and a place by the side of Apollo; for, after all, one must be just. Homer, Cicero, and Petrarch were therefore to be seen on Skelton's Parnassus—

"With a frere of Fraunce men call syr Gagwyne,
That frownyd on me full angerly and pale."[1]

And well he might. Henry VIII. sent as ambassadors to France the cleverest poets of his day, those who best understood the delicate art of sonnet writing, the greatest admirers of Petrarch, and of the French and Italian models, poets who were impregnated with the spirit of the Renaissance, such men as Sir Thomas Wyatt, and " thee "—Bryan—" who knows how great a grace in writing is." But neither helped to spread in France a knowledge of English poetry. Bryan in particular made himself famous only as a matchless drinker. Little importance should be attached to his despatches, wrote the Constable of Montmorency, when he has written them "after supper."[2] The English

[1] "Garlande or Chapelet of Laurell"; "Works," Dyce, i. p. 371.
[2] Letter from Constable de Montmorency, 1538. "Correspondance de Castillon et de Marillac," Paris, ed. Kaulek, 1885, p. 78.

poet, Sackville, was ambassador to France during the reign of Elizabeth ; and the French poet, Du Bartas, was sent on diplomatic missions several times, to the English and the Scottish courts.

Marriages tightened periodically the bonds between the royal and aristocractic families of the French-speaking and English-speaking countries. Mary, the sister of Henry VIII., married Louis XII. ; James V. of Scotland, married first a daughter of Francis I., then the beautiful Marie de Guise ; Marot celebrated in French the first marriage, and Lyndesay deplored in English the early death of the princess.[1] Mary Stuart, great-niece to Henry VIII., began her royal career as Queen of the French ; interminable negotiations prepared a union between Elizabeth and the House of France. Later on a daughter of Henri IV. of France became Queen of England ; a sister of Charles II. married the brother of Louis XIV.

Numerous Englishmen visited Paris in the sixteenth century and appeared either at court or at the University, attracted by the eclat of the fêtes of the one and the teaching of the other ; for the "grand'ville" with her numerous painters, her savants, her royal lecturers recently created by Francis I. (an institution which has developed into the "Collège de France" of to-day), had followed the Renaissance movement eagerly, and attracted foreigners from every part. Henry VIII. sent his natural son, the Duke of Richmond, to be taught

[1] "Chant nuptial du Roy d'Escosse et de Madame Magdaleine première fille de France" (Jan. 1, 1537), by Marot. "The Deploratioun of the deith of Quene Magdalene," by Lyndesay ; "Works," Early English Text Society, 5th part.

there; English Linacre struck there a friendship with French Budée who "opened freely his mind and bosom to him," a thing, Budée said, "he would not do for many people." Surrey spent a year in Paris. The learned Sir Thomas Smith made a prolonged stay in France as ambassador of Queen Elizabeth, and some time as a prisoner in Melun, for ambassadorial privileges were not always a perfect safeguard in those days. Such mishaps did not matter so much then as they would now; Sir Thomas, when liberated, returned very quietly to his functions, remained a few years more in France, kept up his connection with the country, and had his principal works printed in Paris by Robert Estienne: his book on the pronunciation of Greek, and even a work on the writing of English, which he had compiled while taking the waters in fashionable Bourbon l'Archambault. Robert Estienne had to procure some Anglo-Saxon types to print this last book. It was, however, specially written for English people; few others read it; and whatever may have been the case with the rest of the issue, the copy preserved in the National Library at Paris has certainly not suffered from being over-read.[1] Scotchmen, like Major and Buchanan, filled chairs in France; the latter, "prince of the poets of our day," according to Florent Chrétien, wrote Latin tragedies, which were performed by his pupils at Bordeaux (one of them being young Montaigne), and translated later into French.[2] He paid,

[1] "De recta et emendata linguæ Anglicæ scriptione Dialogus," Paris, 1568, 4º.

[2] "La tragédie de Jephtée," translated by Claude de Vesel, Paris, 1566, 8º; "Jephté ou le Vœu," translated by Florent Chrétien,

at times, high compliments to France: "Hail, happy France, sweet nurse of arts, mother country of all nations!"[1] and grateful France repaid his homage in translating, by the hand of Du Bellay, one of his Latin poems:—

> "Adieu ma lyre, adieu les sons
> De tes inutiles chansons . . ."

The religious troubles which caused so much bloodshed throughout Europe helped also to increase the intercourse between the two countries, each being used alternately as a place of refuge by the exiles of the other. The great English Bible of 1539 was printed in Paris by François Regnault, on paper "of the best sort in France," according to Coverdale, who fortunately was present to correct the proofs.[2] Groups of French and English Protestants, moreover, met and lived together in the Low Countries, Strasbourg, and Geneva. Later on groups of English Catholics are to be found at Douai, Saint-Omer, Reims, and Paris.

French visitors, on the other hand, came to England; they were doubtless much less numerous than in Italy

Orleans, 1567, 4°; "Baptiste ou la Calomnie," translated by Pierre de Brinon, Rouen, 1613.

[1] "At tu, beata Gallia,
Salve, bonarum blanda nutrix artium,
Sermone comis, patria gentium omnium
Communis."
"Opera omnia," ed. Ruddimann, Leyden, 1725, 2 vol. 4', vol. ii. p. 292.

[2] The authorities, however, interfered, and the publication had to be finished in London. At the time of Elizabeth and James, the English Catholic Bible, translated under the supervision of Cardinal Allen, was printed in France: Reims and Douai, 1582-1609.

(part of which country was French at that time), but some came, however : diplomates, soldiers, merchants, poets, exiles, and a few sight-seers, the latter being rare enough.

French printers : such men as Jean Barbier and Richard Pynson, crossed the Channel and settled in London ; for while in France there was a superfluity of these craftsmen, in England there were too few. Printing presses existed in forty-one French towns before 1500, but in England at this epoch only Westminster, London, Oxford, and St. Albans were supplied with them. Richard Pynson became printer to the king, preserved his connection with France, ordered his material from Rouen, and used a finch (*pinson*) as his crest. But the English produce of his presses remained entirely ignored in France.

A few tourists were making their appearance in England, and already guide-books were being compiled for them, rude specimens of the Joanne and Murrays' art : Paradin's guide-book in Latin, 1545, Perlin's, in French, 1558.[1] Paradin mentions briefly where

[1] "Angliæ Descriptionis Compendium, per Guilielmum Paradinum," Paris, 1545 ; "Description des Royaulmes d'Angleterre et d'Ecosse, composé par Maistre Estienne Perlin," Paris, 1558. A few more guide-books or relations of journeys might be quoted, such as the "Guide des Chemins d'Angleterre fort nécessaire à ceux qui y voyagent," Paris, 1579, by J. Bernard (author of a "Discours des plus mémorables faicts des Roys et Grands Seigneurs d'Angleterre" (same date) ; or the "Voyage du Duc de Rohan, fait en l'an, 1600," Amsterdam, Elzev., 1644. The Duke took passage at Flushing for Margate ; "Mais je croy, n'ayant déclaré mon intention aux vents, ils ne me furent favorables pour ce dessein," p. 191. It took him four days and five nights to reach England, and even then he did not land where he wanted. Payen,

England is, and how one gets to it, which are its chief ports, and in what a strange manner its affairs are administered by a sort of Senate. He gives a list of the kings who have died a violent death, and a host of details showing small sympathy for the country he visits.

Master Etienne Perlin sojourned in England under Edward VI. (whom, by the way, he calls "Edouard Quint") and Queen Mary. That he was astounded by all he saw is manifest from the confused nature of his impressions. He mingles cooking recipes with appreciations on the Government; flies off to the kitchen and back to Parliament in a fever of bewilderment. He too notes disagreeable details complacently, but he occasionally does justice, according to his views, to his neighbours over-sea. Thus London seems to him "a very fine town, and, after Paris, one of the finest, largest, and wealthiest in the whole world. And one must not talk of Lisbon, nor of Antwerp, nor of Pampeluna." The English have two Universities, "Cambruche" and "Auxonne," and many "milors," such as the "Milors Notumbellant, Ouardon, Grek and Suphor."[1]

Perlin notes several traits which will henceforth

---

later, was three days crossing from Dieppe, owing to a dead calm. "Voyages," 1666, p. 10.

[1] Northumberland, Wharton, Grey, Suffolk. "It falleth out," writes Harrison at that time, "that few forren nations can rightlie pronounce our [language] . . . especiallie the French. . . . It is a pastime to read how Natalis Comes (Conti, the Italian from whom Scarron took the subject of his "Typhon"), in like manner speaking of our affaires, dooth clip the names of our English lords." "Description of Britaine," 1577, book i.

recur continually in guide-books. First, the people do not love the French over much, and when they see a Frenchman they call him "France chesneue" (knave), "France dogue," and even "or son." "French dog" had already been the standard insult for centuries, since we find it in Froissart; it was destined to survive for centuries more. The women of England are very pretty: on that point also there will be unanimity henceforth. That the men are great drunkards, "de grands yvrongnes," is another remark unanimously repeated. When they drink they pronounce cabalistic words, always the same, which, according to Perlin, are, "drind you; iplaigiou"; the reply being, "Tanque artelay."

Their navy is strong. Their artisans earn and spend a great deal: a wealth which is noted by every traveller down to Voltaire; one sees artisans who "stake a crown at tennis"; they go to the tavern and make good cheer "on rabbits, hares, and all sorts of viands." These taverns are remarkable for their comfort; they have "much hay [rushes] on the wooden flooring, and many tapestry pillows upon which the travellers sit." Such were the taverns in which, a few years later, Shakespeare was to meet Ben Jonson; and Falstaff, Prince Hal.

The English are turbulent and fickle. On this point again there is unanimity. That nation which is usually looked upon now as essentially "conservative," passed in the Middle Ages, at the Renaissance, and up to the French Revolution for the most dangerous and hard to manage, "les plus périlleux et merveilleux à tenir," in Europe. The period at which Perlin visited

England was not calculated to give him a different opinion. Nothing, he writes, can be more fickle than the English : "Now they will love a prince, turn your hand, they will want to kill and crucify him." The misfortunes that overtake the "milors" are incredible. "In that country you will not find many great lords whose kinsfolk have not had their heads struck off. Certes, I had liefer (with due reverence to the reader) be a swineherd and keep safe my head." And he adds thoughtfully : "Alack, Lord God, how happy is he who lives under a good king !"

These frequent executions encourage, he considers, the natural ferocity of the nation, for the sight is horrible to behold. Think what it is to see a man like that "Milor Notumbellant," erstwhile master of the whole country and queen-maker, in the hands of the headsman, a headsman who seemed a butcher ! "for I was present at the execution, and the headsman had on a white apron like a butcher. This high and mighty lord made great lamentations and regrets at dying, and said this orison in English, throwing himself on his knees, looking heavenwards and weeping tenderly : 'Lorde God, mi fatre prie fort ous poores siners nond vand in the hoore of our theath.' [1] . . . And after execution done, you would have seen little children receiving the blood which had fallen through some chinks in the scaffold."

England, however, was visited by other people besides printers, courtly gentlemen and diplomates. The best French writers and greatest poets of the period

[1] *Sic* in Perlin.

crossed the Channel. Jacques Grévin, famous as a lyric and dramatic poet, went twice to England, in 1561 and 1567, during the time of the French religious wars—

> "Alors qu'abandonné aux ondes popullaires
> Je naviguoys la mer des civilles misères." [1]

He was welcomed by the French Ambassador, Jacques Bochetel de la Forest-Thaumière, saw the sights, rowed on the Thames, visited the town, and admired its palaces, its places of entertainment, its peerless queen, to whom he sent a rhymed compliment as a new year's gift, 156[1].[2] He found all qualities united in Elizabeth—

> "Vous gardez la doulceur avecque la puissance." [3]

The places of entertainment he visited offered to his sight those sanguinary bull and bear baitings for which the English capital was famous. But the "deaf waters of the Thames, and the silent stones of the palaces," could not assuage the sorrow he felt, far from those he

---

[1] "Le Chant du cigne.—A la magesté de la Royne d'Angleterre," preserved in the MS. Lat. 17,075, in the National Library of Paris, unpublished.

[2] Same "Chant du cigne." He feigns at the end to undergo a metamorphosis and to become one of the swans on the Thames—

> "Je sentis mes deux bras, mes flancs et ma poictrine
> Se charger peu après du plumage d'un cigne,
> Non pour nager les eaux," . . . &c.—(*Ibid.*, fol. 91.)

[3] *Ibid.* fol., 90.

oved :[1] the people of England seemed to him even more "tumultuous" in their peace[2] than the French people in the midst of their civil wars; his heart bled at the thought of the distant mother country, of sweet France, "France, my sweet mother," and he expressed his feelings in verses of matchless tenderness and beauty—

> "France, ma douce mère, hélas, je t'ai laissé,
> Non sans un long regret et une longue plainte,
> Non sans avoir au cœur une douleur empreinte,
> Et un long pensement mille fois repensé."

Ronsard in his youth made two journeys to Scotland and one to England. He spent thirty months in Scotland and six in London. He had performed the long sea voyage between France and Scotland in the company of one of the most famous poets of the latter country, the quick-witted Sir David Lyndesay. Claude Binet, the biographer of Ronsard, goes so far as to affirm that he accomplished

---

[1] "Ores, dans un basteau, je rame la Tamise,
Et voy de mains pallais l'excellante beauté;
Je voy ore un toreau, ore ung ours qui se dresse
Contre l'assault mordant des dogues plains d'adresse . . .
Mais l'onde qui est sourde et la pierre muette,
Les bestes sans raison ne me font qu'ennuyer
Depuis qu'il me souvient de ceulx que je regrette."
See the "Sonnets d'Angleterre et de Flandre," discovered and published by L. Dorez, "Bulletin du Bibliophile," September 15, 1898.

[2] "Qui ne trouve rien bon, à qui rien ne peult plaire,
Que cella qu'il a fait ou qu'il prétend de faire
Et qui pense tout aultre estre défectueux."—"SONNETS," *Ibid.*

the extraordinary feat of learning the language:
"Having learnt the language with great rapidity, he
was received with such favour [in London] that
France was very near losing one whom she had bred
to be some day the trumpet of her fame. But the
good instinct of the true Frenchman tickled him every
hour, and invited him to return home; and he
did so."[1]

He did so, and if a knowledge of English is not
one of the fabulous attainments lavishly attributed to
him by Binet, it can, at all events, be asserted that his
work does not show the slightest trace of any acquaintance with English literature. He does not seem to have
preserved any remembrance of Lyndesay, whose fame,
however, was destined to cross the seas, his English
poems being translated during the sixteenth century,
not into French, it is true, but into Danish.[2]
Greatly admired by Mary Stuart, the "star-eyed
queen" as he calls her, and by Queen Elizabeth,
author of several pieces dedicated to them, panegyrist
of "Mylord Robert Dudley, Comte de Leicester,
l'ornement des Anglois," Ronsard scarcely left, among
the huge mass of his works, so much as a vague
allusion to the possibility of such a thing as an English
poet. He was not aware that "cet ornement des

---

[1] "Discours de la vie de Pierre de Ronsard," Paris, 1586, 4°, p. 5.
Binet says, by mistake, that the journey took place on the occasion
of the *second* marriage of James V.

[2] "Dialogus" (on Monarchy, and other works), by "Herr
David Lyndsay Ridder de Monte," Copenhagen, 1591, 4°. Several
of Lyndesay's works were published in English, "at the command
and expenses of Maister Samuel Jascuy *in Paris*," 1558; but this
seems to be a fancy localisation, as no such printer is known.

Anglois," Leicester, was one of the chief patrons and promoters of dramatic art in England. He had observed the presence of swans on the Thames, and that seemed to him a good omen for the poetical future of the race ; but the way in which he expresses himself clearly shows that he had seen the swans with his own eyes but not the poets.[1] The fact is the more noticeable since Ronsard had been careful, before he wrote, to refresh his memory of England by a conversation with a newly returned French traveller. The traveller had described to him the queen, a youthful, learned, elegant, *beautiful* queen, who loved all arts, knew everything, and spoke all languages—

"On dit que vous savez conter en tous langages."

He had given Ronsard full particulars about the splendid way in which Elizabeth loved to dress and " adonise " herself, to mix gold and pearls with her " longues tresses blondes," and he had told him how she succeeded so well in making herself admirable that the sight would move even "l'estomach d'un barbare Scythois."[2] But the traveller, who had noted all those details and many others given in full by Ronsard, had not had the

[1] " Bientôt verra la Tamise superbe
Maints cygnes blancs, les hôtes de son herbe,
Jeter un chant pour signe manifeste
Que maint poète et la troupe céleste
Des muses sœurs y feront quelque jour,
Laissant Parnasse, un gracieux séjour."

[2] " S'il contemplait la douce mignotise
De votre chef, alors qu'il s'adonise
D'un beau bonnet, où le voyant encor
Couvert d'un ret fait de perles et d'or."

curiosity to open "Tottel's Miscellany," widely read then in London, and whose fifth edition had just appeared (1567), and he did not think fit to give the head of the *Pléiade* information concerning the English rivals of Petrarch, Marot, and Saint Gelais.[1]

Another visitor, and a famous one, keenest of keen observers, came to England during the same reign. Brantôme, whose father had been united by the ties of a "grande amitié" to Henry VIII., appeared twice at the Court of Queen Elizabeth. When, at a later date, wounds obliged him to renounce an active life, and he began to note all he remembered of his chequered career, he found room in his memoirs for three things he had been struck by among all those he had seen in England : a play, a picture, and a breed of dogs. The play was a mask of the wise and foolish virgins performed at Court in 1561 (the year of "Gorboduc").[2] "The lady performers were quite beautiful, honest and well-behaved ; they took us French

[1] "Le Boccage Royal," 1567. Elsewhere Ronsard again mentions England as a land of poetry, but he remains just as vague. Poetry is like a will-o'-the-wisp,

"Lequel aux nuits d'hyver, comme un présage est veu
Ores dessus un fleuve, ores sus une préc. . . .
Elle a veu l'Allemagne, et a pris accroissance
Aux rives d'Angleterre, en Escosse et en France,
Sautant deçà, delà, et prenant grand plaisir,
En estrange pays, divers hommes choisir."
("Discours à Jacques Grévin.")

[2] "The Tragedie of Gorboduc wereof three actes were wrytten by Thomas Nortone and the two last by Thomas Sackvyle." London, 1565 ; first performance, Christmas, 1561 (see *infra*, pp. 33, 35, 217, 383 ff.).

to dance with them. Even the queen danced, and she did so with excellent good grace and royal majesty ; for she was then in all her beauty and grace. There would be only praise for her had she not caused the poor Queen of Scots to be executed."

The picture was a representation of the battle of Cerisoles, painted by order of Henry VIII. and preserved in one of the Queen's closets. But the only sight which seems to have given the visitor a heartbeat was the unexpected encounter, in the Tower, of certain dogs, which suddenly reminded him of his native Périgord. François de Bourdeille, his father, taken to England by Henry VIII., had observed, while shooting with the king, that the royal dogs were " but indifferent dogs either for the partridge or the hare," and said that he would give his Majesty some of his own, " much better looking, better trained, and black as moles all of them." He did as he had said, and sent to the king six dogs, four of them being bitches. With filial joy Brantôme discovered, among the "spaniels of the Queen of England," a quantity of those dogs, as beautiful as before and as black as ever ; they had increased to the number of twenty-four, and the Lieutenant of the Tower certified their origin and pedigree : " Feu M. votre père y envoya cette race." [1] On poets Brantôme is mute ; on dramas and theatres he is mute also. He had been able to see, during his second journey in 1579, the two or three great theatres newly built in London (while there was only one in Paris), but he remembered only the dogs.

[1] "Œuvres," Société de l'Histoire de France, vol. iii., pp. 216, 290 ; x., p. 54.

II.

Very different were the results of this intercourse in the two countries. While English literature continued ignored in France, French literature was familiar to everybody in London. Skelton imitates the "Pèlerinage de la vie humaine," Barclay translates Gringoire, Wyatt derives his inspiration not only from the Italians, but also from Marot and Saint Gelais; Spenser copies Marot, translates the Roman sonnets of Du Bellay, and borrows from French literature the idea of his royal and noble shepherds : Raleigh is in his lines the "shepheard of the ocean," and Elizabeth is the "great shepheardesse," in the same way as Louise de Savoie is, in Marot, "la mère au grand berger," Francis I. Margaret of Navarre is praised by Nash as "a maintener of mirth." Rabelais, "that merry man Rablays," [1] is famous in London ; famous enough to be a cause of anxiety to moralists :

"Let Rabelais, with his durtie mouth . . ."

writes Guilpin in his "Skialetheia" (1598). Ronsard figures on the most elegant desks ; James VI. has a copy of his works, which comes from his mother, Mary Stuart. Montaigne is translated and becomes familiar to Shakespeare ; Du Bartas, owing partly to the similitude of religion, becomes more celebrated in England than in France ; even the "sweete conceites" of Desportes, as Thomas Lodge is pleased to call them, are "englished and ordinarilie in everie man's hands"

[1] "An Almond for a Parrat," attributed to Nash.

(1596)[1]; even Pibrac is translated, line for line, the exquisite platitude of the model being reproduced with unrelenting care.[2]

Kings and princes set the example. Henry VIII. vies "with his good brother of France" in everything; Francis is an able wrestler, so is Henry; Francis founds public lectures, so does Henry; Francis surrounds himself with painters, so does Henry; Francis adopts an elegant cut for his beard, Henry adopts the same; Francis is a musician, so is Henry; Francis writes French verses, so does Henry, and here is a specimen of them:—

> "Adew madam et ma mastres,
> A dew mon solas et mon joy."

The daughter of Henry VIII., Elizabeth, had translated in her youth the "Miroir de l'âme pécheresse" of Margaret of Navarre. In imitation of the king, the English noblemen paid great attention to French customs, fashions, and literature; so much so that Sir Thomas More found in the London francomaniac a fit object for his satire, and described, with his usual humour, the fop of his day, who wore his ribbons and shoe-strings French fashion, who spoke Italian with a French accent, and even English with a French accent, and all languages, in fact, with a French accent—except French alone—

> "Nam gallicam solam sonat Britannice."

---

[1] "Margarite of America."
[2] Like Du Bartas, by Sylvester: "The quadrains of Guy du Faur, lord of Pibrac," London, 1605, 8º.

But there was no reciprocity. English was a language unknown in France; English literature was, to Parisian men of letters, as though it did not exist. None of the English books printed in London by the Frenchman Pynson with types brought from Rouen found any purchasers in France. Anglo-French vocabularies and grammars were compiled during the sixteenth century, sometimes by English sometimes by French people, by Barclay in 1521, by Palsgrave, "Angloys, gradué de Paris," in 1530,[1] by Saint-Lien "gentilhomme Bourbonnois" in the time of Shakespeare: all these works were meant to teach French to the English, and not the reverse. The need of English grammars was by no means felt in France. Palsgrave helped to make known French literature by giving selections from the best authors— Alain Chartier, Guillaume de Lorris, &c. Saint-Lien, who translated his name into English, Holyband, became almost famous; his "French Littleton" had countless editions; he could secure commendatory lines from no less a person than George Gascoigne, lost lines if any! for Holyband's treatises have long ceased to be considered "a most easy, perfect, and absolute way to learne the French tongue—"

> "This pearle of price which Englishmen have sought
> So farre abroad, and cost them there so deare,
> Is now found out within our countrie here,
> And better cheape amongst us may be bought—
> I meane the French, that pearle of pleasant speech," &c.

[1] "Here begynneth the introductory to wryte and pronounce Frenche," London, Copland, 1521, by Alexander Barclay. "Lesclarcissement de la Langue Françoyse" (in English, despite its French title; dedicated to Henry VIII.), 1530, 4°, by Palsgrave.

—a sonnet, complete, "Tam Marti quam Mercurio." Unlike Palsgrave, who would not sell his grammars to all comers, for fear of losing his pupils, Saint-Lien sold his by the hundred and resorted to other means in order to fill his school : he inserted in his books familiar dialogues on himself, in which he gave his address and his terms, and disparaged rival teachers, of whom too many, alas, are "fort négligens et paresseux," quite the reverse of one whom we have given as a master to our boy : "Jan comment s'appelle ton maistre ?—Il s'appelle M. Claude de Sainliens."[1]

Saint-Lien had, in fact, many rivals, and there was more than one school like his own, not only in London but also in the country. The translator of Du Bartas and Pibrac, Joshuah Sylvester, learnt French in Southampton at a school where, says Dr. Grosart, "it was a rule all should speak French ; he who spoke English, though only a sentence, was obliged to wear a fool's cap at meals and to continue to wear it till he caught another in the same fault."[2]

To Saint-Lien's compendious vocabulary succeeded, in 1611, Cotgrave's large dictionary, a work of considerable importance, carefully prepared with the help

---

[1] "The French Littleton : a most easy, perfect, and absolute way to learne the French tongue, set forth by Claudius Holyband, gentil-homme Bourbonnois," London, 1630, 12º. Dedicace dated London, March 25, 1597. The first edition is of 1566 ; other editions in 1578, 1581, 1593, &c. He had published a "French Schoolmaister," to learn French without a teacher, in 1573, and a "Dictionarie French and English" in 1593, London, 4º.

[2] Grosart, "Complete Works of Sylvester," London. 1880, 2 vols., 8º, vol. i. p. x.

of friends, who wrote to the author from France and
supplied him with information as to the real meaning
of words. But this, again, was an English work, printed
in London, and intended specially for an English
public. The dictionary went through numerous
editions in the seventeenth century, all printed in
England. The edition of 1650 was preceded by an
essay on the French language by James Howell, who
had travelled in France, and who, although he did
not acknowledge it, drew from the "Recherches
de la France" of Pasquier all his information, quotations, explanations of proverbs, and comical mistakes,
this one for instance: "Scaliger would etymologize
[Languedoc] from langue d'Ouy (*sic*) whereas it comes
from langue de Got in regard to the Goths and
Saracens." It all came, in fact, from Pasquier,
except the Saracens, who were added by Howell as an
extra ornament. He introduced, moreover, words of
his own in praise of Cardinal Richelieu who "also had
a privat place in Paris called l'Académie des beaux
esprits, where forty of the choicest wits in France used
to meet every Munday to refine and garble the French
language of all pedantic and old words."[1]

There was no room in Paris for any Palsgrave or any
Holyband; a professor of English would have starved

---

[1] "French-English Dictionary," ed. Howell, London, 1650, fol.
Howell addressed himself "to the nobility and gentry of Great
Britain that are desirous to speak French for their pleasure and
ornament, as also to all merchant adventurers as well English as
... Dutch ... to whom the said language is necessary for
commerce and forren correspondence." An appeal was also made
"au favorable lecteur François," by Loiseau de Tourval; but there
was little answer to that appeal.

there. While Saint-Lien, alarmed at the number of his rivals, was charging parents to note well his address, " by Saint-Paul's churchyard, at the sign of the Golden Ball," we find in France, during the sixteenth century, only a few rude grammars and brief lists of words intended to facilitate the trading operations of merchants with England. The chief professor of English at that time, Gabriel Meurier, lived, not in Paris, but in Antwerp, and did not teach English alone. He had founded and directed for fifty years a sort of polyglot institution where French, Spanish, Flemish, Italian, and English could be learnt. It seems evident from the title of his works on the English language that he too had in view English rather than French pupils: one of his books, for instance, is called: " Communications familières non moins propres que très utiles à la nation angloise désireuse et diseteuse du langage François." [1] One of his treatises appeared in Rouen; it is obviously intended for traders alone, as one may learn from it " to speak French and English, as well as to write out missives, bonds, receipts, necessary for all merchants desirous of trafficking." [2]

But an actual smattering of English was a very rare accomplishment. When Rabelais would describe the first meeting of Pantagruel with Panurge "so ill favoured that he seemed to be just off from the teeth of dogs," he was able to represent the queer fellow addressing the giant in all sorts of languages: German, Italian, Dutch, Spanish, Hebrew and even Utopian;

---

[1] Antwerp, 1563, 8º.
[2] Rouen, 1563 (Brunet); a copy of the 1641 edition in the British Museum.

but he had obviously no one near at hand to help him with an English speech. English figures only among the supplementary specimens of Panurge's erudition introduced into subsequent editions. And the printer having added his own mistakes to the incorrections of the master, we have, as a result, the following example of "English as she was spoke" in sixteenth-century France: "Lard ghest tholb be sua virtuiss be intelligence: ass yi body schal biss be naturall relutht tholb suld of me pety haue for natur hass ulss equaly maide : bot fortune sum exaltit hess and oyis depreuit . . ." &c. It must be remembered, however, that Continental printers, when unchecked by English correctors, would put forth garbled texts of this sort even in more serious cases. A dignified treatise by Hooper printed at Zurich in 1547 begins: "For asmouche as all mightye God of his infinit mercye and Goddenys preparyd Ameanes wherby . . .," &c. No wonder Pantagruel, on hearing the strange idiom, simply exclaimed "Less than ever!" cleverer men than he might well have thought that jargon worse than the "language of the Antipodes, which even the devil would not have a try at." [1]

This strange phenomenon will seem stranger still when we remember that, during this great period of the Renaissance, curiosity had been everywhere quickened. In France a thirst for knowledge was felt in all classes of society : foreign arts, strange countries, forgotten literatures, new systems and inventions elicited keen attention, and often caused enthusiasm. People

[1] "Pantagruel," i. 9, text of 1542, ed. Marty-Laveaux, i. p. 261.

were fond of all that was ancient; but as fond also of all that was unexpected and new. At a time when an English grammar was a rarity and remained unknown to all Frenchmen of any account, Villegagnon and Léry compiled dialogues and vocabularies, printed in 1578, to teach the language of Brazilian natives,[1] and Ronsard, attracted by novelties, as all his contemporaries were, warmed at the descriptions of the travellers, and dreamed of going, with Villegagnon, to South America where man lived "innocently, free of garments and wickedness both"—

"D'habits tout aussi nu qu'il est nu de malice." [2]

The importance of foreign languages was sure to be recognized at such a time: and it was; but with no practical result so far as English was concerned. Montaigne wanted young people to be early taken abroad "to rub and polish their brains against others'," and to learn languages on the spot. Ronsard, to whom Boileau attributes opinions exactly contrary to those he really held, insists upon the French tongue being cultivated above all others, " the which should be the nearer thine heart that it is thy mother-tongue." It must be studied, even in its dialects, "without too much affecting the speech of the Court, the which is oft times very bad as being damsels' speech" (*langage de damoiselles*). Its past history should be carefully learnt: "Thou must not reject the old words of

---

[1] Included by Léry in his "Voyage au Brésil," chap. xv.; Heulard, "Villegagnon roi d'Amérique," Paris, 1897.
[2] "Discours contre la Fortune, à Odet de Coligny," 1560.

our romances. . . . Thou shalt not despise old French words. . . . I hold them still in vigour, until they have given birth in their place (like an old stock) to an offshoot ; and then thou shalt use the offshoot and not the stock the which gives all its substance to its little child, to make it grow and finally take its place." Ronsard, however, with all his love for the "parler de France," wills that the 'prentice poet should learn foreign languages too : " Praythee, learn them with care ; it will be a means to enrich thine own, as from an old treasure found under earth. There is no good writing in a vulgar tongue if one does not know the language of the most honourable and famous foreigners."[1] But who were those Most Honourables? Judging from Ronsard's own works, they were Petrarch, Ariosto, Bembo, and even obscure Capilupi ; no room was found among them for any Surrey, Wyatt, Sackville, or Spenser.

Such a view was not at all an isolated one ; it was, on the contrary, the common opinion of the day. Henri Estienne, brother of Sir Thomas Smith's printer, published, in 1579, his treatise on the " Précellence du langage François," written to show that French could

---

[1] " Je te conseille de les sçavoir parfaictement, et d'elles, comme d'un vieil trésor, trouvé soubs terre, enrichir ta propre nation ; car il est fort malaisé de bien escrire en langue vulgaire si on n'est instruit en celles des plus honorables et fameux estrangers." "Art Poétique." This last idea had not crossed the mind of Ronsard at first ; it is expressed only in the edition of 1573 (first ed. 1565). He never tires of recommending people not to speak Latin in French, "de n'écorcher point le Latin comme nos devanciers qui ont trop sottement tiré des Romains une infinité de vocables estrangers, vu qu'il y en avoit d'aussi bons en nostre propre langage."

compare advantageously with all modern languages. This is precisely the subject chosen for competition by the Berlin Academy two centuries later. Estienne declares in his preface that the French language has two rivals—Italian and Spanish. No other language is of any account ; Italian having the richest literature is the one against which the champion of French wages war with the greatest zeal. Spanish is admitted to be worthy of consideration, German is mentioned, and English totally ignored.

The one French poet who came nearest making his compatriots suspect that there was such a thing as an English literature, was that famous Huguenot Du Bartas, who was praised in London above all foreign poets, and who had been sent on missions to England and Scotland. In his second "Semaine" he drew a picture of all literatures. Coming to the English nation and surveying " the spacious times " in which he was living, he could only name three writers, " the pillars," he said, " of the English speech." He knew more concerning the Arabs than concerning his own admirers beyond the Channel. To the familiar names of More and Bacon, he adds only that of the " sweet singing swan," Sidney, whom he knew personally and corresponded with :—

"Le parler des Anglois a pour fermes piliers
Thomas More et Baccon tous deux grands chanceliers . . .
Et le milor Cydné qui, cygne doux-chantant,
Va les flots orgueilleux de Tamise flatant."[1]

[1] Second day of the second week. The comment added by Simon Goulard to Du Bartas's text is not less characteristic. Goulard has a great deal to say about the Arabs, but about the

For one poet alone he did more than merely mention his name. And who was the "eagle" and "phœnix," the sure guide to the heaven of poetry, before whom he chose to bow his genius in an admirable line—

"Ombre je vole en terre et toi dedans la nue"?

None but the conscientious pedant, James VI., whose poem on the Battle of Lepanto he "turned from Latin into French."[1]

It must be observed, moreover, that national animosity, spite, and disdain would not help to explain this peculiar state of things, in the sixteenth century especially; for the English had ceased then to be *the* enemy in France. There were, doubtless, some battles and difficulties; but their import was comparatively small, and the results were balanced on both sides. Henry VIII. took Boulogne, but his son sold it back to France, 1550; Calais was retaken by Guise, 1558; and Warwick had to surrender at Havre, 1563. The great enemy was the Spaniard, who had had the best of it at Pavia and the worst at Cerisoles, who threatened France on all her frontiers—Pyrenees, Pro-

---

English simply nothing. Here is the only information he can give about Sidney: "Quant au Milord Sidné, il a acquis aussi par tout ce mesme los que luy donne le poète." Du Bartas, "Œuvres," Paris, 1611, fol., vol. ii., p. 216.

[1] The modern biographers of Du Bartas (M. Pellissier, M. Bénétrix) affirm that he knew English, but there is no proof of it. Colletet says vaguely that he acquired "l'intelligence des langues mortes et vivantes." M. Pellissier infers that he must have known English since he was sent on a mission to England; but this is no proof whatever, as it was not at all the custom, far from it, with envoys to know the language.

vence, Picardy; who was to be found before Aix
Marseille, Metz, Saint Quentin, Paris, and could
gather in the middle of Burgundy, even at the close
of the century, to be crushed at last by Henri IV.
at Fontaine-Française.[1] Literary knowledge or ignorance had so little to do with national animosities that
Spanish was as familiarly known then in Paris as
English was generally ignored. Spanish grammars and
vocabularies swarmed on French soil; translating from
the Spanish had become a regular trade. Italian spread
no less. "Coustumièrement," says Brantôme, "la plupart
des François d'aujourd'huy, au moins ceux qui ont un
peu veu, sçavent parler on entendent ce langage," meaning
either Italian or Spanish, and his testimony is confirmed in 1617 by no less a personage than Cervantes
himself.[2]

There can be only one explanation for such a singular

---

[1] Ronsard classifies thus the hatreds and rivalries of that time:—

              "L'horrible Mars
Le sang chrestien espand de toutes parts,
Or' mutinant contre soy l'Allemagne,
Or' opposant à la France l'Espagne,
Joyeux de meurtre, or' le païs françois
A l'Italie, et l'Escosse à l'Anglois."
              ("Les Isles Fortunées," 1560.)

See also the "Sonnets d'Angleterre" of Grévin. "Bulletin du
Bibliophile," September 15, 1898. In Sonnet XVI. Grévin
describes the "doleful tragedy" of France; all foreign nations
attend the performance; the English "talk of it," while the others
think of "the booty."

[2] See the learned and charming study by Mr. Morel-Fatio,
"Comment la France a connu et compris l'Espagne," "Études
sur l'Espagne," Paris, 1888, pp. 29, 37, 39.

state of things as those constant relations with England and that absolute ignorance of its language and literature. A tradition, which did not cease to operate for centuries, had established itself in the remote days of the Conquest, in accordance to which all people of any standing in England spoke French, all thinkers and philosophers spoke Latin, and the rest were of no account. For ignorance was strictly limited to works in the English tongue; the thinkers, philosophers, and historians of Great Britain were familiar to every one in Paris, and had there as many admirers as in their own country. But they were known only under their names in *us*—Morus, Camdenus, Seldenus; they exchanged letters with their French brethren, and received epistles from Budæus, Stephanus, and Thuanus. A Paris edition of More's "Utopia" appeared long before there was a London one, and the work was translated into French before it was turned into English. Bacon was renowned alike on both sides of the Channel. But all that he or others had written in English was practically non-existent for the French public. While "Morus" became famous in France, "Sir Thomas More" and his "Workes" remained utterly unknown. Du Bellay translated "Adieu ma lyre" from the Latin of Buchanan, but no one suspected that he would have better served the muses by putting into French—

> "My lute awake, perform the last
> Labour that thou and I shall waste,"

the exquisite and touching lines of the Ambassador Wyatt. That nobleman spoke French, all London spoke it; the king, the court, noblemen, ladies, every one who was anybody at all ; every traveller was struck by the general use of French in English society ; Greek Nucius and Italian Jove concur in their testimony. "All the English almost," wrote Nucius, "use the French language." [1] Two centuries later, in the days of incipient Anglomania in France, something of that tradition still survived. "Tiens," says a marquis in one of Boissy's comedies, "what is best in the English is that they speak French, even though they murder it." [2]

That the fact was connected with the Conquest had not been forgotten in England; protests were addressed to Henry VIII. against the use of French in the law courts, "as therby ys testyfyd our subjectyon to the Normannys."[3] The Conquest was equally well remembered in France, and its bearing on the language of the inhabitants was about all that the ablest French critics could say of their neighbours' speech :—

> "Les Normands derechef, suivant hors de leur terre
> Guillaume leur grand duc, mirent en Angleterre
> Leur coustume et leur langue,"

wrote Vauquelin de la Fresnaye in his "Art Poétique." Fauchet expressed the same thought, and Etienne Pasquier, who seems to have carried his investigations

---

[1] "Travels," 1545, Camden Society, 1841, p. 13. "Aulæ siquidem et foro Gallicus sermo familiaris." Paul Jove, "Descriptio Britanniæ," Venice, 1548, 4°.

[2] "Le François à Londres," performed July 19, 1727.

[3] Dialogue between Cardinal Pole and Lupset, by Starkey, dedicated to Henry VIII., ed. Cooper, 1871, p. 122 (Early English Text Society).

a little further, said: "The English language at this day owes a great quantity of words to the domination of the Normans in England." As for the general opinion, it was well summed up by Perlin: "The English language proper was brought to that island formerly by savage invaders, and its barbarity has always prevented its being taken into account: their language partakes of the German as well as of other languages. For which reason the poets of days gone by have set little store by their generation, and have always esteemed them as a strange and barbarous race, for their fount and origin may not be traced from people who were born in the land, but from strange men, barbarians and fugitives."[1]

III.

Thus it came to pass that, at the time of Shakespeare, the French Stage could be influenced by the ancients, the Italians, and the Spaniards, but not at all by the English. In both countries the starting-points stood very close together. Great differences were doubtless to be expected as dramatic art developed, on account of differences in the genius of both

---

[1] Vauquelin de la Fresnaye, "Art Poétique," 1605, book i., line 619; Claude Fauchet, "Recueil de l'origine de la Langue et Poésie Françoise," 1581, chap. iv.; Pasquier, "Recherches de la France," book vii., chap. i.; Perlin, *ut supra*, fol. 8: "Leur langaige est tant participant sur l'alemant que sur autres. Parquoy les poètes du temps passé ont peu faict de compte de leur génération, et les ont tousjours estimé comme une terre barbare et estrange, car leur principe et origine n'est poinct venu de gens qui soyent estes nais là, mais des estranges et barbares et profuges."

nations; but those differences were increased by the total ignorance in France of what was going on in England.

Both arts followed, for some while, no very dissimilar paths. In the two countries clever people, worshipful critics, men of knowledge, had given their verdict in favour of Renaissance, antiquity, and rules, against Middle Ages, Gothic barbarity, and unbridled freedom. In the two countries certain people protested and rebelled against Aristotle and his exponents; but what of that? They were men who knew " small Latin and less Greek."

The dramatic " Unities " were eloquently defended in England as in France; no Scaliger, no Jean de la Taille, no Vauquelin de la Fresnaye came forward as decidedly in their favour as Sir Philip Sidney. In his " Apologie for poetrie," invoking the authority of Aristotle and of Reason, he proclaims the dogma of the unities: " The stage should alwaies represent but one place, and the uttermost time presupposed in it should be both by Aristotle's precept and common reason but one day."[1] Above all other tragedies written by his compatriots, he admired " Gorboduc," in which some of the precepts of antiquity are followed, sententious counsellors exchange aphorisms, and the catastrophe is told in a narrative three pages long. But he preferred, even to " Gorboduc," the Latin tragedies of Buchanan, in which the little Montaigne " had played the chief parts

---

[1] "An Apologie for poetrie, written by the right noble, vertuous and learned Sir Phillip Sydney Knight,—Odi profanum vulgus et arceo." London, 1595, 4º. Written about 1581, reprinted by Arber.

at the College of Guyenne." To him they appeared as works divine.

The great thinker of the period, Bacon, assists in the construction of an English play according to the classical standard at a time when Marlowe had already produced his "Faust."[1] Seneca is translated into English line for line.[2] The regent of Parnassus, Ben Jonson, withdraws from sight the death of Sejanus, and sends forth a messenger to relate the event, when Shakespeare had already written half his masterpieces. According to Jonson art should reign supreme; those who are found wanting in that respect must not receive more than their due: "Shakespeere wanted arte."[3] Old Ben had the classic models ever before his eyes; if he could not follow them, the fault lay with the public, not with him: he excuses himself for the irregularities in his tragedies, and declares openly that his dramatic ideal is that of the ancients.

The tragedies in antique style of French Garnier were translated into English and published in London, "Cornélie" in 1594, "Marc Antoine" in 1595, when already "Romeo and Juliet" and "Midsummer Night's

---

[1] "Certaine Devises and Shewes presented to her Majestye," London, 1589, 8º, by Thomas Ughes and others. The Misfortunes of King Arthur are the subject of the play, in which we find a chorus, messengers, sentences imitated from Seneca, &c. On that subject, see my "Théâtre en Angleterre," chap. vi., "Théoriciens et Classiques."

[2] By Jasper Heywood: "Senecæ. ... Hercules Furens," London, 1561, Latin and English; "Seneca his tenne Tragedies," 1581, 4º.

[3] "Conversations with Drummond"; "Works," ed. Cunningham, vol. iii., p. 471.

Dream" had been performed.[1] "Marc Antoine" was translated by Sidney's sister, the Countess of Pembroke; "Cornelia" had two editions in two years. Queen Elizabeth herself, who knew, however, how to be merry with Falstaff, gave encouragement on numberless occasions to classically-inclined dramatists by her presence at their plays. She saw "Gorboduc" in 1561, a Latin "Dido" in 1564, "Tancred and Gismund," with passages unexpectedly drawn from Virgil, in 1568,[2] the "Misfortunes of Arthur"—for which Bacon had ordered the dumb-shows—and a host of others. She was a lettered queen if ever there was one, a great admirer of the ancients, and had translated herself, among other things, fragments of Horace's "Poetical Art,"[3] and a tragedy of Euripides.

While Englishmen of renown imitated those models and spread such ideas, without knowing for certain which style would triumph among them in the end, French writers, being still so near mediæval picturesqueness and unruliness, were very far from adhering strictly to classical dogmas.

We are still in the sixteenth century, an age of wars, duels, rebellion, and debauch, the age of Marig-

---

[1] "Cornelia," translated by Thomas Kyd, 1594; another edition under the title of "Pompey the Great," 1595; "The Tragedie of Antonie," printed with care and elegance upon fine paper, translated by the Countess of Pembroke, 1595, 16⁰ (the translation made in 1590).

[2] See, upon that subject, F. G. Fleay, "A Chronicle History of the London Stage," 1559-1642. London, 1890, 8°, pp. 12 ff., and "Théâtre en Angleterre," p. 242.

[3] "Queen Elizabeth's Englishings of Boethius," &c., ed. Pemberton, E.E.T.S., 1899 (issued in 1898).

nano and of the League, of Catholic and Protestant
butcheries, the age of Montluc, Brantôme, and Maugiron; the time when France delighted to follow the
rambling thoughts of Montaigne, the "enormous"
inventions of Rabelais, and the audacious soarings
of Ronsard. This prince of poets found room in his
verses for all sorts of words, many of which would
not be allowed now even in prose; he was afraid of
nothing, admitted in his poems low and subtle expressions alike, and coined new words, reproaching the
Huguenots with following an *empistolled* Christ—"un
Christ empistolé."[1] Nearly all the poets of the time
of the Valois and early Bourbons, cadets of Vendômois,
Gascony, or elsewhere, turbulent fellows, live sword in
hand, fight duels, go to war and die violent deaths, like
Monchrestien at Les Tourailles; or of the effects of
their wounds, in their castles of Bartas or Saumazènes.

Moreover, mediæval "gothicity" still continued to
hold the French stage during all the sixteenth century
and even part of the seventeenth, at the Hôtel de Bourgogne, the only theatre Paris then possessed. Mediæval
art was patented, had privileges; the "Confrères de
la Passion," lessees of that famous playhouse, had a
monopoly which they exerted jealously; the early classical
dramatists in France, Jodelle, Garnier, Grévin, did not
know where to have their plays performed, and were reduced to composing most of them as much with a view

---

[1] "Ne prêche plus en France une Evangile armée,
    Un Christ empistolé, tout noirci de fumée,
    Portant un morion en tête. ..."
(Apostrophe to Beza, "Continuation du Discours de Misères de
ce Temps.")

PART OF THE THEATRES' CORNER IN SOUTHWARK.
From the engraving by Claes Jan Visscher, early seventeenth century.

to their being read as to their being acted. The Middle Ages, incoherent, irregular, rash, with their executions, their bloody martyrdoms, their farcical plays in the fabliau style, their armies on the march, their changes of time and place, thus live on, protected by decrees and letters patent, threatened sometimes with being dislodged, but impregnable as yet in their stronghold of the Hôtel de Bourgogne. Theatres multiplied in London in the days of Shakespeare : at the time of his death, and even long after, Paris still had but one, that of the Confrères ;[1] and if no genius made himself known there, it certainly cannot be alleged that the fault lay with Aristotle's rules.

On the other hand, French dramatists were treating, at the same period, the same subjects as English poets, sometimes the same as Shakespeare. France had thus her "Romeo and Juliet" (by Châteauvieux, 1580),[2] her "Antony and Cleopatra," her "Julius Cæsar," her "Comedy of Errors," her "Winter's Tale" ("Pandoste"

---

[1] "C'est seulement à la fin de 1629 que les Comédiens du prince d'Orange ont établi à Paris un second théâtre." Rigal, "Esquisse d'une histoire des théâtres de Paris," 1887, p. 85. The Passion Brothers, however, as early as the sixteenth century, were wont to let their hall to others when it was in their interest to do so. We shall see an example of it further on, p. 51.

[2] Côme de la Gambe, called Châteauvieux, groom of the chamber to Henri III. This drama, played in 1580, was taken, like Shakespeare's play, from Bandello's novel. Clément and De la Porte, "Anecdotes dramatiques," Paris, 1775, 3 vols., 8, vol. iii., p. 107. In both countries subjects are borrowed from Ariosto and Boccaccio ; Robert Garnier gives a "Bradamante," 1580 ; Robert Greene, an "Orlando Furioso," 1594 (played in 1591). Rotrou's "Les Ménechmes" (drawn from Plautus as "The Comedy of Errors" had been), were performed in 1632 and printed in 1636.

in French). French Antony, like English Antony, shook the blood-stained gown of Cæsar before the assembled Romans :—

> "You all do know this mantle . . ."

> "Voyez, voyez quel tort
> On vous a fait ; voyez cette robe sanglante ;
> C'est celle de César ! "

And Ronsard was inexhaustible in his praise of the youthful glory of Jacques Grévin.[1] "The Winter's Tale" appeared twice on the French stage—such "Winter's Tales" as a Hardy or a Puget de la Serre could write. They offered the peculiarity of being drawn from a novel of Greene's, the same which Shakespeare used, and one of the very first literary works translated from English into French. That story enjoyed an extraordinary popularity in France,

---

[1] "La Mort de César," by Grévin, 1560. Several passages might be compared with Shakespeare's : for instance, the soliloquy of Brutus in Grévin :—

> "Rome ne peult servir, Brute vivant en elle,
> Et cachant dedans soy ceste antique querelle.
> Ce n'est assez que Brute aist arraché des mains
> D'un Tarquin orgueilleux l'empire des Romains. . . ."
> —(Act ii.)

In Shakespeare :—

> "Shall Rome stand under one man's awe ? What ? Rome ?
> My ancestors did from the streets of Rome
> The Tarquin drive when he was called a king. . . ."
> —(Act ii., 1.)

THE MEETING OF DORASTE AND FAUNIA (FLORIZEL AND PERDITA)
From a French engraving, 1722

it was several times remodelled, and, as late as 1722, a new version of it was published with curious cuts, showing a Florizel and a Perdita dressed in eighteenth century dresses and taking part in the shepherds' feast.[1]

Of the two plays, the earliest, by Hardy, is lost. The second, by Puget de la Serre, " Pandoste ou la Princesse malheureuse," was printed in 1631, and is divided into two days, each of five very short acts. It is written in the prodigiously florid and *précieux* style which was then fashionable with many. The play is dedicated to the Lady " Urania " : " Your black locks always in mourning for the death of your slaves are as many chains which keep my pen prisoner."[2] Pandoste opens the play with a ranting speech worthy of King Herod : " Am I not a lucky man not to know what to wish for ? . . . The sweetest pleasures which can be tasted in this nether world are the everyday dishes for my table. . . . O Fortune, when wilt thou change thy face ? thine continuous smiles incline me to go a-weeping . . ." When he thinks he has discovered that he

---

[1] " Histoire tragique de Pandosto," translated by L. Regnault, Paris, 1615 (see " English Novel in the Time of Shakespeare," p. 184). " Le Roman d'Albanie et de Sycile par le S' Du Bail Gentilhomme Poictevin," Paris, 1626, 12º, with cuts ; no mention is made either of Greene or of Regnault ; several changes have been introduced in the story. It was analysed in 1779 in the " Bibliothèque universelle des Romans," Paris, vol. i. " Histoire tragique de Pandolphe," Paris, 1722, 12mo, with plates, one of which is here reproduced.

[2] The author continues thus : " Pour vostre sein que je suis contrainct de comparer à deux petites montaignes de neige parce qu'elles couvrent un cœur de glace, je n'en ay jamais veu que la moitié au travers des grilles d'une prison de toile transparente où il souspiroit à intervale de sa captivité."

is not quite so happy as he believed, his reproaches to
the " Royne Belaire son espouse " are couched in the
same style: " Dost thou continue dragging on the earth
the dunghill of thy body to give the plague to its
inhabitants ? . . . Speak, I charge thee, infamous one,
but speak from afar, lest the wind from thy mouth
poisons me." Belaire, in her turn, descants to her little
daughter on their sad fate : " Thou criest in vain, as
my helplessness makes me deaf. It seems as if thy tears
would drown thee in their waters, to make good the
curse to which thy fate has condemned thee. Let us
mix our tears together and undergo the same ship-
wreck." The child is put to sea, and discovered on the
opposite shore by a well-taught young shepherd, who,
finding it so pretty, wonders if " it is not some new
Cupid to which Venus has given birth in the sea, where
she was born."

In the second day Doraste and Favvye (Florizel and
Perdita) plight their troth and exchange sweet speeches:

"*Doraste.* What character do you want me to sustain in order
to show you the sincerity of my love ?
Faveye. The character of a shepherd.
Doraste. I am one already, for from the first day that I saw
you, my desires and my thoughts have watched the sheep with
you. . . ."

Like the English, the French during the same period
put their national history into dramas, or rather on that
point England followed the example of the Continent.
Before 1450 a mystery play had been devoted in France
to the Maid of Orleans (burnt in 1431), and in it " the
English army left its island . . . landed in France . . .
real battles took place ; whole quarters of the town

were destroyed by fire."[1] The English relate in their plays the "Contention betwixt the two famous Houses of Yorke and Lancaster" (Shakespeare took from this old drama his "Henry VI."); the French relate in theirs "in brief narrations all the troubles of France from the death of Henri II. up to 1566";[2] a play is written by François de Chantelouve, on the Saint Barthélemi three years after the massacre has taken place.[3] On the London stage Queen Elizabeth appears in a play of Shakespeare's; James IV. in a play of Greene's; Marlowe takes for his subject, in 1590, the reign and death of Henri III. of France, assassinated only the previous year; Chapman, the revolt of Biron the against Henri IV. yet on the throne. In France Guises appear in plays by Pierre Matthieu and by Simon Belyard;[4] Mary Stuart in one by Monchrestien; Mérovée, Gaston de Foix, Henri IV. in the tragedies of Claude Billard.[5] In Paris the greatest poets,

---

[1] "Le Mistère du Siège d'Orléans," Paris, 1862, 4º. Petit de Julleville, "Les Mystères," 1880, vol. ii. p. 579.

[2] "The first part of the Contention betwixt the two famous Houses of Yorke and Lancaster, with the death of the good Duke Humphrey," &c., London, 1594, reprinted by Hazlitt, "Shakespeare's Library," 1875, vol. i. "Montgomery, tragédie où sont contenus par brèves narrations, tous les troubles de la France depuis la mort de Henri II. jusqu'en 1566," by Gerland, 1573; de Mouhy, "Tablettes dramatiques," Paris, 1772.

[3] "La tragédie de feu Gaspar de Colligni, jadis Admiral de France, contenant ce qui advint à Paris le 24 Aoust, 1572." 1575, with choruses, messenger, the King's Council, which acts the part of the confidant; in verse. It is an apology of the Saint Barthélemi.

[4] "La Guysien ou perfidie tyrannique commise par Henry de Valois," Troyes, 1592, 8º.

[5] "Tragédies de Claude Billard, Sieur de Courgenay" (dedicated to Marie de Medicis), Paris, 1612.

the most esteemed critics were no more afraid then of national and contemporaneous subjects, than they were in London, where a play was published on "the Tragicall raigne of Selimus sometime Emperor of the Turkes," with the additional information to whet the reader's interest, that the emperor in question was "grandfather to him that now raigneth."[1] "La Soltane," a French tragedy by Gabriel Bounin, printed in 1561, is localised in the palace of Sultan Soliman, who was yet alive.[2] The scruples of Racine and Boileau existed only in the dim future. Ronsard, while giving their full due to Rome and Athens, foresaw that Grévin might dramatise the dissensions with which France was being rent :—

> "D'Athènes, Troye, Argos, de Thèbes et Mycènes
> Sont pris les arguments qui conviennent aux scènes ;
> Rome t'en a donné, que nous voyons ici,
> Et crains que les François ne t'en donnent aussi."[3]

Vauquelin de la Fresnaye, a passionate admirer of Horace, whose "Epistle to the Pisoes" he incorporated into his own "Art Poétique," was nevertheless

---

[1] London, 1594, 4º.
[2] "La Soltane, tragédie par Gabriel Bounin, lieu-tenant de Chasteau-rous en Berry," 1561, 4º (portrait of the author on the back of the title). This tragedy treats of the death of Mustapha, a favourite subject with dramatists in England as in France during the sixteenth and seventeenth centuries (treated in England, *e.g.*, by Fulke Greville Lord Brooke, and by Roger Boyle, Earl of Orrery ; see below, p. 164).
[3] "Discours à Jacques Grévin," 1560 (on the occasion of his "Mort de César").

desirous of seeing Andromeda and Perseus abandoned in favour of Christian heroes. It seems as though he were calling forth Voltaire's Tancrède and Zaïre [1] two hundred years before their time :—

> " Portez donc en trophé les dépouilles payennes
> Au sommet des clochers de vos cités chrétiennes. . . ." [2]

All the national and modern dramas, and even the dramas in antique style written in France at that period, offer a strange combination of classic and romantic tendencies. " The Guisiade, a new Tragedy, in which is represented truly and without passion, the massacre of the duc de Guise," [3] is a French tragedy with chorus, in which the catastrophes are merely narrated and the murder is described by a messenger :—

> " O France violée, O meurtrier exécrable !
> O barbare, O tyran, O homme abominable ! "

---

[1] " Vous aurez sur le théâtre des drapeaux portés en triomphe, des armes suspendues à des colonnes . . . un *Te Deum*." Voltaire to d'Argental, on the subject of " Tancrède," May 19, 1759.

[2] He would have liked to see "on feast days in villages," or "on some beautiful Christmas night " :—

> " Au lieu d'une Andromède au rocher attachée,
> Et d'un Persée qui l'a de ses fers relachée,
> Un Saint George venir bien armé, bien monté,
> La lance à son arrest, l'espée à son costé,
> Assaillir le dragon."

"Art Poétique," ed. Pellissier, 1885, p. 173 ; 1st ed., 1605 ; the work begun, 1574.

[3] " La Guisiade, tragédie nouvelle en laquelle au vray et sans passion est représenté le massacre du duc de Guise," by Pierre Matthieu, 3rd edition, enlarged, Lyons, 1589, 8º.

Thus begins, and in this style continues, a long-winded messenger, giving us a pale foreshadowing of the famous narrative of Théramène in Racine's "Phèdre." A messenger also relates the massacre of the Protestants, all "despatched to the Stygian waters" in Chantelouve's tragedy of "Colligni." A messenger again relates the death of Mary Queen of Scots (whose lamentations had filled a whole act) in "l'Écossaise ou le Désastre" of Montchrestien.[1]

But in spite of their choruses (which we find also in "Henri le Grand," "Gaston de Foix," &c.), their messengers, and their attention to rules, all these French authors are very far from the absolute regularity and decorum exacted at a later date. They produce most unexpected personages on the stage. Long before the ghost of old Hamlet had been placed by Shakespeare on the boards, Jodelle had shown his audience the ghost of Antony—a French ghost, however, who was careful to declare in the opening lines of

---

[1] "Les Tragédies de A. de Montchrestien," Rouen [1601], 8º. The subject was often taken up again in France : by Regnault, 1639 ; by Boursault, 1683 ; by an anonymous author, 1734, &c. "L'Écossaise" had not, as has been affirmed, been written only to be read ; it was performed at Orléans in 1603 (see an article by M. Auvray, *Revue d'Histoire littéraire de la France*, January 15, 1897). The "Écossaise" is ornamented with a portrait of the author ; the verses which accompany the engraving resemble those that Jonson wrote a little later for the portrait of Shakespeare in the first folio :—

> "Son corps et son esprit sont peints en cet ouvrage,
> L'un dedans ce tableau, l'autre en ce qu'il escrit :
> Si l'on trouve bien fait le portrait du visage,
> Je trouve encor mieux fait le portrait de l'esprit."

the play that Cleopatra would duly die within the prescribed number of hours:—

> "Avant que ce soleil qui vient ores de naistre,
> Ayant tracé son jour, chez sa tante se plonge,
> Cléopâtre mourra."[1]

In the "Tragédie de feu Gaspar de Colligni," the ghost of D'Andelot comes forth, a classical ghost which had been suffering in Hades (in company with Calvin) all the most famous torments in antique mythology.[2] In the same play Mercury and the Furies appear. In "Henri le Grand" we meet Satan; in "Mérovée," Tysiphone, a fury. Decorum and the "convenances" are but ill observed; Jodelle's Cleopatra seizes Seleucus by the hair of his head, and says:—

> "Plucked out shall be the hair of thy cruel head. . . . Have at thee, traitor, have at thee!
> *Seleucus.* Hold her back, mighty Cæsar, hold her back, I say!"

---

[1] "Les Œuvres et Meslanges poétiques d'Estienne Jodelle Sieur de Lymodin," Paris, 1574, 4°. In making ghosts appear upon the stage, Jodelle was simply following the example of Seneca:—

> "*Thiestis Umbra.* Opaca linquens, Ditis inferni loca,
> Adsum profundo Tartari emissus specu."
> ("Agamemnon.")

[2] *Ghost of D'Andelot:*—

> "La terre se crevant, je sors hors du Ténare,
> Et du palais ombreux de l'horrible Tartare
> Où rôtissant d'un feu qui ne cognoit la mort,
> Je languis deschiré d'un tenaillant effort . . .
> Ores je roule un roc du haut d'une montagne . . .
> . . . Non moins que moi le cardinal mon frère
> Et l'apostat Calvin ne font qu'heurler et braire."

But Octavius has not the slightest desire to intervene in so dangerous a quarrel, and contents himself with giving good advice : " Fly, friend, fly !"

Those poetical outbursts which occur in the ancient English dramatists, sometimes at the most unexpected moments—comparisons, highly coloured descriptions, flowers of speech—occur also in many old French tragedies. The messenger who relates the Saint Barthélemi in Chantelouve's tragedy puts in his discourse as much irrelevant poetry as he can, and first describes fair-haired Aurora driving away the black horses of Night.[1] Better poetry but no greater appropriateness is found in such lines as these :—

> " Their lips were four red roses on a stalk
> Which, in their summer beauty, kiss'd each other."

In this manner the two rascals hired for murdering the sons of Edward express themselves in " Richard III.," after their " piece of ruthless butchery."

The starting points (not to speak of the common origins—mysteries, moralities, farces, all imported into England from France) stood, as we see, very close in the two countries at the time of the Renaissance ; the " convenances " did not yet reign supreme in France, rules were not without defenders in England. Add to this the remarkable fact that English players came

---

[1] ". . . Lorsque la blonde Aurore
Chassoit les noirs chevaux de la déesse more
Et que, laissant le lict son mari vieillard,
Ses couleurs pour le ciel semoit de toute part."
(" Tragédie de feu Gaspar de Colligni.")

to France in the time of Shakespeare and performed dramas in the city and at court. English dramatists came too, and among others Shakespeare's best friend, Ben Jonson, while some French dramatists, such as Grévin, Montchrestien, and Schélandre, went to England. The English actors who came to Paris were not mere strolling players; they did things on a rather large scale, for there was only one permanent theatre in Paris, and that one they hired. The lease, dated May 25, 1598, by which the "Confrères de la Passion" allow them free use of the "Grande salle et théâtre de l'Hôtel de Bourgogne," is still in existence among the papers of a notary public in Paris. They had at their head "Jehan Sehais, comédien Anglois." Remarkably sanguine and indefatigable as it seems, they invaded the town, so to speak. The Hôtel de Bourgogne was not enough for them; they wanted to, and actually did play outside the hôtel, contrary to the privileges of the Passion Brothers. The judge had to interfere, and the Châtelet passed a sentence "against the said English comedians," obliging them to pay an indemnity to the brothers.[1] The taste for the drama had become so general in Shakespeare's time that the number of players had multiplied beyond belief. Troops of them swarmed; they roamed over the highways of Europe, meeting with the adventurers of premature "Comical Romances" which unfortunately no Scarron has recorded. We meet with them in the Low Countries, in Denmark, in Germany (where French comedians are

---

[1] Eudore Soulié, "Recherches sur Molière," Paris, 1863, 8º, p. 153. A troupe of English acrobats had been seen in Paris in 1583. E. Fournier, "Chansons de Gaultier Garguille," 1858, p. lix.

also to be found),[1] hawking about a *repértoire* which included several pieces of Shakespeare's ("Hamlet," "Lear," "Romeo"), of Greene's, of Marlowe's, and of other great authors. The difficulty of pleasing the audience with dramas in a strange tongue, obliged them to have recourse to all the little talents they might happen to possess; they played different instruments, amused the public with their comical gesticulations, and excited admiration by antics more worthy of acrobats than of dancers. Previous to the arrival of the troupe of 1598 we find in Paris some English "volteadors" in a Spanish company. In Holland and Germany the English comedians are often designated by the name of "instrumentisten." The Duke of Saxony attached to his person, in 1586, a troupe in which figures the actor Thomas Pope, subsequently a companion of Shakespeare's; these comedians are bound to "play music, and amuse and entertain us with their art in leaping and other graceful things which they have learnt." The player Browne is rewarded for "having acted and played divers comedies and histories, as well as for having made divers leaps in the presence of the burgomasters and community of this city" of Leyden, in 1590.[2]

[1] "En 1595, Charles Chautron jouait à Francfort la 'Sultane' de Gabriel Bounin." P. de Juleville, "Histoire de la langue et de la Littérature Française," iv., 195 (this same "Soltane," 1561, of which we spoke above, p. 46).

[2] Cohn, "Shakespeare in Germany," London, 1865, 4°, pp. xxiii., xxvi., xxxi., cxi. The list in which figure several plays of Shakespeare, is a list of plays performed at Dresden by English comedians in 1626. Their quality of actor-acrobats is shown sometimes by their passports, wherein it is stated that they intend to "exercer

We may well believe that in Paris the English actors, who would scarcely have been less understood had they spoken native Brazilian, must have had recourse more than once to their supplementary talents in order to hold an audience. Even then their success does not seem to have come up to their expectations, for we soon loose sight of them, and no one knows now whether the spectators of the Hôtel de Bourgogne saw " Romeo " as in London, or graceful leaps as in Leyden.

Another English troupe appeared, however, in France some years later, and gave representations in the Palace of Fontainebleau, where King Henri IV. and his son, the future Louis XIII., were staying. Héroard, physician in ordinary to the young prince, who was then scarcely four years old, saw the play with his pupil. It consisted of one of those wild and bloody dramas, destined to cause such lively discussions in France, but not till a century and a half later. Héroard writes in his journal : " Saturday 18th [September, 1604] at half-past three, lunch ; then conducted the dauphin to the great new hall "—the famous hall just then finished, where a stage was erected later, and plays were constantly performed in the seventeenth and eighteenth centuries—" to hear a tragedy performed by English players. He listened with coldness, gravity, and patience, till the head of one of the heroes had to be cut off." What took place then ? Was the child indignant as by a prescience of the arrests of Boileau ;

leurs qualitez en faict de musique, agilitez et jocuz de commedies, tragédies et histoires." Passport in French, signed by Lord Howard, February 10, 1591, *ibid*, p. xxviii.

did he lose his coldness or his patience? Héroard is
mute on this point, but he continues: " Taken him to
the garden and then to the kennel to see the quarry of
the hart given to the hounds. . . . He sees the hounds
come to his very feet, busy with the carnage, and he
views the scene with the most remarkable assurance."
The physician observes elsewhere that the child feels
interested only in weapons, " all other pastimes being
as nothing to him." It seems most probable, therefore,
that when he saw the head cut off in the play he was
not shocked; and that it was his coldness and gravity,
not his patience, which vanished.

Young Louis kept, in any case, a most lively
remembrance of the tragedy and of the words, acting,
and attitudes of the English players. He was very
fond of mimicking what had struck him; when
" Maitre Guillaume," the fool of Henri IV., had
been with him, " with mirth and laughter he repeated
his jokes." In the same way, ten days after the play,
" he asks," says Héroard again, " to be disguised, and
with his apron on his head and a gauze scarf, he
imitates the English comedians who were at court
and whom he had seen play." The day after he
thinks again of them: " He says that he wants to
play in a play. 'Monsieur,' I said, ' how will you
say?' He answers, '*Tiph, Toph*,' swelling his voice.
At half-past six, supped. He goes to his room, has
himself dressed in his disguise, and says, ' Let us go
and see *maman*; we are comedians.' " On the 3rd of
October he is haunted still by the lively remembrance
of that memorable performance. " ' Let us dress as
comedians,' he says. His apron was tied on his head,

and he began talking away, saying, '*Tiph, Toph, milord*,' pacing the room in long strides."[1] The rant, the long strides, the head cut off, all this befits many an English drama and many an English actor of the period. Youthful Louis did not prove a bad observer, and if, when on the throne, arms and hunting had not become his only pastimes, he would, in all probability, have given his support to a sort of drama different from the kind that was to be favoured by a certain young man, then nineteen, and very busy with theological studies, the future Cardinal de Richelieu.[2]

It thus seems that an intelligence, or at least a knowledge of the English drama should have been possible in France, since English players had sojourned there, and since Englishmen, the most expert in matters of poetry and of the stage had visited Paris during Shakespeare's lifetime. While Ronsard, Grévin, Brantôme, and Du Bartas were crossing the sea, Sir Philip Sidney, Sackville, and Ben Jonson were crossing it too in

[1] "Journal de Jean Héroard sur l'enfance et la Jeunesse de Louis XIII.," 1601-28, éd. Soulié and de Barthélemy, Paris, 1868, 2 vols., 8vo., vol. i., pp. 88 and following. In a letter to the "Intermédiaire des Chercheurs et Curieux," vol. ii., col. 105, M. H. C. Coote has expressed the opinion that the play was probably Shakespeare's "Henry IV.," on account of a passage where Falstaff says to the Lord Chief Justice, "This is the right fencing grace, my lord, tap for tap and so part fair." (Henry IV., ii. 1.) This is a very doubtful inference, as no one is beheaded in this play.

[2] One of the masters he had was an Englishman, Richard Smith, "un des esprits le plus libres parmi les théologiens de ce temps." Hanotaux, "Histoire du Cardinal de Richelieu," i., p. 77. The "Argenis" of John Barclay was later one of the favourite books of Richelieu.

the opposite direction—the first in all the ardour
and enthusiasm of youth; the second several times
as ambassador; the last in all his glory, author
of "Sejanus," of "The Alchemist," of "Catiline,"
laureate of James I., regent of Parnassus in his own
country.

Sidney appeared at the Court of Charles IX., in
1572, at the very time when Ronsard was staying
there, had an apartment in the Louvre, and was
writing his peerless sonnets for "Helen." Elegant,
graceful, and learned, a poet born, Sidney pleased
everybody, and, though a foreigner, was appointed
by the king gentleman of his chamber. Henri of
Navarre, who was to welcome the English comedians
at Fontainebleau, struck up a friendship with him. He
must surely have known "Helen" de Surgères, who
was then maid of honour to Catherine de Medicis, and
the beloved of Ronsard. Whether he may not have
climbed, in company with the elder poet, the interminable stairs which led to the rooms of the "docte de la
cour,"[1] is left for speculation:—

> "Tu loges au sommet du palais de nos rois,
> Olympe n'avait pas la cime si hautaine."

His sojourn left few traces; but his name, as we shall
see, was not forgotten in France.

Jonson's sojourn had even lesser results, although no
one would have been better entitled to a hearing.
Illustrious as he was among his compatriots, a great

---

[1] Nolhac, "Le dernier amour de Ronsard," 1882 (a reprint from the *Nouvelle Revue*).

admirer of the ancients, a translator of the Poetical Art
of Horace, whose severe precepts were thus put into
English for the second or third time,[1] a personal friend
of Shakespeare, whom he used to meet constantly at
the tavern only a little before, and who had lent him
his assistance as actor and perhaps as poet on the
occasion of his "Sejanus," Jonson might have given
some idea of what the English drama was like. But
old Ben loved a tavern even when there was no
Shakespeare in it, and he appears to have made himself conspicuous in Paris only as a drinker. He
accompanied to France Master Raleigh, the son of the
famous captain and writer. The young fellow, an
enterprising youth who had already killed his man
in a duel (his tutor being the last person who might
have blamed him for it, as he had done the same), gave
himself the pleasure of causing his mentor "to be
drunken and dead drunk so that he knew not where
he was." Young Raleigh placed him then on a car,

---

[1] These, for example (so readily accepted in France) :—

"Take
Much from the sight, which fair report will make
Present anon : Medea must not kill
Her sons before the people.
. . . Not
Any fourth man, to speak at all aspire."

This Poetical Art, finished about 1604 (and accompanied by a
commentary which disappeared in the fire that destroyed Jonson's
library), came out only in 1640. "Ce qu'on ne doit point voir,"
Boileau will say, drawing from the same source, "qu'un récit nous
l'expose." Previous translations : by Elizabeth (incomplete and
left by her in MS., see *supra*, p. 35) ; by Th. Drant, "Horace,
his Arte of Poetrie," London, 1567, 4°.

which was drawn in the streets of the capital, and passers-by were free to admire Silenus asleep. The anecdote is so strange that we might doubt the truth of it, did we not hold it from Jonson himself.[1]

The Bryans and Jonsons could only be remembered as drunkards; the Wyatts, Sackvilles, and Sidneys as model gentlemen, speaking French as all gentlemen did (Hubert Languet notes that Sidney's pronunciation of it was nearly perfect),[2] their English poems and all English literature remained unknown. The knowledge of literary England was so strictly limited to the Latin works she had produced, that writers using the English tongue had no great illusions themselves on that score. Nash notices in 1592 what we observe ourselves three centuries later: that the prodigious impulse received by dramatic art in London at that time remained totally ignored in France, Spain, and Italy. In order that his fellow authors and the actors who performed their plays, might receive their due, he was preparing a work *in Latin* to make their names known beyond the seas.[3] He did not carry out his plan; and so it befell that the only dramatist of Great Britain who influenced the French stage at all was that Franco-Scotchman, George

---

[1] This took place "anno 1613." "Conversations with Drummond," in "Works of Ben Jonson," ed. Cunningham, vol. iii., p. 483. The conversations are dated January, 1619.

[2] Letter dated 1574, "Correspondence of Sidney and Languet," ed. Pears, London, 1845, 8º, p. 38.

[3] "Pierce Penilesse," 1592. "Complete Works," Grosart, vol. ii., p. 93.

Buchanan, the author of "Jephtes, sive Votum," and of " Baptistes, sive Calumnia."

Such was the state of things in 1616, at the time of Shakespeare's death. His writings, his name, those of Spenser, of the Elizabethan lyrists, "Amourists," and dramatists were unknown; scarcely a few short literary works in prose had been translated : "Anglicum est, non legitur."

CHAPTER II

THE TIME OF LOUIS QUATORZE

I.

THE starting points stood very close together, but the roads unfolded in opposite directions. Soon those who followed them could no longer see and hear each other. After having had the same mysteries and the same moralities, having enjoyed the same jokes, laughed at the same pardoners and at the same shrewish wives and silly husbands, London, in the first part of the seventeenth century, had Shakespeare to admire; while Paris was seized with a passion for Mairet. There remained, it is true, in both countries, free lances and rebels who persisted in following their own by-ways far from the high-roads; and thanks to them, as time rolled on, a little neighbourly intercourse was still kept up, an intercourse unproductive and rare, as these independents, who strayed from the national ways, could teach nothing to the strangers they met, because they were too like them. The first English dramatist sincerely admired in France was not Shakespeare, but classical Addison. Dryden in

THE MANSIONS FOR THE PERFORMANCE OF THE PASSION PLAY AT VALENCIENNES, 1547.

Paradise | Nazareth | The Temple | Jerusalem | The Palace | The Golden Gate / The Sea | Hell

England modelled himself not upon the sober elegance of Racine, but upon the grandiloquent heroism of "Monsieur Calpranède."[1] Classical Addison could not teach the French of Louis XIV. anything, nor could grandiloquent La Calprenède instruct in any way the English of the Restoration.

Nothing can better show the difference in the genius of the two nations. The same rigorous doctrine is upheld in both countries, at the same hour, by equally authorized leaders; it is accepted in France by professionals and by the public, and rejected in England. English classical dramatists soon become curiosities; irregular dramatists will become curiosities before long on the French side of the Channel. The stern doctrines of theorists were welcomed in France from the very first by the best thinkers and writers, and gradually by every one, with a growing enthusiasm. The French had not *learnt* antiquity in the sixteenth century; they seemed to recognize what they had known before. Those Greeks, those Romans, were their own flesh and blood, as they thought; Aristotle and Horace were their ancestors; "Aristotle," according to a witty saying of Faguet, "is in truth the earliest French dramatic critic."[2] A perfect and intimate understanding could thus spring up between the theorists and the public, an understanding so dear to the public, that when later a reaction began, in the eighteenth century, and when other theorists tried to teach other doctrines

---

[1] Preface to the "Conquest of Granada."
[2] "Aristote est en vérité le premier des critiques dramatiques français." Faguet, "La Tragédie Française au XVIᵉ siècle," 1883, p. 35.

antagonistic to rules, the main resistance and the hardest to break came from the public; a resistance so stubborn that it took more than a hundred years to subdue it.

The regulars had, however, a struggle to sustain under Louis XIII. and under the regency of Anne of Austria. If the success was decisive, the skirmishes were hot; for the independents, Schélandre, Cyrano, Rotrou, soldiers of la Meilleraye or of Turenne, long-sworded and high-feathered, in whom survived the fighting traditions of the Valois, were not men to submit without a word, nor to surrender their fortress without a struggle; and their fortress was yet to be taken. Jodelle, Garnier, Grévin, neglecting the general public, had written mainly for a public of "connoisseurs." Paris, at the beginning of the seventeenth century, still had but one permanent theatre, that of the Brothers of the Passion, which continued to be influenced by its origin. The inexhaustible Hardy occupied the stage, producing by the hundred incoherent, irregular, romantic plays wherein "Aristotle's rules" were violated, to say nothing of the rules of decorum, where executions, armies on the march, sieges, battles were still seen as in the old mysteries; and the scene-shifter's art being in its infancy, recourse had to be had to the curious process of "simultaneous scenery."

On the public squares where mysteries used to be performed, Jesus was led from Caïaphas to Pilate, Mary Magdalen went from Palestine to Marseilles; the scaffoldings or "mansions" disposed around the square served to figure all the localities in which

"THEBES WRITTEN IN GREAT LETTERS UPON AN OLDE DOORE"
"BABILONIA" IN THE FRESCO OF BENOZZO GOZZOLI AT PISA

the dramatic action took place, as can be seen in the miniature representing the martyrdom of Saint Apollinia, preserved at Chantilly (fifteenth century) [1] and in the illuminated manuscript of the Valenciennes Passion, dated 1547, now in the National Library, Paris. Plays being acted now within a small space, inside a closed building, " simultaneous scenery " was used. On the same canvas were painted, in summary fashion and in close juxtaposition, all the places where the events in the play were located : a forest was represented by a tree, the Lybian Mountains by a rock, Athens, Rome, or Jerusalem by a portico, with the name written above, as in the mystery mansions, as in Gozzoli's frescoes at Pisa,[2] as on the English stage under Elizabeth : " ' Thebes ' written in great letters upon an olde doore," said Sidney. The public had to content itself with these symbols, which was not more difficult than to accept " foure swords and bucklers " as sufficient representatives for two armies which " flye in."

For the performance of that " Pandoste," which Hardy and Puget de la Serre had both put on the stage without suspecting that Shakespeare before them had turned it into his " Winter's Tale," the theatre was decorated, as we learn from the notes of the Hôtel de Bourgogne's scene-shifter, with scenery thus ordered : " In the centre of the theatre there must be a fine palace ; on one side, a large prison

---

[1] By the famous Jean Fouquet. See "Literary History of the English People," p. 470.

[2] Over the door of a city with wondrous palaces : " Babilonia." See the engraving, p. 67 (part of the fresco representing the building of Babel).

where one can be entirely seen ; on the other side a
temple ; below, the prow of a ship, a low sea, reeds
and steps " ;[1] viz., the palace of Pandosto, the prison
in which he will hold captive his unjustly suspected
wife ; the temple of Delphi, where the oracle will be
delivered ; and the vessel in which the forlorn child
will be placed, being "like to have a lullaby too
rough," as a greater master than Puget de la Serre
had said. For the second day, "you want two
palaces, a peasants' house, and a wood"—the palaces
of the two princely fathers, far apart though they
were in reality, the peasants' hut where Favvie
(Perdita) was brought up, and the wood where she met
Doraste (Florizel). Scene-shifter Mahélot is careful
to give also the list of movables necessary for the play,
and they consist of "a chafing dish, a ewer, a chaplet
of flowers, a flask full of wine, a cornet of incense, a
thunder, some flames : at the fourth act you must pro-
vide a child, and you want also two candlesticks and
some trumpets." Notes in a later hand, preserved in
the same album, show how much less was needed for the
performance of Racine's or Corneille's great tragedies.

[1] "Au milieu du théâtre, il faut un beau palais ; à un des costés
une grande prison où l'on paraist tout entier ; à l'austre costé, un
temple, au dessous, une pointe de vaisseau, une mer basse, des
rozeaux et marches de degrés." "Mémoire pour la décoration des
pièces qui se représentent par les commédiens du Roy entretenus
de Sa Majesté," by Laurent Mahélot, on whom some particulars will
be found in Rigal, "Hardy," Append. I. The general title of
the MS. is : "Mémoire de plusieurs décorations . . . commencé
par Laurent Mahélot (about 1631) et continué par Michel Laurent
en l'année, 1673." MS. Fr. 24,330 in the National Library,
fol. 20, unpublished.

SCENERY FOR THE PERFORMANCE OF "PANDOSTE" ("WINTER'S TALE"), AT THE HÔTEL DE BOURGOGNE, 1631. FIRST DAY.
From a contemporary sketch by *Laurent Mahelot.*

[*p.* 71.

In opposition to the "décor simultané," and no less characteristic of the times, the "palais a volonté," palace at will, any palace, recurs at every page. For the Cid all you want is "a room with four doors," and the list of movables contains one single article, "an armchair for the king."[1]

But the two roads, in the early part of the century, were not yet far apart ; the two stages continued to resemble each other. Mahélot's devisings are quite like those which Sidney had derided in London years before, with "Asia of the one side and Affrick of the other," in plays where the heroine, "after many traverces is got with childe, delivered of a faire boy ; he is lost," &c.[2] It seems as though Sidney were scoffing at the "Winter's Tale" that was to be ; while the audience at the Hôtel de Bourgogne admired it unawares.

If, however, the English drama was ignored, every one in Paris was familiar with the Spanish drama, and the chief master of that art, Lope de Vega, had made known his views on the question of rules in the most outspoken fashion : "When I have to write a comedy," he had said in his "New Dramatic Art," 1609, "I put all rules under lock and key ; I send away from my study Plautus and Terence lest I should hear their cries . . . and then I write according to the

---

[1] "Théâtre est une chambre à quatre portes ; il faut un fauteuille pour le Roy." For "Héraclius," "le théâtre est une salle de palais à volonté" ; for "Polyeucte," "le théâtre est un palais à volonté" ; for Racine's "Bajazet," "le théâtre est un sallon à la turque."

[2] "Apologie," 1595, ed. Arber, 1869, pp. 52, 63, 64.

art invented by those whose object was to obtain the
applause of the multitude." Like the "Ligueurs" of
yore, the French independents could thus count upon
the aid of the regiments of Spain; they made sallies
and fought battles, deriding in anticipation the
Académie and her expunged Dictionary: "You
censors of words and rhymes," exclaimed in soldierly
style, the soldier poet Jean de Schélandre, "with your
pumice and files, you give prettiness and rub off
beauty. As a soldier I speak and write. Know you
that strength in the spring, not smoothness in the
surface, makes a worthy lock for a good arquebuse." [1]

Schélandre practised as he preached; he gave in
1628 a new edition of his wild, unruly tragedy of
"Tyr et Sidon," with a preface written for him by his
friend Ogier, and pervaded with the very ideas which
Lope de Vega had expounded in his essay.[2] Ogier
rejects the unities, banishes the insufferable messengers,
retailers "of sorry intrigues" that ought to be left "at
the inn"; recommends a combination of the comic and
tragic elements in the same play: to separate them "is
to ignore the condition of men's lives, of whom the days

---

[1] "O censeurs des mots et des rimes,
Souvent vos ponces et vos limes
Otent le beau pour le joli;

En soldat j'en parle et j'en use;
Le bon ressort, non le poli
Fait le bon rouet d'arquebuse."

Asselineau "Jean de Schélandre, 1585-1635," Alençon, 1856, p. 3.
See below, p. 115.

[2] "Tyr et Sidon," Paris, 1628, 8º. 1st ed. (without the Preface),
1608. It offers a strange medley of tragedy, low comedy, lyricism
and bloodshed, with battles, scaffolds, drunkards, &c.

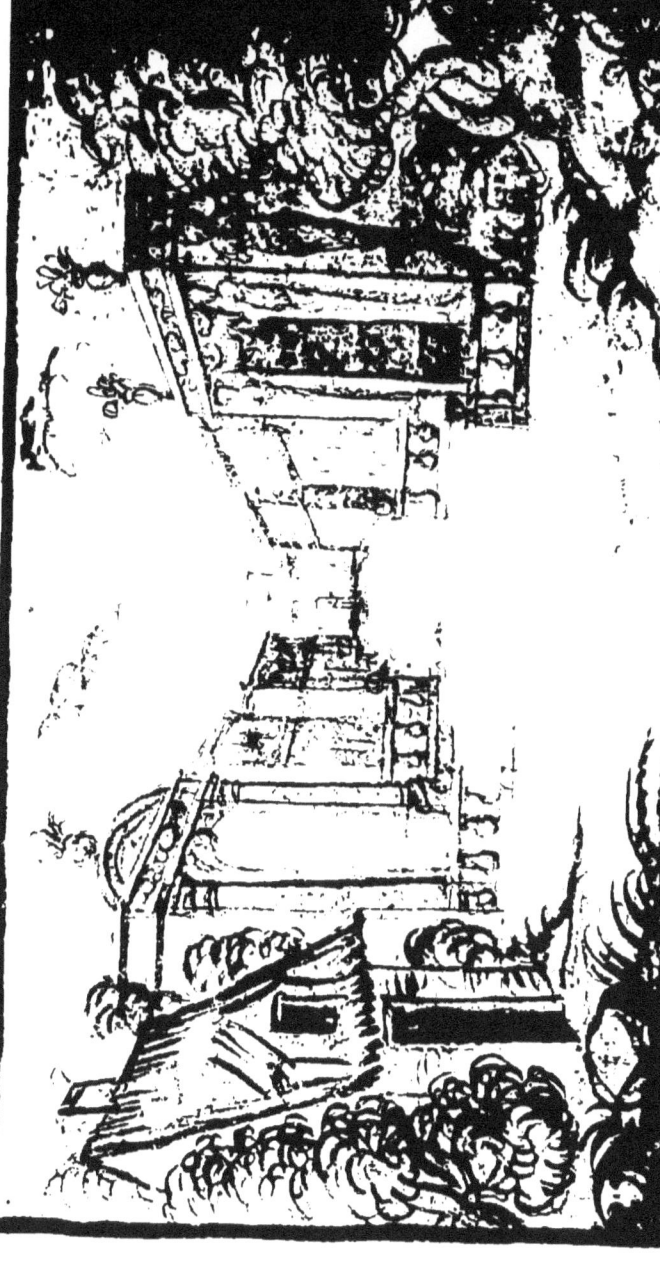

SCENERY FOR THE PERFORMANCE OF "PANDOSTE." SECOND DAY.

and hours are ofttimes intermingled with laughter and
tears, with contentment and affliction, according as they
are moved by good or by evil fortune." Ogier, without knowing it, was defending the poetical creed of
Shakespeare.

There are scarcely any articles of that unknown and
uncodified creed that did not then find some defender
in France : blank verse, the use of prose in a tragedy,
freedom of speech and attitudes, murders on the stage,
scenes drawn from national or contemporaneous history,
representation of sentiments as exalted and as low as
human nature will warrant. D'Urfé, the author of the
famous "Astrée," is for blank verse without rhyme.
"The Italians can boast," he says, " of being to-day
the most exact observers of the laws of dramatic
poetry" ; and they reject rhyme. D'Urfé decides,
therefore, to "clear that path as yet unexplored by
us Frenchmen," and he writes a pastoral drama, where
shepherds express their love in French blank verse.[1]

[1] Of which here is a specimen (beginning of the play) :—

> "Le prix d'amour c'est seulement amour,
> Et sois certain, Hylas,
> Qu'on ne peut acheter
> Si belle marchandise
> Qu'avec ceste monnoye.
> Il faut aymer si l'on veut estre aymé."

"La Sylvanire ou la Morte-vive, fable bocagère de Messire
Honoré d'Urfé," Paris, 1627, 8vo. Other poets were of the same
opinion, Chapelain especially, who would admit on the stage only
prose or blank verse. Rhymed verse is, according to him. "an
absurdity" in a drama, and it "oste toute la vraysemblance." All
foreigners, he adds (meaning the Italians and Spaniards), agree in
that : "Nous seuls, les derniers des barbares, sommes encore en cet

Gabriel Bounin, before him, had used a variety of metres in his tragedy of "La Soltane," even trying the experiment, very uncommon in French, of lines of fourteen feet.[1]

La Calprenède, on the other hand, turns contemporary history into dramas based "on good memoirs which I had received from persons of condition, who were themselves, perhaps, parties to the events therein recorded."[2] Puget de la Serre, author of "Pandoste," who had accompanied Marie de Medicis to London at the time of the marriage of Henrietta of France to Charles I., introduces bloody and horrible spectacles into a tragedy in prose on an historical subject:—

"*The King* (Henry VIII.). Bring me the heads of his companions to show him how I treat his like.

(*An empty charger is brought, and several others filled with heads.*)

The King. You have seen my cruelty only in painting; here it is in relief, and this empty charger, to be filled, awaits your head.

Thomas Morus. O precious relics of martyred bodies!"[3]

---

abus." "Dissertation," 1630; text in Arnaud "D'Aubignac," 1887, Append. IV.

[1] "*Le Soltan*. Sus, sus, muets, courez, volez, aigrissez vos courages,
  Aiguisez vos glaives, seigneurs, vos furiantes rages;
  Or sus occiez, meurdrissez ce traitre deloial,
  Hautain qui m'a voulu ravir mon sceptre impérial."
    ("La Soltane," 1561, 4°, p. 71.)

[2] "Le Comte d'Essex, Tragédie," 1650. He is less scrupulous in his "Édouard," 1640, where the King of England marries the Countess of Salisbury, previously entangled in the folds of this dilemma:—
  "Madame, c'est assez;
  Ou vous estes ma Reyne ou vous m'obeissez."

"Thomas Morus ou le triomphe de la foy et de la constance,"

Cyrano de Bergerac produces an "Agrippine," high flown and high sounding, marred by the most execrable bad taste,[1] but strewn with bold strokes, of a grandeur so truly Shakespearean that some have believed those passages to be the outcome of an imitation of the English master.[2] The resemblance, however, is fortuitous, and Cyrano never knew "Hamlet." "To die — to sleep —" occurs in a tragedy of Gabriel Bounin; and will it be said that Bounin imitated

Paris, 1735, 8vo; first ed., 1642, 4to. After his journey to London, La Serre published an "Histoire de l'entrée de la Reyne, mère du Roy très Chrestien, dans la Grande-Bretagne," London, 1639, folio. Superb engravings: see, *e.g.*, the Guildhall, behind which extends the open country, with a range of green hills and lanes bordered with hedges; sig. E. 2.

[1] Thus he describes how in battle heroic Germanicus dealt "such strokes that he disappeared entire into them."

"Se cachoit tout entier dans les coups qu'il donnoit."

His conquests were so rapid that he "outran the sun who was flying before him" —

"Qu'il devança le jour qui couroit devant luy."

Cf. "The English Novel in the Time of Shakespeare," p. 258.

[2] Including no less an authority than Mr. Sidney Lee, who, in his admirable "Life of William Shakespeare" (1898, p. 347), speaks of Cyrano's having "plagiarised" Shakespeare. But Cyrano never knew English; there is no serious proof of his having ever visited England (the allusion in the "États de la Lune" affords no such proof); the passages quoted below recall Hamlet, to be sure, but they are much more in accordance with Seneca, and with the genius of Cyrano himself. Speeches of this sort were not a rarity with the old French independents; Cyrano, if he wanted models, could find as many as he pleased in his own compatriots' works.

"Hamlet"? He wrote in 1561.[1] The romantics of both countries naturally resembled each other. One cannot read the lines in which the ghost of Germanicus comes to disturb Agrippina's repose in Cyrano's tragedy without remembering the royal ghost of Elsinore :—

> "*Agrippine.* Sanglante ombre qui passe et repasse à mes yeux,
> Fantôme dont le vol me poursuit en tous lieux,
> Tes travaux, ton trépas, ta lamentable histoire
> Reviendront-ils sans cesse offenser ma mémoire?
> Ah ! trêve, cher époux, si tu veux m'affliger,
> Prête moi, pour le moins, le temps de te venger.
> *Cornélie.* Il vient vous consoler de sa cruelle absence.
> *Agrippine.* Il vient, il vient plutôt me demander vengeance."

The hour of the long-expected revenge arrives; Agrippina has Sejanus in her power, and gives vent to the atrocious joy which fills her heart at the prospect of the vanquished enemy's torture. Sejanus remains unmoved, and expresses himself in a way that shows he has long been accustomed to face the awful problem of the dark beyond. His gaze has been as intense as Prince Hamlet's, but his temper is quite different ; he is not a moody thinker, but a man of action, his doubts have been quickly resolved into certitudes, he is insensible alike to spiritual and to physical fear. Why fear? The worst is death, and death is nothing. "Was I unhappy when I was not?" says he (translating Seneca word for word), "An hour after death our dissolved soul will be what it was an hour before life."

[1] "*Moustapha.* A, Sophe, mais encor, mais qu'est ce que mourir
Sinon, chez les aucuns, un perpétuel dormir? . . ."
("La Soltane," 1561, p. 58.)

"*Séjan.* Cela n'est que la mort et n'a rien qui m'émeuve.
Agrip. Et cette incertitude où mène le trépas ?
Séjan. Etais-je malheureux lorsque je n'étais pas ?
Une heure après la mort, notre âme évanouie
Sera ce qu'elle était une heure avant la vie.
Agrip. Mais il faut, t'annonçant ce que tu vas souffrir,
Que tu meures cent fois avant que de mourir.
Séjan. J'ai beau plonger mon âme et mes regards funèbres
Dans ce vaste néant et ces longues ténèbres,
J'y rencontre partout un état sans douleur
Qui n'élève à mon front ni trouble ni terreur ;
Car puisque l'on ne reste, après ce long passage,
Que le songe léger d'une légère image,
Et que le coup fatal ni fait ni mal ni bien,
Vivant parce qu'on est, mort parce qu'on n'est rien,
Pourquoi perdre à regret la lumière reçue,
Qu'on ne peut regretter après qu'elle est perdue ?
Pensez-vous m'étonner par ce faible moyen,
Par l'horreur du tableau d'un être qui n'est rien ?"

Many other elements of the Shakespearean drama can be found in the works of those independents who did not know the English master : his graceful fancies, his realistic details in the midst of comedies that resemble at times lyrical dramas and at other moments fairy tales ; his plots and situations, the very feelings of his grandest characters. Orantée, in Rotrou's "Laure," meeting unexpectedly a "belle inconnue" at a ball, falls in love at first sight. He loves her at once and for ever, as Romeo loved Juliet when he first met her in the hall of the Capulets.[1] He is led

[1] "*Octave.* Un jour donc, en un bal, un seigneur . . .
Orantée. Fut-ce moi ?
Car ce fut en un bal qu'elle reçut ma foi,
Que mes yeux éblouis de sa première vue
Adorèrent d'abord cette belle inconnue.

at one time to think her unfaithful, and his moan, his despair at having been " désabusé," recall Othello's passions : " 'Tis better to be much abused," says the Moor, " than but to know't a little. . . . I had been happy . . . so I had nothing known."[1] Quinault imitates Rotrou, who imitated Spain, and in 1653, remodelling a play of 1636, he gives his charming " Rivales." It is almost a tragedy ; the heroes talk of " their glory " ; it contains lyric monologues in stanzas similar to those in the " Cid " :—

> " Raison, n'en parlez plus, laissez agir ma rage ;
> Bien qu'Alonce tout seul m'outrage," &c.

It also contains hostelry adventures worthy of Don Quixote. The scene takes place sometimes in Lisbon, sometimes elsewhere ; sometimes on a heap of stones, sometimes in the hall of a roadside inn. The little details of everyday life are not forgotten ; the characters yawn, laugh, ask the hour, as they do in Shakespeare :—

> " Je voudrais bien savoir quelle heure il pourrait être."

They fall asleep without blowing out their candle, and it is remarked ; they talk loud : " Bless me ! how she

[1] "*Orantée*.
> Qu'ils livrèrent mon cœur à l'empire des siens
> Et que j'offris mes bras à mes premiers liens."
>   (" Laure," iv. 2, performed 1637.)
> Qu'on m'a fait un plaisir et triste et déplaisant,
> Et qu'on m'a mis en peine en me désabusant !
> Qu'on a blessé mon cœur en guérissant ma vue,
> Car enfin mon erreur me plaisait inconnue ;
> D'aucun trouble d'esprit je n'étais agité
> Et l'abus me servait plus que la vérité."—(*Ibid.*)

screams!" They do not call each other, "You green sickness carrion!" as old Capulet would say to his daughter Juliet, but they are nevertheless sufficiently energetic:—

"Que te dirai-je, horreur des plus abandonnées ?"

cries Don Lope on meeting his daughter in the streets before dawn. The heroines go about in men's garb, wear a sword, and draw it too, mount and ride through forests in pursuit of a fickle lover : the same lover, for they are "rivals." They meet, begin by loving, each finding the other a charming cavalier ; they recognize and provoke each other to a duel. A brother suddenly appears, the lover comes in too, confusion is at its height ; but the wisdom of Solomon brings matters to a satisfactory conclusion. Isabella sacrifices herself, and prefers to abandon Alonce to a rival rather than see him dead ; she is rewarded—it is she who finally marries him. Their adventures end thus "comme au théâtre" ; but life and the stage are very much alike. Shakespeare has said so in a famous line, "All the world's a stage." Quinault says so too, word for word :—

"La vie est une farce et le monde un théâtre."

II.

In spite of all their valiance and ardour, the independent "cadets" were not to win the day ; they were made prisoners or vanquished, obliged to disappear or to disguise themselves. Their stronghold had to surrender ; the stage was occupied by the regular troops. The spirit of vagabond liberty, the taste for romanticism and picturesqueness shone, from that moment, chiefly in literary *genres* of lesser importance, in the immense novels of the day, in La Fontaine's fables, in the "Belles au bois dormant" of Perrault, in memoirs, in the letters of Sévigné, in the opera, which had then more literary importance than now.

But the stage, properly speaking, once conquered, became immediately a hallowed place. Tragedy is capable of rules, and the taste for rules is in the air ; tragedy shall, therefore, be regular. The mere fact of being regular almost ensures success ; and this is so true that Scudéry, to secure the favour of the public, talks of the rules that he follows in his unruly romances.[1] The whole nation, chiefs and all, thirsted for regularity and good order ; Malherbe's poetry had put Ronsard's into the shade ; Richelieu had come, and no one thought of regretting the days of the League and of burly Mayenne. The defeat of the independents was inevitable, because the nation was less and less on their side. The hour had come ; the first man who should write for the general public dramas according to rule would be welcome, even if he lacked genius. He did lack genius, and he was welcomed ; he was Jean de Mairet.

The critics expected and heralded him. We must follow rules, said Chapelain in 1630, while still young and intact (Boileau was not yet born) : they have in their favour "the practice of the ancients, followed,

[1] Preface to "Ibrahim."

PERFORMANCE OF A COMEDY AT THE HÔTEL DE BOURGOGNE, TIME OF LOUIS XIII. ABRAHAM BOSSE INV. ET SC.

with universal consent, by all Italians."—But they
deprive us of pleasures, some will say.—Not at all, for
those are false pleasures, "de faux plaisirs," pleasures
barbarous and Gothic ; eschew Gothism : " We see all
sciences and all arts renew their former lustre. . . .
Every one is now awake with that laudable ambition,
and relinquishes Gothism after having seen what it is."
Should people at this time of day " remain barbarous in
that matter only ? " [1]

Elegant minds, cultivated courtiers, the frequenters
of *ruelles*, thought the same ; they pushed Mairet to
the front. " It is, perhaps, two years ago," he wrote
in 1631, to the Comte de Carmail, "since my lord
Cardinal de la Valette and you persuaded me to compose a pastoral play with all the rigour that Italians are
wont to use in that agreeable kind of work." For the
Italian regulars were not less known in Paris than the
Spanish independents ; their books were read and their
comedies applauded ; eight Italian troupes appeared in
Paris from 1595 to 1624.[2] Mairet, encouraged by that
strange ecclesiastic, Louis de Nogaret d'Epernon,
Cardinal de La Valette, archbishop of Toulouse and
leader of the king's armies in Italy, Savoy, and
Germany, studied the Italians, and saw that " they
had no greater secret than to submit to laws similar
to those of the ancient Greeks and Latins, whose rules
they have observed more religiously than we have
heretofore." Let us follow their example, adopt rules,
and especially " the most rigorous " of all, to wit, " that

[1] "Dissertation" in Arnaud's "D'Aubignac," Paris, 1887,
Append. IV., p. 337.
[2] Rigal, "Hardy," p. 107.

the play shall at least conform to the rule of the twenty-four hours." Mairet gave his "Silvanire,"[1] which pleased the elegants and the lettered; he gave his "Sophonisbe" in 1634, and carried all before him. The general public declared itself; enthusiasm knew no bounds. The play was poor, but regular; it was rapturously extolled. Nothing better shows the real nature and the inward feeling of that public than this prompt success. A Mairet has spoken, and, behold, all agree: here is the true way, the great art, the crowning art, the art which deserves to have care and expense lavished upon it. "The stage," says Perrault, speaking of this tragedy, "was proportionately embellished; acceptable scenery was painted, and crystal chandeliers were introduced to light it," instead of the "few tallow candles in bits of tin-plate" used before, and which, lighting the actors "only from behind, and a little from the sides, made them almost all look black."[2]

[1] "Il paroist donc qu'il est nécessaire que la pièce soit dans la règle au moins des vingt quatre heures." "La Silvanire ou la morte-vive, tragi-comédie pastorale," Paris, 1631, 4° (same title as d'Urfé's; above, p. 77).

[2] "J'ay ouy dire à des gens agez qu'ils avoient veu le Théâtre de la comédie de Paris de la mesme structure et avec les mesmes décorations que celuy des Danceurs de corde de la foire Saint Germain et des charlatans du Pont Neuf; que la comédie se jouoit en plein air et en plein jour, et que le bouffon de la trouppe se promenoit par la ville avec un tambour pour avertir qu'on alloit commencer." (The recollections thus related by elderly people to Perrault, born in 1628, refer to the period when Shakespeare was writing for the London stage.) "Ensuite on joua à la chandelle et le théâtre fut orné de tapisseries qui donnoient des entrées et des issues aux Acteurs par l'endroit où elles se joignoient l'une à l'autre. Ces entrées et ces sortie

"MIRAME," (ACT III.), A TRAGEDY BY DESMARETS DE SAINT SORLIN AND RICHELIEU, PERFORMED IN THE CARDINAL'S PALACE, 1639.

Greater results in that respect were secured when the chief man in France, Cardinal de Richelieu, gave free scope to his taste for dramatic art. A large hall in his palace (Palais-Cardinal, afterwards Palais-Royal) was turned into a theatre of such magnificence that Paris had, at last, little to envy to Vicenza or Parma;[1] and the scenery used in 1639 for the performance of the famous "Mirame," a classical tragedy, written by the Cardinal in conjunction with his favourite poet, Desmarets de Saint Sorlin, might well have been designed by Palladio himself.

"Mirame" was very far, however, from enjoying, as a play, the same success as "Sophonisbe." The fame of

étoient fort incommodes et mettoient souvent en désordre les coeffures des comédiens. . . . Toute la lumière consistoit d'abord en quelques chandelles dans des plaques de fer blanc attachées aux tapisseries, mais . . . elles n'éclairoient les acteurs que par derrière, ce qui les rendoit presque tous noirs." After the "Sophonisbe," "la scène s'embellissoit à proportion, on en fit les décorations d'une peinture supportable et on y mit des chandeliers de christal pour l'éclairer." "Parallèle des Anciens et des Modernes . . . dialogues . . . par M. Perrault de l'Académie Françoise," Paris, 1688, fr. 4 vols., 12°, vol. iii. (1692).

[1] Contrary to the Italian custom (imitated from the ancients, as can be seen at Vicenza, below, p. 99) Richelieu's theatre was not semicircular but square, and the rows of boxes were in straight lines, a fashion long continued in France.

This room was allowed to Molière's troupe when their "salle du Petit Bourbon" was demolished in 1660. The latter had once been the hall of the hostel of the famous Connétable de Bourbon, and occupied the spot where the Jardin de l'Infante now is. The States General of 1614 had been held there. As for Richelieu's stage, it was in a ruinous condition when Molière took possession of it, and important repairs had to be undertaken. See Despois, "Théâtre Français sous Louis XIV.," 1894, p. 30.

Mairet the initiator proved a lasting one; Richelieu had disappeared, Mazarin too, Louis XIV. was in all his glory, and the public still applauded "Sophonisbe." "Despite the thirty years that M. Mairet caused his 'Sophonisbe' to be admired on our stage, she still holds her own; and no more convincing proof of his merit is needed than that longevity, which may be called a forecast or rather foretaste of the immortality she assures to her illustrious author." Thus, in 1663, after having produced all his masterpieces, spoke Corneille himself.

If any one could have saved independent art and irregular drama it would surely have been this same Corneille. To him genius had certainly not been denied, nor the love of liberty. A daring genius was he, if ever such there was, enamoured (like Hugo at a much later date) of Spanish grandeur, deficient in suppleness and the art of management, stumbling on the threshold of doors too narrow for him. But he was not allowed to obey his inclinations; the public, dazzled though they were by the "Cid," would not have followed him, and he had to bow to their decision. Neither the Academy, nor the Cardinal, nor Scudéry could have dominated Corneille, for after all, even among the fashionable leaders of literature and the elegant refiners of speech, he had found partisans, witty and eloquent defenders of the liberties he had taken. The "Cid" is an irregular play? Agreed, wrote Balzac to Scudéry himself, but it is the triumph of truth and nature: "And because what is acquired is not so noble as what is natural, nor man's work so estimable as the gifts of God, one might say further-

KING LOUIS XIII. AT THE PLAY, WITH GASTON D'ORLÉANS, QUEEN ANNE OF AUSTRIA, AND THE DAUPHIN (FUTURE LOUIS XIV.), IN THE THEATRE OF RICHELIEU'S PALACE.

more that knowing the *art of pleasing* is not worth so much as knowing how to *please without art*. . . . But you say that he has dazzled the eyes of the world, and you accuse him of charm and enchantment. I know many people who would be vain of such an accusation." You oblige the author to acknowledge that he has "violated the rules of art," but you are constrained "to acknowledge that he possesses a secret which has succeeded better than art itself." He has deceived the public? "The deception which extends to so large a number of persons is less a fraud than a conquest." [1]

No critic as authorized had ever given such encouragement to Shakespeare; Jonson had grumbled that "Shakespeer wanted arte"; but Shakespeare had continued to follow the bent of his genius because he had the public with him, and it was Jonson, the partisan of the ancients, who was obliged to unbend his in order to keep an audience.[2] With Corneille it was just the reverse; from year to year the public in France was becoming more exacting, and the theorists were of one mind with the public; Corneille murmured at rules as Jonson did at Shakespeare's ignorance of them, but the author of the "Cid" was finally obliged to acknowledge himself beaten and submit to authority. Later on he would never have dared, in a real tragedy, to place his characters, as he had done before,

---

[1] Balzac to Scudéry, Aug. 27, 1637, "Lettres," Book iii., lett. 30 (Elzev.).

[2] In his learned study on d'Aubignac (1887, p. 171), M. Arnaud attributes chiefly "aux puissances" the sovereignty of rules in France; but this explanation is scarcely sufficient: in England, too, "les puissances" favoured rules, and yet rules were rejected.

"on the threshold of a magic grotto"; to make them prepare philters after the manner of Macbeth's witches; to show them "in the air, on a car drawn by two dragons"; to make them die on the stage consumed by an invisible fire, suffering tortures only comparable to the awful ones described in "Vathek," their robes adhering to their burnt and bleeding bodies :—

> "Voyez comme mon sang en coule à gros ruisseaux . . .
> Ah ! je brûle, je meurs, je ne suis plus que flamme." [1]

Still less would he have dared to write: "If some adore this rule [of the twenty-four hours] many despise it"; [2] it would have been accounted blasphemy, and he would have risked stoning.

---

[1] "Médée," 1635; death of Créon and of Créuse, v., 3, 4, and 5; preparation of philters by Medea, iv., 1. The resemblance to "Macbeth" is remarked upon by Voltaire in his "Commentaire": "Ces puérilités," he says, "ne seraient pas admises aujourd'hui." Corneille's fancy continued, nevertheless, to have full play in his lyrical comedies and transformation plays: "Andromède," "La Toison d'Or," &c. The notes in Mahélot's album for the performance of Corneille's plays well exemplify the change that came over the poet. The "palais à volonté" is all that is wanted for his great dramas; for the early ones we find indications such as these: "Au milieu, il faut un palais bien orné. A un costé du théâtre, un antre pour un magicien au dessus d'une montaigne; de l'austre costé du théâtre, un parc; au premier acte une Nuict, une Lune qui marche, des rossignols, un miroir enchanté, une baguette pour le magicien, des carquans ou menottes, des trompettes, des cornets de papier, un chapeau de ciprès pour le magicien." Notes for "Mélite" (performed 1629) with appropriate drawing. MS. Fr. 24,330, in the National Library, fol. 35. See above, p. 70.

[2] Preface to "Clitandre," 1632. He adds: "Que si j'ai enfermé cette pièce dans la règle d'un jour, ce n'est pas . . . que je me sois résolu à m'y attacher dorénavant." Nevertheless he was forced

It was risking, at the very least, being held up on the stage to public ridicule. Schélandre had had rules attacked in earnest by his friend Ogier in 1628. Times are changed ; Desmarets de Saint Sorlin, in 1637, gives to the independents, as a defender, his "Visionary," the ridiculous poet Amidor, who jeers at the unities, and is meant to be laughed at by the public. Why, says Amidor, "subject ourselves to the grotesque chimeras of those people, swaddled in their austere rules, who dare not await the return of Phœbus and care only for flowers that last but a day ?"

> " Pourquoi s'assujettir aux grotesques chimères
> De ces emmaillottés dans leurs règles austères,
> Qui n'osent de Phébus attendre le retour.
> Et n'aiment que des fleurs qui ne durent qu'un jour ?"

He continues, unwittingly praising Shakespearean tragedy, and the public unknowingly condemns it. With those rules, he says, the mind can embrace nothing grand ; when we have a hundred fine inventions in one play, then have we also a swarm of fine ideas : —

> " L'esprit avec ces lois n'embrasse rien de grand ...
> Dans un même sujet cent beautés amassées
> Fournissent un essaim de diverses pensées,
> Par exemple. . . ."

He gives an example ; it is a tragedy as full of action as "Hamlet," with journeys by sea, fights by land, a

---

to take that resolution and to keep it as he could : " Je ne puis dénier que la règle des vingt et quatre heures presse trop les incidents de cette pièce. . . . L'unité de lieu . . . ne m'a pas donné moins de gêne dans cette pièce." "Examen du Cid." performed, end of 1636.

king who dies of grief, a return home, a burial, the election of a new king, a mourning princess, &c. :—

> " Trois voyages sur mer, les combats d'une guerre,
> Un roi mort de regret que l'on a mis en terre,
> Un retour au pays, l'appareil d'un tombeau,
> Les états assemblés pour faire un roi nouveau,
> Et la princesse en deuil qui les y vient surprendre . . .
> Voudrez vous perdre un seul de ces riches objets ? " [1]

The public apparently had no objection to losing one or all of those "rich objects," and laughed heartily at Amidor and his antiquated literature.

All success was for the regulars, all the "Poetical Arts" protected them. Before Boileau's appeared we have the "Pratique du Théâtre" by Abbé d'Aubignac, who proclaims the sacred character of rules, dreams of theatres constructed "after the example of the ancients" [2] (like Palladio's "Olympic Theatre" at Vicenza), and registers in solemn form Corneille's act of submission : " The stage has changed, and has perfected itself to such a degree that one of our most celebrated authors "—printed in full in the margin, that none may ignore it, " M. de Corneille "—" has confessed several times that, in looking over plays that he had given to the public ten or twelve years since with great approbation, he felt shame for himself and pity for his approvers." [3]

---

[1] " Les Visionnaires," ii. 4. The subject had been suggested to Saint Sorlin by Richelieu ; performed with great applause, 1637 ; 2nd ed., 1639.

[2] " Projet de Rétablissement du Théâtre François," 1657, 4°, p. 512.

[3] " Pratique du Théâtre," 1657, p. 26.

AN ITALIAN THEATRE OF THE TIME OF SHAKESPEARE. THE "TEATRO OLIMPICO" OF VICENZA, BUILT FROM THE DRAWINGS OF PALLADIO, AFTER 1580.

Rules and unities must be; anything rather than violate them; anything, even subterfuge, trickery, or falsehood. As far back as 1639 changes of scene in a tragedy seemed to most people unsufferable; Claveret risked some in his "Proserpine," but in fear and trembling. Fear is an evil counsellor, and this is what it induced him to say: "The scene takes place in Heaven, in Sicily and in Hades, where the imagination of the reader can represent to itself a certain unity of place, by conceiving them as on a perpendicular line drawn from Heaven to Hades."[1]

Zealous to combine example and precept, d'Aubignac writes a "Maid of Orléans, tragedy in prose in accordance with historic truth and dramatic rules."[2] He crams in as many difficulties as he can, and he enumerates them complacently; he exacerbates at the same time the asperity of rules; the example will, he thinks, be all the better, and the triumph all the greater: "As the [dramatic] poem, is able to present to the spectators' eyes only what has taken place in eight hours, or at most in half a day, the plot can only be grounded on one of the most capital events: and as they have happened [with Joan of Arc] in divers times and places, and as I cannot take the liberty of advancing the times or confounding the places, the

---

[1] "Le Ravissement de Proserpine," Paris, 1639, 4·; note below the list of characters.
[2] "La Pucelle d'Orléans, tragédie en prose selon la vérité de l'histoire et les rigueurs du théâtre," Paris, Targa, 1642, 12°. There is no author's name on the title-page, but the publisher in his epistle to the reader declares that the play is by "M. l'Abbé Hédelin," i.e., d'Aubignac.

finest actions must of necessity be merely told." Then
there is another difficulty, unforeseen by Aristotle:
"Add also that the Maid was tried by the bishops of
Beauvais, Bayeux, and other ecclesiastics and doctors,
a thing which cannot be suffered on the stage."
D'Aubignac had luckily a happy thought: "I have
changed the clerical assemblies into councils of war."
An intrigue is wanted; there shall be one: "I
have supposed the Earl of Warwick to be in love
with Joan of Arc, and his wife jealous: for although
history does not mention this, it says nothing to
the contrary." Moreover this will be a symbol: in
the earl will be personified "the feelings of the more
reasonable among the English," and in his wife, "the
envy of the English against the Maid." Her death,
"as it cannot be represented," will be related. Nevertheless the death of Bishop Cauchon will be seen on the
stage; it will be a terrible *coup de théâtre*, but being a
bloodless one it can be allowed:—

"*Cauchon*. Good God, I am dead; an invisible shaft has just pierced my heart. . . . (*He falls.*)
The Duke. He has no doubt lost his life."[1]

No doubt he has. Liberty had Corneille on its
side; rules had d'Aubignac on theirs. If d'Aubignac
won the day, it was, indeed, because it could not possibly be lost. His victory was complete; rules imposed

[1] "*Cauchon*. Mon Dieu, je suis mort, un traict invisible vient de me percer le cœur. (*Il tombe.*)
Le Comte. Prompts et merveilleux effets de la prédiction de la Pucelle.
Le Duc. Il a sans doute perdu la vie."

themselves more and more imperiously on the greatest geniuses of the age—upon Racine, upon Molière; and they bore the weight with marvellous ease. But what despot ever thinks his subjects are submissive enough? From year to year the weight increased: so much so that even the regularity of Racine was questioned. Racine, in his turn, found himself in the position of Corneille; all his prefaces, like Corneille's, are apologies; even the preface to that model of regularity, " Andromaque," even the preface to a mere comedy like the " Plaideurs," part of his audience being afraid of not having laughed according to rules : " de n'avoir pas ri selon les règles." Racine protests his respect for decorum and virtue ; he affirms that he could never have dreamt of " polluting the stage by the horrible murder of so virtuous and so amiable a person " as Iphigenia ; he shows how he has " softened a little the ferocity of Pyrrhus," without, however, having done enough, as it seems, since " there have been people who complained of Pyrrhus's angry words to Andromache,"[1] others who affirmed that a

[1] "Quelle apparence que j'eusse souillé la scène par le meurtre horrible d'une personne aussi vertueuse et aussi aimable qu'il fallait représenter Iphigénie ?" Preface to " Iphigénie," 1674. " Toute la liberté que j'ai prise, ç'a été d'adoucir un peu la férocité de Pyrrhus ... encore s'est-il trouvé des gens qui se sont plaints qu'il s'emportât contre Andromaque. ... J'avoue qu'il n'est pas assez résigné à la volonté de sa maitresse et que Céladon (in d'Urfé's " Astrée ") a mieux connu que lui le parfait amour. Mais que faire ? Pyrrhus n'avait pas lu nos romans. Il était violent de son naturel. Et tous les héros ne sont pas faits pour être des Céladons." Preface to "Andromaque," ed. of 1668. (" Œuvres," " Grands Écrivains," iii. 140 ; ii. 35.)

performance of " Britannicus " " could never please an
audience," and finally, others who declared, when
" Phèdre " was given, " that it would have been well to
spare French spectators the horror of it." [1]

Molière, popular though he was, had nevertheless to
struggle in the same way against literary salons, more
exacting in their requirements than Boileau himself;
wits vied with each other in severity. The more severe
they were, the cleverer they thought themselves; so
that a motley crew, in silks and laces, the Marquis
Ignorance and Countess Prejudice, met at the first
performances of his plays, clamouring for rules, Greek
precepts, and Latin examples. The commander complained of the liberties taken; the viscount declared he
was shocked, and made a public exit after the second
act :—

> " L'ignorance et l'erreur, à ses naissantes pièces,
> En habits de marquis, en robes de comtesses,
> Venaient pour diffamer son chef-d'œuvre nouveau . . .
> Le commandeur voulait la scène plus exacte,
> Le vicomte indigné sortait au second acte. . . ."

But what was the ideal of Boileau, the author of those
courageous lines? The ideal of his time and of all
France: unity, clearness, regularity, selection, logic;
all of them qualities rare and noble, placed above all
others in French estimation, but which, carried to
excess, like all qualities, even the best in the world, are
not without serious inconveniences and drawbacks.
One of those inconveniences consists in the difficulty of

[1] Opinions of Saint-Evremond and of Donneau de Visé. Larroumet, " Racine," 1898, pp. 61, 83.

reconciling so studied an art with nature : for the rights of nature cannot be neglected ; no one dreams of contesting them, and Boileau less than any one ; we must learn from nature only :—

"Que la nature donc soit votre étude unique,"

says he.[1] But nature is singularly complex, variable, and checkered ; if she is our only study, we risk putting on the stage many things which have just been forbidden us : after having studied, the playwright will have to select. Tragedy must be simple ; it must have few personages, and only one hero, as there is but one king in the kingdom, and one sun in the heavens. We must make a point of being exclusive, even at the risk of having it said one day "that the French, who understand the sun, are incapable of understanding the moon" (Heine). No matter ; moon-worship will be left to hyperborean dreamers.

In tragedy, Boileau continues, "pompous verse" shall be used ; the spectator will be filled with a "gentle terror," a "charming pity" ; the poet should imitate the brook running over soft sand, "sur la molle arène," rather than the "overflowing torrent" ; there will be no *enjambements* or run-on lines ; regularity is our ideal, and great will be the enjoyment if our lines imitate the ticking of that most regular of

---

[1] On that point all agreed ; the two arch-enemies, Chapelain and Boileau, say the same thing : "Je pose donc pour fondement que l'imitation en tous poèmes doit estre si parfaitte qu'il ne paroisse aucune différence entre la chose imitée et celle qui imite." "Dissertation," by Chapelain, 1630, in Arnaud's "D'Aubignac," Append. IV.

mechanisms, a pendulum. The unities will of course be observed. The first place shall be given to love, that passion being the true way to the heart; love :—

"Est pour aller au cœur la route la plus sûre."

But love must never be so described as to appear "une vertu." What must be "withheld from the eyes" shall be told :—

"Les yeux en le voyant saisiraient mieux la chose ;"

no doubt, seeing would make things more comprehensible, but it is preferable they should be less understood and decorum be better observed. What Boileau said the public thought, and it was not slow now to manifest its feeling if any one, great or small, showed signs of an unruly spirit. Antony kills himself on the stage in a play by Jean de la Chapelle of the Académie Française. La Chapelle is of the Académie, and therefore the more guilty : "This catastrophe is new and striking," wrote the author afterwards with compunction, "but it has not been generally liked by the spectators, who cannot bring themselves to accept the sight of blood on the stage," 1681.[1]

You will be noble, continues Boileau, even in comedy, and be playful with dignity, you must "badiner noblement." Avoid naturalness which is only natural, observes La Bruyère at the same time : "A farce writer may draw comical effects from a scene with a peasant or a drunkard. . . . The characters, it is said, are natural ; but according to

[1] "Frères Parfaict," xii. p. 286.

that rule, the whole amphitheatre will soon be entertained by a whistling valet, a sick man in his closet, a drunken man in his dormition or vomition. Can anything be more natural ? "[1] For your serious plays, resumes Boileau, choose heroes of antiquity, with sounding names, quite different from the "Childebrands" of ancient France. Let your conclusion be abrupt and simple; resort, when you can, to the effective means of a suddenly revealed secret :—

"D'un secret tout à coup la vérité connue,"

will bring about a prompt and interesting ending.

On examining closely this ideal, which was that of all thinking France, one is struck with the real grandeur that appears amidst so many puerilities. This nature, which should be observed unceasingly, must also be restrained; at that cost only is she worthy of constant study; man must overcome himself. The share of picturesqueness in life and art will be diminished : for if we act according to rules our deeds will have nothing unexpected; but the share of nobleness will be augmented. One cannot have too much dignity; dignity may be only a garment, but are there not examples to show that garments have influenced characters? To more than one soldier, who was not born a hero, the uniform has given heart. The dresses worn under Louis Quatorze scarcely allow their wearers to roll on the grass, to fall prostrate on carpets, or even, in the agonies of remorse, on the steps of a church. Man is magnified by the ideas of the time;

[1] La Bruyère. "Caractères," "Des ouvrages de l'esprit," 1688-90.

everything relates to him; what is not man has little interest: let him, therefore, justify the honour done him, and first of all, let him on all occasions be master of himself. He must possess himself even in moments of passion, even in his poetical transports; otherwise he lowers his nature, he approaches to madness, and the beauty of his outbursts can never compensate for the danger of them. "I think that this humour of composing verses," wrote Descartes to a lady (the mother of Prince Rupert) who had herself composed some, "comes from a strong agitation of animal spirits, which might entirely derange the imagination of those whose brain is not firmly settled, but which merely warms the more solid a little and disposes them to poetry." [1]

Man must everywhere preserve his dignity: in the presence of nature, of the woman he loves, and whom he will address as "Madame," and in the presence of God Himself. The best minds acquire thus something chastened and austere which greatly surprises the strangers who visit France at that time. People who want to fritter away their life in amusements go now

[1] "L'inclination à faire des vers que Votre Altesse avoit pendant son mal me fait souvenir de Socrate, que Platon dit avoir eu une pareille envie pendant qu'il étoit en prison. Et je croy que cette humeur de faire des vers vient d'une forte agitation des esprits animaux qui pourroit entièrement troubler l'imagination de ceux qui n'ont pas le cerveau bien rassis, mais qui ne fait qu'échauffer un peu plus les fermes et les disposer à la poésie." He then tries to console her for "la funeste conclusion des tragédies d'Angleterre," the late tragic events in England. To Madame Élisabeth, Princesse Palatine, "Lettres de M. Descartes, où sont traittées plusieurs belles questions," Paris, 1667, 3 vols., 4º, vol. i., p. 83.

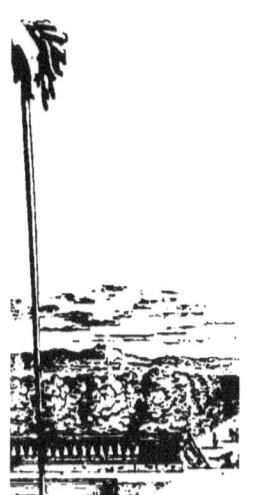

to London, to the Court of the " Merry Monarch," as Gramont does ; Hugues de Lionne, the foreign minister of Louis, sends his son there for la " petite Genins " to sharpen his wit and rub off his shyness.[1]
Meanwhile Racine and Boileau, "after thirty-five years of intimacy," address each other in their private correspondence as " Monsieur," or at most " Mon cher Monsieur."[2] Port-Royal fulminates against Racine himself, and condemns the entire stage : " A theatrical poet is a public poisoner. . . . Sins of this sort are the more fearful, that they are ever living, because those books do not perish."[3] Bossuet does not spare Corneille[4] any more than Lulli, whose " airs so often repeated in the world serve but to insinuate the most deceptive passions " ; his music " is so easily engraved in the memory because it first takes hold of the ear and of the heart." Those noble tragedies of the

[1] 1665, "A French Ambassador at the Court of Charles II.," 1892, pp. 152 ff.
[2] Larroumet, "Racine," p. 107 ; Racine, "Œuvres" (Grands Écrivains), vol. vii., pp. 91, 98.
[3] Nicole, " Visionnaires," 1666.
[4] " Dites-moi, que veut un Corneille dans son ' Cid,' sinon qu'on aime Chimène, qu'on l'adore avec Rodrigue, qu'on tremble avec lui lorsqu'il est dans la crainte de la perdre et qu'avec lui on s'estime heureux lorsqu'il espère de la posséder ? . . . Ainsi tout le dessein d'un poète, toute la fin de son travail, c'est qu'on soit comme son héros épris des belles personnes, qu'on les serve comme des divinités ; en un mot qu'on leur sacrifie tout, si ce n'est peut être la gloire dont l'amour est plus dangereux que celui de la beauté même." Observe that in thus placing " glory " higher than love, the heroes of Corneille showed themselves more manly than many a hero of Arthurian fame : Lancelot, for example, who sacrificed even " glory " to his lady ; a noteworthy change.

classical *répertoire*, so grand, so dignified, so virtuous, as it seems to us, whose only fault, in some eyes, is that they offer intentionally attenuated pictures of realities, were not judged thus in the seventeenth century. Let us, it was said, beware of the dangers of the stage " where everything seems real, where we are shown not lifeless sketches and dry colours, but living personages, real eyes, ardent or tender, steeped in passion; real tears, that draw tears as real from those who look on; in a word, real passions which inflame the whole audience, pit and boxes." [1] Thus spoke that great judge of morals, Bossuet.

Unity, logic, rule, selection. The government tends towards centralisation; religion " rules even desires and thoughts "; [2] the possibility of two religions could only have been considered in an age of confusion; the sixteenth century ended with the edict of Nantes, the

---

[1] " Maximes et réflexions sur la Comédie," 1694, " Œuvres Complètes," Bar-le-Duc, 1863, vol. viii., p. 82. Compare the testimony of the actor Mondory, who writes to Balzac in a tone of triumph, justifying the apprehensions of Bossuet : " Le Cid est si beau qu'il a donné de l'amour aux dames les plus continentes, dont la passion a même plusieurs fois éclaté au théâtre public " (January 18, 1637); and with the testimony of Boileau on the subject of Lulli :—

> " De quel air penses-tu que ta sainte verra
> D'un spectacle enchanteur la pompe harmonieuse . . .
> Et tous ces lieux communs de morale lubrique
> Que Lulli réchauffa des sons de sa musique ? "
> (Satire X.)

[2] Letter from a friend of Port-Royal to Racine, in the quarrel of the " Visionnaires," 1666 ; " Œuvres " (Grands Écrivains), iv., p. 293.

THE MEMBERS OF THE FRENCH ACADEMY ADDRESSING LOUIS XIV. ON THE PUBLICATION OF VOL. I. OF THEIR DICTIONARY, 1694

From a plate in the Dictionary.

seventeenth century with its revocation. Fine, regular, straight avenues are drawn across the parks ; the language, like the parks, is trimmed, cleansed, and chastened ; the Academy prunes it of all those technical terms formerly praised by Ronsard and Malherbe, who wanted a language both rich and strong ; now it is wanted above all noble and dignified. Old words, " les vieux mots," are excluded from the great national vocabulary ; also new ones, " nouvellement inventés " ; also " terms of art and science " ; also expressions of anger or offensive to modesty—" les termes d'emportement ou qui blessent la pudeur." No such improper words have been " allowed into the dictionary because honest men avoid using them in their speech," and academicians do not write dictionaries for clowns. The word "*essor*" (soar) is accepted out of favour, although tainted with " falconry." [1]

Whole families of words are thus driven from the kingdom of poetry ; for them too the edict of Nantes is revoked ; in 1694 the Academy " banished " them, as she expresses it, from her dictionary, and their exile was to last longer than that of the Protestants.

III.

What place could be found in the favour of a public thus formed, for an author who accepts words of all sorts, old or new, lewd, technical, choleric, or learned ; every sentiment and every idea, and far from attenu-

[1] "Dictionnaire de l'Académie." Preface of the first edition, 1694.

ating them in order to keep them within the bounds of nobleness and decorum, carries them to extremes with the view of rendering his contrasts as decided as possible; an author who falls into the most execrably bad taste, reaches the loftiest heights of sublimity, writes plays with or without heroes, plays with whole legions of personages, among which he admits not only the whistling valet and the swearing drunkard, descried as in a nightmare by pessimist La Bruyère, but even dogs, and even a bear ("Exit pursued by a bear"); an incommensurable dramatist now full of tears, now of jokes, who watches the martlets fly (in the middle of a tragedy), wonders whether the crickets are listening ("Yond' crickets shall not hear it"), sings the sweetest love-songs the world has ever heard, divines all our joys, weeps for all our sorrows; coarse beyond endurance, lyrical beyond all possibility of adequate praise; in a word, what place was there for Shakespeare in the France of Louis Quatorze?

A place all the smaller from the fact that the subjects of the "Grand roi," particularly at the beginning of his reign, knew scarcely more English than those of his grandfather, Henri IV., and in the matter of foreign tongues continued to take interest only in Spanish and Italian.[1] Madame de Sévigné never ceased to cultivate the latter; she wrote to her daughter: "Et l'italien, l'oubliez-vous? J'en lis toujours un peu pour entretenir noblesse." Spain was the great fount re-

[1] Ménage, in his "Origines de la langue françoise," Paris, 1650, 4°, makes a few comparisons between French and English (see for instance the words "souiller," "soldat"), but in his recapitulatory index there is only place for Latin, Spanish, and Italian.

sorted to by French dramatists and romance writers in quest of a subject; her language continued to be commonly studied: "Spanish grammars have not been bought to the amount of fifty thousand *livres*, but very near it," wrote Scarron to his friend Marigny. "Sir," said one day old M. de Châlon, late Secretary of the Commandments of Queen Anne of Austria, and now retired to Rouen, addressing young Corneille, "the comic style which you adopt can only procure you a short-lived glory. You will find in Spanish authors subjects which, treated according to our tastes by hands like yours, would produce great effects. Learn their language; it is easy; I am ready to show you what I know of it, and until you are able to read for yourself, to translate a few passages from Guillem de Castro." Corneille followed this advice and wrote the "Cid"; it could never have occurred to him to seek inspiration in that Shakespeare whose contemporary he was for ten years, but from whose works M. de Châlon would have had great difficulty in translating a "few passages." Corneille possessed, however, an English edition of the "Cid"[1] and was very proud of it; it was a great curiosity. England, and the English, figure occasionally in his works; a land and people convenient, because distant and unknown. He wrote a play of which the scene is laid in Scotland, "in a castle belong-

[1] That of J. Rutter, "The Cid, a tragi-comedy, out of French, made English," London, 1637, 12°. But his foreign library mainly consisted of Spanish and Italian books. In 1652, he bought at auction in Rouen, "un Dante italien, in folio, 12 livres." "Œuvres" (Grands Écrivains), i., p. xli.

ing to the King, near a forest"; it is not another
"Macbeth," it is his wild "Clitandre." In the
"Illusion Comique" figures an English lord,
"Théagène, seigneur anglais"; he might just as well
have been a "seigneur" of Argos or of Corinth;
Corneille could never have put "seigneur français,"
or "seigneur italien," because he would not have
commanded the distance necessary for the "illusion."

Racine's letters show him to have been quite imbued
in his youth with Italian literature; quotations from
Petrarch, Tasso, and especially Ariosto, constantly
recur under his pen. Later he is interested in England,
but as royal historiographer. The same love of accuracy
that made him ask the French Ambassador to Turkey
for information on Greece and the fields where Troy
had been,[1] made him seize the opportunity of a meeting with "Monsieur Arbert" at the English Ambassador's, to acquire knowledge about England. On
coming home he took notes which we still possess,
but they bear solely on economic questions and on the
militia; "la milice d'Angleterre appelée trainbans."[2]

---

[1] The ambassador, M. de Guilleragues, describes in reply, with doleful accuracy, the naked rocks, the tiny harbours, that can never have sheltered thousands of ships, the rivers, dry ten months of the year, the poor country: "Les poètes avaient des maîtresses dans les lieux où ils ont fait demeurer Vénus" ("De Péra, au Palais de France," June 9, 1684).

[2] "Œuvres" (Grands Écrivains), v., p. 132. Racine possessed the "Histoire d'Angleterre" of Du Chesne, 1614, a few historical works translated from the English, but none in English. He had, on the other hand, many Italian and Spanish books, a Franco-German-Latin dictionary, a Spanish reader (by Lancelot). See Bonnefon, "Revue d'Hist. Litt. de la France," v., p. 169.

Boileau, who corresponded with Hamilton and Gramont, recommends to French poets the knowledge of foreign lore : "Des pays étrangers étudiez les mœurs"; and he immediately refers his readers to "antique Italy." All the examples he takes from foreign literatures are drawn, without exception, from Spain or Italy ; he condemns "Tasso's tinsel," the "showy folly" of Italian "false jewels"; he quotes in his verses Tasso's religious poem, but not Milton's ; he has heard of satires written against women by Ariosto and Boccaccio, but not by Chaucer ; of "Rocinante cheval de Dom Quichot," but not of the "Faerie Queen"; of the independence of the stage "delà les Pyrénées," but not beyond the Channel. In the "Lutrin," Barbin's bookshop is sacked and its exotic treasures are used as projectiles by the combatants : from dark recesses emerge "Guarinis" and "French Tassos," nothing but the products of southern literatures. Addison visited Boileau in 1700, and found him old and a little deaf, but "talking incomparably well in his own calling ; he heartily hates an ill poet." The conversation turned on Homer, Virgil, Racine, Corneille, Fénelon's "Télémaque," which "is at present the book that is everywhere talked of"; but not a single allusion seems to have been made to English letters.[1]

French was, indeed, more than ever before, the common means of communication in Europe. Howell instructed his "forreine traveller" to learn it first of

---

[1] Addison to Bishop Hough, Lyons, December, 1700, "Works," ed. Hurd, 1854, vol. v. p. 332. According to Tickell, he showed Boileau some verses of his own, but they were *Latin* verses.

all, on account of "the use one shall have of that language wheresoever he passe further." [1] "As I have visited with care every part of Christendom," writes, on his side, Chappuzeau, "it has been easy for me to observe that to-day a prince with only the French language, which has spread everywhere, has the same advantages that Mithridates had with twenty-two." [2]

It was quite an extraordinary event when, in the early part of the century, a few timid translations of English literary works appeared. The translators wondered at their own audacity, and could not conceal their surprise. "Here," says Tourval, speaking of Hall's "Characters," "is the first translation from the English ever printed in any vulgar tongue," and he pompously dedicates so rare a work to that great man, not only the Lord High Treasurer, but the very Treasure of England; that "grand Cécil

---

[1] "Instructions for forreine travell," 1642, Arber's reprint, 1895, p. 19. Jean Blaeu, in publishing "L'estat présent de l'Angleterre, traduit de l'anglois d'Eduard Chamberlayne," Paris, 1671, 16° (first English edition, 1669), thus justifies his undertaking: "Je ne l'ay pas sitost veu en Anglois que j'ay jugé qu'il méritoit de paroistre dans la langue françoise, comme estant plus universelle dans la chrestienté qu'aucune autre" (Epistle to "Monseigneur le Chevalier Temple").

[2] Chappuzeau, "Le Théâtre François," 1674, ed. Monval, 1876, p. 62. This favour continued during the eighteenth century, as is shown by the subject proposed for competition by the Berlin Academy: "De l'Universalité de la Langue Française," 1783 (Rivarol, "Œuvres," 1804, vol. ii.). "La langue Française est devenue celle de toutes les cours et de presque tous les gens de lettres de l'Europe." (De Belloy, "Observations sur la Langue Française," "Œuvres," 1779, vol. vi.) See below, p. 298.

... non le grand Trésorier [mais] plutôt le grand Trésor d'Angleterre." [1]

A greater marvel was in store; the honour of a translation, and even of two translations, was paid to the "Arcadia" of the "cygne doux-chantant," the former guest of Charles IX., Sir Philip Sidney. The two translators, Baudoin and Geneviève Chappelain, who had departed secretly on their incredible voyage of discovery, meeting on the same shore, looked at each other with stupefaction. Fury seized them; they loudly "bawled," to use their own expression, and sent each other challenges, persistently renewed as each successive volume of their translations was given to the world.[2]

Notwithstanding the success of the "Arcadie," facilitated by that of the "Astrée," attempts of this kind continued to be extremely rare; English remained ignored. The unwary traveller could read in

---

[1] "Caractères de vertus et de vices tirés de l'anglois de M. Joseph Hall," new edition, Paris, 1619, 12° (first ed. 1610). The attribution to Tourval is doubtful. Among the other translations of literary works done at that same period, may be mentioned Greene's "Pandosto," translated by L. Regnault, Paris, 1615, 8°, Bacon's "Essays," translated by Baudoin in 1611, Nash's "Pierce," which he affirms had been put (at an earlier date), into French, but abridged and spoilt, &c. No copy of French "Pierce" has yet been found.

[2] "L'Arcadie de la comtesse de Pembrok," translated by Baudoin, Paris, 1624, 3 vols., 8°. The translation by Mademoiselle Chappelain began to come out in 1625, 3 vols., 8°. Mareschal took the subject of a drama from Sidney's work, "La cour bergère ou l'Arcadie de Messire Philippes Sidney, tragi-comédie," Paris, 1640, 4°. On the Baudoin-Chappelain quarrel, see "The English Novel in the Time of Shakespeare," pp. 274 ff.

a guide-book that the chief English coins were called
"Crhon, Alue Crhon, Toupens, Alue Pens, Farden."[1]
Ambassadors themselves, in spite of the lengthy
sojourns they made in London, did not usually learn
a word of the language. Cominges, under Louis
XIV., called a street "rue Rose Street," without suspecting that "rue" and "street" meant the same
thing; the Comte de Broglie, in the following century,
described a curious ceremony at Court which he called
a "drerum." "A French ambassador to England,"
wrote Voltaire in 1727, "does not usually know a
word of English; he can speak to three-quarters of
the nation only through an interpreter; he has not
the faintest notion of the works written in the
language; he cannot see the plays in which the
customs of the nation are represented." The "Journal
des Savants" itself, anxious to justify its title, had
desired to give an account of English books, and
had therefore been obliged to go in quest of an
"interpreter." It published in 1665 the following
note on the Royal Society of London: "This
company produces every day an infinity of fine
works. But because they are mostly written in the
English tongue, we have been unable heretofore to
give an account of them in this Journal. But we
have at last found an English interpreter, by
whose means we shall be able in future to enrich it
with everything worthy of attention produced in
England."

It needs must come to that, since the English persist
in using their own language, causing thereby real grief

[1] "Les voyages de M. Payen," 1666, 12°, p. 24.

to the learned of other countries : " The English are very clever people," said Ancillon, " their works are nearly all good, and many are excellent. It is a pity that the authors of that country write only in their own language, since by that means foreigners, for want of understanding them, cannot profit by their works, or if they read them it is only in translations, for the most part faulty."[1] A third means, which would consist in learning the language, was not thought of.

The country, before the Restoration, was as yet much less visited by tourists than Spain or Italy. Those who appeared in the island, knowing neither the language nor the manners, generally returned greatly dissatisfied with their venture, and the tales they told of it did not encourage others to repeat the experiment. Boisrobert, the dramatist and the familiar of Richelieu, went there, but quarrelled with Lord Holland ; Voiture went and visited the Tower, but, as became the amiable letter-writer, he scarcely tried to remember anything except the Countess of Carlisle's beauty.

Soon, moreover, all Europe was seized with horror at the sight of the unexampled disorders and catastrophes of which the country became the scene : a king brought to trial by his people, and beheaded, a republic proclaimed, a new era inaugurated in the midst of royalist Europe, dating from the first " yeare of freedome by Gods blessing restored." Boileau,

---

[1] " Mélange critique de littérature, recueilli des conversations de M. Ancillon," Bâle, 1698, 3 vols. ; vol. i., " Sur les Anglois."

who was then very young, and already thought he could "pindarise," addressed poetical imprecations to Cromwell.[1] Perlin's predictions had come to pass; the English had indeed killed and crucified their king.

The author of "Moïse," Boileau's future victim, Saint-Amant, whose father held for many years a maritime command in the fleet of Queen Elizabeth,[2] visited England in 1631, and in 1643-44. He met with nothing but disappointments there, and revenged himself by composing epigrams and caricatures in verse. This is, however, the first noteworthy attempt made by any Frenchman of letters to describe English manners.

The English he considers to be now republicans to the core. If Fairfax is still alive, and if the devil has

---

[1] "Quoi ce peuple aveugle en son crime,
   Qui prenant son roi pour victime
   Fit du trône un théâtre affreux,
   Pense-t-il que le ciel, complice
   D'un si funeste sacrifice,
   N'a pour lui ni foudre ni feux?"
(Ode written at eighteen, but, he says, "je l'ai raccommodée.")

[2] "Feu mon père," he says himself, "commanda autrefois, par l'espace de vingt-deux années, une escadre des vaisseaux d'Élisabeth reine d'Angleterre." Adventurous and erratic were all the members of the family. Marc-Antoine de Gérard sieur de Saint-Amant, Écuyer, Gentleman-in-Ordinary to the Queen of Poland, a member from the beginning of the French Academy, was conspicuous as a soldier, traveller, and poet. He visited Africa, America, and most countries in Europe. His father, the seaman, was three years a captive in the Black Tower in Constantinople; one of his brothers fought in Germany, another was killed in the Red Sea. Durand-Lapie, "Saint-Amant," Paris, 1898, 8º, pp. 5, 12, 13.

not yet removed him, it is out of fear that his own kingdom " might be turned into a republic "—

> ". . . craint que par quelque attentat,
> Que par quelque moyen oblique,
> Fairfax n'aille du moins renverser son etat
> Pour en faire une République."

The climate is shocking; there can be no pleasure even in drinking amidst such darkness; a great privation for Saint-Amant, one of the most illustrious drinkers of his day, " bon pifre," as he calls himself:—

> " C'est le pire des climats ;
> La nue y fait un amas
> D'objets tristes et funèbres ;
> Je n'y mange qu'en ténèbres
> Et n'y bois que des frimas."

The inhabitants are morose; life is a burden to them; they hang themselves for the least thing. The Englishman is—

> " Si fait à la pendaison
> Qu'au premier mal qu'il se forge,
> Il se pèse par la gorge
> Aux poutres de sa maison : "

an ever-recurring reproach, repeated by every one, including La Fontaine, who says of the English—

> . . . " le peu d'amour de la vie
> Leur nuit en mainte occasion."

The people are rude : if foreigners cross the street, one will be elbowed out of the way, another insulted :—

> " Et l'autre, avec un *french-dogue*,
> Est entrepris et bravé."

The food is detestable ; the English are known to brew unpalatable mixtures : —

> " Marier dans leurs pâtés
> La confiture à la graisse."

What can be expected from such a people ? What literature can they have ; or rather, what judgment could be passed upon it by a visitor so ill-disposed, and, moreover, ignorant of the language ? To Saint-Amant, as to so many others before and even after him, this language is a *patois* that no one out of the island will ever speak ; peasants' *patois* rarely spreads beyond its village. Any Englishman knows as much :—

> " Il est bien assez matois
> Pour juger que ce patois,
> Bourru, vilain et frivole,
> Est un oiseau qui ne vole
> Qu'aux environs de ses toits."

The traveller could not, however, help noticing that the English had a stage, that they were very proud of it, that they went in crowds to the play, and that one author in particular carried all before him. That author was not Shakespeare, of whom Saint-Amant says never a word, but Ben Jonson, still alive at the time of the French poet's visit, and compared with whom, according to local estimation, Seneca and Euripides were mere babbling poetasters. The Englishman—

> " . . . a néanmoins l'audace
> De vanter ses rimailleurs ;
> A son goût ils sont meilleurs
> Que Virgile ni qu'Horace.

> Sénèque auprès d'un Jonson,
> Pour la force et pour le son,
> N'est qu'un poète insipide,
> Et le fameux Euripide
> N'a ni grâce ni façon."

Saint-Amant visited the different theatres; the acting seemed to him in harmony with the plays, the climate, the food, and everything the country produced. Actors come in before their turn, they mistake their words, and do not know what to do with their hands :—

> " Ici l'un trop tôt se montre,
> Et là, l'autre, rebondi,
> D'un contre-temps étourdi.
> Heurte l'autre qu'il rencontre ;
> L'un disant Goths pour Romains.
> Ou les dieux pour les humains.
> Rougit comme une écrevisse,
> Et l'autre simple et novice
> Ne sait où mettre ses mains."

What do they play? Interludes, dumb shows, masks with dances. They represent Andromeda, Merlin, Arthur and the Round Table. In their interludes they dare—

> ". . . dessous des chiffons
> Jouer la pauvre Andromède ;
> Quelquefois, venus des cieux,
> Ils dansent, droits comme pieux,
> Des moralités muettes,
> Ou, de sottes pirouettes,
> Ils éblouissent les yeux.

> Tantôt l'on revoit au monde,
> Faits comme des bandoliers (highwaymen),
> Artus et ses chevaliers,
> Gloire de la Table-Ronde ;
> Tantôt l'antique Merlin,
> Enfant d'un esprit malin,
> Hurle en ombre vaine et pâle."

As for serious plays, they are remarkable for their murders, battles, bloodshed, and also for the crowds they draw—a moved, distracted, and panting crowd which comes to the theatre and forgets shop, stall, and home, and wishes the play would last two hundred years—

> " Tôt après le tambour sonne ;
> Tout retentit de clameurs.
> L'un crie en saignant : Je meurs !
> Et si l'on n'occit personne.
> Les feintes, les faux combats
> Font trembler et haut et bas
> Le cœur du sexe imbécile,
> Qui laisse œuvre et domicile
> Pour jouir de ces ébats.
>
> L'une voyant l'escarmouche,
> En redoute le progrès ;
> L'autre oyant de beaux regrets,
> Pleure s'essuye et se mouche ;
> L'autre . . .
> Gabant vainqueur et vaincu,
> Gruge quelque friandise
> . . .
> Mère, fille, tante et nièce,
> Bourgeois, nobles, artisans,
> Voudraient que de deux cents ans
> Ne s'achevât une pièce."

Saint-Amant composed his diatribe in London the 12th of February, 1644. He did not publish it, but it gives us an idea of the way in which, on his return to Paris, he must have described English manners, literature, and drama in his conversations with his lettered friends.[1]

The guide-books published about that time were scarcely calculated to correct these impressions. In his "Fidèle conducteur pour le voyage d'Angleterre," printed in Paris in 1654,[2] Coulon warns the reader that this island "used to be the dwelling-place of angels and saints, and is now the hell of demons and parricides. But for all that its nature has not changed; it is still in its place." It is worth the trouble of going there, O traveller! "Thou wilt be able to observe the remains of the former piety as well as the commotions and disorders produced by the brutality of a nation run mad, though at the same time stupid and northern." A description follows, written in a way that recalls the travels " dans la Tartarie le Thibet et la Chine," of Father Huc, a large space being devoted to the wonders which abound in such remote and unknown countries. The land called "Buquhan" in Scotland deserves a visit: "No rat comes to life in this province, and if one is

[1] "Albion, caprice heroï-comique"; "Œuvres Complètes," ed. Livet, Paris, 1855, 2 vols., 12°, vol. ii.
[2] Still less useful information is to be found in La Boullaye le Gouz, "Voyages et observations," Paris, 1657, 4°. He joined the Court at Oxford, a town whose name means, he explained, "le fort des bœufs" (the fortress of the oxen), p. 442, and went to Ireland, where he came near being killed by the inhabitants, who took him for an Englishman.

brought there it cannot live. . . . Birds also are found in this place called *clayks*, whose birth is wonderful in this, that they are produced by trees growing by the seashore. They grow like fruits, and they fall into the sea when ripe, so that branches are to be seen loaded with those imperfect produce, some of which have only their beak and head grown into shape, others half their body finished, while some others, ready to swim or fly, hang to the tree only by a little thread, and the same being broken they swim and fly like ducks." [1] Thus everybody in the Paris of 1654 could know all about the *clayks* or ducks which grow upon trees, but no one had heard of that other produce of the British Islands, William Shakespeare.

IV.

A change began to be seen shortly after the Restoration. The Civil War had forced many English writers to make prolonged stays in France; most of the Cavalier poets had come there; such men as Waller, Cowley, and Lovelace. Sorbières had formed in Paris a friendship with the famous Hobbes, and that friendship brought about a journey to London, of which we possess the curious narrative. Charles II. once re-established on the throne of his ancestors, every Frenchman of distinction who came as an exile or as a visitor

---

[1] On the search instituted for those fabulous animals by Æneas Sylvius Piccolomini (Pius II.) while in Scotland, see "The Romance of a King's Life." Æneas Sylvius was informed at each place that they were to be seen "further north"; he could never go north enough, he says, to find them.

was certain to find a welcome at that brilliant and
pleasure-loving Court, " cette cour toute jeune, toute
vive et toute galante," where Gramont soon went to set
the fashion. Actors and actresses came in numbers,
and were particularly well received.[1] No less well
treated were Protestant refugees at a somewhat later
date.[2] Journeys to England became more frequent.
The impressions brought back by travellers were
pleasanter ; the land no longer seemed so very
" northern," nor the language so barbarous.

That literature of which Saint-Amant had spoken so
disparagingly, making an exception, as usual, in favour
of Bacon alone, began to arouse a certain amount of
curiosity. The example came from above ; it was
given by the king himself. I have related elsewhere
the anecdote taken from the papers of Cominges.
Questioned by his master on the subject of English
famous men, the Ambassador answered that he had

[1] December 10, 1661 ; "Warrant to pay to John Chemnoveau,
300*l*., as the King's bounty to be distributed to the French
comedians."—August 25, 1663 : " Pass for the French comedians to
bring over their scenes, stage decorations, &c.," " Calendars of State
Papers, Domestic, Charles II." Bellerose and Pitel came to London,
See Chardon, " La Troupe du Roman Comique," 1876, pp. 47, 98.

[2] Some of them, such as Boyer, born at Castres in 1667, or
Motteux, born at Rouen, 1660, ended their days in England, after
having learnt English so well that most of their works are in that
language, and that they count among English rather than among
French authors. Their English works (poems, essays, dramas,
newspaper articles) remained practically unknown in France ;
they highly deserved the qualification bestowed upon Chaucer by
Deschamps, of "grands translateurs" ; Boyer translated works by
Racine and Fénelon ; Motteux has remained almost famous as
translator of Rabelais and Cervantes.

a short tale to tell, the whole literary glory of the
English consisting "only in the memory of Bacon,
Morus, and Buchanan," and for more recent times
in the works " of one Miltonius, who had made himself more infamous by his dangerous writings than
the executioners and murderers of their king " (1663).[1]
The time for histories of English Literature in five
volumes had not yet come. We must note, however,
this new curiosity concerning English letters which
begins now, and will spread more and more.

The desire to know the land was spreading too; the
days of Cromwell were past; England was now subject
to a singular ruler who took nothing seriously, and
who, though head of a nation until lately so morose,
seemed to be earnest only in love affairs :—

> " Votre prince vous dit un jour
> Qu'il aimait mieux un trait d'amour
> Que quatre pages de louanges,"

wrote La Fontaine to Lady Harvey. And, whereas
Ronsard had dreamed of chimerical journeys to South
America with Villegagnon, the fabulist lived in the
hope, no less chimerical, of accompanying to England
that beautiful and turbulent Duchess de Bouillon (one
of Mazarin's nieces), who was so fond of animals and
had a weakness for their poet, but who hated Racine

---

[1] "A French Ambassador," pp. 202, 223. Costar, in his
"Mémoires des gens de lettres des pays étrangers," names, among
the poets, only one Englishman, Milton; and even then he merely
remarks that he would doubtless have done better to class him
"au nombre des sçavans." "Continuation des Mémoires de littérature de Salengre," by le P. Desmolets, 1726, vol. ii., p. 353.

THE DUCHESS OF BOUILLON, NIECE OF CARDINAL MAZARIN, FRIEND OF WALLER AND LA FONTAINE.

[p. 133.

and much preferred Pradon. Cæsar composed four despatches at once on four different subjects, wrote La Fontaine to the duchess : " You have nothing to envy him on that score ; and I remember that one morning, while reading some verses to you, I found you at the same time attentive to my reading and to three quarrels of animals. It is true that they were on the verge of throttling each other ; Jupiter the conciliator could not have pacified them."

The duchess has gone, she receives in London the visits of Saint-Evremond and Waller, very old and broken and full of wrinkles both of them, but, as poets, " the youngest of all those around the spring of Hippocrene."

> " Anacréon et les gens de sa sorte,
> Comme Waller, Saint Evremond et moi,
> Ne se feront jamais fermer la porte.
> Qui n'admettrait Anacréon chez soi ?
> Qui bannirait Waller et La Fontaine ?
> Tous deux sont vieux, Saint Evremond aussi ;
> Mais verrez-vous au bord de l'Hippocrène
> Gens moins ridés en leurs vers que ceux-ci ? "

La Fontaine decidedly wants to join her ; as preparation, "I shall have to see first five or six Englishmen and as many Englishwomen ; they say Englishwomen are good to look at." He proposes to Saint-Evremond, exiled in London, and very much enamoured of the no less beautiful and still more turbulent Duchess Mazarin (another niece of the Cardinal's), that they should set forth together. They will make themselves " Knights of the Round Table, as beseems people travelling in the country where that chivalry began." They will go in quest of adventures; but, adds the poet sadly, "we will await the return of the leaves and of my health; otherwise I should have to seek adventures in a litter; I should be called the Knight of the Rheumatism, a name scarcely fit, it seems to me, for a knight errant."[1] La Fontaine never started; even in his youth he had only liked journeys that did not take him far from home, journeys "aux rives prochaines."

But if he stayed, others went. Guide-books, tales of travel, grammars with dialogues multiplied, making known a country that was beginning to arouse interest:—guide-books and travelling impressions by Sorbières, Le Pays, Payen, Chappuzeau, Muralt, Misson, Beeverel (an Englishman), G. L. Le Sage, Moreau de Brasey, and several others;[2] grammars, voca-

---

[1] November, December, 1687. "Œuvres" (Grands Écrivains), vol. ix. La Fontaine never knew Waller personally; he writes to M. de Bonrepaus, the French Ambassador, on the 31st of August, 1687, a few weeks before the death of the English poet: "J'ai tant entendu dire de bien de M. Waller que son approbation me comble de joie." Waller also greatly admired Corneille, and the latter was apprised of it by Saint-Evremond, who served as spokesman for the men of letters of the two countries: "M. Waller, un des plus beaux esprits de ce siècle, attend toujours vos pièces nouvelles et ne manque pas d'en traduire un acte ou deux en vers anglais pour sa satisfaction particulière." Corneille, "Œuvres" (Grands Écrivains), x., p. 499.

[2] "Relation d'un voyage en Angleterre où sont touchées plusieurs choses qui regardent l'estat des sciences et de la religion et autres matières curieuses," by Sorbières, Paris, 1664, 8º. (On Sorbières and his journey, see "English Essays from a French Pen," chap. iv.)—"Relation d'un voyage d'Angleterre," by Le Pays, in "Amitiez, amours et amourettes," new ed., Paris, 1672, 12º, p. 172.- "Les voyages de M. Payen," Paris,

bularies, dialogues by Mauger, Festeau, Miège, Boyer. Even Thomas Corneille could not forbear giving in his great "Dictionnaire Universel" particulars on the "fauxbourg qu'on appelle Sodoark," that is Southwark, where Shakespeare had been seen playing in his own plays, but which was favoured with a mention only on account of the *Bergiardin* (Bear garden) " a great amphitheatre where there are fights of all sorts of animals," and of a meadow close by, " in which, with his spear, St. George killed the dragon that desolated the country." [1]

[1] 1666, 12°.—" L'Europe vivante ou relation . . . de tous ses États jusqu'à l'année présente, 1667," by Chappuzeau, Geneva, 1667, 4° ; one chapter is devoted to the " Iles Britanniques" ; Chappuzeau speaks *de visu:* " J'ai été présent à tout ce qui suit " ; more details in " Le Théâtre François," by the same, 1674 (ed. Monval, Paris, 1876).—" Lettres sur les Anglois et sur les François et sur les voyages," by Muralt (written in 1694-95), Geneva, 1725, 8° ; this, together with Sorbières' journey, is the most important of these documents.—" Voyages du Sieur de la Motraye " (to England, 1697), the Hague, 1727, 3 vols. fol., vol. i., ch. viii.—" Mémoires et observations faites par un voyageur en Angleterre," by Misson, the Hague, 1698, 12°, in dictionary form, curious engravings. —" Les délices de la Grand' Bretagne, par James Beeverel, A. M.," Leyden, 1707, 8 vols. 12°, " le tout enrichi de très belles gravures dessinées sur les originaux."—" Remarques sur l'Angleterre faites par un voyageur en 1710 et 1711," par G. L. Lesage (a Protestant refugee), Amsterdam, 1715, 8°.--" Remarques sur l'Angleterre faites en 1713, par M. de S. G.," in " Recueil de pièces sérieuses," &c., 1721, 16°.—" Le Guide d'Angleterre," par Moreau de Brasey, Amsterdam, 1744 (a series of letters dated 1712-14).

[1] " Dictionnaire universel géographique et historique," Paris, 1708, 3 vols. fol., *sub verbo* " Londres." In the article "Stretford " (on Avon) no mention is made of Shakespeare. Bayle, in his " Dictionnaire historique," 1697, devotes an article to Jodelle and none to Shakespeare ; it is true he omits also Plato and Corneille.

Those travellers, now more numerous, who noted down their impressions, no longer passed such uniformly unfavourable judgments on the country as the Paradins and Perlins of old. They continued having many mishaps and surprises, but nevertheless they mingled some praise with their vituperations. The appearance of the country, which had already propitiated Perlin (who added by way of compensation " Bonne terre, male gent "[1]), elicits raptures from Sorbières. He describes with admiration " its little hills and vales clothed with perpetual verdure . . . and those lawns, some of which are so smooth that one can play at bowls on them as if they were the cloth of a huge billiard table. . . . The country is so covered with trees that even the fields look like a forest when seen from a height, owing to the orchards and to the hedges that enclose the arable land and the meadows." Sorbières observes, too, from the moment he lands, a very characteristic peculiarity: all the houses have bay windows, thanks to which one can see out sideways, "ce qui est à côté," whereas in France "we see from ours only what is before us." If Sorbières had known English and read Shakespeare he might have observed that it was with the stage in the two countries somewhat as with the houses. The author of "Hamlet" required windows

[1] This unpleasant proverb was well known in the sixteenth century, and the English applied it in return to other nations: "Whereas they were woont to saie of us that our land is good but our people evill, they did but onlie speake it, whereas we know by experience that the soile of Italy is a noble soile, but the dwellers therein farre off from anie vertue or goodnesse." Harrison's "Description of Britaine," book i., ed. Furnivall, 3rd part, p. 132.

open in all directions; his house of poetry was full of bay windows, where he liked to sit, and whence he could see not only what was in front of him but also "what was aside."

Strangers are greeted rudely. "French dog" has not gone out of fashion, quite the contrary. At the landing, urchins rush forward as if they had "never seen a Frenchman," and cry, "a mounser, a mounser." The Frenchmen get vexed, the urchins get excited, a crowd collects, the cry of "French dog" resounds, dogs bark, stones are thrown; the first impression is certainly a bad one. Travellers must arm themselves with philosophy, and try to see the good side of things, like Muralt, who, after having noted the use of "French dog," applied, as a matter of fact, to "all sorts of foreigners as well as to the French," adds, "I have no doubt that many think to aggravate the title of dog by the epithet of French," but the French, on the contrary, are so proud of being French that they find "for that very reason the abuse somewhat atoned for."

The women still keep up their reputation for beauty, as we have seen by La Fontaine's remark. All travellers praise them. Le Pays finds them rather cruel: "Les belles de ce pays ici sont furieusement cruelles"; not, he adds, that they always reduce their lovers to despair, but they have a marked liking for horrible sights. Fair youths, "blondins," take their "blondines" to see gladiators; young women in England "like blood and carnage," and are in a great measure responsible for the massacres that take place in English tragedies. Muralt, who has a weakness for dark-haired ladies, is of opinion that there are too many blondes in England, and that they wear too many patches. Chappuzeau, on the other hand, is in ecstasies over them; and Payen finds "their carriage extremely advantageous."

The singularity of the inhabitants' character strikes all travellers; their mind has something independent, rebellious and peculiar, shown in everything they do. Their parliament is a strange assembly, "un corps bigearre," unlike anything known; they are uncontrollable debaters; even the common people discuss public affairs, and have an opinion on the king's acts, and what an opinion! "Going back," says Sorbières, "to the remembrance of the power of their fleets in the time of Oliver, to the glory they acquired on every sea, to the alliances that the whole earth sought to make with them, to the pomp of the Republic toward which came ambassadors from all sides, they cannot help making odious comparisons and showing some disposition toward new disorders." This people is, in reality, ever on the verge of a revolution; no other can be compared to it for the quantity of kings who have died a violent death.[1] "When I am shown here," says Le Pays, "the sad spot where the late king had his head cut off, I give vent to a thousand imprecations against this cursed nation, and I take great pleasure in seeing on the doors and the towers of

[1] A copy of the "Nouvelle Grammaire Anglaise-Française" of Miège, Rotterdam, 1728, preserved at the National Library of Paris, contains manuscript notes of the eighteenth century, on the English kings who have died a violent death: "Cruauté naturel aux Anglois qui est sans exemple par tout le monde qu'aux Anglois seul [*sic*]." This was, in fact, a current aphorism: "Cette nation est cruelle," says Gui Patin, more than once, "Lettres," Paris, 1846, 3 vols., iii., 148, 287, 666.

London so many criminal heads, arms, and thighs. The head of Cromwell, of execrable memory, is much to my liking, placed as it is over Westminster Hall." Nevertheless, " the throne still seems a little shaky."

They do anything that comes into their minds ; they ignore the moderation that a classical education teaches in other countries ; they go at once to extremes. If a king displeases them they cut off his head. If they are bored, they hang themselves. All this "extravagance of ideas," remarks Sorbières, thus proving a precursor of Taine, comes from the soil, " leur vient du terroir." [1] These peculiar dispositions exert an influence upon their amusements ; no doubt they have some pacific ones, like " the ringing of bells, which is practised in no other part of the world," [2] and to which Bunyan addicted

---

[1] The same ideas, which can in fact be traced back to Aristotle, occur in Voltaire, the Abbé Du Bos, and others : " Pourquoi toutes les nations sont elles si différentes entre elles . . . quoiqu'elles descendent d'un même père ? Pourquoi les nouveaux habitants d'un même pays deviennent-ils semblables, après quelques générations, à ceux qui habitaient ce même pays avant eux ?" It is owing to the climate and to the " pouvoir de l'air," according to Du Bos " Réflexions critiques sur la Poésie," Paris, 1719. Voltaire attributes the different forms of genius in part to the way in which countries are governed, but more especially " au terrain et au ciel " of each land : " Il se pourrait bien encore que le gouvernement d'Athènes, en secondant le climat, eût mis dans la tête de Démosthènes quelque chose que l'air de Clamar et de la Grenouillère, et le gouvernement du Cardinal de Richelieu ne mirent point dans la tête d'Omer Talon ou de Jérôme Bignon." ("Dictionnaire Philosophique," "Anciens et Modernes.")

[2] " Nouvelle Grammaire angloise, enrichie de dialogues curieux, par Paul Festeau, maistre de langues à Londres," London, 1672, 8°, p. 164. Citizens and peasants have, besides other sports and pastimes, " la sonnerie des cloches qui est une récréation que l'on

himself with that almost pagan ardour of which he bitterly repented later. But they are specially fond of combats between various animals, cocks, dogs, bears, which, being excited for the purpose, tear each other to pieces, and they are so brave that they "always die on the spot." They also have combats between men, "who do not hesitate sometimes to give each other terrible blows and to swallow half one another's cheek." Fair and rosy ladies flock to this amusement, in which foreigners see "something very ferocious" (Sorbières). The sight diverts English women; they are afraid of nothing, and their reputation for courage is so well established that it is quite surprising if one of them proves an exception to the rule. "The Comtesse de Gramont," writes Madame de Maintenon, "has fallen, since her little attack of apoplexy, into a melancholy, a fear of death, and continual tears; one cannot recognise that superior mind, nor that English courage; all is weak in her."[1]

Other exercises are less dangerous, such as horse-racing, in which the animals run "so fast that it is not conceivable" (Beeverel), or football. "In winter, football is a charming and useful exercise; it is a leather ball, as big as one's head, and full of wind; it is tossed with the foot in the streets by whoever can catch it; there is no further science," write Misson, who simplifies somewhat the rules of the game. Muralt finds that, there again, the people lack reserve: "Sometimes

---

ne connoist point en aucune autre partie du monde." "L'Estat présent de l'Angleterre, traduit de l'Anglois d'Eduard Chamberlayne," Paris, 1671, p. 89.

[1] To the Princesse des Ursins, April 10, 1707.

THE BRITISH MUSEUM (MONTAGUE HOUSE) BEFORE ITS RECONSTRUCTION.

they divert themselves in a manner both inconvenient and mingled with insolence, as when they kick a ball through the streets, and take pleasure in breaking the panes in houses and the glass in coaches."[1]

The inhabitants' religion, like their administration, has something " bigearre " and extravagant about it. Sects are innumerable ; the most curious is that of the Quakers—" Coacres," as Misson calls them. Every traveller goes to see them, and is never at a loss for details concerning the singularities " the spirit " dictates to these enthusiasts. " They are accused," writes the Protestant, G. L. Lesage, " of believing that once the spirit is formed in them they no longer sin, whatever they may do. A soldier, it is said, pursued a Quakeress with his solicitations ; wearied at last by his importunities, she exclaimed, ' Well, since thou wantest to lose thy soul, lose it.' " The ordinary clergy are a pleasure to behold, with their air of prosperity : " It is agreeable," says Muralt, another Protestant, " to consider all those fat and rubicond chaplains. These gentlemen are accused of being a little lazy, and this great corpulency makes one suspect that there is something in the accusation."

The respect for religious things is rare ; free-thinkers, " libertines," are numerous, says G. L. Lesage ; " this comes, in great measure, from the fact that people

[1] Foreigners were unanimous in passing judgments of this sort : " Les estrangers jugent que, parmy ces jeux, celuy de faire combattre les coqs est trop bas et indigne de la noblesse ; le combat des ours et des taureaux, trop cruel pour le peuple et le balon de pied trop incivil, rude et barbare pour les bourgeois." " Estat present de l'Angleterre, traduit d'Eduard Chamberlayne," Paris, 16-1, p. 89. Compare above, p. 13. the opinion of Grévin, time of Elizabeth.

of the lowest class and of the last degree of ignorance are free to talk of religion and ecclesiastics in a scandalous manner. Walking one day with one of my friends in the fields behind Montagu House," now the British Museum, "as far as a new quarter, where a chapel was being built which bears the name of St. George, we approached a carpenter, who was working, after the manner of his country, with a pipe in his mouth. Having asked him what they were proposing to make . . . he replied coolly, without looking at us, ' A priest-shop ' " (" Une boutique de prêtre ").

The coffee-houses, taverns, and theatres count among the curiosities of London. There were coffee-houses in Paris, but they were far from having at that date the importance of the English ones. Noblemen, artisans, men of letters, clergymen, every Londoner went to the coffee-house. Les "coquets ridicules" went too : "In English," says Misson, "those fellows are called *fops* and *beaux*. The theatres, chocolate houses, and the promenade of the park swarm with them. They run after every new fashion ; periwigs and coats covered with powder, as millers are with flour ; faces besmirched with tobacco, *dégingandé* airs, the gait and appearance of true *Mascarilles*, lacking only the title of marquis " (Molière's marquesses and Mascarilles).

In the coffee-houses people talk, quarrel, prepare the fall or triumph of plays, actresses, or ministers, drink tea, chocolate, "a stomachic drink," or coffee, a curious liquor that has " the real taste of a burnt crust," price, one sou.[1]   In short, the " northern "

[1] Dialogues by Miège in "Nouvelle facile Méthode pour apprendre l'anglois," new ed., Amsterdam, 1698, pp. 294, 295.

FRENCH OFFICERS SMOKING THEIR PIPES IN A "TABAGIE,"
TIME OF LOUIS XIII

country has humanised itself; one can find people there to talk to, joke with, and "flirt" with, "à qui conter fleurette." Certain travellers having realised the expedition dreamed of by La Fontaine, come back enchanted, although they have not discovered, in the land of King Arthur, now the land of the " bon roi Stuart," as many giants to conquer and damsels to defend as romances had led them to expect. "We have not yet found a single barrier defended," writes Pavillon, "not the least little giant to fight, and, excepting for a few damsels on palfreys that one meets with occasionally, I should never have thought myself in the kingdom of Great Britain, so entirely have things changed here since the reign of King Arthur. One no longer hears of damsels carried away forcibly : whether it be that love's laws are better obeyed, or that ladies do not accompany their resistance with such loud clamours as of old . . . I know not. . . . Whatever the reason, no one complains, and I find the women of to-day a thousand times more civil than those bawlers of bygone days who yelled like mad and drew from the four quarters of the universe knight errants to avenge their injuries on people who very often had done them more honour than they deserved." Contrarily to what Saint-Amant thought, people eat, drink, laugh, "and the late land of plenty of very happy memory (le defunt pays de Cocagne de très heureuse mémoire) was worth scarcely more than this one." Everything abounds there, and if you do not live in France you cannot do better than go and settle in England—

> "Enfin dans ce pays on voit que tout abonde,
> Et sans exagérer, pour tout dire à la fois,
> Quiconque a le malheur de n'être pas François
> Est ici beaucoup mieux qu'en aucun lieu du monde."[1]

London with its streets, shops, and booksellers, its famous Mr. Hobbes, its "savants," Royal Society, monuments, and walks; Oxford with its colleges; the country with its castles and verdure;[2] the ports with their infinity of ships, are all described by turns in numerous books, and sometimes represented in engravings. A place is given to literature, but a very small one as yet. Chappuzeau, who knows more about it than Cominges, quotes half a dozen names, amongst which dramatic art is represented by Davenant alone: "the Chevalier Davenant whom dramatic poety has made famous."

The language is rich but shapeless; it has neither rules nor limits: a great defect, say travellers; a great advantage, reply the English. "The English tongue," writes Beeverel, "has not the delicacy of the French, but whereas Frenchmen are servilely attached to an Academy which subjects them to its rules in such wise

---

[1] M. Pavillon to Madame de Pelissary, time of Charles II., in the "Mélanges" annexed to the "Œuvres mêlées" of Saint-Evremond, London, 1708, vol. vi. p. 91.

[2] So pleasant to behold that English Le Nôtres dare not modify nature, and they willingly allow trees to grow as they please. English parks, says Pavillon, "sont faits comme il plaît à Dieu, qui en sait bien plus que Monsieur Le Nôtre" (cf. below, p. 409). Hills, woods, and meadows are most beautifully green—

> "Tout vous enchante et l'art humain,
> Respectant de si beaux ouvrages
> N'ose pas y mettre la main."—(*Ibid.*)

that they scarcely dare risk a new word even when they need it . . . . Englishmen, on the contrary, carry their liberty even into their language " ; a phenomenon so strange and so notorious that the rumour of it had reached Fénelon, who speaks of it by hearsay in his " Lettre à l'Académie." [1]

The English let their language grow as it likes, and never in their conversations discuss the choice of a word or the elegance of a term ; the French, on the contrary, ever preoccupied with these problems,[2] are greatly astonished at finding such indifference in London. G. L. Lesage notes the fact as one of the curiosities of the country : " Rarely does the conversation turn upon the appropriateness of a word, or upon the correctness of an expression." In France each new edition of the Dictionary was, and has continued to be, the occasion of endless discussions. The first edition gave rise to a number of books, pamphlets, comments, and epigrams. " Je suis," the long-expected lexicon, was supposed to say :—

" Je suis ce gros dictionnaire.
Qui fus un demi-siècle au ventre de ma mère ;

---

[1] Fénelon, who had an innovating turn of mind, ventures to approve this liberty : " J'entends dire que les Anglois ne se refusent aucun des mots qui leur sont commodes : ils les prennent partout où ils les trouvent chez leurs voisins. De telles usurpations sont permises." 1714.

[2] They have not altered in this respect. We read in the *Temps* (April 6, 1898) : " Nous sommes un peuple de grammairiens et de puristes. Sitôt que, dans un journal, on propose au public une question de langue, d'orthographe ou de prononciation, les lettres abondent, et la discussion, si l'on n'y prend garde, ne tarde pas à s'échauffer." (Sganarelle-Sarcey), on the term "coupe sombre."

Quand je naquis j'avois de la barbe et des dents,
Ce qu'on ne doit trouver fort extraordinaire,
Attendu que j'avois l'âge de cinquante ans." [1]

On the subject of theatres, all travellers are of the same opinion; they are struck by the beauty and comfort of the edifices, and the richness of the costumes; but revolted by the incoherency, the licence, and the ferocity of the plays. There are three excellent troupes in London, says Chappuzeau, without speaking of the country troupes: "I must add that the three London houses are furnished with very well-shaped actors, and particularly with handsome women, that these theatres are superb as regards stage scenery and scene shiftings, that the music is excellent . . . that they have no less than twelve fiddles each for the preludes and entr'actes" —they had only six in Paris—"that it would be a crime to use anything but wax to light the stage, or to fill the chandeliers in such a manner as to offend the spectators' nostrils." They play every day, the three theatres are always crowded, and "a hundred coaches ever choke the surrounding streets."

Chappuzeau, it is true, was by nature an optimist: "Everything in this world goes from good to better,"

---

[1] "L'Apothéose du Dictionnaire de l'Académie," La Haye, 1696. Great exception is taken at the want of those "Remarques" which had long been expected, and without which the Dictionary was finally issued. Fénelon insisted later upon the usefulness of such "Remarques," and Matthew Prior confirmed him in that opinion. See below, p. 181. Among the pamphlets relating to the Dictionary, see, e.g., besides Furetière's "Factums," "Réponse à une critique satirique," by C. Mallement de Messange; "L'Enterrement du Dictionnaire de l'Académie" (a reply to the "Réponse"), 1697, 12°.

A MAN OF QUALITY ON THE STAGE AT THE OPERA. 1687.

[p. 155.

he remarked with conviction. This happy generalisation was inspired to him by the fact of the lemonade girl, at the French Comedy, having replaced by raspberry and cherry-water the " simple ptisane " of yore. But his testimony is confirmed by other travellers: Sorbières and Misson are no less positive: "The stage is quite free, with many changes of scenery and perspectives"; very different from Paris, where noblemen continued to encumber the stage at Molière's and Racine's plays as well as at the opera, hampering the movements of the actors, preventing any illusion, considering themselves as the most interesting part of the performance, talking aloud, and taking, if so disposed, the liberty of bringing their dog to see the play: "Row at the play," writes the lieutenant of police, René d'Argenson, in his Notes; "the day before yesterday there was a stir at the play on account of a Danish dog that M. le Marquis de Livry, the son, had brought there. The dog began to go through his tricks and to show his agility in a hundred different ways. The gentlemen of the pit made every sort of hunting sound that they could bethink themselves of in order to cheer and encourage him."[1]

Another advantage: in London the spectators in the pit are seated, whereas in Paris they stand, which facilitates confusion. "The pit in London," says Misson, " is disposed like an amphitheatre (in Paris it was square) and filled with benches without backs and covered in green stuff. Men of quality, particularly young men, a few honest and respectable ladies, and

[1] "Notes de René d'Argenson," ed. Larchey and Mabille, Paris, 1866, p. 41. January, 1701.

many wenches seeking their fortune, sit there pell-mell, talking, playing, jesting, listening or not listening. Further off, against the wall and opposite the stage, rises another amphitheatre occupied by people of the highest degree, among whom there are few men. The galleries, of which there is but a double row, are filled only with ordinary people, particularly the upper one."[1]

The costumes are splendid; "they have magnificent clothes"; but, on that score, Paris can easily bear comparison, for at the French Comedy a "mere dress *à la romaine* will often go up to five hundred crowns," writes Chappuzeau. There is the same splendour, and also the same indifference to historic accuracy in the two countries. In London, observes Muralt, "the heroes of antiquity are costumed as they are in France; Hannibal appears with a long powdered wig under his helmet, ribbons upon his coat of mail, and holding his sword with a fringed glove."

Resemblances cease there; the plays are as different as can be; the two dramatic arts are now in direct and absolute opposition. The chief point in Paris is to be decent, regular, logical, to open on real life windows which, like the windows in the houses, show what is

---

[1] "Mémoires et observations," 1698, p. 63. Sorbières' description is nearly the same: "Les meilleures places sont celles du parterre où les hommes et les femmes sont assis pêle-mêle, chacun avec ceux de sa bande. Le théâtre est fort beau, couvert d'un tapis vert. . . . Les acteurs et les actrices y sont admirables à ce que l'on m'a dit et mesme à ce que j'en peux comprendre au geste et à la prononciation," p. 166. It must be remembered that the comprehension of Italian comedies in Paris was made easier by the abundant gesticulations of the comedians, who were, in fact, described as "gestueux."

INTERIOR OF THE FRENCH COMEDY, WITH THE STANDING PIT AND GENTLEMEN ON THE STAGE—TIME OF MOLIÈRE

straight before us, "ce qui est au droit devant nous." The chief point in London, at that date, is to be licentious, undisciplined, astonishing ; the Restoration honours Wycherley and Dryden ; tolerates Shakespeare, but Shakespeare altered, with dances inserted in " Macbeth " ; despises Racine, adapts Molière and French dramatists English fashion, adding rodomontades to the part of Titus in Racine's " Bérénice " :—

> " Henceforth all thoughts of pity I'll disown,
> And with my arms the Universe ore-run,
> Rob'd of my Love, through ruins purchase fame,
> And make the worlds as wretched as I am." [1]

Titus becomes another Almanzor ; Alceste the " Misanthrope " undergoes as complete a transformation, and is turned into a swearing, smoking, debauched and nauseous Jack Tar, " that smells like Thames Street " (Wycherley's " Plain Dealer ").

One solitary French critic, Saint-Evremond the exile, attempted at that time to compare, with some care, the two theatres ; only he did not know English, and judged of things by hearsay. As a man of letters, he belonged to the distant days of the regency of Anne of Austria, the days when he was young ; he had consequently a weakness for the independents.[2]

---

[1] " Titus and Bérénice . . . with a farce called the Cheats of Scapin," by Otway, London, 16--, 8°.

[2] " Il faut aimer la règle," he says, " pour éviter la confusion, il faut aimer le bon sens qui modère l'ardeur d'une imagination allumée ; mais il faut ôter à la règle toute contrainte qui gêne, et bannir une raison scrupuleuse qui, par un trop grand attachement à la justesse, ne laisse rien de libre et de naturel." " De la Comédie Angloise."

He was therefore less scandalized than others had been at the sight of the English stage. English comedy pleases him more than tragedy; it is conformable, he thinks, to the comedy of the ancients, "as far as manners are concerned." He has never heard of Shakespeare, it seems, but he knows Jonson well, he regards him as the head of the English drama, and does him the unexpected and incredible honour of imitating one of his plays. "As M. de Saint-Evremond," writes his biographer, Des Maizeaux, "did not understand English, these gentlemen (the Duke of Buckingham and M. d'Aubigny) explained to him the best things composed by the poets of that nation. . . . These readings furnished him with the observations he has made on English comedies in some of his works. It was also that kind of study which gave these gentlemen the opportunity of working together at the comedy of 'Sir Politick Wouldbe.' Each supplied part of the characters, and M. de Saint-Evremond put them into shape."

As for tragedies, Saint-Evremond is aware that the English have "some old tragedies" (in a note: "like Ben Jonson's 'Catiline' and 'Sejanus'"), "from which many things ought in truth to be omitted, but that being done they might be made very fine." People murder each other a little too much in those plays, but if they massacred each other less, no one in London would go to see them: "Eyes eager for cruel sights want to see murders and bloody corpses. . . . Death is so little to the English, that to move them pictures must be shown more baleful than death itself." Shakespeare is nowhere mentioned.

Appreciations of the same sort, but less studied, are to be found in Sorbières, Chappuzeau, Misson, Muralt, and others. Sorbières, who knew no more English than Saint-Evremond, does not think that English dramas would have much success in France, because they are not according to rule. The English " write comedies that last twenty-five years " ; they are insensible to the charms of alexandrines ; their plays " are in a measured prose (blank verse) which resembles ordinary speech more than our verses, and which is not without some melody. They cannot conceive that it should not be a wearisome thing to have the same cadence strike the ear continually, and they say that to hear people talk in alexandrine verse for two or three hours and see them skip from cæsura to cæsura is a way of expressing oneself not very natural or diverting." Be that as it may, Sorbières resolved to show his friends what English plays were like : "I have brought a volume of them," he wrote, and he counted upon that volume to show that " wit good sense, and eloquence are to be found everywhere." The volume brought back by Sorbières contained neither Shakespeare nor Jonson, but it did contain the works of the Marchioness, afterwards Duchess of Newcastle,[1] and it was by reading these pale productions, in which are unfolded the adventures of " Lady Sansparelle " and " Lord de l'Amour," that the traveller's friends were allowed to glean some idea of a stage for

[1] It was the volume modestly entitled : " Playes written by the thrice noble, illustrious, and excellent princess, the Lady Marchioness of Newcastle," London, 1662, fol. ; the plays being preceded by two dedicaces, a prologue, and eleven epistles to the reader.

which, unknown to them, William Shakespeare had also written.

They make one "laugh and cry" in the same play, "which cannot be suffered in France," wrote Le Pays on his side. To end a tragedy, they stab four or five personages; this sight never fails to amuse. Le Pays, who had a grudge against "blondines," affirms that they "clap their hands and burst out laughing at that moment." Chappuzeau assisted "at the death of 'Montezuma, King of Mexico,'[1] and at the death of 'Mustapha,'[2] who defended himself vigorously against the mutes who wanted to strangle him, which elicited laughter"; this constitutes, continues our incorrigible optimist, a comedy "not so regular as ours," but which "has nevertheless its peculiar charms."

Only two of these travellers mention Shakespeare: Muralt, who greatly prefers Jonson, and contents himself with the casual remark: "England is a land of passions and catastrophes, so much so that Schakspear, one of their best ancient poets, has turned a great part

---

[1] In the famous "Indian Emperor, or the Conquest of Mexico," by Dryden. It was translated into French in 1743, and men of taste read with astonishment a play beginning thus: "Dans quel heureux climat la fortune nous a-t-elle conduits? et pourquoi faut-il que l'ignorance nous ait caché pendant tant de siècles ces bords enchantés? Ne dirait-on pas que notre ancien monde s'était retiré par pudeur pour en enfanter un autre en secret?"

[2] By Roger Boyle, Earl of Orrery, performed with success at Lincoln's Inn Fields in 1665, and printed in 1677. It was acted at Court in 1666: "I was invited by my Lord Chamberlaine to see this tragedy, exceedingly well written, though in my mind I did not approve of any such pastime in a season of such judgments and calamities" (an allusion to the Fire and Plague). Evelyn's Diary, October 18, 1666. See above, p. 46, note 2.

of their history into tragedies"; and Moreau de
Brasey, who also praises his historical dramas, and does
it in these terms: "One Shakespear (un certain Shakespear), who lived in the last century, has left the
reputation of a master owing to his excellent historical
plays, and M. Addison has perfected this taste in his
admirable 'Cato.'"[1]

V.

The "certain Shakespear" and the "nommé Miltonius" were still very far, as we may see, from
exciting enthusiasm. Things appertaining to England
were, nevertheless, becoming more familiar; the history
of the country was beginning to arouse interest, and
was related in French by Vanel, Rosemond, Larrey,
and several others.[2] It was one more opportunity for

[1] "Si les Anglois pouvoient se résoudre à y être plus simples (in tragedies) et à étudier davantage le langage de la nature, ils excel-leroient sans doute dans le tragique par dessus tous les peuples de l'Europe. L'Angleterre est un païs de passions et de catastrophes, jusques là que Schakspear, un de leurs meilleurs anciens poëtes a mis une grande partie de leur histoire en tragédies." Muralt, "Lettres sur les Anglois," 1725, 8°, p. 57 (written about thirty years before). "Il n'y a point de nation qui représente l'histoire plus naturellement, plus au vif ni plus conformément à la vérité que les Anglois. Ils ont représenté fort noblement la plupart des événements de leur propre histoire. Un certain Shakespear qui vivoit dans le siècle dernier a laissé une fondation de maitre pour cela dans ses excellentes pièces de théâtre, et Monsieur Addison a perfectionné ce goût dans son admirable Cato." "Le Guide d'Angleterre," by Moreau de Brasey, Amsterdam, 1744, p. 161 (written 1712-14).

[2] "Abrégé nouveau de l'Histoire générale d'Angleterre," by Vanel (who follows principally Gregorio Leti), Paris, 1689, 4 vols., 12°.—"Histoire des guerres civiles de l'Angleterre," by Rosemond,

describing the kingdom, its inhabitants of both sexes, Parliament, the English drama in which may be noticed a great many "criminal intrigues," and the religious sects "so extravagant that one is horrified to see how far they carry their abomination." [1] Works of that kind excited curiosity because they referred to the country "which has ever been the theatre of the strangest revolutions in Europe." [2]

Translations become less rare; the "Histoire de l'état présent de l'Empire Ottoman," translated from the English of Sir P. Rycaut,[3] falls into Racine's hands, and he seeks information in it for his "Bajazet"; Burnet's "History of the Reformation," put into French by Rosemond, is read by Madame de Sévigné. Bacon, Temple, Sir Thomas Browne, Stillingfleet, Locke,[4]

Amsterdam, 1690, 12º.—"Introduction à l'Histoire d'Angleterre, par le Chevalier Temple, enrichie de portraits; traduite de l'anglois," Amsterdam, 1695, 12º.—"Histoire d'Angleterre, d'Écosse et d'Irlande," by de Larrey, Rotterdam, 1697, ff., 4 vols. fol.; a Protestant refugee, he declares that he is "sans païs natal, sans liaisons, sans attachemens, sans crainte et sans espérance, sans haine et sans amour." The great history, long considered as a standard one, by Rapin Thoyras, came out at the Hague from 1724 onwards, 13 vols., 4º.

[1] Vanel, vol. i.; Larrey, vol. i., "Dissertation sur les Parlements."

[2] "Abrégé de l'Histoire d'Angleterre écrite sur les Mémoires des plus fidèles autheurs anglois," La Haye, 1695, 12º. The author (forgetting Vanel) pretends that his history "est l'unique qui a encore paru dans notre langue."

[3] By Pierre Briot, Paris, 1670, 4º. "Bajazet" is of 1672; Racine had, moreover, gathered information from ambassadors to Turkey.

[4] By Le Clerc, "Œuvres diverses de M. Jean Locke," Rotterdam, 1710, 12º.

Clarendon, Shaftesbury, &c., are translated ; Addison also, a little later, and his "Spectator" has an immense success in France ;[1] Jeremy Collier's "Short View of the Immorality and Profaneness of the English Stage" is put into French in 1715.[2]

As the seventeenth century draws to its close, French literary periodicals, published by Catholics at Trévoux or Paris, and by Protestants in the Hague or Amsterdam, open their pages to English works ; eyes are no longer turned only toward Spain and Italy. The "Journal des Savants," aided by its dragoman, has set the example, and publishes, from 1666, a review of works (chiefly scientific) which have come out in England, from the "Natural and Political Observations made upon the Bills of Mortality," by John Graunt, to the "Discours sur le grand cordial du S\`r Walter Rawleigh," a cordial composed " of everything that there is most excellent in other cordials," and of which the principal ingredients are viper's flesh, bezoar, hart's horn, magisteries of pearl and coral . . . prepared gold," &c. Mention of purely literary works is only made later on.

Several other periodicals devoted to French and foreign works are founded before the end of the century, or shortly after.[3] Some place is given to the English

---

[1] "Le Spectateur ou le Socrate moderne," Amsterdam, 1714, ff.
[2] "La Critique du Théâtre Anglois," Paris, 1715, 12 .
[3] "Journal des Sçavans," Paris, 1665, ff. 4\`o, "Table générale," Paris, 1753.—"Nouvelles de la République des Lettres," Amsterdam, 1684-1718, 56 vols. (by Bayle, Laroque, Le Clerc, &c.).— "Mémoires pour servir à l'histoire des sciences et des beaux-arts " (i.e., "Journal de Trévoux"), Trévoux and Paris, 1701-67. 813 vols., "Tables," by Father Sommervogel, Paris, 1864, 3 vols.

in these reviews ; but conformably with the old traditions, contributors busy themselves especially with theologians, " savants," and thinkers—Tillotson, Locke, Boyle, Shaftesbury, Toland. Grave and serious works are discussed ; if the drama is brought into question it is on account of some book like that of Jeremy Collier, who considers the drama from a theologian's point of view. Basnage thus gives, in 1698, an account of Collier's work, published in the same year ; but he chiefly dwells upon the "profaneness" of the English stage : "At the end of a play called the 'Mock Astrologer' [by Dryden] a troop of demons appear ; one of them sneezes, and thereupon they civilly say to him, God bless you, and add the ironical compliment that he has taken cold because he is not used to be so long away from the fire."[1]

Nothing is more uncommon, before 1700, than an English play translated or adapted into French. Otway's "Venice Preserved" was adapted, but La Fosse, the author of this attempt, terrified at his own audacity would never run the risk of having modern names heard on the stage ; he transported the subject into ancient times, turned the action into narratives, dressed Otway's Venetians as Romans, and made of his

---

[160]. "Bibliothèque universelle et historique," Amsterdam, 1686, ff. 12°, by Le Clerc. "Bibliothèque choisie pour servir de suite à la Bibliothèque universelle," Amsterdam, 1703, ff., by the same.— "Œuvres des Savans," by Basnage, Rotterdam, 1695, ff.—"Journal Littéraire" (of the Hague), 1713, ff., by S'Gravesande, Van Effen, Sallengre, &c. Several others are pointed out by Hatin, "Bibliographie historique de la Presse périodique Française," Paris, 1886, 8°, p. 28, "Presse Littéraire."

[1] May, 1698.

tragedy a "Manlius Capitolinus," 1698.¹ The example of Campistron, moreover, was there to restrain him, Campistron, whom the Academy was soon to receive, and who, desirous of producing on the stage "the tragic adventure of Don Carlos, eldest son of Philip the Second King of Spain," had with great decorum transferred this story to antique times, and drawn from it the plot of his "Andronic," 1685. An English comedy was translated at the same period; not "Much Ado," but, as though out of defiance, one of Vanbrugh's most licentious plays, "The Provoked Wife,"² a play fit to make even the criticisms of Jeremy Collier seem indulgent, and to fill with disgust the dignified connoisseurs of Louis Quatorze's day.

The English "think profoundly," La Fontaine had said; they are strong in experience, "forts d'expérience." It was especially their thinkers who attracted attention; they were admired, quarrelled with, written to, translated even: and this preference was so marked that Abel Boyer, that French Protestant who had

---

¹ The play met with great success, precisely on account of its regularity: "La beauté du sujet, la sagesse dont il est traité, sa régularité, sa conduite, les sentiments héroïques qui y sont répandus, tout concourt à la gloire de l'auteur." Frères Parfaict, "Hist. du Théâtre François," Amsterdam, 1735. ff., vol. xiv., p. 89. La Fosse, in his preface, quotes as his sources Titus Livius and Saint-Réal, but says nothing "des obligations qu'il avait à M. Otwai, poète anglois" (ibid).

² "La femme poussée à bout, comédie traduite de la pièce angloise intitulée: The provokd wife," London, 1700, 12°. Coarse actions, coarse sentiments, and coarse words fill the play, which was translated, evidently with the help of interpreters, by that belated independent, Saint-Evremond.

taken refuge in London, and was so well versed in the two literatures, observed as late as 1713 : "Most foreigners are unaware of the genius and taste of the English for poetry." [1]

What, then, was the fate of Shakespeare in France? Did he still remain completely unknown at the close of Louis XIV.'s reign, at a time when, in England, it has been possible to form two large volumes of the English praise and criticism dedicated to him before that date? [2] For we must not forget that Muralt's letters, written in 1694–95, came out only thirty years later, in 1725, and that Moreau de Brasey's, written in 1712, came out in 1744.

Silently and unobserved the great man has crossed the Channel. Already he is in the heart of the capital; a copy of his works figures, next to those of Racine and Corneille, in the library of the "Roi-Soleil" himself. We know it because the copy, which the Paris National Library still possesses, was included by Nicolas Clément, Royal Librarian, in his first methodical catalogue of books, commenced in 1675, and finished in 1684. The original slip, which I discovered some years ago,[3] con-

---

[1] Preface to his translation of "Caton, tragédie par M. Addison," London, "chez Jacob Tonson, à la tête de Shakespeare, dans la rue nommée le Strand," 1713 ; with a frontispiece representing a peri-wigged Cato, dying at Versailles, as it would seem, in the arms of high-heeled Louis XIV. and of Madame de Maintenon. On Boyer, 1667–1729, editor of the "Post Boy" and other periodicals, and a most prolific writer, see above, p. 131.

[2] Ingleby, "Shakespeares Centurie of Prayse," ed. L. Toulmin Smith, 1879 ; F. J. Furnivall, "Some 300 fresh allusions to Shak-spere," 1886 (New Shakspere Society).

[3] "Revue Critique," November 14, 1887.

THE DEATH OF CATO.
A plate by Du Guernier illustrating the translation of Addison's "Cato." 1713.

tains, besides the title of the work, an appreciation on the author's genius ; some enlightenment on a man so little known having been deemed indispensable. Clément's note reads thus :—

"WILL. SHAKESPEARE,
"Poeta anglicus.
"Opera poetica, continentia tragœdias, comœdias et historiolas. Angl^e, Lond., Th. Cotes, 1632, f°.
"Eædem Tragœdiæ et comœdiæ anglicæ. Lond., W. Leake, 1641, 4°.[1]
"Ce poëte anglois a l'imagination assés belle, il pense naturellement, il s'exprime avec finesse ; mais ces belles qualitez sont obscurcies par les ordures qu'il mêle dans ses Comédies."

Such is the oldest appreciation on Shakespeare in the French language ; it does not breathe great enthusiasm : the poet has a rather fine imagination, he thinks naturally, he expresses himself skilfully ; but these fine qualities are obscured by the filth he introduces into his comedies. Nevertheless, here is at last a written opinion on Shakespeare, and here is a library where the master's works are to be found.

We might quote a second one, but not a third : that singular man, equally fond of gathering riches and of squandering them, the surintendant Fouquet, an intrepid collector of books, possessed what was at

[1] This second volume does not in reality contain Shakespeare's works, but various plays by Beaumont and Fletcher. Louis XIV.'s copy, as will be seen from its date, was not the first, but the second "folio."

that time a very unusual number of English works.
Most of them were, it is true, preserved "in his
garret"; but among them figured, besides many
volumes of history, besides the dictionaries of Spelman
and Cotgrave, a quantity of dramatic works. We read
in the inventory, drawn up after his fall, "Inventaire,
prisée et estimation des livres trouvés à Saint-Mandé
appartenant ci-devant à M. Fouquet,"[1] articles like
the following :

"Histori of housse of Douglas, fol.		10d.
14 volumes en anglois d'histoire	30l.	
Deffensio regia Miltoni, folio 164	3l.	
Divers volumes de comédies en anglois ...	3l.	
Comédies de Jazon (Ben Jonson) en anglois, 2 voll., London, 1640	3l.	
Id., comédies angloises		10d.
Shakespeares comédies angloises	1l.	
Fletcher commédies angloises, London, 1647	1l."	

The modest price, one franc, assigned by the experts
to Shakespeare's works (a copy maybe of the first folio,
now worth £600) will be noticed. Such as it was, and
garret or no, Fouquet's library was exceptional. Even
among the richest, for instance, in that of Raphaël Trichet
du Fresne, librarian to Queen Christine, the only English books were works of history, philosophy, or science.[2]

[1] Preserved in MS. at the National Library, MS. Fr. 9,438
(July, 1665).
[2] "Catalogus librorum bibliothecæ Raphaelis Tricheti du
Fresne," Paris, 1662, 4º. We find therein : "Britannia, the
histori, London, 1614.—The Survey of London, London, 1633,
fol.—Chronicles of the Kings of England, London, 1643, fol.,"
&c. But no purely literary works.

In most cases English letters were not represented at all.[1]

Many more years must pass before a *printed* appreciation on Shakespeare can be found in France. The first time the dramatist was mentioned in a French book his name figured without any comment among the celebrated authors of his country, and the fact attracted so little attention that long afterwards lists continued to appear in which "Cassibelane, who twice repulsed the Roman legions," and Jonson, "equal to any of the ancients for the exactness of his pen"[2] were included, but in which the author of "Hamlet" was omitted. It was long thought that the earliest printed mention

---

[1] M. Rathery quotes, as an example, the "Catalogue de Bilaine, libraire fort en vogue, Paris, 1681, 12º." There is a series entitled, "Libri in Anglia impressi"; they are all in Latin. In the "Bibliotheca Colbertina, seu Catalogus Librorum," &c., Paris, 1728, 3 vols. 12º, there are numerous Spanish, Italian, and Portuguese works; a very few English ones, mostly historical or philosophical. English literature proper is represented by "Castara en anglois, Londres, 1640, 8º; Les pas ou démarches du Temple, en anglois, par Richard Crashaw, Londres, 1648; Les Délices des Muses par le même, 1648, 8º."

[2] Guy Miège, "The new state of England under their Majesties King William and Queen Mary," 2nd ed., London, 1694, 12º. The work was periodical, and had a French edition; the "Journal des Savants" gives an account of it in 1706, and reproduces the list of great men that Miège had "tirée de la cosmographie de Heylin," that is: "Cosmography containing the historic of the whole world," 1st ed., 1652, fol. In this, at the time of its publication, very popular work (the fifth edition of which was issued in 1677), Heylin gives a list of ten English poets, Gower, Lydgate, Chaucer, Sidney, Spenser, Daniel, Drayton, Beaumont, Fletcher, and "my friend Ben Jonson, equal to any," &c. (as in Miège). Shakespeare is not mentioned (ed. of 1666, p. 304).

was to be found in the translation of Collier's "Short View," "La critique du théâtre Anglois," 1715, (where his name is printed Chacsper). M. Texte has recently shown, however, that Shakespeare was mentioned in the "Œuvres mêlées" of Sir W. Temple, published in French at Utrecht, 1693.[1] But at least one book came before these, since the name of Shakespeare figures in the "Jugements des Savants" of Baillet, the enemy of Menage, printed at Paris in 1685-86. In the second volume of that work, an article is devoted to English poets, and the author writes: "If we end with the English it is only to follow the order of geographers who mention the islands after the Continent, for one cannot say that this country is inferior, even for poetry, to several of the northern nations. The principal poets of the British Islands in the vulgar tongue, according to the above quoted authorities, are Abraham Cowley, John Downe or Jean Donne, Cleveland, Edmund Waller, John Denham, George Herbert, Chancellor Bacon, Shakespeare, Fletcher, Beaumont, Suckling, John Milton, &c."[2] It will be noticed that the list, such as it is, contains more names than Addison thought fit to include in his "Account of the greatest English poets," as Shakespeare does not figure among those "greatest English poets."

We have, at all events, the name printed for the first time in France. The earliest printed appreciations are even more concise than Nicolas Clement's; the dramatist is evidently only spoken of from hearsay.

[1] "Revue d'Histoire Littéraire de la France," vol. i., p. 463.
[2] Racine possessed a copy of Baillet's compilation. J. Bonnefon, "Revue d'Histoire Littéraire de la France," April 15, 1898, p. 187.

In the "Dialogues familiers" included in his grammar,[1] Boyer makes an English speaker say (in French) : "We have a Pindar and a Horace in Cowley and in Oldham ; a Terence in Ben Jonson ; a Sophocles and a Euripides in Shakespeare ; a Homer and a Virgil in Milton ; and nearly all the poets together in Dryden alone."[2] Boyer was evidently of the same way of thinking as the Englishman who owned the copy of the first folio edition of Shakespeare, now preserved at the Paris National Library, and who wrote opposite the title of the "Tempest," in the list of plays, this appreciation worthy of Mr. Pepys : "Better in Dryden." Boyer stuck to this opinion, for he repeats it in the preface to his "Dictionnaire," where there is a pompous eulogy of the "greatest poet that England has ever had," to wit, Dryden.[3] The "Journal des Savants" had, on the other hand, devoted a line to Shakespeare in 1708, and had declared that he was "the most famous of English poets for tragedy."

[1] Quérard quotes an edition of this grammar of 1700 ; it is neither at the Bibliothèque Nationale, the British Museum, nor the Bodleian. I have followed the Amsterdam edition of 1718 : "Nouvelle double Grammaire " (by Miège and Boyer).

[2] "Nous avons un Pindare et un Horace en Cowly et en Oldham, un Térence en Ben Johnson ; un Sophocle et un Euripide en Shakespear ; un Homère et un Virgile en Milton et presque tous ces poètes ensemble en Dryden seul " (p. 368).

[3] " Dictionnaire Royal François et Anglois," 1702. The British Museum (whose collection is not complete) possesses 41 editions of this dictionary ; the sale of it augmented prodigiously during the days of Anglomania in France. Boyer was helped, while compiling his dictionary, by his friend Savage : " Mon ami M. Savage, gentilhomme anglois, d'esprit et de mérite, qui a eu la bonté d'augmenter mes recueils de plus de mille mots."

Such is, with the exception of a few passages in the "Spectator" translated in 1714,[1] all that I have been able to discover for a whole reign and a whole century: two or three brief and vague appreciations, the most important of which remains hidden among the slips prepared for the catalogue of the "Bibliothèque Royale"; the name of Shakespeare printed by chance in two or three books where no one notices it; nothing more.

French dramatic art, meanwhile, after the incomparable period it owed to Corneille, Racine, and Molière, and which had just ended with "Athalie" (1691) was hastening to its decline. Filled with admiration for those great men, their successors imagined they could divine their secrets; they studied them attentively and composed tragedies, as dishes are prepared, from the right recipe. The important thing for them was the formula; they were intractable in the matter of rules, going even beyond their masters, blaming the excess of independence that they detected in the Greek authors themselves, and never suspecting how little credit they deserved for restraining the starts and moderating the bounds of their own genius. Their docile Pegasus asked nothing better, alas, than to bow his head and follow the well-worn road; no danger was there that he would spring from the ground and lose himself in the blue sky; a sound of monotonous alexandrines, a tinkling of bells, was

---

[1] The first time the name appears, the translator adds this comment: "Il a écrit des tragédies dont la plupart des scènes sont admirables. Mais il n'est pas tout à fait exact dans ses plans ni dans la justesse de la composition," vol. i., p. 84. The "pas tout à fait" shows that the translator had not examined them very closely.

sufficient sign that the author, well seated on his pacific steed, would not leave the straight path. Let us sleep in peace ; we shall find everything in order on awakening. The *convenances* will have been harmed by no one, and the modesty of rules will not have received the slightest affront. The "Venices preserved" are turned into "Manliuses," and the adventures of Don Carlos into "Andronics" : this surpasses the "délicatesse" of the Greeks themselves.[1] "I have given my heroine," writes Brueys, in 1699, "the name of Gabinia, which I have taken from her father's, because it seemed to me that that of Susanna, which the history of our holy martyrs gives her, was too lacking in nobleness for the stage."[2] Let us sleep in peace.

A change, however, is preparing, and it will be great with consequences for French literature. Travellers, more and more illustrious, come to visit England ; they observe, they compare, they note their impressions, to good purpose. They are called Abbé Prévost, Montesquieu, and Voltaire ; in 1734 the latter will publish his famous "Lettres philosophiques ou Lettres sur les Anglais."

[1] On which the abbé Du Bos again congratulates Campistron in the eighteenth century. "Réflexions critiques," Paris, 1746, vol i., p. 149 (first edition, 1719).

[2] "Gabinie, tragédie chrétienne," performed for the first time April 2nd, 1690 (imitated from a Latin tragedy by A. Jourdain, entitled "Susanna").

CHAPTER III

THE EIGHTEENTH CENTURY

Part I.—1715-1750

I.

SOME men have the gift, whatever they say, of being listened to; whatever they write, of being read. They may repeat word for word what has been already expressed, no matter; when others spoke no one paid any attention; now that they open their lips every one is all ears. Their voice is clearer; it seems as though their ink were blacker. This precious gift was at all times Voltaire's; he possessed it from his youth and retained it till his death.

In 1734 he published the French edition of his "Lettres philosophiques ou Lettres sur les Anglais." Nearly all the subjects they treat of had been treated before, and had remained unknown. He spoke, and it was as if he had just discovered them. After him, England was no longer "terra incognita"; people knew where they were going when they crossed the Channel.

Various efforts had indeed preceded his own. The
change, begun at the end of the seventeenth century,
had become much more marked at the commencement of the eighteenth. A poet represented England
at Paris : the same thing had been seen before ; but
unlike Wyatt and Sackville, Matthew Prior found
people to talk to, and he was frequently questioned
on the language and literature of the two countries.[1]

A public was forming who took interest in these
matters, a much more numerous public than the little
group of curious inquirers of former days. Essays on
England were becoming abundant ; periodicals in which
a place was accorded to her literary and scientific men
multiplied. English literary works did not always receive
enthusiastic praise, but they were no longer ignored. The
" Journal des Savants " busies itself with Swift's " Tale
of a Tub," and pronounces it " insipid and coarse " ; it
moreover declares writings of that kind to be " impious,
because they tend to nothing less than establishing the
toleration of all religions," which should not be thought
of (1721).[2] The reviewer gives an account of " Robinson
Crusoe," and wonders very much whether it is a true

---

[1] " M. Prior, Anglois, dont l'esprit et les lumières sont connus
de tout le monde, . . . m'a parlé cent fois de l'utilité du travail
que je propose," *i.e.*, the remarks to be added to the " Dictionnaire de l'Académie." Fénelon, " Mémoire sur les occupations
de l'Académie," 1713. Prior wrote French very well, as can be
seen by a number of his letters (unpublished) preserved in the
archives of the " Affaires Étrangères."

[2] Cf. W. Wotton's opinion : " 'Tis all with him a farce, all a
ladle " ; it shows the author's " contemptible opinion of everything
which is called Christianity." " A Defence . . . with observations
upon the ' Tale of a Tub,' " 1705, 8°.

story. He has doubts, although he points out "some semblance of truth that the author has tried to make interesting by the help of novelty" (1720). A rubric is opened in the same paper for London literary news, and thus readers learn, for instance, in the course of the year 1710, that "the sieur Tonson, bookseller of that town, begins to sell the new edition of the works of Shakees Pear . . M. Rowe has revised and corrected it."

At length appears the unexpected phenomenon of a periodical in French expressly designed to give an account of English books, the which, although very interesting, "are scarcely known outside the island"; it was called the "Bibliothèque ou histoire littéraire de la Grande Bretagne," and was founded by De La Roche in 1717.[1] La Roche gives his readers information on

---

[1] And continued by La Chapelle, who gives as his address, "The Rev. Armand de La Chapelle in White Row, Spittlefields, London"; but the review was printed and issued in Amsterdam; the preface is dated London, November 13, 1716. The "Bibliothèque Britannique" was founded at the Hague in 1733 in imitation of the preceding one; its contributors lived also in London: "L'avantage qu'ont les auteurs d'entendre parfaitement l'anglois, de résider à Londres et d'être au fait de la littérature angloise semble devoir former un préjugé en leur faveur." Henceforth a place is given to English authors in nearly all periodicals, now become innumerable, and in compilations like those of Niceron: "Mémoires pour servir à l'histoire des hommes illustres," Paris, 1727, ff.; of Clément: "Les Cinq Années littéraires, 1748-52 (The Hague, 1754, 8º); in the manifold publications of the prolific and not very competent abbé Desfontaines, the translator of "Gulliver," refuter of Muralt, editor of the "Journal des Savants" from 1724 to 1727, of "Le Nouvelliste du Parnasse," 1731, ff., of the "Jugemens sur quelques ouvrages nouveaux," Avignon, 1744, ff., &c. See also the "Mercure" of, e.g., June, 1722, May and August, 1723, December,

the past and the present, on philosophers, theologians, and poets, on Waller, Denham, and Milton : "Every body knows that Milton was a person of distinguished merit."

The most remarkable of all these scattered essays is the " Dissertation sur la poésie Angloise " (published by the " Journal littéraire " of the Hague in 1717, and containing considerations on the general characteristics of English literature and comparisons between English and French authors from the time of Chaucer. Scarron is compared with Butler ; Boileau with Dryden and with Pope ; La Fontaine with Prior. An essay of some length is devoted to the drama of both nations ; to French rules, which are perhaps too strict ; to English liberties, which are surely too great. Molière and Racine are compared with their feeble imitators. The most minute details as yet printed in French are given (seventeen years before Voltaire's " Lettres ") on the English drama, and especially on Shakespeare, on his " Hamlet," in which speeches "extremely strong and energetic " are found mingled with low touches, " des traits rampants " ; on " Othello " ; " Henry VI." ; " Richard III." ; in a word on that genius whom his compatriots hold in "exorbitant esteem " ; – a lawless genius, observes the " Journal littéraire," who "imitated no one, and drawing everything from his own imagination, abandoned, so to speak, his works to the care of Fortune, without choosing the noble and necessary circumstances

---

1724, July, 1725 (all those numbers contain articles on the English drama, partly drawn, without any acknowledgment, from Saint-Evremond and Muralt).

of his subjects, and without rejecting those that were useless and indecent. It does not even appear from his plays that he educed, by his own reasoning, from the nature of tragedy, the slightest fixed rule for his own use to replace the rules of the ancients which he had neglected to study."

The translation of an English work, even what was formerly so rare, of a literary work, is less and less of a curiosity. Addison's "Cato" is put into French, also Milton's "Paradise,"[1] Defoe's "Robinson Crusoe," Swift's "Gulliver," the "Spectator," the "Tattler" (whose articles have for Continental readers the interest of giving a picture of the English, drawn by themselves), Pope's "Essay on Criticism," which is even translated into French verse.[2] Translating becomes an industry employing many hands; English takes the place that Spanish had held in the sixteenth century. These literary manufactories, established for the most part in Holland, and usually by Protestants, continue, it is true, to give the preference to books of philosophy, history, and science, for it remains an undisputed fact that the English "think profoundly." This judgment continues to be found everywhere, and comes up under every form: "The English have written on all sorts of matters, and have written well; they have their Malebranches, their

---

[1] By Dupré de Saint-Maur and Chéron de Boismorand, Paris, 1727, 3 vols., 12°; by Louis Racine, Paris, 1755, 3 vols., 8° (three or four other translations in the same century).

[2] Amsterdam, 1717; translation in prose, with the "Essai sur l'homme," text on opposite page, by the famous financier Silhouette (the same whose name was satirically used to designate the flat outline portraits in black, *à la mode* in those days).

Fontenelles, their Pétaus. . . . The liberty they enjoy, added to their temperament, makes them go deeply into matters and investigate thoroughly what others only glance at."[1]

This point of view is so generally accepted that Boissy is able to embody it in a comedy and to interest the Parisian public with a play turning solely upon that subject. We have in it a wise French baron, an honour to his country and capable of appreciating the merits of other nations; a French marquis, elegant and giddy, who sees nothing good out of Paris; a "milord" who is very much like the typical American in Alexandre Dumas' plays: practical, determined, sensible, unprejudiced, plain of speech, and prompt of action;[2] and a dull merchant, "Jacques Rosbif," heavy with commerce, who is not to win the hand of Eliante any more than the giddy marquis. The scene is in London. Here, says the baron, conversation is full of sense.

"*The Marquis.* Their conversation? they have none at all. They remain an hour without talking and have nothing else to say than: *How do you?* . . . The three years' stay you have made in London have completely ruined your taste, and you have even caught that foreign air that all the inhabitants of this town have.

The Baron. The inhabitants of this town have a foreign air? What the deuce do you mean by that?

The Marquis. I mean that they have not got the air one

[1] Saint-Hyacinthe, "Mémoires littéraires," The Hague, 1716, 8°, p. 149.
[2] Henceforth a familiar personage, who reappears in Voltaire's plays: part of Freeport (in the "Écossaise"). Freeport unites, however, the qualities of the "milord" and the roughness of Rosbif.

should have, that free, open, prepossessing, engaging, gracious air, the air 'par excellence'; in a word, the air we French have. . . . As there is but one good taste, so there is but one right air, and it is unquestionably ours. . . . Good sense is nothing else than common sense, which runs the streets and is of all countries. But wit grows only in France, which is, so to speak, its native soil; we furnish all the other nations of Europe with it." [1]

In spite of these fine speeches, Boissy lets his marquis do penance alone, and rewards the sensible baron with the hand of Éliante: a first symptom of nascent anglomania, 1727.

For some Anglomaniacs might already be found, several years before the Letters of Voltaire. A few months after Boissy's play, Marivaux, who had just founded his "Spectateur François" in imitation of Addison's, had his "Ile de la Raison ou les petits hommes" [2] performed, with a prologue in which he discussed the same question as Boissy, but pronounced a different verdict. The dispute is again between a marquis and a chevalier, but as the unlucky marquises had been doomed to ridicule ever since the days of Molière, Marivaux's marquis is now made to defend the English, ever lost in their meditations, while

[1] "Le François à Londres," by M. de Boissy of the French Academy, performed July 19, 1727, 4th ed., Paris, 1759. The play was a great success: "Le contraste des caractères des Français et des Anglais est naturel et touché avec vivacité dans cette pièce que l'on donne souvent au public." Clément and De la Porte, "Anecdotes dramatiques," Paris, 1775, 3 vols., 8º, vol. i., p. 397.

[2] In three acts, performed September 11, 1727, printed the same year. Resemblances have been pointed out between "Midsummer Night's Dream" and "Arlequin poli par l'Amour," by Marivaux, in which figures a fairy enamoured of the clownish Arlequin; but these resemblances are faint ones, and seem to be accidental.

the wise chevalier makes fun of him, routs him, and
at last converts him :—

"*The Marquis.* The play we are going to see is no doubt taken from 'Gulliver'?
The Chevalier. I do not know. What makes you think so?
The Marquis. Egad, it is called 'Little Men,' and doubtless they are the little men of the English book.
The Chevalier. But the mere sight of a dwarf is enough to suggest the idea of little men, without the help of that book.
The Marquis (eagerly). What! seriously, you think the play is not about Gulliver?
The Chevalier. Well, what does it matter to us?
The Marquis. What it matters to me? It matters so much, that if it is not about that, I shall presently leave."

His reason is that the English "think"; which we, replies the chevalier ironically, "do not; we have not got that talent." And thereupon he compares the two temperaments: "With them everything is serious, everything is grave, everything is taken literally; one would think they had not been long enough together; other men are not yet their brothers, they look upon them as beings of another nature. If they see customs other than theirs, it vexes them. As for us, we find amusement in all that; everything is welcome to us; we are the natives of all countries; with us, the fool diverts the sage; the sage corrects the fool without spurning him; here nothing is grave, nothing is important, save what deserves to be so. We are of all men in the world, those who have been of most account with humanity." The marquis, convinced, exclaims: "Come, good citizen, come that I may embrace thee"; and he declares he will leave the play if he finds

"Gulliver" in it. Gulliver's absence is, unfortunately, not sufficient to ensure the success of a play, and Marivaux's had only four representations.

England had sent the poet Matthew Prior to Paris; France returned the compliment by sending to London the poet Destouches, formerly a soldier, nearly killed at Landau, wounded at Friedlingen, author already of several plays, and honoured, at the beginning of his literary career, by a letter in which old Boileau incited him to climb Parnassus and "cull the infallible laurels which await you there." Destouches remained six years in London, first as secretary of embassy, then as chargé d'affaires, and many of those fine red leather volumes, stamped with the arms of France, in which the original despatches of French envoys are preserved in the archives of the Affaires Étrangères, are filled with his official correspondence. He married in London, learned the English language, studied the English drama, as may be seen from several plays written by him after his return to Paris, and became the friend of Addison, who liked to discuss with him the merits of rules and decency, about which both held the same opinion: "He told me so himself," writes Destouches.[1]

Shortly after, the Abbé Prévost, in his turn, visited England, examined the country, was pleased with it, and assigned it as a temporary dwelling-place to his "Homme de Qualité." The travelling impressions noted by the Man of Quality in his "Mémoires" are Prévost's own.[2]

---

[1] Preface to the "Tambour nocturne." Stay in London from 1717 to 1723.

[2] Book v. The "Mémoires" came out from 1728 onwards.

The country "is not sufficiently known"; Prévost speaks of it with sympathy; he describes not only London, but many provincial towns, such as the elegant watering-place of Tunbridge Wells, already eulogised by French travellers in the preceding century.[1]

He goes to Oxford, visits castles, sits in the coffee-houses where "milords" and artisans discuss State affairs; coffee-houses "are, as it were, the seat of Anglican liberty." He frequents the theatres, and Mrs. Oldfield seems to him so beautiful, that — triumph of love — he sets himself the task of learning English on her account: "It must be agreed that she is an incomparable woman. She has made me like the English theatre, for which I had but little inclination at first. Charmed with the sound of her voice, with her face, and with her every movement, I made haste to learn enough English to understand her,

---

[1] "Vous voyez un reste de ces enchantements jadis si communs en ce pays; c'est en cet endroit délicieux qu'Amadis et Orianne consommèrent jadis leur mariage et, pour conserver une mémoire éternelle des plaisirs qu'ils y prirent, l'enchanteur qui se méloit de leurs affaires a donné à ces eaux une vertu miraculeuse : —

"Ces eaux portent au cœur de si douces vapeurs,
Qu'une belle en buvant, presque sans qu'elle y pense,
Guérit en un moment de toutes ses rigueurs,
Et le galant de sa souffrance."

Pavillon to Madame de Pelissary, "Mélanges" added to the "Œuvres mêlées" of Saint-Evremond, London, 1705, vol. vi., p. 94, time of Charles II.

and after that I rarely failed to attend the plays in which she appeared."

Soon the sight of the actress was not his chief pleasure; he became an enthusiastic admirer of English dramatic art, and particularly of Shakespeare. The fault in English plays is their want of regularity: "But, for the beauty of the sentiments, be they tender or sublime, for that tragic power which stirs the deepest regions of the soul and never fails to arouse the passions dormant in the dullest mind; for energy of expression, for the art of bringing events about, and of managing situations, I have read nothing either in Greek or in French, which surpasses the drama in England. Shakespeare's 'Hamlet,' Dryden's 'Don Sebastian,' Otway's 'Orphan' and 'Venice Preserved,' several plays of Congreve's, Farquhar's, &c., are excellent tragedies, where one finds a thousand beauties united." He acknowledges that some of them are no doubt "a little disfigured by a mixture of buffoonery unworthy of the buskin"; no matter, he is under the charm. Comedies seem to him no less admirable; he listens to them "with infinite satisfaction. At first the actors' declamation seems to foreigners hard and peculiar, but it does not take long to get accustomed to it, and one ends by finding that they attain to the true and the natural." Prévost, in fact, talks like an "anglomane," and he is one of the first in date.

He is withal not less surprised than the travellers who had come before him, at the strange sights offered by the streets of London, at the ferocity of the wrestlers, boxers, and gladiators, who end by emitting blood from their nostrils, mouths, and ears, or who remove by a

clever sword-cut a slice from their adversary's leg ; as
the celebrated Figg did one day in Prévost's presence.[1]
He notes the independence of manners, and a practice
of equality very surprising to foreigners : " Who could
imagine, for instance, that the most miserable street
porter will dispute precedence with a 'mylord' whose
quality he knows, and that if one or the other refuses
to give way, they will publicly exchange blows until
the stronger remains master of the pavement? This
happens frequently in London. I have heard mylord
H. boast of having overthrown a chair-bearer, although
he confessed that the man was a vigourous rascal who
had made him feel the weight of his arms in more than
one place." This was not a unique example, nor even
a rare one, and many besides Prévost were able to
observe as much : " The late Maréchal de Saxe going
through the streets of London on foot," we read in
another description of the town, " had an affair with a
scavenger that he ended in the twinkling of an eye to
the unanimous applause of all the bystanders. He let
his scavenger come up close to him, seized him by the
nape of the neck and whirled him aloft, directing
him in such wise that he fell into the middle of his

---

[1] "Le sergent (an Irish soldier) porta un coup à Figg qui lui
coupa une pièce assez large de son bras. . . . Figg, dans l'instant
même, lui emporta une grande partie du mollet qui tomba sur la
scène. Tout le monde applaudit à un si beau coup en frappant des
mains et en criant *bravo, bravo, ancora, ancora*, qui est une façon
d'applaudir qu'ils ont prise des Italiens. Le sergent ne pouvant
plus se soutenir demeura assis en considérant son sang, qui coulait
comme un ruisseau." "Mémoires d'un homme de qualité." bk. v.
Figg died in 1734.

tumbrel filled to the top with liquid mud "; a new victory to add to those of Fontenoy and Rocoux.[1]

Guide-books recommended ordinary travellers, who had not won the battle of Fontenoy, rather to employ persuasion if they could, " la voie de la douceur," and discouraged both " les représailles " and the appeal to judges.[2]

" French Dog " was still the fashion, and people in the streets continued to gather around strangers, with aggressive intent ; as the learned La Condamine was enabled to observe : " In the journey he made two or three years since to London, M. de La Condamine was attended, in all his outings, by a numerous cortège attracted by a huge tin ear-trumpet which he constantly held to his ear, a map of London which he carried about unfolded, and his frequent pauses before every object worthy of his attention. In his first walks, often

---

[1] "Londres," by Grosley, 1770, 3 vols., i., p. 149. Many other examples might be quoted. Here is one more : " Si un cocher de fiacre a dispute pour le payement avec un gentilhomme qu'il a mené et que le gentilhomme lui offre de se battre avec lui pour vuider la querelle, le cocher y consent de bon cœur. Le gentilhomme ôte son épée, la met dans quelque boutique, avec sa canne, ses gants et sa cravate et se bat. . . . Si le cocher est bien battu, ce qui arrive presque toujours (*Side note :* Un gentilhomme ne s'expose guère à un pareil combat, s'il ne se sent être le plus fort), le voilà payé : mais s'il est battant, il faut que le battu paye ce qui était en question. J'ai une fois vu le feu Duc de Grafton (*Side note :* Dans le beau milieu de la grande rue du Strand, Le Duc de Grafton était grand et extraordinairement robuste) aux prises en pleine rue avec un pareil cocher qu'il étrilla d'une terrible manière." Misson, " Mémoires d'Angleterre," La Haye, 1698, p. 253.

[2] Expilly, " Description . . . des Isles Britanniques," Paris, 1759, p. 24.

surrounded by the crowd which hampered his movements, he used to shout to his interpreter :—

" ' What do all these people want ? '

" And the interpreter, applying his lips to the ear-trumpet, shouted back :—

" ' They are making fun of you.'

" They became accustomed at last to seeing him, and ceased to gather about his person."[1]

Immediately after his journey to England Prévost employed himself in trying to propagate a knowledge of English literature, and with this intent, independently of his voluminous and far from accurate translations, he published in Paris a periodical, " Le Pour et Contre," 1733.[2] In the first number Prévost wrote (and this shows how the taste for English things was beginning then to spread) : " What will be quite peculiar to this paper, is that I promise to insert, in each number, some interesting particular touching the genius of the English, the curiosities of London and of the other parts of the island, and the progress which is made there daily in science and in art."[3] He kept

---

[1] Grosley, " Londres," i., p. 150.

[2] " Le Pour et Contre, ouvrage périodique, d'un goût nouveau, dans lequel on s'explique librement sur tout ce qui peut intéresser la curiosité du public en matière de sciences, d'art, de livres, d'auteurs, &c., sans prendre aucun parti et sans offenser personne ; par l'auteur des Mémoires d'un homme de qualité."

[3] This interest, of recent date, was already lively, for Prévost counted upon a publication thus planned, " pour gagner du pain," as Mathieu Marais observed in not very flattering terms : " Un certain Prévost, ex-bénédictin, est arrivé là avec une suivante ; il s'est avisé, pour gagner du pain, de faire un journal sous le nom de *Pour et Contre*," July 11, 1733. " Journal et Mémoires," ed. Lescure, Paris, 1863, vol. iv. p. 504.

his word and translated passages from the best authors; he gave information about the literature, the customs, and the manners of the English.

But already the most illustrious of all these travellers had sojourned in England and had returned thence, had familiarised himself with the men of letters there, Swift, Pope, Congreve, and many others, and had learnt English well enough to write it fluently, so as not to be understood, he said, "by people too inquisitive." It was still, at that time, somewhat as though one had corresponded in cipher. Voltaire was very far from seeing a crabbed *patois* in that language, as Saint-Amant formerly had: "I look upon the English language as a learned one which deserves to be the object of our application in France, as the French tongue is thought a kind of accomplishment in England." For his part, he had learnt English as if it had been "Greek or Latin," that is to say, particularly from a grammatical point of view; the pronunciation seems to have offered insuperable difficulties to him.[1] Finally he published in French his famous "Lettres philosophiques," the year after Prévost had started his "Pour et Contre."[2]

---

[1] "It has the appearance of too great a presumption in a traveller who hath been but eighteen months in England to attempt to write in a language which he cannot pronounce at all, and which he hardly understands in conversation. But I have done what we do every day at school when we write Latin and Greek, tho' surely we pronounce them both very pitifully." Preface to "An Essay upon the Civil Wars of France . . . also upon the epick poetry of the European nations," 1727; 2nd edition, "corrected by himself," 1728, "Price 1s. 1d." He improved, however, in his pronunciation during the remainder of his stay.

[2] "Lettres philosophiques par M. de V.," Amsterdam (Rouen),

VOLTAIRE AT TWENTY-FOUR. (1718.)

Voltaire had arrived in the month of June, 1726, and his first impression had been delightful: "When I landed near London, it was in the middle of spring; the sky was as cloudless as on the finest days in the south of France; the air was cooled by a gentle west wind which augmented nature's serenity and disposed the mind to joy, such *machines* are we, and so much do our souls depend upon the action of our bodies. I stopped at Greenwich, on the banks of the Thames. This beautiful river, which never overflows, and whose borders are ornamented with verdure all the year, was covered with two rows of merchant vessels during the space of six miles; all had unfurled their sails to honour the king and queen, who were promenading on the river in a gilded barge, preceded by boats filled with music and followed by thousands of little rowing boats. . . . There was not one of those mariners who did not show by his face, by his dress, and by his corpulency that he was free and that he lived in plenty." Races for girls, young men, and horses take place on the green: "I thought myself transported to the Olympic games." The next day, it is true, he sees nothing but gloomy people; he hears that "Molly has cut her throat," that the English hang themselves "by the dozen, in the months of November and March," and that all this is caused by "the east wind." [1]

1734, 12°; the English edition had appeared the preceding year: "Letters concerning the English nation." London, 1733, 8°.

[1] Letter to M——, 1727 (vol. xliv. of the Kehl edition). The hangings, drownings, and throats cut on account of the east wind or for other motives were celebrated. Jean Baptiste Racine writes to his brother Louis à propos of suicide: "Ce ne sera jamais un

Such were his first impressions and his first surprises. He remained in England until the spring of 1729. Patronised by Bolingbroke, and recommended, exiled though he was, by Morville, French Minister of Foreign Affairs and member of the French Academy (who had given him a letter to the ambassador, Comte de Broglie),[1] Voltaire, with his usual activity, resolved to turn this forced sojourn to the greatest possible account. He observed with especial zeal everything that differed from French customs (religious sects, independence of minds, confusion of ranks, trading "mylords," burial of Mrs. Oldfield the actress, so admired by the Abbé Prévost, at Westminster, "the Saint-Denis of the English"), giving of these singular ways an account as witty, as bitter, often as comical as possible, pretending to blame what was excessive in English customs and to defend the ideas received in France; at bottom, doing just the contrary. At bottom is even saying too much, it is almost on the surface:

péché fort à la mode parmi les gens de bon sens; et je ne crois pas que vous vouliez en cette occasion être le missionnaire des Anglais; laissons-les se jeter tant qu'il voudront dans la Tamise; plût à Dieu que leurs sots écrits y fussent avec eux!" 1741. "Œuvres de Racine" (Grands Écrivains), vol. vii., p. 344.

[1] See the reply of the Comte de Broglie, afterwards marshal and duke, to Morville, à propos of Voltaire and of his "Henriade," printed by me in the "Revue Critique," April 27, 1885; also in "English Essays," chap. v. Cf. the curious letters of the Earl of Stair to James Craggs on the first relations of "my little poet ye author of Œdipus" with England, printed by M. E. Scott, "Athenæum," June 27. 1891. On Voltaire's stay, see especially J. Churton Collins, "Bolingbroke, a historical study, and Voltaire in England," London, 1886; and A. Ballantyne, "Voltaire's visit to England," 1726-9, London, 1893.

GREENWICH AND THE "FELICIOUS LAND" AROUND.
By Rigaud, 1736.

his pleasure to be complete must not be concealed ; it must be witnessed by his reader, even the common reader and the inattentive reader : for Voltaire writes on every subject for every one.

The Voltaire of the "Lettres philosophiques" is already the master-scoffer who made of irony so terrible a weapon ; he is sure of his art, he has quivers full of arrows, he darts them, keeping a smile on his lips ; he sends them straight to the mark, looking the while as though his thoughts were elsewhere and as if he were chatting idly with his neighbours. Under pretence of describing the English nation, he satirises the kingdom of France ; he relates the Quakers' beliefs in such a way as to damage the Catholic faith : and so with everything else. Voltaire has already in hand the pen which will write the story of Candide.

On one point, however, he is sincere, does not scoff, and will bear no jesting ; and this to the very end. On that point this great revolutionist is full of reserve ; he behaves like a liberal conservative ; but he is far more conservative than liberal. The subject on which he early takes such a decided attitude is literary art, and particularly dramatic art. His friends, Bolingbroke, Falkener, and Pope, had made him acquainted with Shakespeare ; he went to see the great man's plays, and assisted with emotion at the performance of "Julius Cæsar," in spite of "the barbarous irregularities" of that tragedy. He contemplated with stupor a poet so different from those of his nation ; he tried to express an opinion upon him, but trod warily on such dangerous ground. His "Lettre sur la Tragédie," with which he reproached himself later, on account of its too favourable appreciations, is far from breathing enthusiasm for English liberty.[1] "Shakespeare," he says, "whom the English take for a Sophocles, flourished about the same time as Lope de Vega ; he created the drama, he had a genius full of strength and fecundity, of naturalness, and sublimity, without the least spark of good taste and without the slightest knowledge of rules. I am going to say a thing very hazardous but true, namely, that this author's merit has ruined the English stage ; there are such fine scenes, such grand and terrible parts interspersed in those monstrous farces called tragedies, that his plays have always been acted with great success. . . . Most of the eccentric or *gigantesque* ideas of this author have acquired, after two hundred years, the right to pass for sublime." Thereupon he sneers at "Othello," "a very touching play in which a husband strangles his wife on the stage," and at "Hamlet," in which "gravediggers dig a grave, drinking and singing ballads." As for the "grand and terrible" parts, he gives a specimen of them by translating the soliloquy of Hamlet. But there, his whim getting the better of him, and delighted to continue his game and shock the good Christians of France by the mouth of Hamlet, he turns the soliloquy into a diatribe against religion :—

> "Demeure, il faut choisir et passer à l'instant,
> De la vie à la mort et de l'être au néant.
> Dieux justes ! s'il en est, éclairez mon courage . . .
> O mort . . .
> Eh ! qui pourrait sans toi supporter cette vie,

[1] He had already published several appreciations upon Shakespeare ; see, e.g., his preface to "Œdipe," 1730 ; below, pp. 245-6.

> De nos prêtres menteurs bénir l'hypocrisie,
> D'une indigne maîtresse excuser les erreurs,
> Ramper sous un ministre, adorer ses hauteurs ? "

Needless to remind the reader that "the just gods, if such there be," and the "lying priests," to say nothing of the "unworthy mistresses," were very far from the thoughts of Prince Hamlet.[1] And yet, in spite of his prejudices, Voltaire's literary sense was too keen for him not to feel all there was of truth, of strength, and of life in that drama ; so he sums up his opinion in a phrase of which the romantic enthusiasts of 1830 themselves would not have altered a word : "The poetic genius of the English is, up to now, like a bushy tree planted by Nature, throwing out a thousand branches and growing unsymmetrically with strength. It dies if you try to force its nature and to clip it like one of the trees in the Marly gardens."[2]

---

[1] " For who would bear the whips and scorns of time,
The oppressor's wrong, the proud man's contumely,
The pangs of despis'd love, the law's delay,
The insolence of office, and the spurns
That patient merit of the unworthy takes."
(iii. 1.)

[2] Letter XVIII., "Sur la tragédie." This impression, such as it is, is the one Voltaire really felt when he began seriously to study the English drama. In his "Essai sur la poésie épique," he placed the irregular Shakespeare above the correct Addison : "Tel est le privilège du génie d'invention ; il se fait une route où personne n'a marché avant lui ; il court sans guide, sans art, sans règle ; il s'égare dans sa carrière, mais il laisse loin derrière lui tout ce qui n'est que raison et qu'exactitude" (ch. ii.). A letter to Thieriot of June 14 [1728] shows that he had already put on paper at that date the additions and corrections which he introduced later in the French text of his "Essai" (first published in English in an abbreviated form, and without the passage here quoted, 1727).

The phrase had not, however, in Voltaire's eyes, quite the same meaning it had to the enthusiasts of 1830. The "Lettres" came out, it must not be forgotten, at a time when Albano was preferred to Rembrandt.

They appeared, and made a great stir. Firstly, the moment they were issued, they were condemned to be "lacerated and burnt in the Court of the Palace [of Justice] at the foot of the grand stairway of the same, by the executor of high justice, as scandalous, contrary to religion, good morals, and to the respect due to the powers," June 10, 1734. Secondly, the book had really all the faults attributed to it in the sentence; the advertising done for it by the executor of high justice was no cheat, and the amateurs who managed to procure it got their money's worth. It was, moreover, written in that style at once sharp and clear, rapid and light of gait, the incomparable style of Voltaire. Finally, it satisfied that growing curiosity, pointed out by the Abbé Prévost, for the things of nebulous England. Voltaire spoke of them after a prolonged stay, as one who had a thorough knowledge of the subject, who knew the language, who had read the books and seen the people. He did not speak by hearsay of Congreve, "infirm and almost dying when I knew him"; nor of Pope, "with whom I passed much of my time"; nor of the Quakers: "I went to see one of the celebrated Quakers of England." In short, he wrote in that tone of authority and with that "blacker ink" which he so well knew how to use.[1]

Adversaries were not wanting, and their diatribes

---

[1] The success, naturally enough, was not quite so great in London. The English edition had appeared first, in 1733. Jordan, who was in England at the time, notes the effect it

THE CUT TREES OF MARLY
From the Plate by Aveline

served to heighten further the success of the book. The "R.P.D.P.B." (Le Coq de Villeray) protested in the name of patriotism and good taste ; his indignation was aroused especially by the eulogiums bestowed on Shakespeare, which seemed to him immoderate. What need to go and praise Shakespeare when there had been a Grévin ? "Jacques Grévin, who died in 1570, at the age of twenty-nine, would perhaps have soared as high as Shakespeare, whose contemporary he was, if death had not so soon cut the thread of his life. The tragedy of 'César' might have ranked with the 'More of Venice,' and I doubt not that M. de Voltaire, who, in dramatic matters, passes for having some taste, would have found some also in that play, he who acknowledges that his Shakespeare was completely devoid of it. Grévin, on the contrary, was one of the finest geniuses of his time ; he put wit into everything he did." Shakespeare died "in 15-6" (a mistake of forty years), the remote period at which he lived is his only excuse for "all the foolish things he put on the stage." [1]

produced : " Pendant le temps que j'étois en Angleterre, les lettres de M. de Voltaire sur les Anglois parurent en anglois sous la direction de M. Tyriot, ami de ce poète. J'ouis parler différemment de ces lettres : les uns en étoient contents, d'autres soutenoient que ce poète parloit d'une nation qui lui étoit inconnue ; la plupart cependant rendoient justice à l'auteur et convenoient qu'il y a des choses curieuses et dites avec esprit." "Histoire d'un voyage littéraire fait en 1733, en France, en Angleterre et en Hollande." La Haye, 2nd ed., 1736, p. 186. The French text of Voltaire's "Lettres" went through five editions within the year of its publication (Bengesco).

[1] "Réponse ou critique des Lettres philosophiques de M. de V." Basle, 1735, pp. 78 ff. On the "César" of Grévin, see above, p. 40.

II.

From that moment, information becomes more precise; Voltaire has spoken, every one listens; he has written, every one reads him; he is admired, blamed, discussed; his shrill trumpet has awakened sleeping energies; people are ecstatic or indignant; his tiniest pamphlet starts a question, and sometimes causes a war. His "Lettres" gave rise to a quantity of other essays on the same subjects. Shakespeare thus became, like the Quakers, one of the curiosities of England; it was difficult henceforth to talk about that country without mentioning him: "I see very well that you expect me at this place to speak to you of the Quakers or Shakers" ("des Quarkers ou des Trembleurs"), wrote Sorbières, who, when he came to the drama, celebrated the Duchess of Newcastle, and did not name Shakespeare. Travellers are now expected to talk, not only about the Quakers, but also about the author of "Hamlet." The grave Montesquieu himself, as early as 1730, had been obliged to hold an opinion on Shakespeare; it does him less honour than his dicta on the government of the nations: "The 5th of October, 1730, I was presented to the Prince, to the King, and to the Queen at Kensington. The Queen, after having spoken about my journeys, spoke of the English drama; she asked milord Chesterfield whence it comes that Shakespeare, who lived in the time of Queen Elizabeth, had made women speak so badly, and had pictured them so silly. Milord Chesterfield replied very aptly that women did not appear then on the stage, and that bad actors played those parts, which was why Shakespeare did not take so much trouble to make them speak well. I could give another reason for it, which is that to make women speak, one must be accustomed to society and to the *bienséances*. To make heroes speak one need only be accustomed to books."[1] These ingenious explanations allowed Queen Caroline (to whom Voltaire had just dedicated his "Henriade") to understand why Beatrice, Rosalind, Portia, and Juliet speak "so badly" and are "so silly."

Historical dictionaries, which, so far, had not said a word about the dramatist, now allow him a few lines. In 1735 the "Supplément au Grand Dictionnaire de Moreri" devotes a notice to him, in which it is said, as in Villeray's book, that he died "in 1576" (the "Supplément" killed him at the age of twelve); that he had eccentric and gigantic ideas, followed "by several modern authors to whom this imitation has done no honour." On this subject one may consult

---

[1] "Le 5 Octobre, 1730, je fus présenté au prince, au roi et à la reine, à Kensington. La reine, après m'avoir parlé de mes voyages, parla du théâtre anglais ; elle demanda à milord Chesterfield d'où vient que Shakespeare, qui vivait du temps de la reine Élisabeth, avait si mal fait parler les femmes et les avait faites si sottes. Milord Chesterfield répondit fort bien que les femmes ne paraissaient pas sur le théâtre et que c'étaient de mauvais acteurs qui jouaient ces rôles, ce qui faisait que Shakespeare ne prenait pas tant de peine à les faire bien parler. J'en dirais une autre raison, c'est que, pour faire parler les femmes, il faut avoir l'usage du monde et des bienséances. Pour faire parler les héros, il ne faut qu'avoir l'usage des livres." "Notes sur l'Angleterre" ; "Œuvres," ed. Destutt de Tracy, vol. vii. Montesquieu says elsewhere : the English theatre resembles those freaks of nature, "dans lesquels elle a suivi des hasards heureux." "Des Anglais et des Français."

"le sieur Arouet de Voltaire and his so-called philosophical letters."[1]

Verdicts more generous were formulated at the same time; first of all by Abbé Prévost, who, in 1738, devoted entire numbers of his periodical to Shakespeare. He spoke of him with a freedom and audacity far greater than Voltaire's, but which attracted much less attention. This abbé was a born heretic; he spoke without respect of the ancients and their rules; and, what was then an unheard of thing, he did it to the advantage of the English dramatist. Shakespeare, he said, did not know the ancients; so much the better, for perhaps the contact "would have made him lose something of that warmth, of that impetuosity, and of that admirable delirium, if one may thus express it, which bursts forth in his slightest productions." He did not observe the unities, "but, if we consider the manners, the characters, the unfolding of passions and the expression of sentiments, we shall find scarcely anything in all his works that cannot be justified; and on all sides abound beauties which cannot be praised too highly." Here follows an analysis of "Hamlet," "Macbeth," the "Tempest," "Les Femmes de Windsor en bonne humeur," "Othello," &c.

Prévost knew the originals of Shakespeare's plays; he knew Greene's novel, from which "The Winter's Tale" was derived; he suspected that the English theatre had had a commencement and a development,

---

[1] This "Supplément," Paris, 1735, 2 vols., fol., had been compiled by the Abbé Goujet, who had revised the R.P.D.P.B.'s "Réponse," whence the similarity of appreciations and errors.

in short a history that might be related. Louis Riccoboni, the famous Lelio of the Comédie Italienne, and the first in date of several Riccobonis, authors and actors, attempted, in the same year, 1738, to relate that history and to give an account of Shakespeare and his times.¹ He had been in London at the same time as Voltaire, and, like him, had been to see old Congreve: "I had more than one conversation with him (in 1727) and I found him learned, and very well informed on literary matters." Riccoboni gathered information to the best of his ability; he had something to say on the performances of mediæval mysteries, on the children of St. Paul's, on the tragedy of "Gorboduc," "which," he observed, "is attributed in one edition to the seigneur Buchurst and in another to Thomas Sachville," adding, "I cannot imagine the reason of it." The reason is of course that the two persons are one and the same; but it was something to be aware, at that date, of the existence of "Gorboduc." The biographical notes devoted by Riccoboni to Shakespeare are not perfect models of accuracy either: "Having devoured his patrimony he took up robbery as his profession." He wrote bloody dramas, "Hamlet" amongst others, and "Othello," in which is seen the incredible strangling of Desdemona. Catastrophes of this sort are very astounding, but it needs no less to keep the too meditative English awake: at tragedies "devoid of the horrors that pollute the stage with gore, the spectators would perhaps fall asleep." For the same motive, English

---

¹ "Réflexions historiques et critiques sur les différents Théâtres de l'Europe," Paris, 1738, 8º.

comedy is laden with incidents, "in order to prevent the attention of the audience from slackening." When he sums up his opinion, Riccoboni cannot help showing that he has been, in reality, more touched and more deeply impressed with admiration than he will acknowledge; but he has not the Abbé Prévost's temerity; he is kept in awe by the thought of rules, inviolable, immutable, intangible, sacred: "If it were allowable to depart from those rules which reason's self has dictated, the English drama would be able to balance the reputation of the ancient and modern dramas. The beauties of English tragedy are above any of the beauties that the European theatres can show us, and if some day English poets submit to the three unities of the drama ... they will, at the very least, share the glory enjoyed by our best modern poets."

Many others directed their attention to the English drama and especially to Shakespeare; their criticisms were nearer the appreciations of Riccoboni than those of the audacious Prévost. Louis Racine took Shakespeare as a point of comparison in order to explain the genius of Sophocles, and, implicitly, the genius of his father.[1]

---

[1] Shakespeare "fit tout à la fois parler prose et vers, rire, pleurer, et heurter Melpomène. . . . On vit sur le théâtre des Anglois . . . des apparitions, des fantômes, des meurtres, des têtes coupées, des enterrements, des sièges de villes, des saccagements de couvents, des maris égorgeant leurs femmes, des patients accompagnés par leurs confesseurs, conduits à l'échafaud. . . . Les Anglois, constants à admirer les étincelles qui sortent quelquefois des brouillards de leur Shakespeare, ne nous envièrent point nos richesses dramatiques." "Remarques sur la poésie de Jean Racine, suivies d'un Traité sur la Poésie Dramatique," Amsterdam and Paris, 1752, 3 vols., 12º, vol. iii. pp. 190, 197.

The Abbé Le Blanc devoted a number of his "Lettres"[1] to minute studies of the English stage and of Shakespeare's genius, an admirable genius, but ruined by his ignorance of rules: "Their famous Shakespeare is a striking example of the danger one runs in departing from them. This poet, one of the greatest who has perhaps ever existed, has failed, either through ignorance of the rules of the ancients, or unwillingness to follow them, to produce a single work that is not a monster of its kind." It may even be said that "not one of them can be read through from beginning to end." His vulgarities are prodigious; in his comedies "the ample paunch and wide hat of the actor are generally the most comical element in his rôle. That Falstaff, so celebrated on the English stage, is scarcely anything more than a buffoon worthy of [Scarron's] Don Japhet of Armenia." In his tragedies, Shakespeare "does not scruple to make Cæsar appear in his nightcap; you feel by that how he must degrade him."[2] Some personages, in this same play of "Julius Cæsar," abuse each other so, "that one cannot take them for Romans." Le Blanc—and this is his great merit—was the first in France to understand the incomparable magic of Shakespeare's style: "As regards style, that is the part which most distinguishes Shakespeare from the other poets of his nation; it is the part in which

---

[1] "Lettres d'un François." The Hague, 1745, 3 vols.
[2] Evidently Sc. ii., Act ii.: "Cæsar's house. Thunder and lightning. Enter Cæsar in his night-gown." There is, however, no direction concerning the night-cap. On "Don Japhet," see "English Essays from a French Pen," pp. 121 ff.

he excels. There is colour in all his pictures, life in all his words. He talks, so to speak, a language of his own ; for which reason he is very hard to translate. It must also be admitted, however, that, while his expressions are at times sublime, it often happens that he does not abstain from the *gigantesque*." This last word, as we have already seen by the way in which Voltaire employs it, was not used then in the same eulogious sense as it was by the romantic writers of the 1830 period.

Up to now the French public knew Shakespeare only by hearsay, from the appreciations of a few men of letters ; it could not form its own opinion ; it had at its disposal only Prévost's short accounts of the principal plays and the few fragments translated by Voltaire. No real translation of the master's works existed. A first attempt was made by La Place in 1745.[1] As yet no one could entertain the idea of translating the complete plays : it was even rash to devote, as La Place intended to do, two volumes to this foreigner, author of dramas both monstrous and " gigantic." In these two volumes some plays were

[1] " Le Théâtre Anglois," London, 1745, 8 vols., 12". La Place (Pierre Antoine de, 1707-93) translated a quantity of English works : novels by Mrs. Behn, by Fielding, by Clara Reeve, &c. He translated Otway's " Venice Preserved " and had it performed without, like La Fosse, transferring the subject to Rome : " Roseli harangua le parterre avant la pièce pour prévenir le public sur la singularité d'un genre auquel l'auteur a conservé le caractère anglais," 1746 ; De Mouhy, "Tablettes dramatiques," Paris, 1752. Otway's drama has enjoyed in France a special favour ; it was recently translated into French verse by M. Marcel, French Minister to Sweden.

translated (a very timid translation, attenuated, toned down, full of mistakes, but nevertheless meritorious for the time); others were simply analysed. The work was prefaced by a "Discours sur le Théâtre Anglois," certainly the best thing La Place ever wrote. He knew the objections which would be made to his undertaking, and the repugnance that people of taste would feel at venturing into that forest, among those brambles, so different from the well-trained trees of Marly. Shakespeare would be blamed for violating the unities, for bloodshed, for his low comic vein, for the use he made of prose. La Place had an answer for everything; he did not ask his readers to admire but to know: "Shakespeare's reputation has held good for a hundred and fifty years. Do comedians see their theatre deserted, and the audience indifferent to the performance of the various works announced? they have recourse to Shakespeare: and people flock to the play in crowds. . . . Would the modern English go to these plays on purpose to be bored, if admiration and pleasure did not attract them?"

If, thought La Place, Shakespeare could charm by means which none of our authors have employed, all the more reason for us to study him, since he will show us ways unknown to us, and we may find it useful perhaps to be able to appreciate for ourselves that sort of flavour, "goût de terroir," characteristic of works produced under skies so different from our own. No doubt this master poet uses rhyme, blank verse, and prose in the same play, which is to us very shocking. The English pretend, however, that that way is "the most natural: since the language, according to them, must be proportioned to the quality of the speakers. ... It results, moreover, from this, that nothing can be less monotonous than their tragedies and that the characters are always natural, distinct, and strongly depicted. We might then compare English plays to pictures in which a deep shading is employed by the painter on purpose to give more relief to the principal objects. Carrying the comparison still farther, we might say that this same painter often throws rays of light on to the distant background to render visible episodes that sometimes are no component part of his subject, but which enliven the picture and cause the spectator to gaze with renewed pleasure on the principal personages." Why, indeed, be prompt to blame? "Let us keep ourselves from condemning unreservedly now, what our nephews will perhaps some day applaud." It seems as if La Place was foreseeing, beyond a Voltaire, a Victor Hugo.

The rule of the three unities is sacred, he continues: this much is granted, and it is scarcely likely it will ever be abolished; and yet who knows? What cannot great minds do? "Are the bounds of genius known to us?" And considering that art which had just received, so to speak, a new birth, La Place added these quasi prophetic words: " In our own days, have not new resources, and new roads into the recesses of the human heart been discovered, so that a new style of novel has been created? Scrupulous criticism may say that these ingenious innovators, by dint of analysing the human heart, have only decomposed it. Perhaps, however, this is only the beginning of a new style which will lead to minute studies of the heart of a kind unknown before. Discoveries may thus be made ; new literary pleasures procured, and our nephews will perhaps witness this unexpected result : that, owing to those attempts, new rules, sanctioning new enjoyments, will be introduced into the drama." [1]

This was predicting very exactly, both the importance that novels were to acquire and the influence they were to exercise upon the stage. The study of Shakespeare had given La Place's mind the habit of observing the *au delà*, of casting looks over the wall of rules ; it had allowed him to perceive how arbitrary were the lines drawn between literary genres and to foresee the reactions of one genre upon another.

He added very eloquently : "Shall we believe that the faculties of the heart and mind are more limited than the properties of matter ? or that their study has been carried further than that of physics, geometry, and anatomy, which we feel to be still so far from having reached their final goal and perfection ? The world that seems decrepit to some and definitively formed to others, is perhaps only in its adolescence, given the centuries which are still to follow ours ; and we are no more justified in considering it as having reached the

[1] "N'a-t-on pas trouvé, de nos jours, de nouvelles ressources et de nouvelles routes dans les replis du cœur humain, pour créer un nouveau genre de roman ? La critique scrupuleuse dira peut-être que ces ingénieux novateurs, à force d'analyser le cœur humain n'ont fait que le décomposer. Mais ce n'est peut-être aussi qu'un premier pas qui mène à le *travailler en grand*. Qui sait si nos neveux ne verront pas éclore de ce travail de nouvelles découvertes et de nouvelles propriétés qui, formant pour eux de nouveaux plaisirs, prescriront aux auteurs de nouvelles règles pour le dramatique."

extreme and unpassable limit of knowledge than were in their day the Egyptian sages, the Greek philosophers and the brilliant geniuses of the time of Augustus."

La Place's appeal was heard, and the success exceeded his expectations. Instead of two volumes, he had, at the request of his readers, to devote four to Shakespeare, and "to make known, by translation or by analysis all that remains of this author's plays." The "Journal de Trévoux" published no less than seven articles about this extraordinary venture.[1]

III.

But to what extent, one may well ask, was the taste of the French public transforming itself; was it really a change of taste, or was it only an increasing curiosity for foreign wares? There can be no doubt that the play-going public, if it read willingly at home the translations of La Place, encouraged but moderately on the stage any imitation of the English independents. The respect for the unities was engraved so deeply in French minds, rules formed such fine avenues in the literary field, that they could not disappear in a day,

---

[1] From August, 1745 (with the usual reservations on the ignorance of rules, the mixture of the tragical and comical, &c.). Fiquet du Bocage, thus showing the audacity of the translator's undertaking, praised La Place highly for having shown a certain moderation and selected "ce qu'il y avait de présentable . . . Quelle apparence y avoit-il d'intéresser le bon goût des François à un assemblage baroque de choses également étranges et ridicules?" "Lettre sur le Théâtre Anglois, avec une traduction de l'Avare de Shadwell et de la Femme de la Campagne de Wycherley," 1752, 2 vols., 12º.

nor even in a century. It was like the paved roads of Louis XIV.; the king expended so much energy to make them that it would need nearly as much to destroy them, and so they still exist. A few sidepaths, however, have been contrived, along those royal roads; and the same was done with regard to tragedies. For the thing was evident even long before the Abbé Yart, a great translator of English works, expressed it: imitation of the ancients could yield nothing more; "on a épuisé toutes les manières d'imiter les anciens." Something else must be found.

It must and could be done. The spirit of independence and of adventure can never die out entirely; traces of it are found in the quietest and most civilised nations, in their moments of deepest tranquillity. It manifests itself where it can: far from sight, in shaded woods, where the inquisitive go and discover it; sometimes beneath the embroidery of "habits à la romaine," where observers detect its presence. Driven from regular tragedy, it had taken possession of the opera, and the opera, under Louis XIV., belonged to the realm of literature; that form of art was cultivated by the greatest minds of the century: Corneille, Molière, La Fontaine. Imagination was there allowed full scope, the place where the action was laid changed every moment and opened to view scenery either picturesque, charming, or terrible: "The stage represents the palace and gardens of the Tuileries . . . the trees are separated by fountains"; or else we have "a village," "a desert," "a sea-port," "a palace in ruins," "a country scene where a river forms an agreeable island." Armide's palace is destroyed, ghosts leave their tombs : "The earth opens and the shade of Hidraot emerges."[1]

However sedate an artist's temperament may be, there always remains, somewhere, under lock and key, in some recess, half smothered but not dead, Folly with her cap and bells, "la folle du logis." She looks through the keyhole, sometimes she breaks in the door. She dictates to the defenders of rules unexpected words or acts. "Will it be said," we read in an old tragedy, that "I have been ofttimes seen in the darksome night, running dishevelled and half clothed, to ransack the sepulchres of the dead, to cull with muttered incantation poisonous herbs, look for serpents amidst the ruins of old palaces, darken the face of the moon, and plunge all nature into perturbation and terror?" All this witchery is not drawn from any French "Macbeth," but from the "Pucelle d'Orléans selon la vérité de l'histoire et les rigueurs du théâtre," by that great promoter of rules and decorum the Abbé d'Aubignac.[2] Thomas Corneille won prodigious applause because he had the gift of evolving on the stage the wildest plots of the great romancers of the day without departing from rules; witness his "Timocrate," 1656, taken from "Cléopâtre," and his "Bérénice,"

[1] Act 5th of "La Comédie sans Comédie (Armide et Renaud)" 1654; prologue of "Alceste," 1674; "Armide," 1686, by Quinault. See also Corneille's "La Toison d'Or," "Andromède," &c.

[2] "Que n'avez vous instruit vos satellites pour soutenir qu'ils m'ont veue souvent au milieu des ténèbres, courir toute eschevelée et sans ceinture, fouiller dans les sépulcres des morts, couper en murmurant des herbes empoisonnées, chercher des serpents sous les ruines des vieux palais, obscurcir le tein de la lune et mettre toute la nature dans le trouble et l'effroy."

THE DESTRUCTION OF THE PALACE OF ARMIDE, IN THE OPERA
BY QUINAULT, MUSIC OF LULLY.
Drawn by Berain, 1686.

1657, taken from the "Grand Cyrus." "La folle du logis" had something to whisper even in the ear of the sapient Boileau, and there were certainly more bells than usual on her cap the day when, under the shape of "Madame de M. and Madame de T.," she persuaded him to forget his grievances against the opera and to compose one himself:—

"*Poetry.* Well, then, my sister, let us part.
Music. Let us part.
Poetry. Let us part.
Chorus of poets and musicians. Let us part, let us part." [1]

At the very moment when classical art was at its zenith, doubts as to the value of that style had crossed certain minds. Perrault, whose "Parallèle" swarms with ingenious ideas and wise observations [2]

---

[1] We have only a fragment of this opera, the subject of which was the fall of Phaethon. Racine and Boileau worked together at it; Racine's verses have been destroyed. Boileau published the Prologue which he had composed. It is a "disputoison" or strife between Poetry and Music.

[2] Here is an example: "Quand le comédien qui contrefaisoit le cochon à Athènes plut davantage au peuple que le cochon véritable qu'un autre comédien cachoit sous son manteau, on crut que le peuple avoit tort, et le peuple avoit raison, parce que le comédien qui représentoit cet animal en avoit étudié tous les tons les plus marqués et les plus caractérisés et, les ramassant ensemble, remplissoit davantage l'idée que tout le monde en a." This is true of all the arts. Instantaneous photographs have fixed on paper movements of a horse's gallop that the eye cannot perceive; painters have thought they were doing well in transferring the same to their canvas, conforming thus, as they believed, to truth and to nature; but the spectator stands perplexed, the sight is meaningless to him, and does not arouse in his mind the slightest idea of rapidity.

mingled with many paradoxes, had expressed those doubts better than any one else in his days. Art is not so limited as people pretend, he wrote as early as 1692 : " When, in ancient times, a traveller had reached the Straits of Gibraltar, he thought himself at the end of the world. Here were Hercules' pillars, there was no going beyond. But the modern traveller will never be stopped by the thought that, arrived at those pillars, he is at his journey's end ; he is only just beginning it, he crosses the ocean and passes into a new world more spacious than the one he has left." [1]

As years go by, the claims of dramatic art to extension become more and more definite ; they are supported, however, by a minority. The spirit of the independents of the early seventeenth century reappears at the beginning of the eighteenth. Boyer protests, in the very terms used formerly by Schélandre, against the excessive refining of the language : " The French language, enervated and impoverished by refiners, always timid and always the slave of rules and customs, never allows itself the slightest licence and admits no happy temerities." He praises, like d'Urfé, the merits of blank verse : the English language " has a sort of measured prose, which, being limited to a certain number of feet composed of long and short syllables, sustains itself without the feeble support of the rhymes' jingle." This prose " is called blank verse." [2]

---

[1] " Parallèle des Anciens et des Modernes . . . dialogues par M. Perrault de l'Académie Françoise," Paris, 1688, 4 vols., 12°, vol. iii., 1692, p. 227.

[2] Preface to " Caton, tragédie par M. Addison," London, 1713. This translation appeared shortly before the " Caton d'Utique " of

La Motte-Houdard, a few years later, goes much farther still. He openly declares war on rules, verses, narratives, confidants, and nearly all received ideas: "To establish the necessity [of the unity of place] it is vainly alleged that the spectators, being themselves stationary, cannot imagine that the actors change from place to place: but what then, do those spectators, for knowing that they are in reality at the theatre, transport themselves less easily to Athens or to Rome, where live and move the heroes shown to them?"

An unwarrantable use, according to the same La Motte, is made of the *coulisse;* all actions and sights worth seeing are dismissed from the boards and take place behind the scenes: "Most of our plays are only dialogues and narratives, and what is astonishing, is that the very action by which the author was struck, and which decided the choice of his subject, always takes place behind the scenes. The English have a quite opposite taste; people say they carry it to excess, which is very possible"; for certain kinds of action must, after all, be excluded from the stage, on account of "the horror of the objects represented."[1]

F. Deschamps, Paris, 1715. At the end of Deschamps' drama we see Portia, anxious to die on the stage, but restraining herself:—

"Caton n'est plus. Hélas! pour comble de malheur,
  Je ne saurois sans crime expirer de douleur."

The "Mercure Galant" published a comparative study of the two plays and placed Deschamps' far above Addison's, promising the English, however, a fair dramatic future if they observed rules and abstained from "certaines bassesses que les poètes grecs n'ont pas assez évitées." Number of March, 1715.

[1] "Discours sur la Tragédie, à l'occasion des Machabées. . . . A l'occasion de Romulus" (performed 1721, 1722), "Œuvres," Paris

An easy matter it was for theorists to talk; dramatists did not find their own path so smooth; they had to deal with a public that the greatest geniuses of the nation had rendered exacting, that came in crowds to the performances of "Athalie,"[1] that clamoured no doubt for novelty (for without novelty the stage dies), but forbade the discarding of rules. It laughed at La Motte, who had tried to join example to precept, and had written an "Œdipe" in prose; anything rather than such platitude, was the cry on all sides; give us back our rules; "qu'on nous ramène aux carrières!" In some English plays, writes Destouches, à propos of the "Tempest," there is "perpetual magic. And what incidents cannot be brought about by the force of magic? How happy we should be in France, we comic authors, if we could be permitted to use so convenient an art!... But as soon as we want to take our imagination as our guide, we are hissed unmercifully.... 'Tis the taste of the nation, it will have nothing but truth; all that swerves from truth is rejected and hooted without pity."[2]

1754, ten vols., vol. iv. Victor Hugo finding, a century later, the dispute at the same point, says also: "Nous ne voyons en quelque sorte sur le théâtre que les coudes de l'action, ses mains sont ailleurs." Preface to "Cromwell."

[1] "Le 17 Dec. (1739) il y eut tant de monde à la représentation d'‘Athalie,' et le théâtre et le parterre se trouvèrent si excessivement remplis que la pièce, se trouvant à chaque instant interrompue par le tumulte, ne put être achevée." De Mouhy, "Abrégé de l'Histoire du Théâtre," Paris, 1780, vol. iii., p. 38 (the first *public* performance of "Athalie" had taken place in 1716).

[2] "Scènes Anglaises" (Dedicace). These scenes are taken from the "Tempest," as remodelled by Dryden and Davenant, and embel-

AN UNPOPULAR AUTHOR. "L'AUTEUR SIFLÉ."

The foremost tragic author in France, at the opening of the century was Crébillon, who studied to satisfy the public in its desire to be moved according to rule, but by means either new, or supposed to be new. He succeeded very well, limited to the required twenty-four hours his appalling medleys of love and bloodshed reigned by terror, and lived long enough to be the hero and god of the radical reformers of the drama in the second half of the century. Youthful literary revolutionists came to consult him as an oracle in his dilapidated temple: "I was nineteen years old," wrote Mercier, "and in those days the fame of Crébillon, the tragic poet, was at its height. People opposed him to Voltaire, for the public ever seeks to find a rival to every illustrious man, and balancing them one against the other, thus rids itself of a too-considerable weight of esteem.... He lived in the Marais, rue des Douze-Portes. I knocked: immediately the barking of fifteen or twenty dogs was heard; they surrounded me, open-mouthed, and accompanied me to the poet's room. The staircase was filled with awful signs of their presence. I entered, announced and escorted by them. I beheld a room with bare walls; a pallet, two stools, and seven or eight torn and dilapidated arm chairs, composed all the furniture.... The dogs had seated themselves upon all the arm chairs and growled in chorus. The old man, his legs and head bare, his bosom uncovered, was smoking a pipe. He had large blue eyes, spare white hair, a physiognomy full of

lished according to the taste of the times: rôle of the youth who has never seen a woman.

expression. He silenced his dogs, not without trouble, and, whip in hand, made them yield one of the arm chairs to me. He removed his pipe from his mouth as if to salute me, and began to smoke again with a delectation which was depicted on his strongly characterised features.

"The dogs were uttering low growls, showing their teeth at me. The poet at last put down his pipe. I asked him when 'Cromwell' would be finished. 'It is not yet begun,' he replied." (The play had been expected forty years.)

"I begged him to recite some lines of his own. He said he would do so after a second pipe."

The poet smokes. He finishes his second pipe. "He put down his second pipe and then recited to me some very obscure lines from I know not what romantic tragedy he had composed from memory, and which he recited from memory, too.[1] I understood nothing of the subject or the plan of his tragedy. His lines contained a great many imprecations against the gods, and especially against kings, whom he disliked. . . .

"The poet having recited his lines, did nothing but smoke. I rose, the dogs rose too, resumed their barking, and accompanied me thus to the street door. The poet only reprimanded them gently; tenderness shone through his rebukes."[2]

---

[1] As was his custom. His memory was prodigious, he composed whole tragedies without writing a line of them. When he had to read his "Catilina" to the French comedians he produced no manuscript, but recited his tragedy from memory.

[2] Mercier, "Tableau de Paris," vol. x. (1788), chap. 774; the visit to Crébillon took place in 1759.

The thirst for novelty and the respect for rules appears as well on the comic as on the tragic stage. The great innovator in comedy was then La Chaussée, who had reversed Boileau's famous maxim on the antagonism between comedy and tears—

"Le comique, ennemi des soupirs et des pleurs."

His plays are nothing but sighs and tears. The English works which his friend the Abbé Le Blanc had interpreted to him, had shown him the way; it was edged with cypresses; he followed it, and many others followed it with him. Richardson's novels were the rage, Pamela was the heroine of the day. La Chaussée drew from the novel one play, by no means his best, and Voltaire another. English domestic comedies found enthusiastic translators: "Away, exclaims one of these, away, minute wits, not so delicate as finical and frivolous; dry and ungrateful hearts, lost in debauchery and in reflections. You are not made for the pleasure of shedding tears."[1] The age of sensibility was beginning; Rousseau was yet unknown, but it seemed as if he were expected. Collé read the drama thus announced to the public, and

---

[1] Preface to the "Marchand de Londres, ou l'histoire de George Barnwell, tragédie bourgeoise, traduite de l'anglais de M. Lillo," by M. [P. Clément], Paris, 1748, 12°. The work was placed under the patronage of the Abbé Prévost. "The London Merchant, or the History of George Barnwell," in prose, 1730, had had in London such a success, and was held in such esteem, that its performance was recommended for periods of the year when young men most frequent the theatres, on account of its great moralising influence. "The Companion to the Play House," London, 1764, vol. i., Appendix. See below, p. 320, note 1.

wrote in his journal: "I have also read the translation of [Barnwell] ... it moved me to tears. What scenes are that of the assassination of the uncle, and that of the two friends in the prison! What truth, what warmth, what interest! It is withal a very badly written play. There is, however, a great deal of genius and wit in it."[1]

The reader is thus tossed about in opposite directions: What lack of art! What genius! As for the spectator, one could not be too prudent with him. Of his two desires, the desire to see rules respected remained the liveliest. The instant rules were too openly infringed he noisily revolted; before condemning the innovators of that time for their timidity, we must remember the playgoer's state of mind. All dramatic authors knew it by experience: the translator of "Barnwell" dared not even *print* the end of the play.[2]

Destouches seeks among English dramas the one which comes nearest to ours, "it is by the late M. Addison."[3] In London the lines in the picture were

---

[1] "Journal," November, 1748, ed. H. Bonhomme, 1868, 3 vols. 8º.

[2] "La plume me tombe de la main. Les scènes suivantes représentent le lieu de l'exécution; on y voit la potence, le bourreau, la populace, &c. Milvoud meurt en enragée et Barnwell en saint." The French independents of yore had however offered such sights to view. A scene on the scaffold is in Schélandre's "Tyr," 1608. See above, p. 74.

[3] "Le Tambour nocturne, Comédie Angloise," printed in 1736, performed in 1762; taken from "The Drummer, or the Haunted House," of Addison, 1715. "The reader," Steele writes in his preface to Addison's play, "will see many beauties that escape the audience, the touches being too delicate for every taste in a popular assembly." Petitot thought (but wrongly) that he had discovered

MLLE. CLAIRON'S VISIT TO VOLTAIRE.
From a contemporary plate by Huber.

judged not deeply drawn enough, and the play met with little success ; in Paris, Destouches attenuates those lines, and fearing lest they still seem too marked, he does not venture to have the play performed. It was given only after his death in 1762, and succeeded thanks to the progress made by the spirit of reform.

IV.

For this public and in this *milieu* writes the great innovator, the most active revolutionist of the century, the author of the " Lettres Anglaises," Voltaire. To him nothing is more beautiful, more holy, more sacred than literary art, and in literary art than dramatic art. He cannot exist without a theatre ; wherever he goes he builds one, forms troupes, plays himself in his own plays, on his " little green and gold theatre " ; while his niece, the fat Madame Denis, appears as Idamé or Zaïre. In his enthusiasm for all that is his, Voltaire considers her as another Clairon.[1] He invites

an imitation of " Timon " in " Le Dissipateur," of Destouches. The " Drummer " was also translated by Descazeaux Desgranges : " La prétendue Veuve ou l'Époux magicien," in verse, Paris, 1737.

[1] Marmontel went to see him at the Délices (close by the Lake of Geneva, where he lived before he built Ferney), and gave him a glowing account of the fame won for herself of late by Clairon : " J'épuisai le peu que j'avais d'éloquence à lui inspirer pour Clairon cet enthousiasme dont j'étais plein moi même ; je jouissais, en lui parlant, de l'émotion que je lui causais, lorsque enfin, prenant la parole : ' Eh ! bien, mon ami, me dit-il avec transport, c'est comme Madame Denis ; elle a fait des progrès étonnants, incroyables. Je voudrais que vous lui vissiez jouer Zaïre, Alzire, Idamé ! le talent ne va pas plus loin.' Madame Denis jouant Zaïre ! Madame

actors to visit him and gives them lessons in declamation: "To him [Voltaire] I owe the first notions of my art," writes Le Kain.[1] Voltaire congratulates the English on having laid two of their actresses to rest in Westminster,[2] when there was certainly no question of opening to French ones the vaults of Saint Denis; he admires the noble conduct of a "gentleman of your country [England], who enjoys fortune and consideration, and who has not disdained to play upon your stage the part of Orosmane."[3] The least performance, organised with his guests, seems to him an event of mighty importance; he makes it known to all Europe. Rebellious to hostile criticism, he hastens to take advantage of friendly advice; he discusses, remodels, experiments: "I have not the stiffness of mind that goes with old age; I am as flexible as an eel, as quick as a lizard, and always as busy as a squirrel. No sooner is any mistake of mine pointed out to me, that I hasten to remove it and put another in its place."[4]

Dramatic art has for Voltaire something almost divine; its perfection matters to the State; a tragedy does more good than a sermon: "A mage," relates his Babouc, "appeared in a high machine, and talked

Denis comparée à Clairon! Je tombai de mon haut." He took Marmontel to his little "gentilhommière" of Tornay, hard by: "Là je vis ce petit théâtre qui tourmentait Rousseau et où Voltaire se consolait de ne plus voir celui qui était encore plein de sa gloire." (Marmontel "Mémoires," Bk. vii.)

[1] "Mémoires . . . précédés de réflexions par F. Talma," Paris, 1825, 8º, p. 427.

[2] First "Épître dédicatoire" of "Zaïre," to Falkener, 1733.

[3] Second "Épître dédicatoire," 1736.

[4] To d'Argental, October 22, 1759 (à propos of "Tancrède").

very long about vice and virtue.... He proved methodically everything that was clear, he taught everything one knew. He worked himself coolly into a passion, and went off perspiring and breathless. The whole assembly then woke up and thought they had attended an instruction." A tragedy is given; great personages figure in it: "Their language was very different from the people's; it was measured, harmonious, and sublime. No one slept.... The duties of kings, the love of virtue, the danger of passions were expressed in a fashion so lively and touching that Babouc shed tears. He did not doubt but that the heroes and heroines, the kings and queens he had just heard were the preachers of the empire."[1] Everything that touches the drama has a sacred and salutary character; histrionic art cannot be too much encouraged: "There are more than twenty houses in Paris where tragedies and comedies are represented.... It is hard to believe how useful that amusement which demands much care and attention really is; it forms the taste of the young, gives gracefulness to the body and to the mind, contributes to the talent of speech; it diverts young men from debauchery by accustoming them to the pure pleasures of the mind."[2]

Voltaire busied himself with every branch of literary art, cultivated every science, spoke foreign tongues, made himself an opinion on every subject and forced it upon others; changed, and wanted others to change too; gave cause for admiration and for laughter;

---

[1] "Le monde comme il va, ou Vision de Babouc," 1746.
[2] "Le Temple du Goût" (note).

carried on innumerable wars, and was the author or the subject of innumerable epigrams. Of him it was said : "His sign is 'The Encyclopædia.' What will you have ? English, Tuscan, verse, prose, algebra, opera, comedy ? Epic poems, history, odes, or novels? Speak, and it is done. You give him a year ? You insult him. In three or four evenings, subjects spoilt by the elder Corneille, subjects filled by proud Crébillon, he recasts everything. . . ."

> " Son enseigne est à l'encyclopédie,
> Que vous plaît-il ? de l'anglais, du toscan ?
> Vers, prose, algèbre, opéra, comédie,
> Poème épique, histoire, ode ou roman ?
> Parlez, c'est fait. Vous lui donnez un an ?
> Vous l'insultez. En trois ou quatre veilles,
> Sujets ratés par l'aîné des Corneilles,
> Sujets remplis par le fier Crébillon,
> Il refond tout. . . ."

He resumes, remodels, contradicts, attacks generally received ideas, proposes others, all in an instant ; he lives in a whirl : he would have liked to remake the world, and remake it in *less* than a week :—

> " Il eût voulu refaire l'univers
> Et le refaire en moins d'une semaine." [1]

Dramatic art cannot continue in the same narrow groove ; such is the universal opinion. Voltaire knows the masterpieces of foreign literatures ; he has

---

[1] Epigrams by Piron (Collé " Journal," 1805, i. 155, 187). Last lines of the first of those epigrams :—

> " Il refond tout.—Peste, voici merveille !
> Et la besogne est elle bonne ?—Oh ! non."

no superstitious respect for the Romans, the Greeks, the Italians, or for anybody: "One cannot discuss matters of taste," he says, "but certainly such scenes (in Euripides' 'Alcestis') would not be suffered here even at the fair." [1] He is a revolutionist to the core; it would be in no wise displeasing to him to " remake the universe."

Writing for the stage, thus armed and at such a moment, contrary to expectation, he upsets nothing; he is prudent; he is seized with fear. He has to deal with an art so holy in his eyes that his hand hesitates. This audacious reformer becomes circumspect; he cannot turn aside from the high-road without trembling. He will go and attack God on His altars without fear of hell, nor even of the Bastille—less remote; but the idea that it might be possible to renounce alexandrines makes him shudder; [2] he veils his face, he protests against the impiety of La Motte: [3] he

---

[1] "Dictionnaire Philosophique," "Anciens et Modernes." Euripides and Sophocles have "des beautés"; but "ils ont de bien plus grands défauts." The "farceur Aristophane" is very roughly handled.

[2] The mere choice of names had the same importance in Voltaire's eyes as in Boileau's (Commentary on Corneille's "Attila"). He was even shocked at the familiarities of Bossuet: "L'éloquent Bossuet voulait bien rayer quelques familiarités échappées à son génie vaste, impétueux et facile, lesquelles déparent un peu la sublimité de ses oraisons funèbres" ("Temple du Goût").

[3] Preface to "Œdipe"; first edition of the play, 1719, of the preface, 1730 (Bengesco). He has recourse also to the theological argument of "universal testimony": "Toutes les nations commencent à regarder comme barbares les temps où cette pratique [of the rules] était ignorée des plus grands génies, tels que Don Lope de Vega et Shakespeare" (*Ibid.*).

cannot view the sacrilegious deed. He will forgive his friends any sins they please, but never a tragedy in prose. That, in his eyes, is the sin against the Holy Ghost, the sin for which there is no remission. Unities to him have a super-human character; he speaks of them as a theologian speaks of the ten commandments; nothing can be more dangerous than to compound with such laws: one may extend, at most, "the unity of time as far as twenty-four hours, and the unity of place to the enclosure of an entire palace . . . further indulgence would open the way to too many abuses. For, if once it were established that the dramatic action could take place in two days, soon some author would be taking two weeks. . . . We should see, in a short time, plays like the ancient 'Julius Cæsar' of the English, where Cassius and Brutus are at Rome in the first act, and in Thessaly at the fifth." [1]

His keen glance has, however, discerned all the points on which reforms are necessary: monotony of the verses, excessive use of love, absence of action, superabundance of discourses and narratives, lack of movement, the most striking scenes taking place in the coulisses, exorbitant respect for the rules of decency and "all those petty trifles which in France are called *bienséances*." [2] For each of these articles, without exception, he proposes reforms, but limits himself to the most modest, to those which depart least from the ancient ideal. He has the timidities of a lover.

Foreigners have tragedies in prose; never will

---

[1] Same preface to "Œdipe."
[2] To d'Argental, à propos of the "Écossaise," July 14, 1760.

Voltaire allow of prose in a tragedy. He remains the staunch partisan of verse, and of rhymed verse; verses without rhymes are nothing: " Blank verses cost only the trouble of dictating them. It is not more difficult than to write a letter."[1] There is, however, some truth, he admits, in the reproaches addressed to alexandrines; an innovation is possible; he risks it, but with what anxiety! He composes, later in life, " Tancrède" in alternate rhymes, and says: " This kind of poetry escapes from the uniformity of the symmetric rhyme, but that style of writing is dangerous . . . and the kind of verse I have employed in ' Tancrède ' comes perhaps too near to prose."[2] He is struck by the number of personages Shakespeare puts on the stage: thirty-nine in " Richard III.," forty in " Henry V.," twenty-eight in " Macbeth," without counting, " lords, gentlemen, officers, soldiers, murderers, attendants and messengers, ghost of Banquo and other apparitions " (whereas Racine had only seven characters in " Britannicus " and " Bajazet," and eight in " Andromaque" and " Phèdre "). All this Shakespearean population moves and acts with extraordinary independence; Voltaire could not think of taking such liberties. He only aspires to " introducing more than three persons talking together," and to representing, if need be, murder on the stage; for, he remarks somewhat apprehensively, " it is not with the rules of *bienséance*,

---

[1] Preface to the translation of " Julius Cæsar " (translation written to show the superiority of " Cinna ").
[2] Dedicace to Madame de Pompadour, Ferney, October 10, 1759.

always rather arbitrary, as with the fundamental rules of the stage, which are the three unities." [1]

Voltaire felt, and with reason, some doubts as to the welcome these modest attempts would receive: they still revolted the public. He tried in vain, in 1724, to make Mariamne die on the stage: "The death of Mariamne," he himself wrote, "who at the first performance was poisoned and expired on the stage, revolted the spectators. . . . I might have held out on that last point . . . but I would not go against the taste of the public." This is why Herod, in the revised text, says to his wife, "Go!" and remains on the stage until Narbas comes to narrate in classical style the circumstances of Mariamne's death :—

> "Aux larmes des Hébreux, Mariamne sensible,
> Consolait tout ce peuple en marchant au trépas ;
> Enfin vers l'échafaud on a conduit ses pas," &c., &c.

She dies far from sight, "par le fer," instead of by poison.[2]

Nevertheless, the effect of contact makes itself felt, for the contact is incessant. Voltaire is much more preoccupied with Shakespeare than he will admit; the English dramatist is oftener in his thoughts than he will

---

[1] Preface to "Brutus," first ed., 1731 ; first performance, December 11, 1730.

[2] In order to fully understand the slow evolution of dramatic taste, compare the style used on the occasion of a similar catastrophe by one of the French independents of former years. Agrippina and her adversary Sejanus, in Cyrano's tragedy of "Agrippine," are both sent to the block by Tiberius. There is no narrative, and though the execution takes place out of sight, it may be doubted whether the actual view of the scaffold on the

acknowledge, and yet, on many occasions he mentions his name, if only to condemn him, to boast of the dissimilarity between Shakespeare and himself, and to render thanks to the god of letters for the same. The monster scares and attracts him at the same time.

In "Brutus," begun in England at a time when he had " almost become accustomed to think in English,"[1] and was so imbued with the spirit of the place that one could observe in his play "republican ideas as if he had been still living in London,"[2] he introduces lively scenes; shows a crowd on the stage; and even risks one of those changes of place, from one part of a town to another, for which Corneille had had to do penance and offer excuses: ancient liberty was awakening once more. "The stage represents a part of the consuls' house on Tarpeian mount; the temple of the Capitol is seen in the background. The senators are assembled between the temple and the house, before the altar of Mars. (Act I.)—The stage represents, or is supposed to re-

stage would be more impressive than the few pregnant words exchanged, as the curtain falls, by Tiberius and his man :—

"*Nerva.* César!
Tiberius.   Nerva?
Nerva.   J'ai vu la catastrophe
    D'une femme sans peur, d'un soldat philosophe . . .
    Et déjà le bourreaux qui les ont menacés. . . .
Tiberius. Sont ils morts? Tous les deux?
Nerva.   Ils sont morts.
Tiberius.   C'est assez.
        (*The curtain falls.*)"

[1] "Dicours à mylord Bolingbroke" (prefacing "Brutus").
[2] "Des traits républicains, comme s'il avait encore été à Londres," Marais "Journal et Mémoires," letter of February 7, 1730.

present, an apartment in the consuls' palace." (Act II.)
—This is exactly the kind of sight that the independents had offered their public a hundred years before : " The Capitol opens, in which the Tribunes come to hold council.—In the distance is seen the Senate where Amphidius accuses Coriolanus of treason." [1]

It is impossible to read " Brutus " without thinking of " Julius Cæsar " ; " Eryphile " without thinking of " Hamlet " ; or " Zaïre " without remembering " Othello." [2] The " Mort de César," a play without love, that Voltaire dared risk in public only twelve years after its composition, is directly imitated from Shakespeare : "Instead of translating," say the publishers (in reality Voltaire himself), " Shakespeare's monstrous work, he composed, after the English manner, the ' Julius Cæsar' that we are giving to the public." [3]

[1] " Le véritable Coriolan," by Chapoton, 1638 ; beginning of Act IV., and Act V., sc. 5.

[2] Which Voltaire does not speak of ; he contents himself with attributing to an imitation of the "théâtre anglais la hardiesse [qu'il] a eue de mettre sur la scène les noms de nos rois et de nos anciennes familles du royaume. Il me paraît que cette nouveauté pourrait être la source d'un genre de tragédie qui nous est inconnue jusqu'ci." (First " Épître dédicatoire." This style, as we have seen, was in no wise unknown in France, but was in disfavour. " Nous avons fait," wrote the Abbé Du Bos, " monter sur notre scène, lorsqu'elle était encore grossière, nos souverains encore vivants " ; it was not, at all events, to satirise them, observed the Abbé, as had been done elsewhere, for the French "respectent naturellement leurs Princes ; ils font même davantage, ils les aiment." This is why, when they put them on the stage, " ils n'ont péché que par grossièreté." (" Réflexions critiques," vol. i. ; first edition, 1719.)

[3] " La Mort de César," begun at Wandsworth in 1726, finished in 1731, was performed on private stages in 1733 and 1735. The

It is a very attenuated English manner. Instructed by the fate of Marianne, Cæsar does not hesitate, from the first performance, to retire behind the scenes there to be murdered: "I had rather die than fear death. Let me go." And he disappears in the coulisse.

But the coulisse is, so to speak, transparent; one can almost see what goes on there, and one can, at all events, hear what is said:—

> "*Dolabella.* What clamours, oh heavens, what cries are those I hear?"
>
> *The conspirators (behind the scenes).* Perish, expire, tyrant! Have courage, Cassius!
>
> *Dolabella.* Ah! let us fly to save him.
>
> *Cassius (entering, a dagger in his hand).* 'Tis done, he is no more."[1]

This semi-realism was doubtless a concession to what Voltaire called the "English taste." Eryphile dies in the same manner "behind the stage," but she is heard protesting against her fate. In "Zaïre," again, 1732, the heroine does not die within sight of the spectators, but she comes very near indeed to doing so:—

> "*Orosmane (running to Zaïre).* I am betrayed by you; fall at my feet, perjured one!

first public performance took place in 1743, "after the success of 'Mérope.'" (H. Lion, "Les Tragédies de Voltaire," Paris, 1895, pp. 53 ff.) In "Brutus," inspired also by "Julius Cæsar," we still find the ineluctable lovers' parts.

[1] "*Dolabella.* Quelles clameurs, ô ciel, quels cris se font entendre?
Les conjurés (derrière le théâtre). Meurs, expire, tyran. Courage, Cassius!
Dolabella. Ah! courons le sauver.
Cassius (qui entre en scène un poignard à la main). C'en est fait, il n'est plus."

Zaïre (falling in the coulisse). I die, merciful God!
Orosmane. Now am I avenged."[1]

The great principles were thus respected, but they had a very narrow escape; the stage was not flooded with blood, but it received splashes. In " Adélaide du Guesclin" more audacious experiments were tried: Nemours appeared wounded, his arm in a sling, and in the fifth act a cannon was fired. It was going too far; at the first performance, in 1734, the cannon and the arm in a sling were hissed and the play fell. Voltaire was reproached with having " armed himself with the cleaver of the English stage," and with having produced " gory imitations of that stage butcher called Shakespeare."[2]

English influence, Shakespeare's in particular, is more apparent still in " Eryphile," 1732, and in " Sémiramis," 1748; the two plays turn, in fact, on the same subject, taken up twice by Voltaire, and transported from Argos to Babylon. It can even be said that the original place was Elsinore, for the story is essentially that of " Hamlet"; but Voltaire had not yet rid himself entirely of the scruples entertained by La Fosse, who had made a " Manlius" out of a " Venice Preserved."

In " Sémiramis" an important place is assigned to scenic effect: " The stage represents a vast peristyle,

---

[1] " *Orosmane (courant à Zaïre).*
        C'est moi que tu trahis; tombe à mes pieds, parjure!
Zaïre (tombant dans la coulisse).
        Je me meurs! ô mon Dieu!
Orosmane.   J'ai vengé mon injure."

[2] Collé, " Correspondance inédite," ed. H. Bonhomme, Paris, 1864, 8o, " Préface garnie de ses digressions," p. 337.

A PLAY AT THE THEATRE OF THE LITTLE COMEDIANS, ON THE BOULEVARDS, WITH GENTLEMEN SEATED ON THE STAGE.

From Gravelot's engraving.

at the further end of which is Sémiramis's palace. Terraced gardens are raised above the palace. The magi's temple is on the right, and a mausoleum on the left, ornamented with obelisks." Voltaire ventures changes of place in the same city, and even a scene-shifting : " The closet where Sémiramis was changes to a large salon magnificently ornamented." Unfortunately, the old custom of encumbering the stage with spectators still existed in France. Voltaire had already protested against that habit on the occasion of the performance of " Brutus " : " The benches on the stage, intended for the spectators, make the scene narrower and render all action nearly impracticable. . . . How could we dare, in our theatres, to make, for instance, the ghost of Pompey or the genius of Brutus appear in the midst of so many young men who never consider the most serious things otherwise than as an occasion for a *bon mot ?* " [1]

When "Sémiramis" was given, things remained as they had been, so that, says Marmontel, "distracted Sémiramis and the ghost of Ninus emerging from his tomb were obliged to cross a dense row of young fops." Voltaire continued to protest, and would no doubt have done so for ever if the Comte de Lauraguais had not offered the French Comedy to take upon himself the expenses resulting from the alteration of the theatre.

[1] Discourse to Bolingbroke, prefacing " Brutus." Madame d'Épinay complains in her Memoirs of being neglected by her husband, whom she rarely saw at all, and when she did, only at the play and at a distance, as he was seated on the stage : " Il ne soupe presque jamais chez lui et toutes les fois que je l'ai rencontré au spectacle, c'était toujours sur le théâtre." " Mémoires," Paris, Charpentier, i., p. 85.

The work was done, and the stage was freed in 1759. Voltaire tendered his thanks to M. de Lauraguais in the preface of the "Écossaise"; the young count was unanimously declared a public benefactor. Playgoers breathed at last; they were surprised to think they could so long have tolerated such a terrible inconvenience, and it was surely astonishing enough. "The effect is excellent," wrote Collé in his Journal, "the theatrical illusion is now complete; one no longer sees Julius Cæsar ready to brush the powder off a fop seated in the front row of the theatre, Mithridates expire in the midst of all the people of our acquaintance, and Camille fall dead in the coulisse on top of Marivaux and Saint-Foix." If ever the need is felt of showing the forty-three personages of a Shakespearean play, there will be room for them all: "This new form of theatre opens to tragic authors new ways for putting show, pomp, and more action into their poems."

Voltaire was, in fact, hazarding the experiment of a Shakespearean drama and an antique tragedy fused into one play when he wrote "Sémiramis." The manner of exciting emotion and the structure of the play recall both English "Hamlet" and Greek "Œdipus." Terrors and horrors, crimes, incests, ghosts, recognitions, vengeances, mausoleums, subterranean passages, labyrinths are all to be found in "Sémiramis." Like the future romantics for whom he opens the way, Voltaire makes the most of the mystery of tombs and the terror of underground hiding-places:—

> "Du sein de ce sépulcre inaccessible au monde . . .
> Les mânes de Ninus et les dieux outragés
> Ont élevé leurs voix . . .

> Au fond de ce tombeau, mon père était mon guide ;
> J'errais dans les détours de ce grand monument . . .
>
>   Dans les horreurs de la profonde nuit,
> Des souterrains secrets où sa fureur habile,
> A tout événement, se creusait un asile,
> Ont servi les desseins de ce monstre odieux."

Semiramis, assisted by Assur, a prince of the royal blood, has poisoned King Ninus, her husband (as in "Hamlet"); but, contrary to the expectation of Assur, who counted, as it seems, upon the precedent of Hamlet, she has not married her accomplice, and for fifteen years has reigned alone, to the great displeasure of Assur. Ninias, the son of Ninus and Semiramis, was to have perished, and every one believes him to be dead, but he has been spared (like Œdipus). Grown to manhood, he saves the empire and appears at Court under the name of Arzaces. Semiramis feels attracted towards the youth, and wants to marry him ; but Arzaces prefers, naturally enough, the amiable Azema, a young princess whom he had delivered from the hands of the barbarous Scythians. Assur becomes, in consequence, jealous of Arzaces, and Azema of Semiramis.

The queen, meanwhile, has lost (after those fifteen years) her peace of mind, and begins to feel the first pangs of remorse. She complains, moreover, of the terrors caused her by the ghost of the late king. Voltaire, taught by Shakespeare's example, seeks to prepare the spectre's apparition ; the Shakespearean method seems to him ingenious but somewhat vulgar ; he tries to raise it to tragical dignity. No familiar dialogue ; no sentinel giving the pass-word on the terrace of Elsinore. We hear first a few growls uttered by the ghost in its tomb. Arzaces, left alone by his companion, was busy, according to the wont of classical heroes on such occasions, making a speech to himself, when he is interrupted by the noise his father is making in the mausoleum :—

> "Mais quelle voix plaintive ici se fait entendre ?
> Du fond de cette tombe, un cri lugubre, affreux,
> Sur mon front pâlissant fait dresser mes cheveux ?"

Semiramis, further on, relates her fears to a confidant : she has seen her husband's ghost :—

> "Je l'ai vu ; ce n'est point une ombre passagère
> Qu'enfante du sommeil la vapeur mensongère . . .
> Je veillais . . ."

The miscreant Assur alone shrugs his shoulders and makes jokes in the worst taste upon the phantom, "born of fear and who in its turn gives birth to it" :—

> "Qui naquit de la crainte et l'enfante à son tour."

At length the ghost comes forth, an audacious ghost indeed, for it does not appear in the silent night, "the bell then beating one," but in the middle of the nuptial ceremony, to prevent another Œdipus from marrying another Jocaste. It is "quite white, in gilt armour, a sceptre in its hand, and a crown on its head." Voltaire himself had assigned to it this festive costume.[1]

[1] To d'Argental, August 15, 1748.

"*Ghost.* Thou wilt reign, Arzaces; but crimes there are which thou must atone for. . . ."[1]

And so on. Ghost withdraws; it does not vanish, but goes back to its place of abode, the huge tomb which filled half the stage. A letter written by Ninus before his death replaces the play in "Hamlet," and serves to make the guilt of the queen manifest. Arzaces, however, like Hamlet, is loth to kill her, and turns his fury against Assur. The final catastrophe takes place far from our sight, amid the windings of the sepulchral labyrinth which becomes in the last act a general meeting-place. We see the people as they walk out of it, one by one. Arzaces comes first, his sword red with blood; he has vaguely discerned his enemy "in a darksome recess, near a column," and has killed him. He does not drag his corpse on to the stage, though he would have liked to do so; the groans and sighs of the mortally wounded

---

[1] "*L'Ombre.*   Tu régneras, Arzace,
Mais il est des forfaits que tu dois expier,
Dans ma tombe, à ma cendre, il faut sacrifier,
Sers et ton père et moi; souviens toi de ton père,
Écoute le pontife.
Arzace.   Ombre que je révère,
Demi-dieu dont l'esprit anime ces climats,
Ton aspect m'encourage et ne m'étonne pas.
Oui, j'irai dans ta tombe, au péril de ma vie,
Achève, qui veux-tu que ma main sacrifie?
     (*L'Ombre retourne de son estrade à la porte de son
          tombeau.*)
Il s'éloigne, il nous fuit."
(Arzaces is not aware at that moment that he is himself the son of the late king.)

miscreant have moved him, and he has left " the gory victim " behind.[1]

At this word, Assur comes forth; it is not he who was hiding behind the column, but Semiramis. She is not quite dead; she comes out, bleeding, from the tomb, and is "placed in an arm chair." She blesses Arzaces and Azema, while Assur is led away to be hanged, being unworthy to die by the sword.[2]

The success of the play was contested. Voltaire had expected opposition and had filled the theatre with friends, to whom he had given free tickets in even greater abundance than usual. " In spite of this precaution," says Collé, " two or three young men of this packed assembly clapped their hands, yawning aloud the while, which made every one laugh except Voltaire. As for me, I found the play bad, but it is bad Voltaire; I could not do as much, nor M. l'Abbé Le Blanc either." [3]

"Eryphile," a sort of first sketch of Semiramis, had a nearly similar plot, with adventures just as romantic, while the author's methods were equally classical. There was, however, this difference, that the hero had no Princess Azema to occupy his heart, and that he aspired at once to the love of the queen his mother.

[1] ". . . Je vous l'avouerai, ses sanglots redoublés,
　　Ses cris plaintifs et sourds et mal articulés . . .
　　M'ont fait abandonner la victime sanglante."
"Qu'il meure dans l'opprobre et non de mon épée,
　Et qu'on rende au trépas ma victime échappée."
[3] "Journal," September, 1748. On the debates provoked by the play and on the agitation which troubled even the adjacent streets, see " Mercure de France," same date.

A PERFORMANCE OF VOLTAIRE'S "SÉMIRAMIS" AFTER THE REMOVAL OF THE BENCHES FOR GENTLEMEN ON THE STAGE.
Drawn by Gravelot, 1768.

His state of mind recalls that of Ruy Blas, for he believes himself born of a slave :—

"*Alcméon.* Victim of a fate which even now I defy, I conceal it no more, I am the son of a slave.
Eryphile. You, my lord?
Alcméon. Yes, madam; and though of such low condition, remember that, at least, I would not conceal it; that I was magnanimous and high-souled enough to make before you that crushing confession, and that the blood given me by the gods has warmed a heart too high not to love you."
Eryphile. A slave——!"[1]

Eryphile, at the end, dies by the hand of her son, like Semiramis, and like Lucrèce Borgia later in Victor Hugo's romantic drama. "Spare me, my son," Eryphile cries. "Ah! thou hast killed me! Gennaro, I am thy mother," Lucrèce will exclaim. Voltaire was indeed supplying the stage with romantic dramas in classical clothing.

The signal was given, and even the example; the

---

[1] "*Alcméon.* Victime d'un destin que même encor je brave,
Je ne m'en cache plus, je suis fils d'un esclave.
Eryphile. Vous, seigneur?
Alcméon.   Oui, madame, et dans un rang si bas,
Souvenez vous qu'enfin je ne m'en cachai pas;
Que j'eus l'âme assez forte, assez inébranlable,
Pour faire devant vous l'aveu qui vous accable;
Que ce sang dont les dieux ont voulu me former
Me fit le cœur trop haut pour ne vous point aimer.
Eryphile. Un esclave!
Alcméon.   Une loi fatale à ma naissance
Des plus vils citoyens m'interdit l'alliance.
J'aspirais jusqu'à vous dans mon indigne sort;
J'ai trompé vos bontés; j'ai mérité la mort."

experiments were renewed; authors dared not venture upon every sort of liberty at once, but all were tried one after the other. In 1740, Gresset, the author of "Ververt" and of the "Méchant," put a murder on the stage in his "Édouard III.," "a spectacle," he affirms, "offered in France for the first time," forgetting, he too, like Voltaire, the independents of the age of Louis XIII., towards whom he was moving back unawares. The evolution was indeed complete. A hundred years previously, Coriolanus had been massacred on the French stage, and put an end to by degrees, discoursing in the intervals left him by his murderers, the whole forming, it is true, a picture little calculated to encourage people of taste to follow the example thus given them by the dramatist Chapoton[1]:—

"*Coriolanus.* Ye Gods! my thread is cut!
Amphidius. Receive this other blow . . .
Coriolanus. Ere death deprives me of my sight, know that your chief, by this his cruelty, causes my goodwill to die with me, for had I lived . . . But I die without saying——"[2]

Thereupon he died, without saying, no one knew what. Gresset, at the other end of the cycle, alarmed at

---

[1] "Le véritable Coriolan, tragédie représentée par la troupe royale, par le Sr Chapoton," Paris, 1638, 4°. (Fine frontispiece: Roman scene.)

[2] "*Coriolan.* Dieux! ma trame est couppée!
Amphidie.   Reçois ce coup encor . . .
Coriolan. Avant que le trespas me prive de la veue,
Sçachez que vostre chef, par cette cruauté,
Fait mourir avec moy ma bonne volonté,
Car si j'eusse vescu : mais je meurs sans le dire."

his own daring, takes pains to justify himself; he will not invoke "the rights of English tragedy," although they have something to do with his attempt; he looks for reasons of a higher sort and more general bearing; he deems that the rule forbidding bloodshed on the stage "should apply only to cases where the deed is contrary to justice or humanity." The murder of a scoundrel is permitted, therefore, by the laws of good-taste, and Volfax shall be stabbed by Arundel under our eyes:—

"Voilà ton dernier crime, expire, malheureux!"[1]
(*He throws away the dagger.*)

President Hénault is likewise struck by the necessity of renewing the ancient French style; the old soil is exhausted; its fecundity must be restored and new seeds sown. " Must nothing be ventured? And have all *genres* been tried, so that it be impossible to think of new ones?" In his turn he attempts to innovate and publishes, in 1747, his " Nouveau Théâtre François.— François II., roi de France." The influence he obeys is Shakespeare's, he declares from the first line: "The English drama of Shakespehar gave me the idea of this

---

[1] Act IV., sc. viii.—"Je ne me sers point des droits de la tragédie anglaise pour répondre à quelque difficulté qu'on m'a faite sur le coup de théâtre du quatrième acte, spectacle offert en France pour la première fois; je dirai seulement, autorisé par le législateur même ou le créateur du théâtre français, que la maxime de ne point ensanglanter la scène ne doit s'entendre que des actions hors de la justice et de l'humanité." "Avertissement." First performance, January 22, 1740.

work; but as I have not been able to flatter myself I could attain to the true and touching beauties of that great poet, particularly writing in prose, so I had no difficulty in avoiding his coarseness and extravagance." For Shakespeare is extravagant, he is ignorant of rules, and his plays are, consequently, "monsters of their kind." They are, however, deserving of some attention: "As monsters themselves are useful for anatomy, Shakespehar's tragedies have made me perceive a use in dramas which I should never have thought of without him." Of all "Shakespehar's" plays, "Henry VI." is the one which has most struck the president. "Why is our history not written thus?" he asks himself; and he tries the experiment. He departs therefore, on many points, from the frequented routes, but without, however, launching forth into the open sea; he follows the coast: "The rule of twenty-four hours is not observed, it is true, since that reign [Francis II.'s] lasted seventeen months, but the undertaking is less shocking than if I had chosen the reign of Francis I., which lasted thirty-two years." Assuredly, he has put into his drama an astrologer and various individuals who are neither princes nor confidants of princes: "If I have found room for some episodical personages, I have not, at least, chosen them, as Shakespehar does, among street porters and the military rabble." Let us, therefore, be grateful to him, as he seems to desire it, for his reserve; let us thank him for not having chosen the reign of Francis I., and even more for having discarded the reign of Louis XIV., which lasted seventy-two years; let our gratitude apply to all he did *not* do, and especially to all the national dramas which he might have written and did not write: for he stopped after his dull and solitary "François II."[1]

Audacious attempts, however, went on multiplying and, what was most significant, they were tried by conservative minds and partisans of rules. The taste for English literature was increasing, knowledge of the language was no longer so rare. On that point, as on all others, the example of Voltaire had been decisive. Destouches or Prévost had known English, it is true, but no one had paid the slightest attention to this minute phenomenon. Voltaire learnt English, and his example "incited many people to learn how to speak it, so that this language has become familiar to men of letters," 1736.[2] Translation after translation was published; poems of Pope, satires of Swift, novels of Defoe, Richardson, and Fielding, all that attracted attention north of the Channel, obtained almost as much south of it. The taste even for political discussions began to spread. "Fifty years ago," said d'Argenson, "the public was not at all curious of State news. To-day, every one reads his Paris Gazette, even in the provinces. They discuss politics; they do it at random, but they busy themselves with such questions. English liberty grows upon us. Tyranny is better watched, and is obliged, at least, to tread secret

---

[1] He left, however, some tragedies on classical subjects, a "Marius," a "Cornélie."

[2] We have it, it is true, on the testimony of Voltaire himself, for the "Préface des Éditeurs," of the "Mort de César," 1736, was not written by his publishers, but by him. Bengesco ("Bibliographie," i., p. 26). The praise he bestows upon himself seems, however, to be justified.

paths and use involved language."[1] Richardson was
in the highest favour, his works had revealed new ways,
elegant ladies were as enthusiastic as men of letters:
"It is very modish to have a 'Pamela,'" wrote, in
1743, La Chesnaye des Bois in his "Lettres amusantes
et critiques sur les Romans en général Anglais et
Français"; "I am waiting impatiently until some
other novel forces her to decamp from ladies' dressing-
tables to go and occupy the ante-rooms, and be used,
perhaps, as curl-paper by the hairdresser of some
fop, or of some young woman in a hurry to get to
the play." Pamela "decamped," but only to be replaced by Clarissa, and then a delirious enthusiasm
was seen; rivers of tears flowed on both sides of the
Channel. "There never yet has been written in any
language whatsoever, a novel equal to 'Clarissa,'" said
Rousseau; and Diderot, dissolved in tears, exclaimed,
"Oh, Richardson, Richardson, man unique in my eyes,
thou shalt be my reading for all time! Forced by
pressing needs, if my friend falls into poverty,
if the slenderness of my means prohibit me from
bestowing a sufficient education on my children, I will
sell my books: but from thee I will not part. Thou
shalt remain on the same shelf with Moses, Homer,
Euripides and Sophocles, and I will read you all in
turn."

This was going very far. Hitherto the movement
had been slow, and had given rise to scarcely any pro-

[1] "Mémoires et Journal inédit du Marquis d'Argenson";
"Loisirs d'un ministre," Paris, 1857, i., 137. (René Louis
d'Argenson, son of Marc René d'Argenson who had been
Lieutenant-General of Police; he died in 1757.)

tests. The number of people acquainted with England and Shakespeare had increased, but had alarmed no one; there were those who knew the great man and those who did not; there were as yet no partisans and opponents; there was not a Shakespeare question. That began in the second half of the century. Boissy, in his comedy "La Frivolité" (January 23, 1753), rallies the pensive English ladies, and the Frenchmen enamoured alternately of England and of Italy, warming at one time for Shakespeare and at another for the opera: "Here is our Frenchman: the other day he was a raving anglomaniac; nothing without an English dress could please him; above Corneille he placed Shakespir. Now a new frenzy has seized him, Italian music is his craze." [1] Boissy was only joking; but the time was coming when the question would no longer be a laughing matter; storms were gathering, war threatened. "I speak it with truth," d'Argenson wrote on the occasion of a translation of "Tom Jones," published with great approbation in 1750, "Anglicism is gaining upon us." Many echoed these words; the alarm was given.

Tragedy being more highly prized, and submitted to stricter rules than novels, Shakespeare, not Richardson, was to bear the brunt of the impending war.

[1] "Son transport l'autre jour était l'anglomanie;
Rien sans l'habit anglais ne pouvait réussir;
Au-dessus de Corneille il mettait Shakespir.
Une nouvelle frénésie
Aujourd'hui vient de le saisir,
C'est la fureur des accords d'Italie."

CHAPTER IV

THE EIGHTEENTH CENTURY

Part II.—1750 to the Revolution

I.

D'ARGENSON had spoken with truth; Anglicism was now pervading France. Complete was the change; the rough and rude "patois" derided by Saint-Amant had become the fashionable language of the day. Each and all prided themselves upon knowing it; ladies played their part in the movement; they wrote translations from the English, dissertations and comments; they were becoming learned. "On their toilets Newton replaced the 'Grand Cyrus.'"[1] Madame de Pompadour had a Shakespeare in French; Madame du Barry had one in English. Louis XVI. translated into French Walpole's essay on Richard III. Some even tried to overcome the difficulties offered by the pronunciation of a language which surpasses all others in this respect, "with the solitary exception of the language of cats." So says Abbé Galiani, writing

---

[1] Abbé Le Blanc to Buffon, letter xciii. ("Lettres d'un François," La Haye, 1745, 3 vols.).

to Madame de Belsunce: "They have killed my cat! Ah! what a sad loss, the loss of dogs and cats. . . . Three weeks have passed, and I remain inconsolable. He had been my master in the cattish idiom (mon maître de langue chatoise); and though I could not speak it, because it is more difficult to pronounce than English, yet I could understand it pretty well." [1]

Anglicum est, non legitur, people thought in the sixteenth century; *Anglicum est, erudimini*, they say now. It seemed as if there was some particular virtue in an English book; they ordered from London "des livres anglois," they bespoke from publishers "des comédies angloises," without entering into more particulars,[2] in the same way that a century earlier Scarron used to order "des comédies espagnolles."[3] For the generality of people in society who busied themselves with literature, all those books were the work of one and the same author, called England. The more a book seemed to be characteristically English, according to the standard of the time, the more it was liked.

---

[1] "Correspondance," ed., Percy and Maugras, Paris, 1881, 8°, Naples, May 11, 1776.

[2] La Place asks Monnet to send him from London various books "and the plays of the last six months—I mean the new plays—as well as short tales and pretty new pamphlets; novels ditto if they are said to be pretty." ("Correspondence of David Garrick," 1831, vol. ii., p. 474.) Patu edits a "Choix de petites pièces du Théâtre Anglois, traduites des originaux," Paris, 1756, 2 vols.; Madame Riccoboni prints a "Nouveau Théâtre Anglois," Paris, 1769, 2 vols. They are "Anglois" plays; no need to say more.

[3] "Je vous suis bien obligé de la peine que vous prenez de me faire trouver des comédies espagnolles." To Marigny, "Dernières Œuvres," 1730, vol. i., p. 62.

The "Night Thoughts" of Young were received with
boundless admiration ; the poems of Ossian with
rapturous enthusiasm, an admiration and enthusiasm
so vigorous that they outlasted the Revolution. "I
have begun a canto on Brutus," wrote Lucien Bonaparte to his brother Joseph, "one single canto in the
style of Young's 'Night Thoughts.' Young is my
model ; by a thousand darts he penetrates to my very
soul."[1] Lamartine, later, took Ossian for his master in
poetry : "Ossian was the Homer of my younger days ;
I owe him part of the melancholy of my pencils."[2]

Some grumblings, it is true, were heard, from the
first. "As for novels," said Collé with a shrug, "if
they are not translated from the English, they are not
read."[3] "Miss Fanny, Miss Jenny, Miss Polly,"
wrote Beaumarchais, "delightful beings ! My Eugénie
would, doubtless, have been better if she could have
had you for a model, but she existed before you had
received life yourself, failing which one can serve as a
model to nobody."[4] Fashion, however, was the stronger,

[1] Year IV. of Liberty, "Revue de Paris," March 15, 1895.
[2] "Ossian fut l'Homère de mes premières années ; je lui dois
une partie de la mélancolie de mes pinceaux." Preface of the
"Méditations."
[3] "Journal historique," September, 1764. Cf. Saurin's "L'Anglomane," 1772, first called "L'Orpheline léguée," 1765. Abbé
Prévost never tired of translating, but curtailed his originals for
the sake of his readers, to the great indignation of Richardson, who
complained, of course, that the *best* parts had been left out. La
Place evinced also an unceasing zeal ; his "Collection de Romans
imités de l'anglois" fills 8 vols. 8º. For poetry, there was the
selection of Abbé Yart, also in 8 vols., "Idée de la poésie Angloise,"
Paris, 1753.
[4] "Eugénie, avec un essai sur le drame sérieux," Paris, 1767, 8º.

and for all his ill-humour, Collé mentioned expressly on the title of one of his plays that he had composed it "in the free style of the English theatre," a very free style indeed.[1] Beaumarchais, in spite of his banter, gave his readers to understand that his play "Eugénie" had an English plot, "était tirée d'un sujet anglais." Préville, the actor, hoped for a success, but had some doubts: "As there is a wench with child in that play, and we are not accustomed to indecencies of that sort, I do not know how the audience will take it."[2]

Everything was done "à l'anglaise;" people rode "à l'anglaise" and boxed "à l'anglaise"; Ollivier represented in a charming picture, now in the Louvre, a "thé à l'anglaise" at the Prince de Conti's; "matinées" were spent "à l'anglaise"—that is, without saying a word. "We have spent the morning, to-day, English-fashion," wrote Saint Preux to milord Édouard in "La Nouvelle Héloïse," "we were together and remained silent; we enjoyed, at the same time, the pleasure of being with each other and the sweetness of meditation."[3] "Bets were made, *ponche* was drunk, *rosbif* and *pouding* were eaten with relish, claret was

---

[1] "Les Accidents ou les Abbés, comédie dans le goût libre du Théâtre Anglois," Paris, 1786, 8º. The Countess flirts with a young chérubin of an abbé, who proves to be a woman.

[2] Monnet to Garrick, January 26, 1767. "A play fell yesterday at the Français; the author, M. de Beaumarchais; Préville played like an angel." Madame Riccoboni to Garrick. "Correspondence of D. Garrick," ii., 508, 511.

[3] "Nous avons passé aujourd'hui une matinée à l'anglaise, réunis et dans le silence, goûtant à la fois le plaisir d'être ensemble et la douceur du recueillement." "Nouvelle Héloïse." Part V., letter iii.

preferred to champagne and burgundy, fights were fought with the *forts de la halle*," in the same way that "mylords" wrestled with scavengers or cabdrivers in the streets of London. Some even went the length of preferring "Shakespeart" to Corneille.[1] Dresses also were modified; men of fashion gave up embroidered coats, "small hats under the arm," laces. "It is now the craze among young men," wrote Mercier, "to copy England in her dress. The son of a financier, a young man of family as it is called, a commercial clerk, alike don the long narrow coat, carry their hat on their head, sport a flowing scarf, with gloves, cropped hair, and a stick."[2]

English fashions were welcomed in France, while French ones were followed in England, for there was reciprocity. What would have become of Garrick without French reviews, novels, and pamphlets, without the "Année Littéraire" of Fréron?[3] What would have become of Mrs. Garrick without the full books of coiffures despatched from Paris by trusty Monnet, as well as ready-made petticoats and a thousand other ornaments, Paris fashion? Monnet

---

[1] "L'Observateur Français à Londres," Paris, 1769-72, 32 vols. 12°, by Damiens de Gomicourt; Letter from London, 1768. "M. de Voltaire en avait jeté les fondements" (*i.e.*, of Anglomania). "Corneille fut placé au deuxième rang par l'Anglomanie; elle mit Shakespeart au premier." Cf. Saurin's "Anglomane," sc. xii.

[2] Renouncing lace, gold, "deux montres avec leurs breloques" and the "petit chapeau sous le bras." "Tableau de Paris," 1782, vii., ch. 548. See dress of Damis in "L'Anglomane," sc. i.

[3] Noverre, a ballet master, secures for him, besides dancing girls, Fréron's paper, "J'aurai soin de vous porter la suite de 'l'Année Littéraire' et de l'acheter à mesure qu'elle paroîtra."

is ever on the move ; he keeps accounts, receives, packs, sends forth, recommends a "new flambeau with spirit of wine and powder," said to give excellent light for the theatre ; he sends cartloads of French books and prints, gives news of all Paris, not forgetting his own dog : "Your friend, my knave of a dog, gives me more trouble than he is worth ; he has ravished the favourite little bitch of M. le duc de Choiseul, for which deed he is threatened with the Bastille. I do not know whether I shall be able to obtain a reprieve." [1]

People travelled more than before. "Is it possible to live for ever in Paris?" exclaimed Voltaire ; "what stay-at-home people you are ! . . . I rage to think that I shall die, and not have seen the Pyramids and the ruins of the theatre of Æschylus." [2] Without going so far, people flocked to England ; guide-books were becoming numerous, detailed, practical, illustrated. Men of letters came and went in numbers ; after those great stars, Voltaire, Montesquieu, and later Rousseau, a cluster of minor luminaries and secondary abbés went to shine in Great Britain : Abbé Expilly, Abbé Coyer, Abbé Bonnet, Abbé Morellet. Reviews and gazettes were filled more than ever with translations and accounts of English works : "Mémoires de la Grande Bretagne," "Journal Étranger," "Gazette Littéraire de

---

[1] "Correspondence of Garrick," December 17, 1766 ; July 6, 1767. Concerning the stay of Monnet in London with a troupe of French actors in 1749, see his "Supplément au Roman Comique," London, 1772, 8°, with portrait.
[2] To Madame d'Argental, July 20, 1759.

l'Europe" of Suard and Arnaud, "Année Littéraire" of Fréron, "Journal Encyclopédique,"[1] "Observateur Littéraire," "Magasin Anglais," "Journal Anglais," "Papiers Anglais," "Journal Français, Italien et Anglais," in three languages (a forerunner of the modern "Cosmopolis")[2] "Annales politiques civiles et Littéraires" of Linguet, "Journal du Lycée de Londres" of Brissot; not to speak of a quantity of others, of many older publications still continued then, such as the "Journal des Savants," the "Mercure de France," the "Journal de Trévoux," &c., or of all those which were created later—for example, that "Bibliothèque Britannique," begun at Geneva in 1796, of which Napoleon possessed a set, and in whose first volume he may have read, all unconscious of the tragic interest the subject would one

---

[1] Whose articles of October 15 and November 1, 1760 (being parallels between Shakespeare and Corneille; Otway and Racine, "traduits de l'anglais"), elicited Voltaire's answer: "Appel à toutes les Nations de l'Europe," 1761.

[2] Begun August, 1777. The French part of this number contained a letter on Cubières (see below, pp. 342 ff.), an analysis of Baretti's answer to Voltaire concerning Shakespeare, some short poems, &c. The second part was filled by "A Dessertation by M. Mercier on . . . Othello"; the third, by a "Dialogo tra Omero e una ricamatrice" the work of the "célèbre comte de Gozzi." The cosmopolitan tastes of the period are again well exemplified by such compilations as the "Bibliothèque d'un homme de goût ou tableau de la littérature ancienne et moderne, étrangère et nationale, dans lequel on expose le sujet . . . de tous les livres qui ont paru dans tous les siècles, sur tous les genres et dans toutes les langues," Paris, 1777, 4 vols. 12º. There are notices even on Chinese epic and dramatic poets; needless to say that they are worthless, but so is also all the rest of the compilation.

day have for him, "a sketch of the island of Saint Helena."[1]

The "Journal Anglais"[2] has England for its only subject; it gives information on the past history, the literature, and the present politics of the country. Some space is reserved for society news, for births and deaths, for curious inventions, such as boxes "to remove plants and shrubs and to allow of their being safely transported by sea" (illustrated). But, above all, this paper offered the peculiarity of giving in each number, according to its original programme, the biography of some English poet or man of letters. The first essay was, as of right, dedicated to Chaucer, "father of English poetry," whose biography, it is true, has been somewhat rectified since: "The birthplace of Chaucer is still an enigma as Homer's was"; he died "at Donnington Castle, near Newbury, in Berk-

---

[1] The last of the series was the "Revue Britannique, ou choix d'articles traduits des meilleurs écrits périodiques de la Grande Bretagne," founded in 1825 by Saulnier fils and P. Dondey-Dupré, and best known as associated with the name of the two Pichot, father and son. The first article of the first number treats: "Du transport par les canaux, les routes à rainures de fer et les voitures à vapeur"; in other words, steam engines and railways. "Nous avons pensé," the editors observe, "que cet article, où les avantages et les inconvénients des différents modes de transport sont habilement discutés, présenterait un intérêt particulier dans un moment où l'on examine si on joindra Paris au Havre par une route en fer ou par un canal qui serait accessible aux batiments de mer." This last problem is still under discussion, and the Review is still alive.

[2] A fortnightly review, begun October 15, 1775, by Ruault. Le Tourneur, La Guerrie, and Peyron are announced as contributors from October, 1776.

shire." The summing up is expressed in the terms which were then considered the most flattering: "To say everything in a single word he was a philosopher, according to the true meaning of the name; he had religion and morals." In the second number appeared a life of Spenser, "an old poet"; then came lives of Jonson, of Shakespeare (containing enthusiastic praise of his genius),[1] and of a multitude of others, down to Hume and Goldsmith. The "Journal Anglais" goes even so far as to give specimens of certain "detached pieces" we owe to Shakespeare, deeming that one may discover "in those slight, unstudied sketches the qualities and characteristics of his energetic, sensible, and graceful muse." By "detached pieces" the translator means the sonnets; and without troubling himself in the least about the famous "Mr. W. H.," he describes them as addressed, one and all, by Shakespeare, to his lady-love, "à son amante."

In other reviews, as well as in the "Journal Anglais," numerous articles are dedicated to Shakespeare: "Whosoever knows Shakespeare well, better understands English minds, for his genius is the genius of the whole island." "Contes Moraux" are extracted from his works;[2] "Beauties" are selected from "Tout est bien qui se termine bien," "La Correction d'une

---

[1] And a keen satire on his enemies or clumsy friends: "L'un l'habille à la française et, après l'avoir défiguré, nous dit: *Voilà Shakespeare*. L'autre, s'armant de l'épigramme pour faire la guerre au génie, travestit en platitude sa noble simplicité et veut aussi être cru quand il nous dit: *Voilà Shakespeare*" (November 30, 1775).

[2] By T. B. Perrin, London, 1783, 12°.

Femme de mauvaise humeur" and "Comme vous voulez."[1] It was even a law, "une loi," in the "Journal Étranger" to quote texts in the original. As "several of our readers have become familiar with the English language," they will be enabled "to compare at a glance the three styles of Racine, M. l'Abbé Metastasio, and M. Whitehead." The sample, as printed by the Journal, still has affinities with English "as she was spoke" by Panurge :—

> "Be strictly just ; but yet, like heaven, with mercy
> Temper thy justice. From thy purged ear
> Banish bale flattery."[2]

One thinks of the reader looking for words in his dictionary and picturing to himself Joas "yelling like heaven."

A Frenchman was found, in the same period, who already contemplated, a century before Taine, and, what is more remarkable, many years before Warton, writing a complete history of English literature. Admiration for Shakespeare had led him to assume this tremendous task ; he wanted his work to be " an accurate and thoughtful history, written without prejudice," but not without enthusiasm.[3] All his thoughts

---

[1] "Journal Étranger," July and September, 1754.

[2] Joad to Joas in Racine's "Athalie." "Journal Étranger," June, 1775. See, in the number of December, 1755, an article by Fréron (who had succeeded Prévost as editor of the paper) on "Romeo." He greatly praises Garrick, who had altered the catastrophe.

[3] "Je travaille maintenant à un ouvrage sur votre littérature qui me donnera lieu de m'expliquer sur ce génie merveilleux" (Shakespeare). Patu to Garrick, May 6, 1755. He recurs in a letter of

were centred upon it, he read English books unceasingly, and learnt to write English.[1] He went to stay in London, though threatened with consumption; but the disease got the better of his plans; he soon began to spit blood—and death, which overtook him at Saint Jean de Maurienne, when he was only twenty-eight, prevented Claude-Pierre Patu from being honoured, French though he was, as a forerunner of the poet laureate and famous critic, Thomas Warton.

Travellers continued more than ever to note and publish their impressions. Grosley, a barrister of Troyes, who " brought back only two words from England, namely, *very good* and *very wel*," and translated " Blac Friars " by " Moines Blancs," *black* and *blanc* being obviously the same word, printed a " Londres " in three volumes, full of amusing anecdotes, one of which put Garrick quite beside himself. Grosley supplies a number of details on games, fights, theatres, performances of " Macbet, Richard III., le Roi Lawe et autres pièces de Shakespéar." [2] Expilly, La Tour,

June 18, 1755, to the "idée où je suis d'exécuter un jour mon grand projet d'une histoire exacte et réfléchie de la *Littérature angloise*. . . . J'ai mille choses à dire, sans préjugés ce me semble, sans mauvaise humeur, sans partialité nationale, sur cette divine *action* sur cette *chaleur d'intérêt* qui caractérise tant de vos pièces."

[1] " I will write sometimes in English, pitifully to be sure, but what is that to me, since error is the only way to truth, and besides, a true Englishman considers thoughts more than words." Letter (in English) to Garrick, February 25, 1755.

[2] " Londres," Lausanne, 1770, 3 vols., 12°, " augmenté des notes d'un Anglois," Neufchâtel, 1774. Grosley reports that Garrick having increased the price of the seats in his theatre, had to kneel before the public and beg pardon. Suard pacified Garrick by inserting in the "Avant-Coureur" a note rectifying the story circu-

Coyer, print descriptions, guides, and observations.[1] Sentimental travellers, encouraged by the fame of Sterne, addict themselves in preference to autumnal walks, "Promenades d'Automne," and, in their English travels, go to the open fields there to shed tears : "I abandoned myself without reserve to the sweet emotions which the English country had already made me experience. I recalled to mind the descriptions of Camden, Pope and Shakespeare, and the English ballads which I had wept over in my youth."[2]

Another wants to return Sterne's visit, and writes,

lated by "ce voyageur de caffé qui, d'ailleurs, est un assez galant homme." "Correspondence of Garrick," ii., 570, August 12, 1770.

[1] "Description historique-géographique des Isles Britanniques," by the Abbé Expilly, Paris, 1759, 12º.—"Nouvelles observations sur l'Angleterre, par un voyageur" (Abbé Coyer), Paris, 1779, 12º, in the shape of letters.—"Londres et ses environs," by de Serre de La Tour, Paris, 1788, 2 vols., 12º (a real guide-book with particulars concerning the inns, the precautions to be taken against pickpockets, &c., fine engravings). Many other books, meant to make England better known, might be quoted, such as "Essai géographique sur les Isles Britanniques," by Bellin, Paris, 1757, 8º, with maps ; "Les Nuits Anglaises, ou recueil de traits singuliers, d'anecdotes, &c., propres à faire connaître le génie et le caractère des Anglais," by d'Orville, 1770, 4 vols., 8º ; the letters of Madame du Bocage in the "Recueil" of her works, Lyons, 1764, 3 vols., 12º (some translations from Milton and Pope are also to be found in that "Recueil") ; the pseudo-novel of Lescure : "Les Amants Français à Londres ou les Délices de l'Angleterre," London, 1780, written to show "la façon de vivre dans ce pays Républiquain," and to give to Frenchmen "de nouvelles raisons d'estimer et d'aimer leur Gouvernement," &c.

[2] J. Cambry, "Promenades d'Automne en Angleterre," Paris, 1788, 8º. He imitates the meandering ways of Sterne ; he took his notes, he says, "en voiture, dans une auberge, au pied d'un arbre."

as a parallel to his "Sentimental Journey," a "Voyage philosophique,"[1] describing a journey to the land of thinkers and philosophers. He is at once recognized and saluted, on account of the foreign cut of his fur coat, with the words, "Oh! a French dog!" shouted in chorus by the little philosophers of the street; but he has, he too, some philosophy of his own, and his good humour is not abated. He goes to the play, admires Mrs. Siddons, but protests, at the same time, against the absence of the unities, and against the liberties taken by English players with Shakespeare's text; he belongs obviously to the eclectic school of philosophy. He looks with an observing eye at the audience in the pit: "As for the manners there, much better ones are to be found with us in the booths at the fair: people sing, whistle, scream, drink, eat oranges, and throw the rind straight before them, without the slightest intention of insulting the cheek which receives it; and no one takes offence."

Sterne having done our "grisettes" the honour of paying great attention to them, La Coste, author of the "Philosophical Journey," returns the compliment to their English sisters, sups with them, and listens with emotion to the story of those beautiful persons, all of them "filles d'honneur comme il plait à Dieu," as La Tour said in his guide-book. The philosophical raveller devotes a chapter to the "splin," has nothing to say of the king, who is of no account in this country, as he is nothing but the State crown-bearer, "le porte-couronne de l'État." La Coste sometimes draws vig-

[1] "Voyage philosophique d'Angleterre, fait en 1783 et 1784," London, 1786, 8º (by De La Coste).

nettes which recall the minute sketches of his model. He describes an ale tavern frequented by seamen, drivers, and dockers, and gives an outline portrait of some of the customers : " To my left was a man, five or six feet in circumference, with a short and wide red wig, his hat on his head, a cold composure, his hands in his pockets, his legs apart, and his mind, in truth, I know not where : for he offered a perfect image of inert matter ; he smoked not, drank not, read not, and yet he existed "—John Bull at rest. The scene becomes more lively ; seamen and dockers begin to discuss " in vehement but orderly fashion the bearing of M. Fox's Bill on the East India Company. . . . It struck me as very surprising to hear matters of that sort treated by a class of citizens which its social status seems to bind to the grossest ignorance." The warmth of the debate increases ; upon a contradiction and a denial high words resound, the disputants remove their coats, go into the street, choose seconds, and then follows a regular fight, the conclusion of which is not less remarkable than the origin. When the weaker had fallen, " I thought his enemy would leave him a prey to the laughter of the bystanders and go away bragging and singing his own victory. What was my astonishment when I saw him stretch out his hand, take his adversary's and shake it strongly : a token of attachment used by English people of all ranks ; and I heard them make friends again in words showing esteem for each other. I was the more surprised as the cause of their reciprocal praise was neither the strength nor the skill, but solely the valour that had just been displayed."

An enthusiastic reception awaited English men of letters in the Paris salons of that day; Walpole was the idol of Madame du Deffand; Chesterfield sent his son to Madame de Tencin: "Certain examples," he wrote to that former nun, "are more instructive than all possible precepts. As you have resolved not to have boys yourself" (a resolve not very well kept, as she had given birth to and forsaken the child that was to be d'Alembert), "adopt this one, for some time at least.... I do not wish him to win provinces, but only hearts."[1] Gibbon, sent to do penance at Lausanne, after his reading of "two famous works of Bossuet" had made of him a Catholic for a while, went to see Voltaire play in his own tragedies, and soon became an enthusiastic admirer of French classical art: "Voltaire," he says in his Memoirs, "represented the characters best adapted to his years, Lusignan, Alvarez, Benassar, Euphemon. His declamation was fashioned to the pomp and cadence of the old stage, and he expressed the enthusiasm of poetry rather than the feelings of nature. My ardour, which soon became conspicuous, seldom failed to procure me a ticket." One visitor, at least, did not share Gibbon's admiration, and has left, in the shape of an engraved sketch (here reproduced), a lasting memorial of the impression created upon him by Voltaire in those famous days when he donned the classical helmet.

Sterne, on the other hand, amused, "par son originalité piquante," a society which prided itself upon wondering at nothing. This "minister of the Anglican religion had a wife lawfully belonging to him; he

[1] Year 1751, the original in French. "Miscellaneous Works," ed. Maty, London, 1777, 2 vols., 4º, vol. ii., p. 161.

VOLTAIRE AS A TRAGIC ACTOR.
A caricature drawn in 1772.

was in love with Eliza, who was the wife of another, and neither the one nor the other, nor both together, could prevent his being again and again captivated by any woman whose charms had elicited his admiration."[1] Mademoiselle de Lespinasse tried to write "in the vein of Sterne," and Diderot did not abstain from appropriating some of Yorick's peculiarities,[2] his desultoriness, his dialogues started on the sudden about unexpected subjects, and even his monkey tricks, for there is no other word. Hume was received with open arms, when scarcely out of his chaise :—

> "Ah ! permettez de grâce,
> Pour l'amour de l'anglais, Monsieur, qu'on vous embrasse " ;

Greek was no longer in question.[3] "Lord Beauchamp," wrote Hume to Dr. Blair, "told me that I must go instantly with him to the Duchess of La Vallière. When I excused myself on account of dress, he told me that he had her orders, though I were in

---

[1] Garat, "Mémoires historiques," 2nd ed., 1821, vol. ii., p. 135.

[2] He alludes himself to those resemblances in "Jacques le Fataliste," and makes mention of his "estime toute particulière" for Mr. Sterne. Shandeian reminiscences are innumerable in the French literature of the day, testifying to the great influence and popularity of the Dean : "On sait quel abus on a fait de la société en France ; aussi personne n'y conserve-t-il plus rien de son originalité naturelle ; toutes les physionomies sont les mêmes et l'empreinte de la nature en est effacée. A cet égard encore, on sait combien les Anglais diffèrent de nous." Thus writes a Frenchman, who does nothing but appropriate a famous passage in the "Sentimental Journey" (*Character-Versailles*); "Journal Anglais," August 15, 1776.

[3] "Que pour l'amour du grec, Monsieur, on vous embrasse."
Philaminte to Vadius, "Femmes Savantes," iii. 5.

boots. I accordingly went with him in a travelling frock, where I saw a very fine lady reclining on a sofa, who made me speeches and compliments without bounds. The style of panegyric was then taken up by a fat gentleman, whom I cast my eyes upon and observed him to wear a star of the richest diamonds—it was the Duke of Orléans. The duchess told me she was engaged to sup in President Hénault's, but that she would not part with me—I must go along with her. The good President received me with open arms, and told me, among other fine things, that a few days before, the Dauphin said to him, &c., &c., &c."[1] The philosopher declares he is weary of so many compliments and tired by that unceasing agitation. He adds, however, that he is half inclined to settle in Paris, thus making the comedy complete.

Garrick, too, came to France, and enthusiasm reached its highest pitch. People envied the fate of the British nation who possessed such a man, and consoled themselves somewhat with the thought that he was of French origin. Cochin preserved his features in a fine engraving for his French admirers. Garrick acted in salons scenes from Shakespeare or expressed them in dumb show, and it was like a revelation. Some went to London in order to hear him, and admiration knew no bounds. Collé saw him in Paris in 1751, and wrote in his Journal : " I dined yesterday, 12th of this month (of July), with Garrick, that English comedian ; he played a scene from a tragedy of Shakespeare's, from which we could easily gather that this actor

[1] Paris, April 6, 1765, "Life and Correspondence of D. Hume," ed. Hill Burton, Edinburgh, 1846, 2 vols., 8º, vol. ii., p. 268.

amply deserves his wide reputation. He sketched for us the scene in which Macbeth thinks he sees a dagger leading him towards the chamber where he will assassinate the king.[1] He filled us with terror. It is not possible better to picture a situation, to render it with more warmth, while remaining perfectly self-possessed. His face expressed every passion in succession; and there was no grimacing, though this scene is full of awful and tumultuous movements."

Collé and Garrick met again in 1765; but this time the meeting ended (for Collé) in a disaster: "On Saturday, the 5th of January, I gave a dinner to Garrick, that famous English comedian whom I had already seen in Paris fourteen years ago. I had every reason to flatter myself he would give my wife and my guests an idea of his talents, by acting some scenes in dumb show; so that a knowledge of English should not be necessary. I had seen him do that on his previous journey. But it proved impossible to allure him to do it again; he was in a bad humour, and in such a mood that we had the dullest dinner I ever saw in my life." Collé had crammed him with attentions, had paid him a number of visits, and had even read to him, on his asking, his comedy, "La Vérité dans le vin"; nothing was of any avail. "The day I was simple

---

[1] "Is this a dagger which I see before me,
   The handle towards my hand? Come, let me clutch thee;
   I have thee not, and yet I see thee still.
   Art thou not, fatal vision, sensible
   To feeling as to sight? or art thou but
   A dagger of the mind, a false creation
   Proceeding from the heat-oppressed brain?" (ii. 1.)

enough to receive him at my house, I busied myself only with him and his wife, and I bored myself to the best of my powers, speaking only of England and of all that could concern those two animals. At dessert, and though I had a cold, I sang some of my songs, and did not spare myself, in order to induce him to do the same; it was all in vain." Garrick alleged, with a politeness which put Collé quite beside himself, that he had eaten too well " to be able to act anything." The measure is full; the paper at least must know the bitter feelings of the host, and the Journal[1] receives accordingly the confidence that Garrick is a fop, a mere comedian, "and even a good comedian is nothing much," he does not count in society; "common consent has assigned him a rank above that of the hangman, while considering him as less useful." Indeed! . . .

But those before whom Garrick did not refuse to perform Macbeth were of a different opinion. Marmontel, who was among the privileged ones during this journey, wrote to him the next day: "Sleep has not removed, sir, the impression you left on me, and I hope it will ever abide; the image of Macbeth always present before my eyes will be to me the intellectual model of theatrical declamation at its highest point of truth and vigour. . . . If we had actors like you, there would not be so much empty talk in our plays; we should allow their silence to speak, and it would be more eloquent than our verses. . . . I can say that I have seen together the first actor and the first actress in the world (Clairon); but I see with sorrow that the

[1] "Journal historique," 1805, vol. i., p. 411, and vol. iii., p. 152.

same theatre will never hold them." Garrick, for his part, would have liked such a dream to be realized, notwithstanding the difficulties of the French language and the impossibility of acquiring the right accent, "d'en prendre l'accent." He would have liked, mixing as he did with French actors, "to play French tragedy and comedy with them." He wished also the two capitals might have exchanged, at times, their best complete troupes, so that it would have been possible to see "French dramas in London and English dramas in Paris."[1]

As those dreams were not fulfilled, people went to London and saw Garrick on the stage. Madame Necker went in 1776 and surpassed even Marmontel in her enthusiasm: "I do not know, sir, where I shall find words to render the terrifying impression you left upon me yesterday [in 'Lear']; you made yourself master of my whole soul; it was convulsed by your acting; it was filled with terror and pity. I

---

[1] "Touché de la reconnaissance la plus vraie pour l'accueil qu'il recevait en France, Garrick regrettait beaucoup qu'il ne lui fût pas aussi possible d'en prendre l'accent que d'en apprendre la langue. Mêlé aux acteurs de Paris et sans autre rétribution que le plaisir qu'il aurait donné et le succès qu'il aurait pu avoir, il eût voulu jouer avec eux la comédie et la tragédie françaises.... Un autre vœu de Garrick ou le même avec plus de grandeur et cependant plus facile à remplir, c'est que la France et l'Angleterre, pour faire un échange de leurs plus belles jouissances, s'envoyassent de temps en temps leurs meilleures troupes complètes et qu'on pût voir le théâtre français à Londres et le théâtre anglais à Paris. Eh! pourquoi, dans une si grande proximité serait ce plus difficile d'en faire l'essai que d'entendre les bouffes et les *opera seria* de l'Italie sur tous les théâtres de l'Europe?" Garat, "Mémoires historiques," Paris, 1821, vol. ii., p. 133.

cannot, even now, recall the various expressions of your face without my eyes filling with tears. . . . Oh! why have I no longer the authors of my days; why can I not pour out at their feet the sentiments which you awoke in my mind, and shed there the heartrending tears which you called forth?"

She comes back, and the French drama seems to her a tasteless amusement, "after the wonders she has seen in London." She receives a letter from Garrick "and shows it with pride to all her company." Her friends say: "Tell us something more of that great man; how did he play Hamlet, King Lear, Sir John Brute? I tell them, and they weep, and they laugh. . . ." Garrick answers in the same style: the epistle he has received is "the most flattering, charming, bewitching letter that ever came to my hand. . . . It shall be left by my will to be kept in the famous mulberry box with Shakespeare's own handwriting, to be read by my children's children for ever and ever." Gibbon was present when the letter came: "Mr. Gibbon, our learned friend and excellent writer, happened to be with me when I received the bewitching letter." The paper was handed to him: "He read, stared at me, was silent, then gave it me with these emphatical words emphatically spoken: *This is the very best letter that ever was written*, upon which *à la mode d'Angleterre*, the writer was remembered with true devotion, and in full libations." (November 10, 1776.)

Garrick had become a power in France. Young authors appealed to him: "This letter, sir, is sent to you by a man who has the honour of knowing you only by reputation, but who has heard from London that he had a debt of gratitude towards you. . . . I am the author of that drama of 'Eugénie.' . . ." Thus wrote Beaumarchais at his *début* (March 29, 1769). He became acquainted with Garrick later, wanted to have his opinion on "Le Barbier de Séville" before it was performed, read it to him, and followed his advice: "Your idea of opium being given to L'Eveillé and of showing him asleep on the stage has been adopted without demur." He took hints even from the "smiles full of finesse and meaning of Madame Garike" (July 23, 1774). French comedians in trouble appealed to their English brother and asked for his help. They did so especially on the occasion of the great mishap of 1765, when they were all sent to the For-l'Evêque prison for having arrived after the appointed hour at the play-house, where a numerous audience was waiting for the performance of the "Siège de Calais."[1] The play was

---

[1] By De Belloy; first performance, February 13, 1765. The success was prodigious. History as well as grammar had greatly suffered at the hands of the author; but enthusiasm once kindled went on increasing; everything in the play was admired, even such terrible lines as these :—

"Le Français, dans son prince, aime à trouver un frère
Qui né fils de l'État en devienne le père." (iii. 4.)

"'The answer to all criticisms," says La Harpe, "was: Are you not, then, a good Frenchman? . . . Marshal de Noailles alone had the courage to retort, speaking to the king himself: I wish the verses in the play were as truly French as I am." People went to see Calais on account of the tragedy; Grosley did so; De Belloy had received the freedom of Calais. Then a reaction set in and never stopped: "'The Siege of Calais' is no longer admired except at Calais," Voltaire wrote in 1768 (to Walpole, July 15th).

having the greatest run in the whole century; it was given as a free entertainment in garrison towns, and was honoured three times with the presence of the king. The players were therefore the more inexcusable. Letters were sent to Garrick by Molé, Préville, Le Kain, the impetuous Clairon, who availed herself of the occasion to unburden her heart and to inform Garrick that the "worst scoundrel, the falsest and wickedest of men was M. Le Kain."

Morellet addressed Garrick as: "mon cher Shakespeare," and Grimm as: "illustre Roscius"; Patu, as early as 1755, prophesied that he would have some day "a mausoleum at Westminster." Ducis wanted to have his portrait before his eyes while at work, and wrote to him: "My soul tries, when composing, to assume your vigorous attitudes and to penetrate within the energetic depths of your genius." His help was asked in favour of the Calas family and of the Sirvens. He was truly a power in the State, the high priest of a religion, or, according to others, of a heresy whose adherents grew in numbers, and sang his praises: "Posterity will place the minister by the side of the idol, in the same temple."[1]

The French mind, in the meanwhile, reacted upon English literature to a degree scarcely known before. Anglomania had its counterpart in London. English critics submitted to the decrees of Pope, who had himself accepted Boileau's. Classical ideas gained ground in England among educated people, while their hold on

[1] Abbé Bonnet to Garrick, April 19 (1766?). "Correspondence of David Garrick," London, 1831, 2 vols., 4º, vol. ii., pp. 427, 439, 476, 559, 608, 609, 617, 624, 625.

the French nation began to slacken. In Paris, Voltaire was for the maintenance of rules, but tolerated a few liberties; in London, Blair was for the acceptance of the unities mitigated by a few licences.[1] A sort of equilibrium seemed to be within reach; following opposite directions, the two roads had now circled the globe, and, after a century, they were very near meeting again.

The distance was now so small that people could hear each other, and it was possible to exchange, according to the hour or temper, blows or caresses, insults or compliments. Madame du Deffand placed English novels above French ones; Walpole answered with praise of "Athalie" and of French tales;[2] the same courteousness was shown as at Fontenoy. French ideas had made such progress in London that it was considered possible to play "Venice Preserved" there, not as it had been written by Otway, but with the emendations introduced in it by La Place in view of a Paris audience.[3] Though De Belloy owed his fame to the patriotic feelings of his Parisian hearers much more than to his own talents, his celebrity as an author spread beyond the Channel, and Garrick made arrangements for one of his tragedies to be performed at

[1] "Lectures on Rhetoric," London, 1783.
[2] "Depuis vos romans, il m'est impossible de lire aucun des nôtres." Madame du Deffand to Walpole, August 8, 1773. Walpole answers: "Dans 'Gil Blas' rien n'est forcé. . . . Je conviendrai de tout ce que vous me dites d' 'Athalie,' mais 'Tom Jones' ne me fait pas la moindre impression."
[3] The "Venise" of La Place "a eu ici (in London) le plus grand succès." "Observateur Français," London and Paris, 1769 ff., vol. iv., p. 396.

Drury Lane. There was a *lutte de générosité* : Garrick was not stopped by the remembrance of De Belloy's anti-English lines, and De Belloy declined to receive any royalty.[1] Madame Riccoboni, on the other hand, gave up the idea of translating English tragedies: the old ones are too well known in France, she said, "and the new ones are too much like ours."[2] Gibbon began his literary career with an "Essai sur l'étude de la Littérature," which he wrote in French and printed in London, 1762. In the English capital, writes a visitor, who takes an optimist's view, "three-quarters of the inhabitants speak or understand French."[3]

The opinion of critics on Shakespeare was becoming more and more similar in the two countries. While the amount of praise bestowed upon him was on the increase in France, many a literary man in London

---

[1] De Belloy to Garrick, November 2, 1772 : "Je ne demande rien que la gloire de plaire à votre nation . . . toute idée d'intérêt dégraderait la noble ambition dont je suis animé. . . . Encore une fois, je ne veux absolument rien." Garrick had alluded to the "conditions à faire" between them.

[2] Preface of her "Nouveau Théâtre Anglois," 1769.

[3] Monnet, "Supplément au Roman Comique," London, 1772, vol. ii., p. 32. The "universality" of the French language was in fact scarcely contested in the eighteenth century, and it was nothing but a commonplace subject the Berlin Academy proposed to competitors in 1783. "On parle aujourd'hui français à Vienne, Stokholm et Moscou," wrote Voltaire to Madame du Deffand (October 13, 1759); and Rutledge, who did not bear any great love to France and to the French, said : "Une preuve qui ne leur paraît pas moins convaincante de la grande idée que l'Europe a d'eux, c'est le vaste empire de leur langue qu'ils regardent comme un aveu général de sa perfection." "Essai sur les caractères des Français," London, 1776.

gloried in scorning the gigantomachies of the Stratford bard. "We do not deserve," wrote Chesterfield to Madame de Tencin, "the honour you do us of translating our plays and novels. Your theatre conforms too closely to rules, is too chastened to admit most of our dramas; our authors carry not only liberty but licence far beyond the limits of decency and probability. I do not think we have as many as six which could be accepted by you in their original state. It would be quite necessary to recast them." He declared elsewhere that he preferred the French theatre to all others, including even the drama of the ancients, "with all the reverence I owe them."

Hume thinks "there may remain a suspicion that we overrate, if possible, the greatness of the genius [of Shakespeare], in the same manner as bodies often appear more gigantic on account of their being disproportioned and misshapen." He considers him, as Voltaire did, a prodigy, given the time when he lived and his total want of "any instruction"; but "if represented as a poet capable of furnishing a proper entertainment to a refined or intelligent audience, we must abate much of this eulogy." Hume tries, however, to show that he is capable of judging with impartiality the produce of a semi-barbarous age, and he finds, therefore, some extenuating circumstances and excuses for Shakespeare's "total ignorance of all theatrical art and conduct."[1]

---

[1] "History of England, containing the reigns of James I. and Charles I.," Edinburgh, 1754, 4°. Pope deplored in the same way that Shakespeare had composed his plays in view of "the people and writ, at first, without the patronage from the better sort . . .

The pleasure Gibbon felt in seeing Voltaire play in his own tragedies increased his fondness for classical dramas: it "fortified my taste for the French theatre, and that taste has perhaps abated my idolatry for the gigantic genius of Shakespeare, which is inculcated from our infancy as the first duty of an Englishman."[1] Even in the land of its birth the Shakespearean religion had its nonconformists, who were, as we see, men of account.

Garrick even, Garrick the minister of the idol, who wrote to a young actor, "never let your Shakespeare be out of your hands or your pocket; keep him about you as a charm,"[2] was sometimes, in his inmost soul, ashamed of his hero. He would never have confessed it in the presence of a disrespectful foreigner, and if some Abbé Morellet or other raised his voice, he flew to the defence of his god: "He rushed towards me," says the Abbé in his "Mémoires," "like a madman, calling me *French dog*." But, left to himself, he expurgated the theatre of Shakespeare, made it more regular, polished it according to his own taste, and tried to cover the nakedness of his master. He put Shakespeare's plays on the stage, not as they were, but

without the knowledge of the best models, the ancients." The dramatist improved when he had secured "the protection of his prince and the encouragement of the Court." Preface to the "Works of Shakespeare . . . by Mr. Pope," 1725. Cf. Gildon: "The highest praise we can justly give our magnified Shakespeare is only that he was a great master of dialogues, but not that of a tragic poet." "The Complete Art of Poetry, in Six Parts." London, 1718, 2 vols., 12", dial. iv., p. 222.

[1] "Memoirs of my life."
[2] To Powell, Paris, December 11, 1764.

as he would have wished them to be ; he suppressed the grave-digger's scene in "Hamlet," running the risk of having "the benches thrown at his head" by the rabble, but sure thereby to obtain the approbation of Voltaire.[1] He gave a "King Lear" with a happy ending; he awoke Juliet before the death of Romeo; and never allowed old Capulet to call his daughter "green-sickness carrion," nor any such names. "Winter's Tale" became in his hands "Florizel and Perdita"; "Midsummer Night's Dream" became "The Fairies"; "Taming of the Shrew," "Catherine and Petruccio"; Bianca lost her lovers and the play its drunkard.[2] He built a temple to Shakespeare in *Greek* style, a rather alarming honour. "On an artificial hill overlooking the banks of the Thames, and divided from the garden by a continuous row of laurel trees and evergreens, rises a little temple built with as much solidity as elegance in fine Portland stone. It is round-shaped, surmounted by a cupola of about twenty feet in diameter. The gate is adorned with a pro-

---

[1] As well as the praise of Morellet, La Place, &c. La Place wrote to him : "Recevez tous mes compliments sur vos succès nouveaux et surtout sur celui de la très hasardeuse entreprise que vous avez tentée dans la reprise de la tragédie d'Hamlet. J'aurois, d'honneur, frémi pour vous (car je connois la populace angloise) de vous voir assez téméraire pour la priver de la scène des fossoyeurs qui, de tout temps, a fait ses délices." January 24, 1772. Congratulations of Morellet, January 14, 1774. Voltaire declared himself "enchanté" with the catastrophe in "Romeo" as Garrick "en a peint les circonstances" (Patu to Garrick, Genève, November 1, 1755). He rejoiced at the disappearance of the grave-diggers (Letter to the Academy on Shakespeare, 1776).

[2] "Dramatic Works of David Garrick," London, 1798, 3 vol. 8º.

truding pediment, supported in antique fashion by two detached columns. Inside the temple stands a lifesize statue of Shakespeare, the work of Roubillac, in fine Carrara marble." Grosley, who gives these particulars and had visited the temple in 1765, adds: " M. Garric does the honours of the building in a way that brings out still more its merit : ' I owe everything to Shakespéar,' he says ; *si vivo et valeo, suum est:* this is a slight token of a boundless gratitude." The temple was Greek and the statue French,. Roubillac being a native of Lyons and a pupil of Coustou. The temple soon became one of the shrines most frequently visited by the literary pilgrims who now flocked in large numbers to England. Le Kain went to see it, and could not find words to express his rapture, " peindre son extase ; "[1] while Delille " interrogated the harmonious grotto " of Pope, and others went to visit the famous summer house of Hammersmith, and weep over the inkstand of Richardson.

For people wept profusely. In spite of low morals, wars, the growth of scepticism, the partition of Poland, the impending Revolution, Europe was becoming sentimental. Rousseau had come ; tears were the fashion ; tears had revealed to him his vocation : " I saw the

[1] To Garrick, April 4, 1766. Statues (not to speak of temples) erected to famous writers were not so common then as now, and Garrick's undertaking excited a proportionate wonder. The French admirers of Shakespeare were loud in their praise ; his detractors not less loud in their blame. Patu, an admirer, congratulated Garrick upon " his noble enterprise at Hampton. Our actors have not the same zeal for the memory of Corneille, the reason being that they have not your gifts and are not so high-souled as you are," May 6, 1755. He recurs to the subject on June 18, 1755.

THE SECOND STATUE RAISED TO SHAKESPEARE, THE WORK OF A FRENCHMAN, LOUIS FRANÇOIS ROUBILLAC, OF LYONS, ORDERED BY GARRICK.

front of my vest all wet with tears, though I had not felt I was weeping." He made hereupon his *début* in the world of letters, and published his " Mémoire " to the Academy of Dijon (1750). The die is cast; Emile will weep, Sophie will sob, and Julie faint; good company will be seized with "a frantic appetite for strong emotions."[1] Mistelet prints an essay on "Sensibility with reference to Dramas, Novels and Education," and teaches methodically that, above all, one must be *sensible*: "Whoso loves well a lover, loves well also a father and a mother, and will love well children, friends, and humanity."[2] Voltaire reading his own "Tancrède," shed a flood of tears, and the fat Madame Denis a torrent;[3] Marmontel paying a visit to Voltaire at Les Délices, was asked by his host to read the play, and when he returned the manuscript his face was "soaked with tears."[4]

People admired nature, and dreamed of living the life of shepherds. Worldly Voltaire discovered that "poets had been quite right to praise pastoral life; the

---

[1] Preface by Chastellux for "La Fausse Sensibilité," by the Marquise de Gléon, "Recueil de Comédies Nouvelles," Paris, 1787, 8°.

[2] "De la sensibilité par rapport aux Drames, aux Romans et à l'Éducation," Amsterdam and Paris, 1777, 8°, p. 49.

[3] "La nièce de Voltaire est à mourir de rire : c'est une petite grosse femme toute ronde, d'environ cinquante ans ... laide, et bonne, menteuse sans le vouloir et sans méchanceté ... criant, décidant, politiquant, versifiant, raisonnant, déraisonnant, et tout cela sans trop de prétentions et surtout sans choquer personne."
—Madame d'Épinay to Grimm, "Mémoires de Madame d'Épinay," Paris, Charpentier, ii., p. 421.

[4] Marmontel, "Mémoires d'un père," book vii.

happiness attached to rustic occupations is not an idle
fancy; and I find more pleasure in ploughing, sowing,
planting, and gathering than in writing tragedies and
having them represented." That was saying much.
Men tried to live the life of the heroes in "Astrée,"
the famous pastoral of d'Urfé, which had never ceased
to be fashionable, and the royal shepherdesses of
Versailles went to milk cows in the hamlet of Trianon.
They spent whole nights dreaming under the stars,
they enjoyed the coolness of the morning, and went
to bed after having partaken of onion soup in the
fashion of real shepherds. Madame Victoire, daughter
of Louis XV., writes to the Countess of Chastellux:
"You know that I spent the night of Thursday
to Friday in the garden. How beautiful the sun
was when it rose, and what fine weather! I went
to bed at eight o'clock in the morning after having
eaten for my breakfast an excellent onion soup. . . .
I was truly pleased with the fine weather, the beautiful
moon, the dawn, the beautiful sun, and then with my
cows, sheep and poultry, and with the movement of
all the workmen who began their task gaily." [1]

Such sentiments, very unfrequent formerly, were
now extremely common. Parks were adorned with
artificially disposed sites, and artificially simple build-
ings, meant to appeal to the nice sentiments in tender
hearts. The Comte d'Albon, Prince of Yvetot, had
had a "retreat for shepherds" erected in his park

---

[1] From Bellevue, near Paris, August 7, 1787. J. Soury, "Les
Filles de Louis XV.," in the "Revue des Deux Mondes," June 15,
1874.

L'AZILE DES BERGERS.
The Retreat of Shepherds in the Parc à l'Anglaise of Count d'Albon,
at Franconville. p. 307.

at Franconville in the Montmorency Valley; he had also there a number of temples, columns, pyramids, and grottoes, all with a touching meaning. An altar was erected in the park to his only love: strange to say, and rare sight for the epoch, the bust on the altar displayed no other effigy but that of the Countess d'Albon, his wife. Pastoral life won unexpected adepts. "Wander in the country," we read in a work of the same period, "take shelter in the lowly hut of the shepherd; spend the night stretched on skins, the fire burning at your feet. What a situation! the clock is heard striking twelve, all the cattle of the neighbourhood come out to graze; their lowing mingles with the voice of the herdsmen. Remember it is midnight. What a moment to retire within yourself and meditate on the origin of nature while tasting the most exquisite delights!" The author of these effusions, of this "very dream . . . the work perhaps of a man of feeling," as the academicians said who had to pass judgment upon it, was a lieutenant of artillery, called Napoléon Bonaparte.[1]

The former austerity in manners and tastes was waning. The time is no more when Racine and

---

[1] "Égarez vous dans la campagne, réfugiez vous dans la chétive cabane du berger; passez y la nuit couché sur des peaux, le feu à vos pieds. Quelle situation! minuit sonne: tous les bestiaux des environs sortent pour paître; leur bêlement se marie à la voix des conducteurs: il est minuit, ne l'oubliez pas. Quel moment pour rentrer en nous-mêmes et pour méditer sur l'origine de la nature en savourant les délices les plus exquises."—"Discours sur la question proposée par l'Académie de Lyon," in Masson, "Napoléon inconnu," vol. ii., p. 303.

Boileau addressed each other as "Monsieur" after an intimacy of thirty-five years. From the first meeting the word is now considered too stilted : "Let us drop the *Monsieur*, dear Moulton," writes Rousseau, "I cannot bear that word between men who love and esteem each other ; I shall do my best to deserve that you should not use it any more with me." If *Monsieur* disappears, sentimental nicknames swarm in conversations and private letters of the period : Panpan, Panpichon, Beloved-Panpichon-of-the-Indies (Panpichon chéri des Indes) ; d'Argental is the "cher ange" of Voltaire. No more gardens "à la française," nothing of that former love for straight lines and rectitude ; high ways themselves should not be in a straight line. "The country," observes with regret a tender-hearted officer of dragoons, "is crossed in all directions by the long, straight lines of highways bordered with trees pruned into the shape of brooms ; the protracted monotony of those straight-line roads is most wearisome for the traveller . . . Their artificial regularity is in absolute opposition to nature. . . . Laying out by line as well as pruning ought to be proscribed."[1] Saint Preux, on the other hand, writes to "milord Édouard" (in Rousseau's "Nouvelle Héloïse ") : " The man of taste will give nothing to symmetry that enemy of nature. The two sides of his alleys will not always run parallel ; their direction will not always be

[1] "De la composition des paysages ou des moyens d'embellir la nature autour des habitations en joignant l'agréable à l'utile," by R. L. Gérardin, "Mestre de camp de dragons, chevalier de l'ordre royal et militaire de Saint Louis," Geneva and Paris, 1777, 8º, pp. 59, 127.

in a straight line ; there will be something vague about them recalling the gait of an idle man who wanders in his walk." And these winding alleys, with their "je ne sais quoi de vague," laid out by philosophers, led the nation, amidst rivulets and flowers, to the song of birds, no one knew whither. It was like a springtide, a thawing of the snows ; no one remembered that the time of melting snows is also the season of avalanches and over-flowing torrents.

II.

The theatre, as might be expected, felt the influence of this new state of mind. Plots, scenery, costumes, acting were modified ; there was a visible shifting of the dramatic ideal. Abbé Du Bos, full of the old ideas, still made, in the first part of the century, the apology of the theatrical conventions of the past age. He did not contest their arbitrariness, far from it : he praised them as conventions, and because they swerved from nature : "As the object of tragedy," he said, "is to excite terror and pity, and as the marvellous is a component part of the poem, all the dignity possible must be bestowed upon the persons acting in it. Such is the reason why those persons are usually dressed to-day in costumes which are the produce of pure fancy (imaginés à plaisir)"—those costumes *à la Romaine* spoken of by Chappuzeau, and which cost five hundred crowns—" The first idea of those costumes is derived from the war garments of the ancient Romans, a garment noble in itself, and, it would seem, connected, to some extent, with the glory of the nation which wore it. The dresses of the actresses are as rich and majestic as imagination can invent." Imagination was, in fact, the mainstay of the *costumier's* art in those days. The delivery suited the dresses : " The French do not consider that dresses are enough to give the tragic actors a befitting nobleness and dignity. They want them also to speak in a tone of voice higher, deeper, and better sustained than that of ordinary conversation." This " style of delivery is, it is true, harder to enjoy," but it has more dignity. Acting must accord with the voice : " We want the actors to give an air of grandeur and dignity to all they do."

These counsels were exactly followed. The Abbé Du Bos, member of the French Academy, a diplomate and a man of letters, honoured with the praise of Voltaire, was an acknowledged authority ; between 1719 and 1746, his book had been issued five times.[1] Towards the middle of the century, Cæsar might still be seen on the stage, amply periwigged, " en perruque carrée " ; Ulysses " came out of the waves, carefully powdered " ; Pharasmane (in Crébillon's " Rhadamiste "), dressed in cloth of gold, descanted before the ambassador of Rome, on the wild nature of his own

---

[1] "Réflexions critiques sur la Poésie et la Peinture par M. l'abbé Du Bos, l'un des quarante de l'Académie Française," Paris, 1746, 3 vols., 12º (5th ed.). The sale of the book decreased in the second half of the century. Abbé Du Bos, 1670-1742, knew foreign countries, spoke English, and fulfilled numerous diplomatic missions in England, Italy, and Germany. He translated into French the first scenes of Addison's " Cato."

THEATRICAL DECLAMATION.
By Eisen, 1764.

country where they knew nothing but "iron and soldiers":—

> "La nature marâtre, en ces affreux climats,
> Ne produit, au lieu d'or, que du fer, des soldats."[1]

A tragic actor never forgot what dignity and manners demanded of him: "The actress Duclos was playing in 'Les Horaces'; towards the end of her imprecations she has to go away in a passion as everybody knows; she got entangled in the folds of her train, which was a very long one, and fell. The audience saw thereupon the actor who played the part of Horace take off his hat courteously with one hand, offer the other to the actress, lead her to the coulisse, and then, putting on his hat again with great dignity, kill her according to the book."[2]

Some attention is now paid to truth, nature, and history, and a change begins during the second part of the century: but a slow and feeble change, so powerful was fashion. The encyclopædists scarcely hoped to see it altered: "We know that our remarks will be fruitless," they said in 1754. But their remarks produced some fruit, however, and in Voltaire's "Orphelin de la Chine," Mademoiselle Clairon was seen to appear "en chinoise," which consisted in playing with bare

---

[1] "Encyclopédie," word "Déclamation," by Marmontel, 1754.
[2] Mercier, "Tableau de Paris," chap. 208. Marie Anne de Châteauneuf, called Duclos (1670-1748), made her *début* at the French Comedy in 1693, and left the stage in 1733. She was considered as another Champmeslé. She made herself ridiculous in the latter part of her life, by marrying at 55, the young actor Duchemin, aged 17.

arms and no paniers: the knowledge of China went no further. Le Kain also tried a few timid reforms, but without carrying them very far. "Had he," wrote Talma later, "risked bare arms, hair without powder, long draperies, woollen garments, had he dared shock to that degree the rules of decorum followed in those days: that severe garb would then have been regarded as a very untidy and more particularly as a very indecent style of dress." To complete the reform, it required the authority of Talma himself, the help of "our celebrated David" the painter, who accustomed the eye to plain Roman costumes, and above all it required the lapse of years.[1]

It was the same for declamation. Some efforts with a view to following nature more closely were made, but very timidly, for these attempts were far from meeting with universal approbation. If you limit yourself to following nature, declared the old connoisseurs, you are no longer artists. "The natural acting which M. Diderot recommends," wrote Madame du Deffand, "has produced the excellent result of causing Agrippina to be acted in the style of a fish-wife. Neither Mademoiselle Clairon, nor Le Kain are real actors, they all play according to their nature and condition, and not according to that of the personages they represent."[2]

---

[1] "Mémoires de Le Kain, précédés de Réflexions par Talma," 1825, pp. xviii., ff.

[2] L. Perey and G. Maugras, "Voltaire aux Délices," 1885, p. 127. For a long time those attempts had little effect; as late as the days of "Corinne," 1807, Madame de Stael could write: "Il faut

In a measure more marked, the very essence of plays, their aim, composition, and dramatic springs, were being modified. The old gaiety of comedy and the old rigour of tragedy were being gradually attenuated in France; a period of equality was beginning; Melpomene was loosening her belt; Thalia was shedding tears. La Chaussée had become the head of a school, and the movement showed itself so strong that the most rebellious were carried away by it; Voltaire passed indignant judgments on La Chaussée, but wrote, nevertheless tearful "larmoyantes" comedies, an "Écossaise" and a "Nanine," yielding, like every one, to the influence of Richardson.[1] Tragedies in

d'autant plus de génie pour être un grand acteur en France qu'il y a fort peu de liberté pour la manière individuelle, tant les règles générales prennent d'espace. Mais en Angleterre on peut tout risquer si la nature l'inspire. Les longs gémissements qui paraissent ridicules quand on les raconte font tressaillir quand on les entend. L'actrice la plus noble dans ses manières, Madame Siddons, ne perd rien de sa dignité quand elle se prosterne contre terre." Bk. xvii. chap. iv. The true reform of tragic declamation took place very late. Talma himself had, we hear, a sing-song declamation: "Talma n'est sublime que dans des mots; ordinairement, dès qu'il y a quinze ou vingt vers à dire, il chante un peu; l'on pourrait battre la mesure de sa déclamation." (Stendhal, "Racine et Shakespeare," 1st ed., 1823.)

[1] "Nanine ou le Préjugé vaincu" (in verse, 1749); the "préjugé" is that of birth; it is the story of Pamela; it had been that of Griselda. In the "Écossaise" (in prose, 1760), there were the "larmoyant" rôle of Lindane, and the ignoble rôle of Frelon (Fréron; he was present at the first performance with his wife, who fainted). Many Pamélas, not to mention La Chaussée's (and Goldoni's), many Clarissas and Tom Joneses, were put on the stage in France: "Paméla ou la Vertu récompensée, par le citoyen François de Neufchâteau, Paris, an III." (ideas have progressed;

prose were multiplying in spite of his protestations; he could sometimes prevent their being played, but not their being written. Sedaine, who counted upon a success equal to that of the "Siège de Calais," had, thanks to him, to be content with the applause of the Swedes and Russians for his "Maillard ou Paris sauvé, tragédie en prose, tirée de l'histoire de France, année 1358." [1]

After Rousseau, every one in turn indulged in the pleasure of discovering humanity: every type of the human race was studied and became interesting to tender-hearted naturalists: bourgeois and commonplace people were admitted to the honours of heroship in plays which were neither comedies nor tragedies

mylord Bonfil declares in this play that his mésalliance "honours" his race); "Paméla mariée ou le Triomphe des Épouses," by Pelletier Volmeranges and Cubières-Palmezeaux, an XII., dedicated to Fanny de Beauharnais (aunt to Joséphine):—

"Fanny, qu'il est doux pour nos cœurs
D'avoir excité vos allarmes
Et d'avoir vu couler vos larmes."

Boissy had made a caricature of Pamela: "Paméla en France ou la Vertu mieux éprouvée," 1743 (the marquis disguises himself as a woman to approach Pamela). "Clarisse Harlowe," 1786, by Née de la Rochelle, a great partisan of the "drame" and of moralising plays. "Tom Jones, comédie lyrique," 1766, by Poinsinet, music by Philidor; "Tom Jones à Londres," 1782, in verse, by Desforges (great success at the Théâtre des Italiens; see La Harpe, "Correspondance Littéraire," 1801, iv., 140); "Tom Jones et Fellamar," 1787, &c.

[1] Sedaine, in his preface, openly accuses Voltaire of having caused the interdiction of his play because it was in prose; it was published in 1788 with a dedication to the Empress of Russia.

and which ended by being called "drames," in spite of Cubières and Desfontaines, who proposed to name them "romanédies."[1] Diderot, Saurin, Beaumarchais, Mercier, all tried their hand at this style, which Diderot, on his side, baptised "the serious genre," and the theory of which he established in terms that already make one think of the romantics of 1830: "I shall call this genre the serious genre. This genre once established, no conditions in society, no important actions in life need be excluded from the drama. Do you wish to give this system all the scope it is capable of; to include in it truth and fancy, the imaginary world and the real world? You may, and for that you have only to add the burlesque below the comic style, and the marvellous above the tragic one." No more principles; no more rules; they are not wanted any more than straight-line alleys in gardens: "And above all remember that there is no general principle; I know of none among those I have just mentioned, which a man of genius may not infringe with success."[2] Saurin gave a "domestic tragedy imitated from the English," had the happiness of seeing "Son Altesse Sérénissime le Duc d'Orléans, premier prince du sang" shed tears, and thought that

[1] "On est presque convenu de nos jours d'appeler Drames les pièces qui tiennent le milieu entre la tragédie et la comédie ... Il vaudrait mieux, je crois, qu'on adoptât celui de *Romanédie* qu'avait inventé l'abbé Desfontaines."—Cubières, "La Manie des Drames sombres," 1777, Preface.

[2] "Entretiens sur le 'Fils naturel'" (the play is of 1757; the "Père de famille," written in the same spirit, is of 1758). "C'est donc une des suprêmes beautés du drame que le grotesque," says Victor Hugo (preface to "Cromwell").

he too, like Diderot, and after Sedaine, had enlarged the boundaries of art: "The domestic tragedy is a new field ... the boundaries of art have been laid too hastily. Is [Sedaine's] 'Philosophe sans le savoir,' a tragedy, or is it a comedy?" And Saurin inserted in his play an imitation of Hamlet's soliloquy delivered by a bourgeois about to commit suicide: "To sleep ... What if the tomb, instead of a place of rest, should be an eternal and awful awakening?"

> "M'endormir! ... Si la tombe, au lieu d'être un sommeil,
> Était un éternel et funeste réveil!
> Et si d'un Dieu vengeur ... Il faut que je le prie:
>   Dieu dont la clémence infinie ...
> Je ne saurais prier ...
>   (*He takes the glass and drinks.*)
> Oh! si l'homme au tombeau s'enfermait tout entier! ..."[1]

The same personage, seeing his son "Tomi," who is going to remain in the world poor and despised, pities his fate, and to save him from such misfortunes determines to stab him. "Barbarism!" cries Collé, "Ostrogothism!" The play had none the less an immense success:

---

[1] "Beverley, tragédie bourgeoise, en cinq actes et en vers libres," 1768. Molé was admirable in it: "Le rôle est d'une violence qui fait craindre à chaque représentation qu'il ne se casse un vaisseau," wrote Collé. It was an adaptation of the "Gamester" by Edward Moore, London, 1753, 8°, in prose. The rôle of Beverley had been created by Garrick. The lines quoted above correspond to this passage of Moore's text: "How the self murderer's account may stand, I know not. But this I know.—The load of hateful life oppresses me too much. ... The horrors of my soul are more than I can bear—(*offers to kneel*)—Father of Mercy—I cannot pray." Cf. the "Barneveldt" ("Barnwell") of La Harpe, another domestic tragedy; adapted from Lillo's "London Merchant" (already translated before; see *supra*, p. 237).

"You doubtless know of the success of the 'Joueur' ('Beverley')," writes Préville ; "it is astounding, and I am astounded ; but one must be prepared for anything, our taste is changing." [1]
The play was as successful with the reading as with the playgoing public. Bonaparte, at twenty-two, had read the play and wrote : "One must appeal to sentiment in its own language. You will sometimes show young men Beverley ; let them draw from the sight a horror for the pleasures we forbid them. Many other plays of that kind might also be beneficial, were there not too much love in them. Nature inspires it sufficiently without your blowing upon these live coals." [2]
Beaumarchais, on his side, prefaced his " Eugénie " with an " Essay on serious drama," and exclaimed in the same words as Perrault : " The new world would still be non-existent for us if the bold Genoese navigator had not trampled under foot the *ne plus ultra* of Alcides' columns as mendacious as proud." [3] He little suspected that he would be doing very nearly what he thus announced, the day when he should write, for his

---

[1] To Garrick, July 1, 1768.
[2] "Discours de Lyon," 1791, in Masson, "Napoléon inconnu," vol. ii., p. 311. Thoughts of suicide had been entertained a few years before by Bonaparte himself, then second lieutenant in the La Fère regiment. "Toujours seul au milieu des hommes, je rentre pour rêver avec moi-même et me livrer à toute la vivacité de ma mélancolie. De quel côté est-elle tournée aujourd'hui ? Du côté de la mort. . . . Puisque je dois mourir, ne vaut-il pas autant se tuer ? . . . La vie m'est à charge parce que je ne goûte aucun plaisir et que tout est peine pour moi."— Fragment written in 1786. *Ibid.*, vol. i., p. 145.
[3] Preface to " Eugénie," 1767.

amusement, dramas less "serious"—his "Barbier," or his "Figaro."

Meanwhile people were melting, their hearts overflowed. Going beyond the "serious," Baculard d'Arnaud, secretary of embassy, novelist of the "sensible" school, and dramatist of the funereal genre, was establishing the theory of the "sombre": "I am speaking of the *sombre*, the spring one ought to touch most often in tragedy." Crébillon knew nothing about it; he was almost rose-coloured in comparison with the new ideal; the old French tragic writers were but babblers; we must know better how to use the resources that art and nature place at our disposal, and those resources include graveyards, vampires, and ghosts. The model, from this point of view, is Shakespeare: for the sombre side of his genius was the one by which most minds in France were then struck. Summing up, much later, impressions which went back to the days of his youth, Delille sang the praise of him "whose black pencil painted the awful picture of grand calamities, who darkening the stage with sombre hues, clothed Melpomene in a blood-stained raiment, and by the pale light of sepulchral lamps, to the low groans of subterranean shades, amid ruins, ghosts, and tombs, displaying the tattered purple of the royal mantle, surrounded his muse with spectres and assassins. All nature was for him only an ample tomb inhabited by Terror, Anguish, and Gloom."[1] Such was the Strat-

---

[1] "Je ne t'oublirai pas, toi dont le noir pinceau
    Traça des grands malheurs le terrible tableau,
    Qui, de sombres couleurs rembrunissant la scène,

MOLIÈRE'S "AVARE"
Illustrated by Hogarth: Van der Gucht sc.

p. 323.

ford bard in the eyes of that great admirer of Pope, the Abbé Delille.

Baculard, for his part, quotes as an example of the perfect sombre, "a terrible scene of Shakespeare's, that faithful imitator in many respects of Æschylus," the one in which the ghosts appear to Richard III. He gives the English text and a translation in verse; the model is even ultra-perfect and the translator abridges a little : " I do not think it will be imputed to me as a great crime not to have made use of all the ghosts that this great poet causes to appear." Baculard, too, flatters himself, like all the authors of that time, that he has passed the columns of Hercules : " I have perhaps pointed out to the stage a new road." [1] It was not, at all events, the one recommended by Boileau, who had written for the benefit of all Baculards past and future :—

> " Il est certains esprits dont les sombres pensées
> Sont d'un nuage épais toujours embarrassées ;
> Le jour de la raison ne les saurait percer ! . . ."

The sombre had none the less many adherents among men of letters, and long before Victor Hugo and his

> D'une robe sanglante habillas Melpomène . . .
> A la pâle lueur des lampes sépulcrales,
> Aux gémissements sourds des ombres infernales,
> A travers des débris, des ombres, des tombeaux,
> De la pourpre des rois promenant les lambeaux,
> De spectres, d'assassins, ta muse s'environne :
> La nature pour toi n'est qu'un vaste cercueil
> Que parcourent l'effroi, la douleur et le deuil."

" L'Imagination," Canto V. This passage is a late addition.

[1] " Le Comte de Comminge ou les Amants malheureux," Paris, 1768, 3rd ed., with three preliminary discourses.

peers placed the action of their dramas in the tomb of Charlemagne and other darksome places, such scenery as this was offered to the eyes of the habitués of the French Comedy : " The theatre is draped in black, and is very faintly lit. A lamp hangs in the middle. On one side is a sort of funereal couch, with the body of Lothario on it. On the other, a table, on which stands a poisoned cup." A truly Shakespearean sight Colardeau, the author of the play, must have thought,[1] and the Delilles and Baculards of the time cannot have failed to be of the same opinion.

The roads had become contiguous ; never had the French stage had so many partisans in London, never had Shakespeare been so praised in Paris ; but the fundamental differences of temperament could not, for all that, have really disappeared ; contact is not metempsychosis. The contact of Molière cannot change the temperament of a Hogarth, and when Hogarth illustrates Molière, he insists in such a way on the sins, faults, and oddities of the personages, as to leave (like

[1] But here again the public was slow in accepting the new methods, and the play had but little success. Many among the spectators were " révoltés " at the sight it offered—" Caliste, tragédie, représentée pour la première fois par les comédiens français, le 12 Novembre, 1760," by Colardeau, Paris, 1771 ; Act V. In the midst of such scenery enters Caliste, who says :—

> " Ces terribles objets dont mes sens sont frappés,
> Des voiles de la mort ces murs enveloppés,
> Ce lugubre flambeau dont le jour pâle et sombre
> Luit à peine et s'éteint dans l'épaisseur de l'ombre," &c.

The play was written in imitation of Rowe's " Fair Penitent." Colardeau, of the French Academy, d. 1776.

THE PLAYERS' SCENE IN "HAMLET."
Engraved by Gravelot.

Wycherley in his plays) the impression of men to be shunned rather than to be laughed at. Let us come and laugh, say Molière's habitués. Let us shun all such people, shall we say, looking at Hogarth's engravings.[1] Neither can the contact of Shakespeare transform a Gravelot, and when Gravelot illustrates Shakespeare, Hamlet becomes a slight, sentimental young prince, with curly hair, while Othello recalls those wooden negroes, all enamel and glitter, who hold plateaus under the *Procuratie* at Venice.[2] Women might wear "the head-dress called 'Union of France and England,'" without preventing differences of views, interests, and characters ; or wars for a few acres of "snow between bears and beavers," as Voltaire wrote to Madame du Deffand (little dreaming that one day, beneath those Canadian snows, would be discovered the veritable Eldorado of Candide) ; for "some horrid cod-fish," quoth Madame Riccoboni.[3] And the latter, who was constantly studying English literature, without losing her French temper and way of thinking, could not forbear protesting against this new taste, sprung from northern climes, for the sombre and the lachrymose : "In our brilliant capital," she wrote, "where airs and

---

[1] "Select Comedies of Mr. de Molière, French and English." London, 1732, 8 vols., 12º, engravings by Hogarth and others.

[2] "The Works of Shakespeare," ed. Theobald, London, 1757, 8 vols., engravings by Van der Gucht from designs by Gravelot ; "Works," Oxford, 1744, 6 vols. 4º, engravings by Gravelot from sketches by Hayman.

[3] Born Marie-Jeanne Laboras de Mézières, wife of Antoine-François Riccoboni, son of Louis Riccoboni, all actors and authors, like Marie-Jeanne herself. She died in 1792. "Œuvres complètes," new ed., Paris, 1816, 6 vols.

fashions reign, to wax tender, to be moved, to be
sorrowful, is the 'bon ton' of the moment. Goodness,
sensibility, tender humanity, have become the universal
craze. One would willingly make men unhappy to
enjoy the pleasure of pitying them. People believe
themselves good when they are sombre, excellent when
they are sad. . . . At present, Molière's plays are called
farces, they are given on off-days, and actors who think
well of their own talent, disdain all his rôles, except
that of the Misanthrope. To laugh at a comedy is an
absurdity with us, sheer foolishness, a ridicule worthy
of mere bourgeois. Tears are shed at the comic-
opera." She adds: "Young's 'Night Thoughts' have
made a fortune here; there is no better proof of the
change in the French mind."[1]

The "sombre" which was gaining ground, had
not yet, however, invaded everything; English
liberties had their partisans, but also their detractors, more and more impassioned and attached to
their system, on both sides, as years went by and as
the dispute waxed hotter. War was inevitable; it
began by being sham war, *la guerre pour rire*. Abbé
Le Blanc had, early in the day, opened fire with an
amusing satire, carrying war into the enemy's camp.

He had been shocked, like many others, at the
freedom with which London dramatists borrowed from
the great men of France, without paying any tribute to
their genius, and sometimes (especially in former days)
even denying they had any genius. For if Shakespeare
was destined to appear upon the French stage (as he

[1] May 3rd, September 12, 1769, "Correspondence of D.
Garrick," vol. ii., pp. 561, 566.

"TENDER HUMANITY." A PAUPER CARRYING HOME SOUP FROM
COUNT D'ALBON'S PLACE AT FRANCONVILLE.
"*A study from life.*"   Second half of the eighteenth century.

sometimes appeared on the English boards) strangely transformed, Racine, Corneille, and Molière underwent in London no less curious remodellings. Tastes were undoubtedly becoming more alike in the two countries, but especially the tastes of critics, theorists, and dilettanti. In the upper regions of thought, great were the similitudes ; in the nether regions of practical life, of real boards and actual representations, the two nations no longer seemed to be so very near each other. Playwrights had necessarily to take into account, to a greater extent than critics, the whims and dispositions of the theatre-going public ; and that public, although willing, on both sides of the Channel, to admit some few reforms, continued to preserve a warm feeling for opposite æsthetics and time-honoured systems. Critics have a comparatively easy task ; they read, they learn, they open up a vista, they draw a veil ; new things excite their interest ; new theories invented, or old forgotten ones circulated anew by them, increase their reputation ; they easily secure thereby a public of readers. The playhouse public follows them only at a distance, and the distance must be accurately gauged by dramatists, egregious failure being the penalty for any miscalculation. An English critic of the Chesterfield stamp could very well praise French regularity ; a French critic of the Diderot sort could as warmly praise "the irregular, rugged, and wild air of the English genius." But this transposition of views did not take place to the same extent with spectators. In France they remained long indignant at the undue liberties taken by the reformers, and in London Garrick needed all his authority, and ran at times serious risks when he imposed upon his audience his remodelled and thoroughly toned-down versions of Shakespeare. The real feeling of the English public had been pointed out, years before, by Mrs. Centlivre with meritorious frankness and in terms similar to Lope de Vega's : " The criticks cavil most about decorums, and cry up Aristotle's rules as the most essential part of the play. I own they are in the right of it ; yet I dare venture a wager they'll never persuade the town to be of their opinion. . . . I do not say this by way of condemning the unity of time, place, and action ; quite contrary, for I think them the greatest beauties of a dramatick poem ; but since the other way of writing pleases full as well and gives the poet a larger scope of fancy with less trouble, care, and pains, serves his and the player's end, why should a man torture and rack his brain for what will be of no advantage to him." [1]

For such reasons (like Mrs. Centlivre), Otway, Dryden, Wycherley, Fielding, Cibber, Shadwell, Whitehead, vieing with each other, had turned to the French drama now famous all over Europe, but without forgetting the differences of taste in the audiences of Paris and of London. They had taken two comedies to make one, two characters to make one, certain of interesting with a combination of contrasts and a parallelism of intrigues, fusing into one woman two such opposites as Molière's Arsinoé and Célimène,[2] allowing old Horatius, to use the blunt language of old

[1] Preface to "Love's Contrivance, or the Médecin malgré lui," "Works," London, 1761, 3 vols., vol. ii.
[2] In Wycherley's "Plain Dealer," 1676.

Capulet, and laying down their pen with triumph, exclaiming, "I think I may say without vanity that Molière's part of it has not suffered in my hands; nor did I ever know a French comedy made use of by the worst of our poets, that was not better'd by 'em." So speaks Shadwell in his preface to "The Miser"; he takes also various scenes from Corneille and Molière's "Psyché," "which," he says, "without vanity, are very much improv'd." Mrs. Centlivre resorts to the same fount, and acknowledges her debt in these words: "Some scenes I confess are partly taken from Molière, and I dare be bold to say it has not suffered in the translation." [1]

A whole theatre cannot, in truth, be filled with Chesterfields; there the multitude lays down the law. The simple language of Corneille could not, in spite of the new literary tendencies, suffice for a London audience; still less that of Racine. Whitehead's old Horatius, at the news of his son's flight, cannot stand; he chokes, he rolls in his chair; he can scarcely speak; he repeats three or four times the same insult, and is led away wanting air; a very false idea is conveyed of Corneille's hero:—

"*Horatius.* By flight! And did the soldiers let him pass?
 Oh! I am ill again!—The coward villain! . . .
  (*Throwing himself into his chair.*)
Valeria. What could he do, my lord, when three oppos'd him?
Horatius. Die!
 He might have died.—Oh! villain, villain, villain!
 And he shall die, this arm shall sacrifice

---

[1] "Love's Contrivance, or the Médecin malgré lui."

> The life he dar'd to preserve with infamy.
> (*Endeavouring to rise.*)
> What means this weakness? 'tis untimely now . . .
> . . . So young a hypocrite!
> Oh! shame, shame, shame!
> . . . Pray lead me forth,
> I would have air." [1]

Needless to say that "Oh! I am ill again," and the want of air, as well as the vituperative exclamations of the old man, his feeling faint in his chair (and his witticisms when he is happy again),[2] are embellishments introduced by Whitehead into Corneille's masterpiece.[3] The play thus adapted, obtained, according to contemporary testimony, "the just approbation of repeated and judicious audiences"; [4] it passed through numerous editions and is still reprinted.

---

[1] "The Roman Father," London, 1750, 8º, Act III.

[2] After the death of Camille:—

> "My son, my conqueror! 'twas a fatal stroke,
> But shall not wound our peace."

[3] "*Le vieil Horace.* Et nos soldats trahis ne l'ont point achevé?
Dans leurs rangs, à ce lâche, ils ont donné retraite?
Julie. Je n'ai rien voulu voir après cette défaite.
Camille. O mes frères!
Le vieil Horace. Tout beau, ne les pleurez pas tous,
Deux jouissent d'un sort dont leur père est jaloux.
Que des plus nobles fleurs leur tombe soit couverte;
La gloire de leur mort m'a payé de leur perte;
Ce bonheur a suivi leur courage invaincu
Qu'ils ont vu Rome libre autant qu'ils ont vécu" . . . ("Horace," iii. 6).

[4] "Companion to the Playhouse," 1764.

Corneille's old Horatius using the strong language of old Capulet, Racine's Titus adopting the ranting style of Almanzor, and all other transformations of the same kind, could not but seem sacrilegious. Abbé Le Blanc was one of the first to satirise these strange combinations of contradictory æsthetics. He wrote, for the use of the English authors of his day, a sort of manual to help them in composing their plays from a proper mixture of Racine and Shakespeare : " Le Supplément du Génie, ou l'art de composer des poèmes dramatiques, tel que l'ont pratiqué plusieurs auteurs célèbres du Théâtre Anglois." [1] The Abbé took Swift for his model : in the selfsame tone of humorous gravity the Dean of St. Patrick had composed his ironical " Directions to Servants " and his " Complete Collection of genteel and ingenious Conversation." Le Blanc was careful not to acknowledge the authorship of the work : " It fell into my hands by chance," he said ; " a copy of it was taken, not without difficulty, the author is considered here (in London) an authority in theatrical matters ; discretion forbids me to name him." English criticism itself was led astray and attributed at first the work to Swift.

Young authors, said the Abbé, for the choice of a subject, " take simply any tragedy you like of Corneille's or of Racine's ; change its title and the names of the personages ; call Bajazet, the Sultana ; Iphigénie, the

---

[1] "Lettres de M. l'abbé Le Blanc . . . Nouvelle édition de celles qui ont paru sous le titre de Lettres d'un François," Amsterdam, 1751, 3 vols., vol. iii., pp. 145, ff. In this new edition Le Blanc declares himself the author of the " Supplément." The " Lettres d'un François" had appeared at the Hague, 1745, 3 vols.

Victim"[1] (as La Fosse had done for his "Manlius," taken from "Venice Preserved": for there was reciprocity, and both countries had their pirates), but be careful to alter the style : "You can let the first act subsist just as it is in your original, without adding to it anything of your invention ; but as the French are content to be natural in their stories, and as they are too simple for us, you must not fail to swell your voice and use as turgid a style as you can. You will go to Shakespeare and take from him as many strong and bold epithets as you need, that is, on an average, two in each line. French verses are bad models, they are cold enough to freeze us ; ours, on the contrary, are like thunder, they have its fire, its roar and glare."

The number of characters should be increased in order to secure greater intricacy of plot ; mingle tears with laughter, verse with prose, people of the street with people of the court : "You will introduce in your play two or three personages of your invention to double the intrigue and thicken the coils of the chief action, always too simple with French authors. . . . These personages will arouse all the more curiosity inasmuch as no one will know where they come from or what they are driving at." One of them must be a comic character, that is the way to break the monotony of a play ; thus you can walk happily, "with a buskin on one foot and a sock on the other. . . . Shakespeare ever did so."

In the second act, some striking sight should be offered : " It would not be bad to finish that act by a

---

[1] An allusion to Charles Johnson's tragedies adapted from Racine.

night scene ; then it is that wonders in the heavens are most effective and that ghosts inspire most terror. . . . If you treat a subject as terrible as the avenging of Laius's murder, do not withhold from sight, as the French do, what is most pathetic in this play ; but expose to view the touching picture of the plague. Verses can give but a feeble idea of it. You will try to render all its horror by strewing the stage with dead bodies, and showing almost inanimate figures scarcely able to walk, who augment at every moment the number of the corpses. . . . Here is one of those grand scenes which exist in nature and which the French would not have wit enough to imagine. . . ."

"The fourth act, according to all probability, for want of action will lack warmth in your original. To give it some, try to introduce one or two battles in it ; model them on Shakespeare's memorable battle of Agincourt, the pattern of all battles on the English theatre. . . . Then darken your stage, represent wonders in the air, a sky of blood, two suns, aerial spirits fighting together. . . . Now make a spectre in a bloody shirt emerge from the ground ; the dead of the last battles will furnish you with half a dozen subaltern shades to serve as a *cortège* to it. For the politeness with which spectres wish to be treated, when it is necessary to make them explain the reasons for their apparition, consult Shakespeare ; no man has known better how to talk to ghosts ;"—an obvious allusion to the reverential address of Prince Hamlet to the Royal Dane, his father : "Ha, ha, boy ! say'st thou so? art thou there, truepenny ? . . . Well said, old mole."

If the heroine has lost her hero, you will draw from this mishap the most charming effects : " It is natural that the excess of her grief should derange her reason ; in that case, you will make her come back on the stage, crazy, dressed as a shepherdess, or in undress, just as you like. Make her dance and sing as long as you think fit. We owe this happy invention to Shakespeare." Corneille was wrong not to make Camille go mad : " What can be more interesting than to see a young and beautiful person whom grief has bereft of reason, and who can neither laugh without making us weep, nor weep without making us laugh ? "

Finally one must think of the catastrophe ; it is there especially that the French model must be improved upon : " You will speak more against kings for whom the French entertain too much respect ; add a satire against the ministers, a tirade on the laws, two words upon religion and a long eulogy on the English Government. When your personages shall have nothing more to say, make them all kill each other ; but in order to observe theatrical decency, which wills that virtue should be treated differently from crime, make the most guilty perish first."

Throughout his discourse Le Blanc shows a dramatic erudition astonishing for the period ; he knows every author, from the greatest to the least, from Shakespeare to Cibber ; he has read their prologues, epilogues, and prefaces ; many of his ironical directions are translated, word for word, from prefaces by Dryden, who had given the same advice in earnest. From tragedy the Abbé passes on to comedy : Molière is flat, it is necessary to flavour his characters and exhibit also some striking sights : for instance, "an abandoned woman in her bed and a libertine in his shirt," who falls "through a trap-door into a cesspool, from which he emerges a moment after, all covered with filth;" this is how an author behaves who knows his trade. Such plays are sure to draw large audiences; they have a great moral value, as they teach young men "to beware of bad women."[1]

MICHEL DE CUBIÈRES-PALMEZEAUX.
By Denon, 1785.

War of this same sort, that is, war "pour rire" and not war to the death, is waged again on Shakespeare by

[1] Le Blanc refers his readers to the comedy of "The Rover" (by Mrs. Behn : "The Rover or the banisht Cavaliers," 1677, several editions in the seventeenth and eighteenth centuries ; scene between Blunt, "an English country gentleman," who reappears, "his face, &c., all dirty," and Lucetta, "a jilting wench," act iii. In spite of such coarseness, a very favourable judgment is passed on this comedy,

the Chevalier de Cubières-Palmezeaux later on in the century. He, too, wants only to amuse, and writes in a tone of banter. Time, however, has played some of its tricks on him, and several of the theories which he puts, ironically, in the mouth of his ridiculous Prousas, have since enjoyed the widest popularity.

Cubières had been struck by the increasing gloom of the French stage : people went to the theatre, even to Voltaire's plays, even to the performance of comedies, to weep. Few women had, like Poinsinet's Araminta, the courage to stay at home and speak out what they thought : "No, sir, certainly not ; you will not see me there" (at Voltaire's "Mérope"). "Do not presume that you will catch me at your lamentable tragedies. Why, fie ! a woman only comes away from that sight, her eyes swollen with tears and her heart with sighs. I have found sometimes that there remained on my face and in my soul, after such plays, an impression of sadness that all the vivacity of the nicest supper could not dispel." [1]

For the "bourgeois," "tearful," or "serious" attempts of Sedaine, Diderot, or Beaumarchais, Cubières still has some indulgence : "I have seen you," he writes in his "Lettre à une femme sensible," [2] "often

full of an "infinite deal of sprightliness," by the "Companion to the Play House," 1764). Several plays by Mrs. Behn, Mrs. Centlivre, and other English authoresses, were translated into French in the eighteenth century. See the "Parnasse des Dames, contenant le théâtre des femmes Françaises, Anglaises, Allemandes et Danoises," Paris, 1777, ff.

[1] "Le Cercle ou la Soirée à la mode," performed in 1764.
[2] "La Manie des Drames sombres, comédie en trois actes, en vers, représentée à Fontainebleau, devant Leurs Majestés, par les

weep at the performances of the 'Père de famille,' of the 'Philosophe sans le savoir,' of 'Eugénie.' . . . I have myself wept by your side." What he condemns are " those sepulchral farces where, to employ an expression of M. de Voltaire's, skulls are used to play bowls with, where gravediggers make silly jokes on ancestral skulls ; where spectres, and ghosts still shrouded in their palls, come forth to address pathetic remarks to the bystanders, where the most abundant use is made of scaffolds, coffins, gallows, poisoned cups, and a thousand other puerile means of terror." It is indeed against Shakespeare that Cubières goes forth to war. He had his play performed on the 29th of October, 1776, " at Fontainbleau, before their Majesties, by the French comedians," a tardy answer to those English actors who had played in the same hall of the same palace their bloody dramas before Henri IV. and his son : " Tiph Toph Milord ! "

At Fontainebleau, Cubières had given only a first abridged sketch of his comedy, and he had not

comédiens françois sous le nom du Dramaturge, le 29 Octobre, 1776," Paris, 1777, 8º ; preceded by a " Lettre à une femme sensible." In the "Almanack des Spectacles de Paris" the play is quoted under the title of the "Dramomane," 1777. The "Année Littéraire " praised it most highly ; it spoke of "dramaturges " and of "dramomanie" with the same contempt as the classicists did in the days of Hugo, and congratulated Cubières, who sought to " dissiper ces vapeurs sombres répandues sur le caractère national," 1778, p. 270. The "Année Littéraire" was continued then by Fréron the son, the future member of the Convention. Against the "dramaturgie" à l'anglaise, see also Saurin, "L'Anglomane," sc. xii., and Palissot, "Dunciade," 1764, i. and ii. Shall I see at last, says " la Sottise,"

" Phèdre et Tartufe et Chimène
Ensevelis sous mes drames anglais ! "

obtained great success. One of his friends, who was present at the performance, M. Le Roz, a clerk at the War Office, published an account of it in the "Journal Français, Italien et Anglais." He informs us that the first scenes were much applauded: "The other scenes were not heard because of the multitudinous coughs and sneezes in the pit, where, as it seems, colds abounded on that day."[1] But the true reason was that the court, who held for La Chaussée and the larmoyants, had not very well understood what Cubières was driving at, or whom he meant to ridicule. Hence the care taken by the chevalier, when he published his play, remodelled and divided into three acts (instead of one), to explain clearly to the "femme sensible" and to the public his real intentions.

Cubières draws the picture of a ridiculous dramatist called Prousas, who has the mania of writing lugubrious plays, in prose, and whose views on æsthetics are so dear to his heart that he will give his daughter only to a son-in-law who shares his ideal. Hence a struggle between Sainfort, a true gentleman and a loyal mind, who admires the young girl and Racine; and Sombreuses, who pretends to love the lady and tearful dramas, but who is a vile hypocrite and, at heart, cares only for money. The friends of the drama are painted very black indeed in this play.

Prousas, when it opens, talks with Cornet, his secretary, whose task consists in going through the news-

---

[1] August, 1777. La Harpe gives an even less flattering account in his "Correspondance littéraire adressée au Grand Duc de Russie," afterwards Paul I. (Paris, 1801, letter 56), but he was not present at the performance, and he hated Cubières.

papers in order to find dark and vulgar crimes which might furnish subjects for plays. Has he made any good find?

"*Cornet.* Alas! no : there are only comical stories in them.
Prousas. Such paucity confounds me. What? nothing remarkable under the rubric : 'London'? And yet the English. . . .
Cornet. Alas! Those poor folks have degenerated very much of late."[1]

They only occupy themselves with politics; they have ceased to be disgusted with life and to hang themselves.

"*Prousas.* And the rubric : 'Paris'?
Cornet. What can you be thinking of? It is less fertile in accidents than any other; the Frenchman lives in the midst of pleasures and amusements. Do you expect people to kill themselves when they are happy?
Prousas. What! not even a little suicide?
Cornet. Not the least.
Prousas. So much the worse. Some fine parricide would have been most welcome. No rape, no murder?
Cornet. Not even a theft.
Prousas. Times are very bad.
Cornet. Formerly, for their mistresses who did not give them tenderness for tenderness, lovers killed themselves, and jealous

---

[1] "*Cornet.* Hélas non, on n'y voit que des contes plaisants.
Prousas. Une telle disette a lieu de me confondre.
    Quoi! rien de remarquable à l'article de Londres? Les Anglais cependant. . . .
Cornet.   Hélas! les pauvres gens
    Ont bien dégénéré depuis un certain temps.
Prousas. Qu'est-ce à dire?
Cornet.   Ah! monsieur, l'altière Politique
    Remplace tout à fait leur manière héroïque.
    Tous, des crimes bourgeois viennent de se lasser;
    Aucun d'eux ne se tue, ils aiment mieux penser."

husbands, skulking around their homes like wolves, more than once, giving way to their dark frenzy, cut to pieces their better halves; but all is changed. Morals make frightful progress, everything degenerates in these unlucky days; husbands and lovers are equally placid." [1]

A scene takes place between Sainfort—the upright man, friendly to Racine, alexandrines, and regular tragedies—and Prousas, who defends his favourite ideas; ideas which have since met with a success that Cubières little anticipated. There especially we see his irony turn against him; he wanted to make Prousas ridiculous; time has avenged Prousas, as well as Amidor, the *Visionnaire* derided of old by Saint Sorlin, and nothing better shows the change which has

[1] "*Prousas.* Et l'article Paris ?
  Cornet.   Quelle idée est la vôtre ?
        Il est en accidents moins fertile qu'un autre :
        Le Français vit au sein des plaisirs et des jeux.
        Voulez-vous qu'on se tue alors qu'on est heureux ?
  Prousas. Eh quoi ! pas seulement un petit suicide ?
  Cornet. Pas le moindre.
  Prousas.   Tant pis. Quelque beau parricide
        M'aurait fait grand plaisir. Point de rapt, point de viol,
        Pas un assassinat ?
  Cornet.   Pas seulement un vol.
  Prousas. Les temps sont bien mauvais.
  Cornet.   Jadis, pour leurs maîtresses,
        Qui ne leur rendaient pas tendresses pour tendresses,
        Les amants se tuaient, et les maris jaloux,
        Autour de leur logis, rôdant comme des loups,
        Plus d'une fois, suivant leur noire frénésie,
        D'immoler leurs moitiés avaient la fantaisie ;
        Tout est changé. Les mœurs font des progrès affreux,
        Tout dégénère enfin dans ces temps malheureux ;
        Autant que les amants les maris sont paisibles."

come about than this prodigious and almost incredible shifting of views :—

> "*Sainfort.* So, then, each object that strikes your eye will furnish you with the theme for a serious drama? Everything will seem good to you?
> *Prousas.* Yes, despising protests, I shall go and seek my heroes on the market-place; and if any one finds fault, I shall do more, and carry my pencils even into hospitals.
> *Sainfort.* That will be touching!
> *Prousas.* How blind we are! The poor, my dear sir, are they not *men*? Why should we abstain from depicting those good folks? Nothing in this world is vile save the wicked!"[1]

People laughed at these words in 1776; this scene was judged "amusing by the mere unfolding of the principles of dramaturgy, which it suffices to state in order to excite laughter.[2] Sainfort, the upright man, shrugs his shoulders; no doubt, he says, "men of the people are respectable," but why depict their manners or their faults? "The faults of a clown can correct no one; those of sovereigns serve as lessons to us. The learned nurslings of the chaste sisters should, therefore,

---

[1] "*Sainfort.* Ainsi donc, chaque objet qui frappera vos yeux
    Vous prêtera le fond d'un drame sérieux?
    Tout vous paraîtra bon?
Prousas.   Oui, bravant le scandale,
    Je veux aller chercher mes héros à la halle;
    Et si l'on me chicane, armé de mes pinceaux,
    Je ferai plus; j'irai jusqu'en des hôpitaux.
Sainfort. Cela sera touchant!
Prousas.   Aveugles que nous sommes!
    Et les pauvres, monsieur, ne sont-ils pas des hommes?
    Pourquoi n'oserait-on peindre ces bonnes gens?
    Il n'est rien ici-bas de vil que les méchants!"

[2] "Année Litt.," 1778, p. 262. Cf. "Les Visionnaires," above, p. 97.

to their exquisite lutes and on our brilliant stages, sing of princes rather than shepherds.

"*Prousas.* Let them sing, let them ; I cannot do as much. But the kings of yore, those you are so pleased with, when they wanted to say, I love you, did they use grandiloquence ? Had they the art of stitching to the end of each phrase a rhyme and the boredom of those double refrains ? Did they address their servants in alexandrine verse ? Did they follow your silly methods in everything, and did they make love as one makes an ode ? "[1]

Prousas holds good. The arrival of Sombreuses is announced ; Sainfort's affairs are in a bad way. Encouraged by the mocking Dorimène, sister to Prousas, he feigns a conversion. Dorimène does the same : "We are cured of those old prejudices which made us admire Regnard and Molière ; the stage must be turned into a graveyard, Thalia shall wear crape and place a dagger in the hands of the loves."

Sainfort follows in her wake : "If people listened to me, that pitiful Bajazet would be sent back to the

---

[1] "*Sainfort.* Les fautes d'un manant ne corrigent personne ;
Celles des souverains nous servent de leçons.
Ainsi des chastes sœurs les doctes nourrissons,
Sur leurs luths ravissants, sur nos brillants théâtres,
Doivent plutôt chanter des princes que des pâtres.

Prousas. Qu'ils chantent, c'est fort bien ; je n'en puis faire autant.
Mais les rois d'autrefois, ceux qui vous plaisent tant,
Pour dire : Je vous aime, employaient ils l'emphase ?
Avaient-ils l'art de coudre, au bout de chaque phrase,
Une rime et l'ennui de ces doubles refrains ?
Parlaient-ils à leurs gens en vers alexandrins ?
Ne suivaient-ils en tout qu'une sotte méthode
Et faisaient-ils l'amour comme l'on fait une ode ?

Turks, and our dramatic authors, disciples of Young, would turn all his Nights into comic operas."[1] If the "Night Thoughts" were not exactly turned into comic operas, they were, in fact, as Madame Riccoboni had noticed, none the less popular. They were several times translated; Colardeau began a translation in verse, and "Young's Cave" was thought a fit object to adorn such a place as the beautiful park "à l'anglaise" of Count d'Albon, at Franconville.[2]

Sombreuses appears at last, as late in the play as Tartufe in Molière's comedy. He is in mourning from head to foot: "He looks like the ghost in a famous English drama":—

> "Il ressemble au fantôme
> D'un fameux drame anglois."

He has gone into black because one of his travelling companions has been killed by brigands :—

---

[1] "*Derimène.* Nous sommes revenus de ces vieux préjugés
  Qui nous faisaient aimer et Regnard et Molière,
  Il faut que de la scène on fasse un cimetière,
  Que d'un crêpe Thalie enlace ses atours,
  Qu'elle mette un poignard dans la main des Amours.
Sainfort. . . . Si l'on me croyait
  On renverrait aux Turcs leur triste Bajazet,
  Et, disciples d'Young, nos auteurs dramatiques
  Mettraient toutes ses Nuits en opéras comiques."

[2] Le Tourneur's translation, in prose, enjoyed a wide popularity (queer, romantic frontispiece). Colardeau translated into verse, very freely, the two first Nights :—

> "Toi, le dieu du repos et que l'ombre environne,
> Sommeil, viens m'assoupir . . ."

He adapted also Pope's "Epistle from Eloisa."

"*Prousas.* Was he related to you?
Sombreuses. No, but his title of man had made him my brother."

Sainfort's chances lessen every moment, in spite of his pretended conversion. Sombreuses praises Prousas' dramas that his father has had performed in Lyons :—

"In the temple of memory, your pictures are all engraved *à la manière noire.*
Prousas. That is the right hue; Albano lived but a few days; Rembrandt's touch will charm us ever.
Sombreuses. An English coal stands you in lieu of pen.
Dorimène. Yes, but his coal never takes fire."

Sombreuses is unmasked at last by some means or other, unlikely and awkward, and Sainfort marries Sophie; we may be sure there will not be many Rembrandts in their drawing-room.

Thus, before Louis XVI. and Marie-Antoinette, in the presence of the assembled court, spoke the Chevalier Michel de Cubières de Palmezeaux, younger brother of the Marquis de Cubières. He derided sombre dramas; he depicted the French living "in the midst of pleasures and amusements," and unable to take interest in anything save the adventures of kings. He little thought then that he should see dramas enacted more sombre than those of Prousas, that he, Cubières, should one day be "secrétaire-greffier" to the Commune, sign wine tickets for the slaughterers at the Abbaye, on the 2nd and 3rd of September, 1792, and live long enough to sing the Eighteenth Brumaire, Marengo, and the return of the Bourbons. He was able, between whiles, to dedicate "to her Imperial Highness Stéphanie Napoléon, now Electoral Princess of Baden," daughter

YOUNG'S CAVE, IN COUNT D'ALBON'S "PARC À L'ANGLAISE," AT FRANCONVILLE. SECOND HALF OF THE EIGHTEENTH CENTURY.

by adoption to "the greatest prince in the universe," a "Roméo et Juliette, tragédie lyrique," wherein he declared that "Juliet is the masterpiece of nature," and, heedless of the sombreness of the catastrophe, offered at the end the spectacle of Romeo dying in frightful contortions from the effects of a "subtile poison." The stage is planted with "cypresses and other funereal trees;" the "tune of a lugubrious march is heard;" Juliet "speaks in a weak and lugubrious voice. . . . The effect of the poison is rendered by Romeo with the verity of nature; he bows himself, stands erect again and presses his hands to his suffering bosom; from time to time cries of agony escape him."[1] Cubières, who had made his peace successively with the people, with emperors and with kings, had also made his peace with Shakespeare.

[1] "Roméo et Juliette, tragédie lyrique," by Moline and Cubières, Paris, 1806, 8º. See among other works by the same, "Les deux centenaires de Corneille, pièces en un acte et en vers, par M. le Chevalier de Cubières, de l'Académie de Lyon," Paris, 1785, 8º. Cubières advocated in it the same ideas as in his "Manie des drames sombres"; he showed False Taste promoting the emancipation of the tragic Muse :—

"*Le Faux Goût.* Point d'unités ! bravo ! C'est ce que j'aime.
  Où se passe l'acte premier ?
L'Auteur tragique. Dans le sénat romain.
Le Faux Goût. Le second ?
L'Auteur tragique. A la Chine.
Le Faux Goût. Le troisième ?
L'Auteur tragique. Au sérail ; c'est le plus régulier.
Le Faux Goût. Le quatrième ?
L'Auteur tragique. A Sparte, au Japon le dernier."

There are five intrigues instead of one, and the work is, of course, in prose.

III.

"For several years past, the most perfect harmony, the most touching union, reigned between France and England; never had there subsisted, between two neighbouring and rival nations, a more flourishing commerce of ridicules, fashions, and tastes. If our swords, our carriages, our gardens are 'à l'anglaise,' all Great Britain is no less fond of our feathers, our top-knots, and our trinkets of every kind. . . . Thus, little by little, disappear those barbarous prejudices which prevent nations from instructing and civilizing one another.

"We see, with great bitterness and sorrow, that a harmony so desired and so precious is in great danger of being troubled, and of being troubled by a circumstance which seemed calculated to augment it still more; it is the unfortunate translation of Shakespeare which has just raised this storm. M. de Voltaire, although he doubtless had more reason than any one else to love the glory of this great man, could not learn, without indignation, that the French had had the weakness to sacrifice to this foreign idol the immortal wreaths of Corneille and Racine. His patriotic resentment has already burst forth, in the liveliest manner, in a letter to M. le Comte d'Argental.[1] . . . He has now appealed to the justice of the French Academy itself. Must not this step be regarded as a declaration of war in due form? It is difficult to

---

[1] Infra, p. 375. The letter was a manifesto, written to be shown. La Harpe sends a copy of it to the Grand Duke of Russia: "Correspondance littéraire adressée au Grand Duc;" letter 51.

PIERRE FÉLICIEN LE TOURNEUR.
By Pujos, from life, 1787.

foresee its consequences, but they cannot fail to be
extremely serious. We know the entire English
nation idolatrously worships Shakespeare's genius.
Will it allow the French Academy to quietly discuss
the title deeds of that worship? Will it recognise the
competence of these foreign judges? Will it not try
to secure adherents among our own literary men? Can
one forget how much wrath, hatred, and fury quarrels
of that kind, and for causes far less interesting, have
produced?" Thus reads the "Correspondance littéraire"
of Grimm and Diderot in July, 1776.

It was, indeed, no longer a matter of skirmishes nor
of make-believe war. Real war was beginning and
had been declared in "due form." All the troops
were out, and old Marshal Voltaire had taken the
command of them. The cause of the quarrel was
an intolerable encroachment of Shakespeare's.

Hitherto he had preserved an attitude modest
enough; he had been translated, but incompletely;
many of his plays had been only analyzed by La
Place, besides which the latter's undertaking was a
private work which had nothing to do with the public
powers. In 1776, the Comte de Catuelan, Le Tourneur, and Fontaine-Malherbe, announced a complete
translation of the works of Shakespeare.[1] The
announcement made a great stir; the young king,

---

[1] "Shakespeare traduit de l'anglois," Paris, 1776, ff. 20 vols., 4º.
The work was due especially to Le Tourneur; his name appears
on the title page from vol. iii.; it was very superior to La Place's
work, although far from attaining the scrupulous exactness which
is required in our day. Even then, a few liberties attracted attention and were censured. There is no doubt that the "Journal de

anxious to please everybody, not forgetting even De Belloy, whom he had just made a present to,[1] accepted the dedication of the work, which was published by subscription, as Voltaire's "Henriade" had been, and more lately his "Théâtre de Corneille avec des Commentaires." A series of engravings, under separate covers, were to accompany the new Shakespeare. The artist selected was "M. Moreau, whose name needs no praise," but whose zeal needed encouragement, and who never got beyond a single plate representing the "Tempest." At the beginning

politique et de littérature" (June 5, 1778) could think with some reason that the vague lyricism of Iago's song in Le Tourneur :—

"Dans la bassesse où tu respires,
N'affecte point l'orgueil d'un vêtement nouveau," &c.,

was but an indifferent rendering of the English original :—

"King Stephen was a worthy peer ;
His breeches cost him but a crown. . . ."

On Le Tourneur's translation, see M. Beljame's (very severe) appreciations, "Macbeth, texte critique," Introduction, Paris, 1897. Since the French edition of the present book was issued, M. Beljame wrote to its author : "Je ne crois pas avoir été sévère pour Le Tourneur. Peut-on l'être, d'ailleurs, pour un homme qui attribue à Shakespeare des phrases comme celle-ci : 'Déterminé comme un rat sans queue ?' Il n'y a pas à être sévère, il n'y a qu'à le citer. Et il a bien d'autres méfaits sur la conscience" (December 29, 1898). No doubt he has. But can it be contested that all a man needs, to deserve indulgence, nay gratitude, is to have improved, not at all upon the men who came after him, but upon those who came before ? This, Le Tourneur did, and, for all his blunders he nevertheless deserves, as I think, some indulgence and gratitude.

[1] Ducis to Sedaine, January 25, 1775.

of the first volume figured a list of subscribers ; it included the King, the Queen, Monseigneur le Comte d'Artois, the princesses of the House of France, Monseigneur le Prince de Condé, the King of England, "Sa Majesté l'Impératrice de toutes les Russies," followed by a quantity of celebrities : the Comte d'Argental (Voltaire's friend), the Duc de Choiseul, " M. Turgot, Ministre d'État," the Comte de Vergennes, " M. Necker, Ministre de la République de Genève," " M. le Chevalier de Cubières de Palmezeaux," Diderot, Ducis, Garrick, d'Holbach, Mercier, " six English gentlemen, lovers of old Shakespeare " (in English in Le Tourneur's list), Russians, Germans, Spaniards, Dutchmen, princes and commoners, secretaries of embassy, consuls, comedians ; the most famous names in France and abroad : the new Shakespeare was a European event.

In their epistle to Louis XVI. the authors expatiated on the greatness and originality of Shakespeare's genius, and displayed an enthusiasm unknown till then : "Never did a man of genius penetrate more deeply into the abysses of the human heart, or make passions better speak the language of nature. Prolific as nature herself, he endowed his innumerable personages with that astonishing variety of character which she dispenses to the individuals she creates. Born in a low condition and in a yet barbarous age, he had only nature before him. He divined that she was the model he must follow, and that the great secret of dramatic art consisted in creating on the stage men resembling in every respect those modelled by her hands." He thought he might paint men of the people after men of the Court ;

he interested himself in "humanity" long before the days of eighteenth century philosophers. Leaving palaces and "descending to the poor man's hut, he saw humanity there and did not disdain to depict it in the lower classes. He painted nature wherever he found her and disclosed all the recesses of the human heart, busying himself with scenes in real life. These naïve and true pictures will not be without charm in the eyes of your Majesty, who is pleased to descend sometimes from the throne, in order to seek, under the humble roof of the ploughman or of the artisan, truth, nature, and objects for his benevolence. Should the philosopher and the man of letters be more disdainful than kings, and should they blush to descend to these lowest classes of society? No: it would be barbarity to hold one half of the human race to be but a vile scum unworthy of the pencil of genius and devoted to its scorn."

We may imitate the art of Louis XIV., but we cannot restore it to life; our copies are paler and paler: "Thus we are condemned to crouch before the great men who came before us. Herds branded with the name of imitators, we all belong to masters. Our thoughts, the aspirations of our soul, are chained, and this servitude, transmitted to our descendants, will perpetuate itself from age to age. . . ." Let us then try to react, and see if there exist no other means to move and to please; we can do it without neglecting the cult of our ancestors: "Shakespeare can appear with confidence in the country of Corneille, Racine and Molière, and demand of the French that tribute of glory which every nation owes to genius and which he would have received from those great men had he been known to them." Foreseeing, however, the storm that such an audacious enterprise could not fail to raise, Le Tourneur added: "You will not share these vain alarms, oh you, revered shades of our great dramatic poets. Freed from the prejudices and petty interests of our critics, sure of your immortality, you prefer the stranger who has known how to invent in your art, to the insipid incense, the cold copies of your servile imitators; and like the Romans, you behold the gods of other nations enter the Capitol, without fearing the desertion of your altars or any abatement in the worship due to the mother country."

All the eloquence of these appeals could not touch Voltaire, whose indignation had been growing for years and was ready to overflow. Had he not granted the monster enough? Had he not introduced certain liberties on to the French stage? Had he not ventured into those darksome foreign woods, pruning, trimming, and reducing them to regularity (forgetting what he had said himself about the wild trees that die if you try to force their nature and to trim them like the trees in the Marly gardens)? And now more still was wanted; not content with his displacement of the landmark, they objected to any landmark at all; his revolt was not enough, and a revolution was threatening.

Numerous symptoms had foreshadowed the event from the middle of the century. Imitations, intended for the stage, had multiplied; studies more and more minute and judgments more and more eulogistic upon Shakespeare and the English drama had come out.

Men of fashion, *esprits forts*, Counts de B* * * would now possess a Shakespeare, sometimes an English one, as Sterne once discovered, to his great advantage— ". . . And does the Count de B* * *, said I, read Shakespeare? . . . *C'est un esprit fort*, replied the bookseller"—and thanks to Shakespeare and to the Count's partiality for the great man, the traveller could at last, as everybody knows, secure the famous passport "directed to all lieutenant-governors, governors, and commandants of cities to let Mr. Yorick, the King's jester, and his baggage, travel quietly along." Festivities had been organised, a jubilee had been celebrated in honour of Shakespeare; it had been held in remote Stratford (September, 1769), but the noise of this unwonted solemnity had spread throughout Europe: "A festival worthy of ancient Athens," said Suard; and the "Journal Anglais" published in French prose: "'Shakespeare's Mulberry Tree,' a song sung at the festival of Shakespeare's jubilee by M. Garrick who held in his hand a cup made out of the wood of a mulberry tree planted by the poet." [1]

The echoes had sent the sound of applause as far as Ferney, and people were beginning to wonder whether it would not be well to do something, and follow, for national authors, the example given by Garrick in favour of his idol. Hence a "great stir (in Paris) among the amateurs of Apollo's divine art . . ." Efforts must be made to re-establish the equilibrium.

[1] "Le Mûrier de Shakespeare, chanson que M. Garrick chanta à la fête du Jubilé de Shakespeare, en tenant à la main une coupe faite du bois d'un mûrier que le poète avait planté."—"Journal Anglais," April 15, 1776.

VOLTAIRE'S STATUE.
By Pigalle, 1776. Preserved in the Library of the Institute, Paris.

"Men of letters suggest an immense rotunda ; fanatics propose a single column which should be dedicated to Voltaire. Some obstinate old things call that a sacrilege : What then of Corneille? they say ; where shall we put him, pray? The sceptics have ended the dispute ; let us do nothing, they said ; their sentiment has prevailed. We shall have, nevertheless, Voltaire's statue by subscription."[1] They had it, chiselled by Pigalle, who represented the great man as lean as nature made him and as nude as a Roman god.[2] But no column, no rotunda, no jubilee.

Shakespeare's festival was being renewed in a thousand different ways. Suard, soon after member of the French Academy, had inserted in his "Variétés littéraires,"[3] an "Essai historique sur l'origine et les

[1] Madame Riccoboni to Garrick, October 1, 1770.
[2] Begun at Ferney in June, 1770 ; finished in 1776 ; it is now in the library of the Institute in Paris. The skin is almost transparent ; the skull and skeleton are visible. When Voltaire's tomb was opened in 1897, M. Berthelot noticed the exactness of Pigalle's chisel. The head alone, however, was modelled from nature, and not without difficulty, as Voltaire would not keep quiet, dictated letters to his secretary while sitting, and made faces, "grimaces mortelles pour le statuaire." The body was copied from an old soldier whose build had the greatest similitude to Voltaire's. "Après avoir cherché la tête du patriarche à Ferney, il a pris ici un vieux soldat sur lequel il a modelé sa statue avec une vérité surprenante, mais qui paraît hideuse à la plupart de nos juges. Leur délicatesse, qui est vraiment nationale, est blessée de tout ce qui est prononcé en quelque genre que ce soit."—"Correspondance Littéraire de Grimm, Diderot," &c., ed. Tourneux ix., 285 (April, 1771).
[3] "Ou recueil de pièces tant originales que traduites," Paris, 1768, 4 vols.

progrès du drame Anglais," containing details even on the obscure predecessors of the great man, on Mysteries, Moralities, Interludes, on l'"Éguille de Dame Gurton" ("Gammer Gurton's Needle"), "Gorboduc" and the dramas of Euphuistic Lyly. He had given, in the same collection, some "Observations sur Shakespeare," translated from Dr. Johnson:[1] he thus contributed to the glory of Shakespeare, whom he himself, however, judged very severely.[2] All the dictionaries and encyclopædias now contained flattering notices: Bayle's Dictionary, formerly silent, informed its readers, in its "Supplément," that Shakespeare's characters are so exactly nature itself that it is a kind of insult to give them so distant a qualification as that of copies of nature.[3] The Encyclopædia of Diderot, d'Alembert, and Voltaire himself recurred constantly to Shakespeare under the words Genius, Stratford, Tragedy, &c., and in these two last articles, written by the Chevalier de Jaucourt, the dramatist was compared "to the stone, set in Pyrrhus's ring, which, according to Pliny, repre-

[1] "Observations sur Shakespeare, tirées de la préface que M. S. Johnson a mise en tête d'une nouvelle édition des œuvres de ce poète."

[2] "Je voulus faire un morceau sur [Shakespeare] et je me suis mis à le relire ; mais je fus si épouvanté des extravagances et des puérilités qui défiguraient les plus belles choses que la plume me tomba des mains." To Garrick, 1776, Corresp., II., 471. Same severity, but same preoccupation of the great man in La Harpe, very hard on Le Tourneur, "Corresp. litt. avec le Grand Duc," 1801, I., 345.

[3] "Nouveau Dictionnaire historique . . . pour servir de Supplément au Dictionnaire de Bayle," by J. G. de Chaufepié, Amsterdam, 1750, ff. *Sub verbo* Shakespeare, vol. iv., 1756 ; the article (translated from the English) fills ten folio pages.

sented, in the veins which nature had traced in it without any help from art, the figure of Apollo with the nine muses." Marmontel made doctoral reserves, but he too was taken with vertigo and gave way to the attraction of the abyss.[1] Mercier went to the verge of idolatry in his book, " Du Théâtre ou nouvel essai sur l'art dramatique."[2] He had the audacity to take up La Motte's theories, to strengthen them, to add to them, to carry them so far as to make them blasphemous; and honest De Belloy, who, since the success of the "Siège de Calais," thought himself a poet, cried louder than Voltaire : " La Motte rises again from his ashes, he is a hydra that it is almost impossible to destroy ! . . . La Motte is reproduced in a crowd of sectators whose credit augments every day."[3]

Mercier declared himself a partisan of prose, of the mingling of the comic with the tragic, of the rabble, and of Shakespeare : " Our superb tragedy, so highly praised, is only a phantom clothed in purple and gold, but with no life in it. . . . Our haughty poets have been guilty of widening still more the inhuman distances that we have placed between fellow citizens. He should rather lessen them, but he would have

---

[1] " Shakespeare a un mérite réel et transcendant qui frappe tout le monde. Il est tragique, il touche, il émeut fortement. Ce n'est pas cette pitié douce qui pénètre insensiblement . . . c'est une terreur sombre, une douleur profonde . . ."—" Chefs-d'œuvre dramatiques," Paris, 1773, dedicated to Marie-Antoinette, then dauphiness ; superb engravings.
[2] Amsterdam, 1773, 8º.
[3] " Traité de la Tragédie " (" Œuvres," 1779, vol. vi.).

thought himself a man of the people if he had
condescended to write for the people; he has been
punished by failing really to understand Nature."
Our art has been cramped in too narrow a field:
"They have taken a vein for the whole mine, and they
have tried to make believe the mine was exhausted,
whereas it has immense ramifications." People laugh
at the drama, they are wrong; it is the style that best
suits the stage; Corneille has the merit of having
written a drama—the "Cid." Mercier's work did not
pass unperceived, quite the contrary; it was greatly
discussed, for in it might be found, it was said, "some
strong and true ideas, a great love of humanity," that
love which had become a fashion, "some of those
general and exaggerated maxims that fire the enthusiasm of youths, and would make them run to the
world's end, and abandon father, mother, brother, to
come to the assistance of an Esquimau or a Hotten-
tot." [1]

Diderot also, Diderot the encyclopædist, Diderot the
friend of Voltaire, already told every one he came across
and was soon to write to Tronchin, another friend
of Voltaire's, and who was preparing a "Catilina":
"Ah! sir, that Shakespeare was a terrible mortal; he
is not the antique gladiator, nor the Apollo Belvedere,
but he is the shapeless and rough-hewn colossus of
Notre Dame (St. Christopher)—a Gothic colossus, but
between whose legs we could all pass." [2]—*All?*

---

[1] "Correspondance Littéraire de Grimm, Diderot," &c., ed. Tourneux, July, 1774, vol. x., p. 463.

[2] December 18, 1776. H. Tronchin, "Le Conseiller François
Tronchin," Paris, 1895, 8º, p. 227. Diderot would have liked

thought Voltaire, and his indignation waxed. He expressed it of course in the name of Racine and Corneille. Discord was in Agramant's camp.

The state of mind of the Ferney hermit had already been made apparent in the " Appel à toutes les Nations de l'Europe," [1] published in 1761, and in several essays, various skirmishes, and a quantity of letters : skirmishes with Mrs. Elizabeth Montagu, " la Shakespearienne," the friend of Hannah More and of Dr. Johnson, who regretted as early as 1755, that she could not " burn Voltaire and his tragedy " (the " Orphelin de la Chine "),[2] but who had to content herself with a vengeance less complete ; skirmish with Walpole, who, being a dilettante, chose to praise " Athalie " and " Hamlet " in turn ; but had made fun of Voltaire very freely in the second preface to his " Castle of Otranto "—an unlucky preface for Shakespeare himself, as Walpole made him responsible for the style of his novel, and even Voltaire's diatribes contain no worse abuse. Voltaire replied, this time,

Tronchin to give the crowd a place in his "Catilina," to insert some of those little scenes which at first render the spectator anxious and then carry him away ; in a word, to derive inspiration from the example of Shakespeare.

[1] Reprinted in 1764 under the title " Du Théâtre Anglais," by Jérôme Carré (Voltaire replies in it to two articles of the " Journal Encyclopédique," of October 15 and November 1, 1760. Bengesco, " Bibliographie," ii. p. 96).

[2] Letter to her sister, Mrs. Scott, November 18, 1755, " Letters of Mrs. Elizabeth Montagu," London, 1810, 4 vols., 8º, 3rd ed. Her reply to Voltaire appeared in 1769 : "An Essay on the writings and genius of Shakespear compared with the Greek and French dramatic poets, with some remarks upon the misrepresentations of M. de Voltaire " ; 6th edition in 1810.

with perfect good grace,[1] "for one follows the rules of courtesy when fighting against captains who are men of honour."[2]

But real war, without mercy, was certain, inevitable, and already, on the occasion of this very incident, Voltaire was writing to the Duchesse de Choiseul : " The wife of the protector is protectress ; the wife of the minister of France can take sides with the French against the English with whom I am at war. Deign to judge, Madame, between M. Walpole and me. . . . You will think me very bold, but you will forgive an old soldier who is fighting for his country, and who, if he displays any taste, will have fought under your colours."[3]

The time for caution and reserve is passed. Shakespeare is henceforth, to Voltaire, a maniac, a buffoon, a grotesque ; he is Gille of the fair : "Gille, in a country fair, would express himself with more decency and nobleness than Prince Hamlet." What is Gille ? for since the palmy days of the "Théâtre de la Foire," the personage has lost a little of his reputation. Voltaire has defined him incidentally : " France," he writes to Baron de Constant, " is beginning to imitate your Swiss government. Some care is taken of the people, the corvées are being abolished : every one cries Hosanna ! For myself, I am like silly Gille, who performs his little tricks six inches from the ground while rope dancers tread the middle region of

---

[1] To Walpole, Ferney, July 15, 1768.
[2] To Madame du Deffand, *à propos* of this incident, July 30, 1768.
[3] July 15, 1768.

SILLY GILLE.
From an eighteenth century plate.

the air. I have the vanity to finish my little town." [1] But usually Voltaire does not apply this name to himself; he reserves it for everything he hates; he sticks it on " that Gille called Piron." As for Gille-Shakespeare, to show what he is worth, he translates "nearly line for line and very exactly," in his " Lettre à un journaliste," the monologue, " O that this too solid flesh," and we find in it verses like these :—

> "Oh ! si l'Être éternel n'avait pas du canon
> Contre le suicide ! . . . ô ciel ! ô ciel ! ô ciel !"

Heaven's decrees are transformed into pieces of ordnance in Voltaire's "very exact" translation.[2] On a judge thus disposed, full of glory, but jealous of the glory of all others, living or dead, equally hard on Euripides, Corneille, Petrarch and Milton, we may readily imagine the effect produced, after the jubilee, by the announcement of an integral translation of Shakespeare, dedicated to the king, honoured with the subscription of all the princes, the lettered and the

---

[1] To the Baron de Constant, August 9, 1775. He refers to Ferney, which is getting to be " une ville singulière et assez jolie."

[2] Walpole translates with the same facetious inaccuracy two lines of Racine's :—

> " De son appartement cette porte est prochaine
> Et cette autre conduit dans celui de la reine,"

which become in his English :—

> " To Cæsar's closet through this door you come,
> And t'other leads to the queen's drawing-room."

Second preface to the " Castle of Otranto." See Voltaire's reply, July 15, 1768.

great of the earth, preceded by high-flown prefaces and sounding speeches. And from these speeches one might have inferred that the French stage was at that moment empty, and the list of great dramatists closed ; Corneille, Racine, and Molière were, it is true, placed on a pinnacle, but not a word was said about the men of the day : as if the century had not had " Zaïre," and as if the list did not include Voltaire. For Voltaire was not even mentioned : it was assuredly an injustice. The injustice appeared so monstrous to the party most concerned, that not finding his own name, it seemed to him he had found none at all, and in the polemics which followed he never ceased to reproach Le Tourneur with having not even mentioned Corneille and Racine.

The philosopher of Ferney was not accustomed to being thus passed over in silence ; he was at the height of his glory ; he was usually quoted on every subject ; he was praised, and in what strains ! "The ' Henriade' will be our Iliad, for, given equal talent, what comparison, may I say in my turn, can there be between the great Henri and the little Ulysses or the proud Agamemnon ? " This parallel was not drawn by any mean flatterer ; it was Buffon who thus expressed himself at a meeting of the Academy, when receiving the Maréchal de Duras, who was replacing De Belloy.[1] Many, and among those most qualified to judge, thought

---

[1] " La Henriade sera notre Iliade ; car, à talent égal, quelle comparaison, dirai-je à mon tour, entre le bon et grand Henri et le petit Ulysse ou le fier Agamemnon." May 15, 1775, " Recueil des harangues prononcées par MM. de l'Académie Françoise," Paris, 1714, ff., vol. iii., p. 67.

like La Harpe, who said later in his " Cours de Littérature " : " I am very far from comparing to 'Sémiramis' a monster of a tragedy like Shakespeare's 'Hamlet.' " And a smearer of paper, a nobody, a Pierrot of the fair, a Le Tourneur, dared to bring Gille-Shakespeare to court and to talk about dramatic art, without remembering that a Voltaire had been born! This was indeed, it must be observed, only one grievance the more, for in this indignation there was a great part of sincerity ; Voltaire took sides with Voltaire first, but he was also very sincerely for Racine against Shakespeare.

" Have you by any chance read," he writes from the first to d'Argental, " two volumes by that wretch (Le Tourneur) in which he tries to make us regard Shakespeare as the only model for real tragedy? There are already two volumes printed of that Shakespeare which seem a collection of plays meant for booths at the fair and written two hundred years ago. . . . There are not enough affronts, enough fool's caps, enough pillories in France for such a knave. . . . The worst of it is that the monster has a party in France, and, worse than the worst, I was myself the first to speak of this Shakespeare ; I was the first to show the French a few pearls that I had found in his enormous dunghill," July 19, 1776. Ten days later, another letter ; the hour of battle is near, the engines of war are got in readiness : " My dear angel, the abomination of desolation is in the Lord's temple. Le Kain . . . tells me that nearly all the youth of Paris is for Le Tourneur . . . and that a tragedy in prose is to be given in which an assembly of butchers is shown with wondrous effect. I shall die leaving France barbarous; but happily you live, and I flatter myself that the queen (Marie-Antoinette) will not let her new country, of which she is the charm, be the prey of savages and monsters. I flatter myself that M. le Maréchal de Duras will not have done us the honour of becoming a member of the Academy to see us eaten by Hottentots. . . . I must try and avenge the French before dying. I have sent the Academy a little piece of writing, in which I have endeavoured to smother my legitimate grief, and to let only my reason speak."

Voltaire had, in fact, a few days before, on the 26th of July, sent his "little piece of writing" to d'Alembert: "Secretary of Good Taste even more than of the Academy, my dear philosopher, my dear friend, to my help! Read my factum against our enemy Monsieur Le Tourneur; make M. Marmontel and M. de La Harpe, who have an interest therein, read it too. . . . I plead for France." Voltaire's intention was thus to make the Academy give a lesson to the court who had so lightly taken sides. There existed a precedent: the Academy had once passed judgment on Corneille and his "Cid"; it was now Shakespeare's turn. Voltaire wanted his letter to be read at a solemn public meeting, by d'Alembert, the most perfect reader of his day.

A preliminary reading took place privately before the assembled academicians, and d'Alembert informed his friend that a few alterations were requested: first, "offensive personalities" must be suppressed, and Le Tourneur must not be named. "Let that be no hindrance," replied Voltaire, "pray, have the kindness not to pronounce his horrid name." Then

ENGLISH VAUXHALL
By Canaletto, 1751

there were terribly coarse passages taken from Shakespeare, which were difficult to read in public. What must be done? You must, said Voltaire, pretend to stop from shame; the hearer "will let his imagination run far beyond" even the realities. We are at war, all means are good, even ruse. "The great point, my dear philosopher, is to inspire the nation with the disgust and horror it ought to have for Gille-Le Tourneur, *preconizer* of Gille-Shakespeare; to hold back our young men from the abominable slough into which they are rushing. . . . But I conjure you not to suppress my appeal to the Queen and to our Princesses. They must be induced to take our side," for nothing should be neglected, and women's opinion is of account. All is settled; the reading will take place in a solemn *séance*, on St. Louis's day; the time is near; d'Alembert sounds the charge: "At last, my dear master, the battle is about to begin and the signal is given. Shakespeare or Racine must remain on the field. . . . Unfortunately there are many deserters and false brethren among [our] men of letters, but the deserters shall be taken and hanged."

At length the day arrived. "Of the Sunday, 25th of August, 1776," we read in the Academy's records: "the company repaired in the morning to the chapel of the Louvre, where it heard mass, during which the Sieur Francœur had a motet performed. Then Father Elisée, preacher to the king, pronounced the panegyric. In the afternoon, the Academy, to the number of twenty-four academicians, held its usual public assembly. M. le Chevalier de Chastellux, director"—author of a "Romeo" with a happy ending—"opened the *séance* by a discourse relating to the prize for poetry." M. de La Harpe read the prize poems; "M. l'abbé Arnaud then read some reflections on Homer." At last the turn came for M. le Secrétaire to read "a writing by M. de Voltaire on the tragedies of Shakespear."[1]

The hall was crowded. Many celebrities, a number of foreigners were present, and among the latter, that same Mrs. Montagu, "la Shakespearienne," who had once wanted to burn Voltaire and now found herself on the gridiron. So, in his best voice, attentive, "not to see this cannon miss fire, when he had undertaken to fire it," d'Alembert did honour to his friend's essay. Voltaire protested at first, on the occasion "of a few foreign tragedies recently dedicated to the king our protector," against Anglomania in general, and against the troublesome jubilee: "A part of the English nation has lately erected a temple to the famous poet-comedian Shakespeare, and has founded a jubilee in his honour. A few French people have tried to feel the same enthusiasm. They transport among us an image of god-like Shakespeare; as certain other imitators have erected a Vaux-hall in Paris, and others have made themselves conspicuous by giving the name of roast-beef to their aloyaux, and prided themselves on serving on their tables roast-beef of mutton," *du roast-beef de mouton.*[2]

---

[1] "Les Registres de l'Académie Française, 1672–1793"; ed. Camille Doucet, Paris, 1895, 3 vols. 8º, vol. iii., p. 399.

[2] "Une partie de la nation anglaise a érigé, depuis peu, un temple au fameux comédien-poète Shakespeare et a fondé un jubilé en son honneur. Quelques Français ont tâché d'avoir le même enthou-

FRENCH VAUXHALL, ERECTED IN THE FOIRE SAINT GERMAIN.

Moderation is needful in all things; the author of the "Lettres Philosophiques," had formerly said about everything it was proper to know on England: "A man of letters, who has the honour to be your confrère, was the first among you to learn the English language, the first to make Shakespeare known." He was derided then; but afterwards an exorbitant reaction took place: "Soon all the books printed in London were translated. People went from one extreme to the other. They cared for nothing but what came, or was supposed to come, from that country." The worst thing of the kind yet seen is this new translation in which the author "endeavours to sacrifice France to England." Not one Frenchman "is quoted in his preface of a hundred and thirty pages. The great Corneille's name is not once to be found in it."

Now, what is this English drama, about which so much noise is made? A collection of "wild" plays; Shakespeare has the barbarity of his day; and, in his day, people liked "the tragedy of 'Gorboduc.' 'Twas a good king, the husband of a good queen; they divided in the first act their kingdom between two children, who quarrelled about this division: the youngest gave the eldest a box on the ear in the second act; the eldest, in the third act, killed the youngest; the mother, in the fourth, killed the eldest; the king, in the fifth, killed Queen Gorboduc;

---

siasme. Ils transportent chez nous une image de la divinité de Shakespeare; comme quelques autres imitateurs ont érigé depuis peu à Paris un Vaux-hall et comme quelques autres se sont signalés en appelant les aloyaux des roast-beef et en se piquant d'avoir à leur table du roast-beef de mouton."

and the people stirred up, killed King Gorboduc; so that, at the end, no one was left." Living in such an age, what could Shakespeare do? He did "Hamlet." "Some of you, gentlemen, are aware that there exists a tragedy by Shakespeare called 'Hamlet.'" A few heads, doubtless, bowed at this passage in sign of assent. The play swarms with anachronisms and absurdities; the burial of Ophelia is seen on the stage, a sight so monstrous that " the celebrated Garrick has lately suppressed, at his theatre, the scene of the grave-diggers." But the translator "sides with the grave-diggers." The play is full of abominable vulgarities, and from the very beginning. The sentry in the first scene declares: "Je n'ai pas entendu une souris trotter" (not a mouse stirring). Can such incongruities be allowed? Doubtless, "a soldier may speak thus in a guard-house; but not on the stage, before the first persons of the nation who express themselves with nobleness and before whom he must express himself in the same manner." But my soldiers, Shakespeare might have replied, talk among themselves and are not addressing Louis Quatorze. No matter.

No observance of rules in Shakespeare, continued d'Alembert, reading, no decency; a few merits however: " Truth, which cannot be disguised before you, compels me to confess that this Shakespeare, so savage, so low, so unbridled and so absurd, had sparks of genius." Sentence must nevertheless be passed against him: " Picture to yourselves, gentlemen, Louis XIV., in his gallery of Versailles, surrounded by his brilliant court; a 'Gille' in tatters, pushes his way through the crowd of heroes, great men and beauties who compose that

VOLTAIRE AT FERNEY, 1777, FOUR MONTHS BEFORE HIS LAST JOURNEY TO PARIS.

From life. p. 385.

court ; he proposes to them to leave Corneille, Racine, and Molière for a mountebank who has happy flashes and can make contortions. How, think you, would he be received ? "

He was very badly received on that memorable occasion, and Voltaire's triumph was complete. "M. le Marquis de Villevieille must have started early yesterday morning, my dear master, for Ferney," wrote d'Alembert at once to the hero of the day ; "he meant to drive a few post-horses to death, so as to have the pleasure of being the first to give you an account of your success. It has been such as you could desire. Your reflections gave great pleasure, and were much applauded. The quotations from Shakespeare . . . King Gorboduc, &c., highly diverted the assembly. Several parts I was made to repeat. I need not tell you that the English who were there went away displeased. . . . I read you with all the interest of friendship and all the zeal inspired by a good cause."

The protests of a sturdy boy of twelve, had, however, very nearly interrupted the proceedings : "There was in the assembly," wrote La Harpe to the Grand Duke of Russia, "an English youth of ten or twelve, brought up in the worship of Shakespeare, as every good Englishman is. He boiled with rage at M. de Voltaire's sarcasms and at the laughter of the assembly. He asked those who were in his company for a whistle : 'I want to hiss that Voltaire!' he repeated."[1] He was with great difficulty kept quiet.

Success, however, failed to unbend Voltaire. He remained unrelenting to the day of his death ; it was

[1] "Correspondance," 1801, i.. 53.

his war; he had some vague apprehension of an offensive campaign from the enemy. Far from going to sleep on his laurels, he began at once to prepare new engines, "a second letter more interesting than the first" (October 7th). The publishing of the former had not been such an easy matter as he expected: "Moureau, to whom I gave your Letter to the Academy, as you had commissioned me to do," wrote d'Alembert, "printed it at once, never doubting that permission to sell it would be granted him. M. le garde des Sceaux has refused that permission. . . . They say that the godly people at Versailles have persuaded [the king] that your essay on Shakespeare was injurious to religion, although at the public reading all the indecent passages from the English dramatist had been carefully omitted." Keen was the disappointment of Voltaire, though long since accustomed to such mishaps: "Poor old Raton, the miserable Raton," he answered, assuming the name of the cat in La Fontaine's fable, "is quite bewildered to have burnt for once his paws when he was acting so honestly." "Bertrand (the monkey) must a little reassure Raton, who will not be absolutely burnt," replied d'Alembert, "but only hanged by the mercy of the court. The prohibition from saying anything against the English drama and Shakespeare has apparently been revoked, for I saw, a few days ago, the letter exposed for sale at the Tuileries."

But sadness had invaded Raton, and he refused to be comforted. Carrying on his epistolary conversation with d'Alembert, he wrote to him on October 22, 1776: "You know that Doctor Franklin's troops have

By Moreau
de Villette.

THE CROWNING OF VOLTAIRE AT THE FRENCH COMEDY, MARCH 30, 1778.

been beaten by the King of England's. Alas! the philosophers are beaten everywhere. Reason and Liberty are ill received in this world." D'Alembert replied : " Sad Bertrand to lean Raton, greetings. Raton, lean though he be, will do very well in continuing to scratch Gille-Shakespeare. . . . Philosophy and Reason must at least have the upper hand in their little realm since they are beaten at 'la Nouvelle Yorck.'" (General Howe had entered New York, on the 15th of September, 1776.)

Voltaire prepared, therefore, without delay, the second campaign, which he regarded as indispensable, for the monster had not disarmed any more than he. " I succomb under the weight of my woes," wrote the octogenarian to Madame de Saint-Julien, " I am crushed by my enemies, by the factious abettors of Shakespeare."

On the 10th of February, 1778, Voltaire, aged eighty-four, re-entered Paris for his last triumphs. He remained firm and immovable in his literary beliefs ; his faith had not deserted him ; the apostle of every liberty, he continued to make an exception for tragedy alone, and the French comedians were preparing the performance of " Irène," his last work, a play according to rules, in which the heroine relates her troubles to Zoé, her confidante, and instead of using such a vulgar word as " husband," prefers to say : "a worthy mortal, one to whom I plighted my troth " —

" Un mortel respectable, et qui reçut ma foi."

This visit was one long fete. When Voltaire came to the performance of " Irène," on the 30th of March, the

crowd rushed towards him, opened the door of his coach;
those nearest "stretched forth their arms, seized that
dear idol, and without giving him time to take breath,
raised him up and carried him to the stairway." He
appeared in his box, and bursts of applause broke
forth; he bowed right and left; Brizard, the actor,
seized this favourable moment, entered suddenly, placed
a crown of laurel on his head," and the applause re-
doubled. After the play, the curtain rose again; "the
bust of M. de Voltaire was seen, placed in the centre of
the stage, surrounded with all the actors and actresses
in gala dress, all holding laurel wreaths in their hands,"
which they placed, "each in turn, upon the bust of that
immortal poet."[1] A soubrette "even went so far,"
relates Mercier, "as to caress and stroke with her hand
this triumphant bust." The Sieur Moreau le Jeune
was present, and on going home that same evening,
made "a perfect drawing" which represented this
apotheosis, and has been engraved.

But the triumpher did not forget his quarrel; he
dedicated his tragedy to the French Academy, and
took advantage of the occasion to make a last inroad
into the enemy's territory. "Irène," he said in his

---

[1] De Mouhy, "Abrégé de l'histoire du Théâtre Français," 1780,
vol. iii., pp. 96, ff. Palissot had composed for this solemnity an
à propos in prose: "Le Triomphe de Sophocle"; but the
comedians pretended they had not time enough to learn it: the
reason invoked does honour to their politeness and the refusal to
their good taste. The comedy was not performed, and Palissot
published it (Paris, 1778, 8º) with a preface full of rapturous praise
of Voltaire and the king. The first performance of "Irène" had
taken place on the 16th of March; Queen Marie Antoinette was
present, but Voltaire was not, being then ill in bed.

new letter to his colleagues, has only one merit ; it is according to rules : " I feel how unseemly it is, at my age of eighty-four years, to dare arrest for a moment your looks upon the degenerate fruits of my latter days. The tragedy of ' Irène ' cannot be worthy of you or of the ' Théâtre Français,' it has no merit save fidelity to the rules given to the Greeks by the worthy preceptor of Alexander." Thereupon he reopened the discussion and began war afresh, making the Academy take part in it : " You enlightened my doubts and you confirmed my opinion, two years ago, by consenting to hear, in one of your public meetings, the letter I had had the honour to write you on Corneille and on Shakespeare. I blush to join these two names together, but I hear that this incredible dispute is being renewed in the midst of Paris. . . ." Many answers and counterblasts to Voltaire's first essay had in fact appeared ; the gazettes had taken sides, and the " Année Littéraire " in particular had not missed so good an opportunity for making fun of its old enemy.[1] Voltaire concluded as he had formerly : " Shakespeare is a savage with sparks of genius which shine in a horrible night." This letter was read at the Academy on the 19th of March, and was " accepted with gratitude. M. le Directeur left at the end of the sitting to go and compliment M. de

---

[1] It gave its own account of how Voltaire's fury rose. The translators of Shakespeare in their long preface had had "l'imprudence et l'impolitesse de ne pas dire un seul mot à la louange de M. de Voltaire. L'exemplaire destiné pour Ferney se présente sans ce passeport littéraire. On l'accueille fort mal ; le maître du château s'emporte, sonne un de ses secrétaires, et dicte sur-le-champ sa diatribe à l'Académie." (" L'Année Littéraire," 1776, vol. vi.)

Voltaire on his success, and to return to him his dedicatory epistle, read and approved by the company." At the Academy as at the theatre, exceptional honours were awarded him. He attended the *séance* of the 30th of March : " M. le Directeur and all the academicians who were present went as far as the first room to meet him. He entered the assembly hall, and M. le Directeur invited him to sit at the head of them all." The same ceremony was observed at his departure ; he was escorted to the door of the first room, " the Academy being persuaded that honours rendered to a man of his age and celebrity could not be invoked in any other case." A few days afterwards the Academy unanimously decided " that every time M. de Voltaire came to the sitting after the hour had struck, he should nevertheless have his presence fee, and that the academicians who arrived before him should enjoy the same privilege, but not those who arrived after him." He was indeed considered as a man above men, and treated as a " dear idol." The " unhappy Raton " could at last forget his sorrows ; he too had had his jubilee, and he had had it during his lifetime.

His vivacity, his readiness of pen and of speech, his astonishing quickness, remained unimpaired. The poet Saint-Marc had rhymed the compliment delivered at the theatre the night of the apotheosis ; Voltaire would not be outdone by him ; ill and almost dying, he found means to reply :—

> " Vous daignez couronner, aux jeux de Melpomène,
>   D'un vieillard affaibli les efforts impuissants.
> Ces lauriers dont vos mains couvrent mes cheveux blancs
>   Étaient nés sur votre domaine.

> On sait que de son bien tout mortel est jaloux ;
> Chacun garde pour soi ce que le ciel lui donne ;
> Le Parnasse n'a vu que vous
> Qui sût partager sa couronne."[1]

His spirit of enterprise remained likewise the same as ever ; he continued the Voltaire of old times who would have liked "to remake the universe, and to remake it in less than a week." He had barely one month left to live : he had immense plans. He proposed to the Academy to remodel, if not exactly the universe, at least the French language, to emancipate it, to return to the freedom of the independents of yore. The dictionary of the Academy, compiled in an aristocratic and disdainful spirit, excluding from the literary realm innumerable families of plebeian words, was no longer sufficient ; a new one was needed which should be based on quite opposite principles, and should contain "all the picturesque and energetic expressions of Montaigne, Amyot, Charron, &c., which it is desirable to revive, and which our neighbours have turned to their own use."[2] Voltaire's proposal was accepted on the 7th of May ; he died on the 30th. Up to the last it was really and truly to tragedy alone that he had refused freedom.

IV.

War had not come to an end. In a moment of optimism, in August, 1776, Voltaire had said of Le Tourneur : "All honest folks are irritated against that

---
[1] "Journal politique et littéraire" (of Linguet, continued, after 1776, by La Harpe), April 15, 1778.
[2] "Registres de l'Académie," vol. iii., p. 432.

man; several have withdrawn their subscriptions." But the event had not justified Voltaire's anticipations. The third volume of the translation came out in 1778; it contained the names of one hundred and forty-nine new subscribers, such as the Duchesse de Boufflers, M. Boissy D'Anglas,, the " Marquise du Deffant, à Saint-Joseph, rue Saint-Dominique," the Princesse de Ligne, Préville the actor, Suard of the Academy, &c. In the fifth volume, published in 1779, another new list was appended, with the Duc d'Aumont, Madame Necker, and, who would have thought it? the great, the faithful friend, whose tragedies Voltaire used to correct, " M. Tronchin, ancien Conseiller à Genève," who, in his turn, was deserting and going over to the enemy. Truly the " abomination of desolation" was in the temple of the Lord. "The translation of Shakespeare's plays by M. Le Tourneur is in everybody's hands," said Ducis a little later; while Sedaine went into ecstasies over it, and talked Shakespeare to every one he met. " Baron de Grimm, who was one day a witness of his enthusiasm, said to him aptly enough: 'Your transports do not surprise me, you feel the happiness of a son who finds a father whom he has never seen.'"[1] The translation was destined to enjoy

---

[1] Life of Sedaine by Auger, prefacing the " Œuvres Choisies," 1813, 3 vols., 12º. The gazettes had devoted to Le Tourneur's undertaking long and numerous articles, and had helped to make an event of it. The "Année Littéraire," the property, from March, 1776, of Fréron, the son, had published on each play studies, which offered the amusing peculiarity of concluding almost in the same words as Voltaire, but Voltaire in his first manner. The obstinate opposition of the English to the unities, considered by them as " lois arbitraires et despotiques auxquelles un fier républicain n'est pas

the most lasting success; remodelled by Guizot, it is in current use to this day.

The "factious abettors of Shakespeare" had not disarmed. Voltaire's letter had made a great noise in England as well as in France; replies to it were written, before and after his death, in several languages and by people of every country. The essay composed in former years by "cette Montagu la Shakespearienne," as Voltaire called her, was translated into French, and La Harpe undertook to answer it.[1] The

obligé de se soumettre," was protested against; but the conclusion was: "Les ouvrages du génie ressemblent à ceux de la nature qui n'a point dans ses travaux la froide régularité des productions de l'art" (1776, vol. i., p. 31). Voltaire had said the same; see above, p. 209. Great praise was bestowed upon Le Tourneur in the "Journal Anglais," the "Journal Français, Italien et Anglais," &c. In this last paper, Mercier (who buries Shakespeare in Westminster, "where royal dust mingles with that of great men"), is very hard upon Voltaire, who has represented the English dramatist "as little superior to an intoxicated savage" from jealousy of his "towering genius," August, 1777.

[1] "Apologie de Shakespeare, en réponse à la critique de M. de Voltaire, traduite de l'Anglois de Madame de Montagu," London and Paris, 1777, 8º. Voltaire warmed La Harpe's zeal: "J'attends avec impatience la suite de votre réponse à cette Montagu la Shakespearienne" (January 14, 1778). From the first Garrick had written to Madame Necker: "I have no room left for Voltaire and Shakespeare. There are rods preparing for the old gentleman by several English wits" (November 10, 1776). In 1785 appeared in French: "Dramaturgie ou observations sur plusieurs pièces de théâtre ... ouvrage intéressant, traduit de l'allemand de feu M. Lessing, par un François, revu par M. Junker," Paris, 2 vols., 8º. The essays thus offered to the French public had originally appeared some eighteen years before; they furnished more fuel to the Voltaire-Shakespeare quarrel, the latter being one of Lessing's literary gods.

"Chevalier Rutlidge,"[1] addressed some "Observations à Messieurs de l'Académie Française," in which he spoke in favour of Shakespeare against Voltaire and the unities : " If the violation of the three unities which Shakespeare was guilty of has not destroyed theatrical illusion, it shows that the laws laid down by Aristotle and his adherents are neither the great nor the indispensable laws of good sense." Joseph Baretti, an Italian living in London, "Secrétaire pour la Correspondance étrangère de l'Académie Royale Britannique," and to whom we owe some curious relations of journeys, wrote in 1777 a "Discours sur Shakespeare et sur Monsieur de Voltaire," in which he alleges that Voltaire did not know English, that his letters in English are not by him, and that, in spite of his classical theories, he could but corrupt the taste of the young generation : " Woe to the young men who shall have read Monsieur de Voltaire's works before having read Homer, Virgil, and the others whom we call classic authors. Woe! Woe!"[2]

[1] James Rutledge, son of a shipowner of Dunkirk, upon whom the Pretender had conferred a baronetcy. He had just published an "Essai sur le Caractère des Français" (London, 1776), not over-indulgent to the French, but in which he happened to have loudly praised Voltaire.

[2] All these replies gave rise to new discussions in the literary newspapers. Thus Baretti's essay was reviewed in the "Journal Français, Italien et Anglais" (August, 1777), Rutledge's and Mrs. Montagu's in the "Journal Français" of Palissot and Clément (March and December, 1777), who, in their enthusiasm for the Greek ideal, ended thus : "Il suffirait, pour terminer ce procès littéraire . . . d'examiner lequel des deux peuples a su le mieux plier son goût national au goût de l'antiquité, sur lequel il n'est pas de nation lettrée qui n'ait formé, le sien." La Harpe, as a friend

"THE MODERN EROSTRATES WRITING ABOUT ART."
A caricature of Sébastien Mercier.   p. 401.

Mercier, the defender of prose and of Shakespearean drama, took up his pen again and reiterated his blasphemies. In a new essay: "De la Littérature et des Littérateurs, suivi d'un nouvel examen de la tragédie Française," 1778, he scoffed at the unities, at confidants and at antique tragedy: "There are things which time has changed.—I have copied the ancients, some poet will say.—Well, then, my friend, may they read you!" We must enlarge our stage, "which is only a parlour," get rid of the twenty-four hours to which we owe so many absurdities, and observe nature and not the Romans: "While a thousand different characters surround us, with their striking features, inviting the warmth of our pencil and a truthful rendering, should we blindly turn away from a living nature whose every muscle is discernible, full of life and expression, to go and draw a Greek or Roman corpse, colour its livid cheeks, clothe its cold limbs, raise it staggering on its feet, and give to that glazed eye, that frozen tongue and stiffened arm, the look, speech, and gesture customary on our boards? What an abuse of the dummy!"[1] He defended himself on the ground of patriotism where Voltaire had insidiously led the quarrel: "Some have gone so far as to say that those who admired Milton and Shakespeare were bad citizens, enemies of the nation, detractors of France. . . . When there are no good reasons to give, puerile extravagances are put forward. Need we say that to fight well

of Voltaire, had little praise for Baretti, "une espèce de fou nommé Baretti," and for his "brochure écrite à faire pouffer de rire." ("Correspondance adressée au Grand Duc," ii. 179.)

[1] "Tableau de Paris," ch. 333.

against a nation it is not necessary to combat Addison, Pope, and Milton?" It was the time of the American War of Independence, and the United States had just been recognized by France. The enthusiasm was great; Mercier tried to show that it was a possible thing to share it, and yet admire Shakespeare : " Perhaps it is in America that the human race will transform itself, adopt a new and sublime religion, improve sciences and arts, and become the representative of the ancient nations. Haven of liberty, Grecian souls, every strong and generous soul will develop or meet there, and this great example given to the universe will show what men can do when they are of one mind and combine their lights and their courage." [1] Chastellux, another Shakespearian, replied still better to adverse critics by taking part in the War of Independence as Major-General in the army of Rochambeau.

Up to, and even after, the Revolution, the skirmishes continued ; but Voltaire was dead, and it was no longer real war. La Harpe, Marmontel, the literary gazetteers, approved, blamed, weighed their words :—

"Sans vouloir faire cas ni des ha ! ni des ho !"

Deeply penetrated with the importance of the part they played and of the sentences they passed, they sat as in

[1] "C'est peut-être en Amérique que le genre humain va se refondre, qu'il doit adopter une religion neuve et sublime, qu'il va perfectionner les sciences et les arts et représenter les anciens peuples. Asile de la liberté, les âmes de la Grèce, les âmes fortes et généreuses y croîtront ou s'y rendront, et ce grand exemple donné à l'univers prouvera ce que peut l'homme quand il met en commun son courage et ses lumières." ("De la Littérature," Yverdon, 1778, pp. 19, 139.)

a congress, and negotiated impossible agreements about this disconcerting *lusus naturæ*.[1] Some few made audacious raids, like Rivarol, who attacks the old independents, French or English, and treats them most cavalierly: Chaucer "deserved, about the middle of the fifteenth century, to be called the English Homer; our Ronsard merited the same compliment, and Chaucer, as obscure as he, was even less known." So many words, so many mistakes. As for Shakespeare, he has become, but only at a recent date, "the idol of his nation and the scandal of our literature."[2] Mere skirmishes still; real war will only break out again later, at the moment of the romantic mêlée, in 1830.

V.

Shakespeare, translated by Le Tourneur, had been winning his way into libraries and drawing-rooms, but not into theatres. A mere translator could not secure for him admittance to the play-house. Efforts were being made, however, to adapt him to the tastes of the day and to render him acceptable to a Parisian audience. Blamed, praised, discussed, he was now known of all;

---

[1] La Harpe does so in his "Cours de Littérature" (1st ed., 1799): "S'il eût connu [les règles] d'Aristote comme notre Corneille, s'il eût suivi l'exemple des Grecs comme notre Racine, je ne suis pas sûr qu'il les eût égalés (car cela dépend du plus ou moins de génie), mais je suis sûr qu'il aurait fait de meilleures pièces." He gives vent more freely to his opinions, and is far more severe in his "Correspondance adressée au Grand Duc," 1801, letters 43, 51, 53, 76, 151, &c.

[2] "De l'Universalité de la Langue Française, sujet proposé par l'Académie de Berlin en 1783." "Œuvres," Paris, 1808, 5 vols., 8º, vol. ii.

but to make him sufferable on the stage was no slight matter, and great precautions were necessary.

Many authors tried, in the second half of the eighteenth century; they all surprised the public then by their rashness, and surprise us now by their timidity. Licences are considerably easier when it is a question of plays to be read in an arm-chair than when it is one of dramas to be performed on the stage. Le Tourneur had secured numerous partisans without any trouble; the adapters for the play-house found a less accommodating public. In spite of recent experiments, the majority continued in favour of the unities, and the rules still seemed to the mass of spectators as necessary for a tragedy as for a sonnet. Regular tragedies were still the fashion; a traveller like Sterne was struck by their popularity, and he admired them as heartily as any one in Paris, but from different motives: "They are *absolutely* fine;—and whenever I have a more brilliant affair upon my hands than common, as they suit a preacher quite as well as a hero, I generally make my sermon out of 'em; and for the text,—Cappadocia, Pontus and Asia, Phrygia and Pamphylia—is as good as any one in the Bible." Even in a comedy, and after all the domestic dramas that had been represented, authors ran great risks in venturing out of the beaten paths. Saurin shortened Beverley's speech to his son because, at the first performance, "several persons had been revolted by it."[1] Desforges suppressed the Latin quotations of the pedantic Partridge because

---

[1] Speech to his sleeping son, whom he intends to kill. Saurin, in printing his play, gave both versions: "Voici," he said, "la première leçon, qui était, je crois, plus théâtrale, mais dont plusieurs

they had aroused "violent murmurs" from a public, more touchy, it would seem, than the audience before whom Molière represented "Le Médecin malgré lui." [1] Lemierre, in 1767, did not yet dare to make William Tell shoot his arrow on the stage; the episode was made the subject of a narrative :—

"Dans la place d'Altdorff, près d'un arbre attaché,
Aux yeux de tout un peuple interdit et touché," &c.[2]

Only later a different version was introduced, and the spectator could see the thing with his own eyes: "He shoots his arrow kneeling, strikes down the apple, rises and falls back as though fainting against a rock."

Shakespeare's adapters were constrained to use great prudence to avoid being hissed; even with all their prudence they were sometimes hissed all the same, so great are the differences in the genius of the two nations, and so lacking in merit, truth to say, were most of these innovators. But the former of the two reasons was the only one that struck the reformers.

We have thus a queer collection of Othellos, Romeos, Richard the Thirds, and Hamlets, each stranger than the other, by Chastellux, Douin, Butini, Mercier, De Rozoi, Ducis, and anonymous authors.[3]

---

personnes ont été révoltées," in spite of the enthusiasm of a first performance which was one of the great successes of the day, May 7, 1768. See *supra*, p. 320.

[1] "Tom Jones à Londres," comedy in five acts, in verse, 1782. "J'ai rétabli, en partie, à l'impression, le Latin qui avait excité de violents murmures à la première représentation."

[2] "Guillaume Tell, tragédie," Neufchâtel, 1767, 8º ; speech of Fust to Cléofé, wife of Tell, iii. 2.

[3] A (very incomplete) list of them is given by Thimm : "Shakespeariana," 2nd ed., London, 1872, p. 105.

The Chevalier, afterwards Marquis, de Chastellux, of the French Academy, colonel at twenty-one of the regiment de Chastellux, a brilliant officer, a favourite with every one, and especially with the beautiful Marquise de Gléon, tried to win the "salons" over to Shakespeare. He chose with this view Romeo, whose passion was calculated to touch the female heart ; but he modified the plot so as not to shock his audience : " I have arranged Romeo for a French stage ; I think I have produced the greatest impression. I have altered much of the intrigue, and have left out all that is comic " [1]—and even all that is tragic, for the Chevalier's play ends as merrily as possible. It was performed at that famous Château de La Chevrette, in the valley of Montmorency, the property of M. and Madame d'Épinay, the rendezvous of men of letters and of a society which was, says Mademoiselle d'Ette, as a live novel, " comme un roman mouvant." The financier Savalette, uncle to the Marquise de Gléon, had hired La Chevrette from the d'Épinays, and displayed there his magnificence. Desirous, like the wealthy financier he was, of following the fashion, he wanted everything about him to be "à l'anglaise," whether dramas or gardens ; he had scarcely settled at La Chevrette when he hastened, like Saurin's "Anglomane," to transform the parterre into a " parc à l'anglaise." M. d'Épinay was forced to acquiesce, but did so in an epistle which showed he was less short of wit than of money :—

> " Savalette a fort bien tourné
> Le parc de la Chevrette,

[1] To Garrick, June 15, 1774.

> Mais son goût anglais a coiffé
>   Mon parterre en vergette (brush-like).
> En fait de goût, soit mal, soit bien,
>   Chacun trouve un apôtre ;
> Je fais un très grand cas du sien,
>   Mais j'aime mieux Le Nôtre." [1]

On the stage of La Chevrette,[2] then, which had already seen such actors as Rousseau playing, when a *débutant*, in one of his own plays,[3] not to mention Madame d'Épinay and many others, Savalette caused the drama "à l'anglaise" of Chastellux to be performed. It was a literary and worldly event ; people fought for invitations, the road was lined with coaches, all Paris flocked to La Chevrette. A spectatress of a satirical turn of mind, but no bad judge in such matters, has left us a description of the entertainment : "The Chevalier de Chastellux has become a decided and confirmed author. . . . His masterpiece, if you please, is 'Romeo and Juliet.' The whole town set out to see this pretended imitation of Great Britain's beloved and revered poet. I followed the stream with two English friends of mine." As the performance went on a growing feeling of disappointment was felt ; the play was no longer either English or French :

[1] Percy and Maugras, "Dernières années de Madame d'Épinay," 1883, p. 309. Needless to recall how famous Le Nôtre was as a designer of gardens in the French style. Cf. above, p. 152.

[2] La Chevrette has been destroyed ; only the stables are left (close by the railway station of La Barre-Ormesson). Cabbages, turnips, and carrots are grown where the ancient gardens were laid ; in the open fields some sculptured stones, half-covered with grass, still mark the place where the ornamental waters used to be.

[3] "L'Engagement téméraire."

" Wit where there should be thoughts . . . the last act a real take in. Instead of amusing themselves with self-poisoning and stabbing, Juliet and Romeo go gaily forth from the abode of death to get married

no one knows where, to live together no one knows how, and to be happy in any way it may please you to imagine. People look at each other, wonder what has become of that terrible catastrophe, of the pathos, of the emotion; the curtain falls and leaves the astonished spectator to wonder as much as he likes." [1]

All judges were not so severe, and the performance bore some fruit. Shortly afterwards we find the critic, whose opinion Chastellux cared most about, the beautiful and learned Marquise de Gléon, deep in the study of Shakespeare, " working by herself and consulting the most lettered English she could find," sending Garrick the note-book in which she had marked the difficult passages whose real meaning escaped her; and finally acting the part of Juliet in society theatres.[2]

"Othello," at the same time, was put on the rack by another officer of the royal armies, " M. Douin, capitaine d'infanterie." " This play," he says, " is the masterpiece of the great Shakespéar, and only the unities of place and time are wanting to make it as regular as any of the Greek and French tragedies. . . . I have tried to bring the Moor of Venice into the exact limits of these two unities." The original contains scenes of low comedy : " I have also remedied, as far as possible, that essential fault." This done, the captain consulted his friends with regard to a performance. " But what was my surprise on hearing my modern Aristarchs declare that the Moor of Venice could not decently figure on the French stage." The friends' objections were remarkably deep : Othello's

---

[1] Madame Riccoboni to Garrick, November 27, 1770. See also " Correspondance Littéraire " of Grimm, &c., ed. Tourneux, vol. x., p. 31.

[2] Suard explains that it was the Juliet of his own adaptation of " Romeo." To Garrick, May 18, 1774.

skin and Iago's soul are both too black ; "the French stage does not admit in profane tragedy the terms heaven, angel, devil, or Sovereign Being ; one should use the general terms of the gods of mythology." Douin replies very gravely on each point and appeals from the Aristarchs to the public : " If this play is to my compatriots' taste, I may decide to employ my leisure in giving them successively the whole of Shakespéar's dramas, reserving to myself only the liberty of cleansing his plays, both comic and tragic, of pruning them of their superfluities, and of reducing them to the limits of the three unities." A slight liberty. He concludes saying : " As I shall be opening for myself a new path, I intend to give even those of Shakespéar's plays which we have already. . . . Alexander would have no other painter but Apelles. I do not flatter myself that Shakespéar would have chosen me to be his interpreter, but I have done my best." Whatever Shakespeare might have thought on the subject, Douin's contemporaries showed no enthusiasm, and our captain was not encouraged to follow to the end the new path he had tried to open for himself.[1]

Butini, a magistrate, proceeds no less cavalierly than Captain Douin : " I shall not waste time in explanations upon a few changes indispensable in Shakespeare's plays. Everybody must feel that it was necessary to whiten

---

[1] "Le More de Venise, tragédie angloise," Paris, 1773 ; in verse. A continual effort is made by Douin to conciliate the tastes of the two countries. Desdemona dies on the stage, but stabbed, not smothered ; Cassio "charge Rodrigue qui tombe dans la coulisse, mais *de façon à être vu*." The scene takes place in Cyprus, all the previous events are made the subject of narratives.

Othello's swarthy face, to soften the ending, suppress a few scenes, simplify the action, and reduce the whole to the three unities. . . ." All this is evident. Like Douin, he admits the murder on the stage, but without going so far as strangulation ; Desdemona does not die smothered, Othello stabs her, " la frappe." Butini, too, had the stage in mind when he wrote : " If this piece proves to be not displeasing to real men of taste, that is to say to the friends of nature, if they judge it worthy of the honour of being performed, the glory of this will be due chiefly to Shakespeare." [1]

With the comedies, which were much less appreciated in France, authors take even greater liberties ; the most popular of these, " The Merry Wives," was remodelled many times for the French stage. La Place had turned it into a three-act play with divertisements and " intended it as a carnival play for the Théâtre Français," but a friend lost his manuscript.[2] Another author, who, like Cubières, was destined in the course of his life to become familiar

---

[1] " Othello, drame en cinq actes et en vers, imité de Shakespeare, par M. Butini, ancien procureur général de Genève," 1785, 8º. On "une rhapsodie de Richard III.," by De Rozoi, 1782, performed at the Théâtre Français, "au grand scandale des honnêtes gens, revoltés qu'une farce si plate et si barbare fût tolérée," see La Harpe, " Correp. adressée au Grand Duc," iii., 251.

[2] " Collection de Romans," Paris, 1788, Preface to "Lydia," vol. iv., p. xiv. The " Merchant of Venice " was translated into French prose : " Le Marchand de Venise comédie traduite de l'anglais de Sharkespeare," London and Paris, 1768, 8º. The translator declares that his only aim has been accuracy ; he is even afraid of having been " too scrupulous," as he tried to render the very " fautes de goût," as " rentrant pour beaucoup dans le caractère original de Shakespeare."

with "sombre dramas" no less terrible than Shakespeare's, Collot d'Herbois to wit, published in 1780, at the Hague, an "Amant loup-garou ou M. Rodomont, pièce comique en quatre actes et en prose, imitée de l'anglais, représentée au théâtre du Casuaristraat," a vulgar farce, with a few comical traits, such as this remark of Rodomont's: "The surest way to fear nothing is to begin by frightening others; here I am, dressed up fit to make the devil himself turn tail." Collot presented his comedy to his readers as a chastened adaptation from Shakespeare: "Shakespeare's play entitled 'The Merry Wives of Windsor,' is a mine of comical situations; a few have been preserved here, as it would be a pity if they were entirely lost to our stage. Those who know the English play will understand how difficult it was to reduce the action to a simpler plan."[1]

These were isolated attempts. An effort far more sustained was made by Jean François Ducis,[2] who

---

[1] "Œuvres de théâtre de M. Collot d'Herbois," the Hague, 1781, 8º. The resemblances which have been pointed out between Shakespeare's play and Barthe's "Fausses Infidélités" (1768) are insignificant. The "Tempest" was transformed into a pastoral play by Rochon de Chabannes, music by Gossec: "Hilas et Silvie, joué par les comédiens ordinaires du Roi," December 10, 1769. "Je dois à Shakespear l'idée de mon monstre et malheureusement je ne lui dois que cela: le célèbre Anglais, dans sa tragédie de la 'Tempête,' introduit l'épisode d'un certain Prosper, retiré dans une forêt avec deux filles et un garçon qu'il a constamment tenus séparés et à qui il a inspiré une aversion réciproque"; in other words, Chabannes follows unawares Dryden instead of Shakespeare.

[2] "Œuvres" (and "Œuvres posthumes"), Paris, 1827, 6 vols. 12º "Lettres," ed. P. Albert, Paris, 1879, 8º. Ducis was born in Versailles in 1733, and died there in 1816

throughout his life took Shakespeare for his ideal, and set himself the task of acclimatizing his sombre dramas on the French stage, beginning with "Hamlet," in 1769, and following with " Romeo " in 1772, " Léar " in 1783, " Macbeth " in 1784, " Jean-sans-Terre " in 1791, and "Othello " in 1792. A singular being was this Ducis, at once ridiculous and charming : in reading his terrible plays one feels irresistibly inclined to laugh; in reading his letters one envies those of his contemporaries who knew him and who counted among his friends. His sincerity is flawless ; his ignorance of English is absolute. He admires Shakespeare passionately, and labours to mutilate his plays in order to increase the fame of the great man and induce the French public to appreciate him. By an irony of fate, at the very time when Voltaire was leading his furious campaign, Ducis's adaptations of Shakespeare were about to win for him a seat in that Academy which Voltaire had chosen as arbiter, and where he was to replace Voltaire himself. This was one of Shakespeare's revanches.

Calm and tranquil by nature, a man of feeling, as people were wont to be in those times, a lover of flowers, springtide, and sunny days, he deepens the sombreness of his model when transporting his dramas on to the French stage; he adds manifold horrors to them, but they are only told ; they are heard of and not seen. Pacific and inoffensive, he resists Bonaparte, who called him familiarly " bonhomme Ducis," invited him to the Malmaison, and, supreme flattery, had had " Macbeth " performed at the Théâtre Français. Bonaparte offered, relates Campenon, to put a little comfort into his life : " ' General,' replied M. Ducis, on perceiving a flight of wild ducks passing through a cloud above his head, 'you are fond of shooting. Do you see that flight of birds cleaving the heavens? There is not one of them but scents from afar the smell of powder and feels the danger of the sportsman's gun. I am one of those wild birds.'"

He chose "Hamlet," the most famous of his master's plays, for his first endeavour. He entered upon this great undertaking in an almost religious spirit, and with the sincerity at once comical and touching that he carried into everything. "In treating this character, I have regarded myself as a painter of sacred subjects working at an altar-piece. But why, sir, do I not know your language?"[1] Being unable to consult the original, he wanted at least to have the portraits of the author and of his interpreter, and caused a mutual friend to write to Garrick, begging the actor "to send us the engraving of Shakespeare and that of yourself in the character of Hamlet. My friend wants to breathe the fire of the dead Shakespeare and of the living one; but he conjures you to send the best engravings and consequently the dearest; he is rich, and one or two louis more or less are nothing to him."[2] Ducis was not rich at all, far from it, but he made his friend pass him off as wealthy in order to be the more sure, in his religious zeal, of obtaining the best copies possible.

Thus armed, the two engravings "under my eyes and before my table," he proceeded, with a mixture of audacity and fear yielding unexpected results, to the

[1] To Garrick, April 14, 1769.
[2] Cailhava d'Estandoux to Garrick, February 6, 1769.

GARRICK AS HAMLET.
From the painting by Wilson. Engraved by J. MacArdell.

fabrication of a hybrid drama, Greek and Danish, French and English, all at once. His Hamlet, imbued with the examples of antiquity, readily invokes *the gods*, and parades through the palace of Elsinore " the redoubtable *urn*" containing the late king's " deplorable *ashes*"—which does not prevent him from speaking elsewhere of that prince's *coffin*.[1] The unities are observed ; Claudius has a confidant, Polonius ; the queen has a confidante, Elvire. King and queen relate their past to the confidants, and declare their intentions with the most dangerous simplicity : Ducis's monsters are black, but not complicated. Claudius opens the drama with the plain statement that he means to overthrow young Hamlet and wear the crown himself :—

> " Oui, cher Polonius, tout mon parti n'aspire,
> En détrônant Hamlet, qu'à m'assurer l'empire."

Elvire reminds the queen that, as she has a confidante, she is bound to confide secrets to her :—

> " Expliquez-vous enfin, c'est trop vous en défendre,
> Avez-vous des secrets que je ne puisse entendre,
> Madame ? "

---

[1] The question of the urn was the cause of lively discussions : " Les aveugles enthousiastes de la Melpomène anglaise purent trouver mauvais qu'on osât altérer ainsi l'un des principaux objets de leur culte. . . . Que signifiait cette urne sur laquelle Hamlet exige que sa mère jure qu'elle est innocente de la mort de son père ? " " Costumes et Annales des grands Théâtres de Paris," by De Charnois, 1786, ff., vol. ii., No. xxiii. The urn was preserved ; Talma used it, and when he was painted as Hamlet (by Lagrenée fils) the urn figured in the canvas as a necessary attribute. The picture is now preserved at the Théâtre Français.

The queen doubtless blushes a little, and informs
Elvire that some time ago she murdered her husband.
All through the play conversations replace the action ;
but the plot is made darker : Ophelia is the daughter
of Claudius, so that Hamlet will be obliged, like the
Cid, to kill his mistress's father in order to avenge his
own. On the other hand, the ghost remains nearly
all the time in the coulisse, and there Hamlet discovers
it :—

"*Hamlet (dans la coulisse).*   Fuis, spectre épouvantable,
    Porte au fond des tombeaux ton aspect redoutable."

Instead of the play performed before the guilty pair,
a tale is told in their presence of how a crime of the
same sort as their own was committed in London :—

"*Hamlet.* Raconte devant eux, pour démêler leur crime,
    L'attentat dont un roi dans Londres fut victime."

At the end, Claudius, in open rebellion, besieges the
palace, takes it, and reaches Hamlet, who kills him ;
but a variant allows the players, if they prefer, to
replace actual killing by a narrative. And Hamlet,
who will no doubt marry Ophelia (" This heart till
the grave will burn for thy charms ") resigns himself
" to be " :—

"Je saurai vivre encor ; je fais plus que mourir."

The play was a success. Molé displayed an extraordinary spirit, and carried all before him—excepting
Diderot, however ; excepting also Collé, the song-

MLLE. FLEURY AS OPHELIA IN DUCIS'S "HAMLET."
"RÔLE D'ORFÉLIE DANS HAMLET."

writer Collé, the "good Collé," so merry in real life, so morose in his Journal, who only kept his good temper, as was seen later, on condition of pouring out the bad in his memoirs: "Molé is exaggerated in that play," Collé wrote after the first performance; "he bellows his part, he is like a madman, he frightens one; but that is enough for this flat abomination to be found admirable and for it to draw crowds. He has made [Diderot's] 'Pere de Famille' succeed by dint of his wild acting; and so he only plays 'Hamlet' twice a week, as he did the 'Pere de Famille.'"[1]

From this we, at any rate, gather that people ran to see the play, and this, for the author, was the chief point. Ducis pursued his plan. Shortly afterwards the tragedy of "Roméo," "read, accepted, learnt, and performed in a fortnight's time," had at first a rather doubtful success, then it was remodelled and "went to the skies," thanks especially to a scene in the fourth act, which was "applauded furiously." Romeo, in this play, is a young man of feeling and a lover of humanity, according to the fashion of the time. He declares from the first that he could not hate a Capulet, for a Capulet is a man, and all men are brothers :—

"Puisqu'il est homme, hélas, peut-il m'être étranger?"

[1] September 30, 1769. The play came out in print shortly after: "Hamlet, tragédie imitée de l'anglois," Paris, 1770, 8º. The advertisement begins: "Je n'entends point l'anglois." Ducis used the French text of La Place. The similitude of Molé's acting in Ducis's play and in Diderot's did not render the latter more indulgent: "Laissez-là le théâtre," he wrote, alluding to Ducis, "je m'accommoderai encore mieux du monstre de Shakespeare que de l'épouvantail de M. Ducis." ("Œuvres," ed. Assézat, vol. viii., p. 476.)

He feels toward "this mortal" the same sentiments which Sombreuses felt for all mortals. "The author obtained the honours of a triumph, that is to say, he was pushed by a comedian on to the stage to make his bow to the public." The writer of the "Correspondance littéraire" adds that he had seen the original play in London: "I still remember with delight a certain conversation by moonlight, full of tenderness and charm, between Romeo and Juliet, when she is on a terrace above, leaning over a balcony, and her lover in the garden at the foot of the terrace"[1]—a scene generally remembered nowadays.

In "Roméo" Ducis is faithful to his method: narratives and confidants allow him, nearly all through the play, to avoid putting the action under our eyes. Shakespeare's sombre plot is rendered blacker still: Hamlet was at the same time the Cid; old Montagu is at the same time Ugolino; he once upon a time devoured all his children, except Romeo, in Famine's Tower, and he relates to the sole survivor the details of this calamity due to the Capulets' ferocity.

English plays must "necessarily be remodelled" to become presentable for you, Chesterfield had said; —Ducis remodelled with right good will, modifying the tone, the style, and the plot. Shakespeare's old Capulet dared call Juliet "carrion"; Prince Hamlet exclaimed, addressing his father: "Well said, old mole"; Ducis's old Capulet dares not use the word

[1] "Correspondance Littéraire de Grimm, Diderot," &c., ed. Tourneux, vol. x., p. 27. First performance, July 27, 1772, second, with alterations, July 29th.

bread, and when describing his wants in the tower, says he lacked even " the aliments granted merely to sustain existence." [1]

The "Correspondance littéraire," and not without reason, judged Ducis' sombre inventions severely : "Our poets commit the same fault of which Comptrollers General of finance are sometimes guilty. Because they have learnt that one and one make two, our financiers persuade themselves the taxes need only to be doubled, and that two and two will make four. They are mistaken, and soon find out that, in spite of their arithmetic, two and two hardly make three. In the same way our poets, to produce terrible effects, pile up horrors upon horrors, and, instead of making people shudder, they make them laugh." Genius does not require all that ; one word is enough for it, " but the question is how to find that word."

Neither the laughter of some nor the indignation of others could stop the " bonhomme Ducis," who had on his side the public, very fond of frightful events, provided it heard of, and did not see, them ; his story of Ugolino had excited in the audience that " charming pity " eulogised by Boileau, and had determined the

---

[1] " *Montaigu.* Dans une tour fatale on me vint enfermer.
  Roméo.   Avec vos enfants ?
  Montaigu.   Oui, prête l'oreille, au reste . . .
         Nous nous levons, on vient, nous attendions d'avance
         L'aliment qu'on accorde à la simple existence.
         Chacun se tait, j'écoute et j'entends de la tour
         La porte en mur épais se changer sans retour . . .
         Je dévorai ces mains . . . Raymond, Dolcé, Sévère
         M'offrirent à genoux leur sang pour me nourrir."

success of the play.[1] Ducis, moreover, was far too sincere in his admiration to allow himself to be intimidated by a few dilettanti; he continued to transcribe for the French stage the works of that "singularly fertile, original, and extraordinary genius," of "that poet, finally, whose work I am." He realized the excess of his temerity; he quaked at the thought; but he persevered. "I trembled more than once, I confess," he writes *à propos* of "Léar," "when I had the idea of showing on the French stage a king whose reason is deranged." He trembles, also, when he ventures the scene of Lady Macbeth's somnambulism, "a singular scene, hazarded for the first time on our stage," in which Madame Vestris was admirable, and, according to Ducis, equalled even Mrs. Siddons.[2]

---

[1] It is the scene in the fourth act mentioned above. This "belle scène," according to Collé, who blames all the rest, saved the play. "Il s'est adroitement servi," we read on the other hand in the "Année Littéraire," "d'un morceau admirable de Dante pour donner plus d'énergie à la haine des Montaigus et des Capulets; mais la délicatesse des spectateurs français l'a contraint d'affaiblir la catastrophe. (1778, vol. vii., p. 105.)

[2] It was then, and for a long while, Mrs. Siddons' great part. A Frenchman who saw her in it in May, 1810, notes in his journal: "Mistress Siddons approche de plus près le beau idéal de son art qu'aucune actrice ou aucun acteur que j'aie jamais vu." "Voyage d'un Français" (L. Simond), Paris, 1816, i., p. 187. Cf. "Corinne," xvii., ch. iv. Châteaubriand, while an *émigré*, saw her too: "Mistress Siddons dans le rôle de Lady Macbeth jouait avec une grandeur extraordinaire; la scène du somnambulisme glaçait d'effroi les spectateurs." He saw her again late in life, when she had left the stage: "Elle était habillée de crêpe, portait un voile noir comme un diadème sur ses cheveux blancs et ressemblait à une reine abdiquée." "Essai sur la Littérature Anglaise."

DUCIS WRITING LEAR.
Engraved by J. J. Avril from the picture by Mme. Guiard of the French Royal Academy of Painting.   p. 427.

To understand all there was of audacity in these attempts, we must remember not only the opposition made to them by the ultra-refined, but also the state of mind in Paris, just before the Revolution. Never was anything seen so gentle, so attenuated, so delicate, and so polished. The contemporaries themselves noticed it : how could horrible sights please a people so full of amenity ? Already Le Tourneur, in his dedication to Louis Seize, had said : " Your Majesty will see the tragic pictures of the divisions which only too often have rent England. It will be for you an agreeable and flattering relaxation to let your imagination wander in the midst of these foreign scenes, while you have at your feet a gentle and submissive people." When the witty authors of the " Correspondance Littéraire " saw Ducis' dramas on the stage, it seemed to them that, even by contrast, those tragedies could hardly please : " Why," they said, speaking of " Hamlet," " this continual repetition of great crimes in our theatrical representations and in a century where the petty manners (*les petites mœurs*) are so far from the energy such crimes demand ? " No one will understand the hatred of the Montagus and Capulets : " To what intent can these horrible pictures be offered to a nation which can scarcely conceive their possibility ? There are no doubt in France hearts born for hatred, and they have made themselves sufficiently known, but their vengeances are characterized by a refinement and, I venture to say, a pettiness conformable with these weakly manners of ours—*nos mœurs fluettes.*" Besides, and for many of the most prominent people in society this was another sort of grievance, these dramas treated of not very interesting persons. Every one knew the Atrides, but not the Capulets. "The Marquis de Brancas went off highly displeased after the first performance. What are to us, he said, all those Capulets whom nobody knows, and who are related to no one? —If Romeo was to have married a Juliette de Brancas, it would no doubt have been different." [1]

Marmontel is no less emphatic. The powerful tragedies, the vigorously-drawn comedies of the English theatre, may very well please a London audience; but how could they be accepted in France? "A gentle and polished nation, where each one considers it his duty to conform his sentiments and ideas to the ways of society, where habits are law, should present only characters softened by good manners and vices palliated by *bienséances*." [2]

Ducis remained immutable, and pursued his own plans. He risked "Léar" in 1783, and showed a crazy king on the stage; he discarded the unity of place and offered the most romantic sights to view: "The stage represents the most sinister spot in an ancient

---

[1] "A quel dessein peut-on donc tracer ces horribles tableaux à une nation qui à peine en doit concevoir la possibilité? Il y a sans doute en France des cœurs nés pour la haine, et ils se sont assez fait connaître, mais leurs vengeances portent un caractère de raffinement et, j'ose dire, de mesquinerie conforme au reste de nos mœurs fluettes."—"Le Marquis de Brancas sortit très mécontent de la première représentation.—Que nous font, dit-il, tous ces Capulets que l'on ne connaît pas, et qui ne tiennent à personne?—Si Roméo avait dû épouser une Juliette de Brancas, c'eût été différent, sans doute." "Correspondance Littéraire de Grimm, Diderot," &c., vol. x., p. 30.

[2] "Éléments de Littérature." *Sub verbo* "Comédie."

forest, rocks, caves, precipices, a fearful site. The sky is dark and threatening." In the second act is seen "a vast and ancient palace, where long and darksome vaults meet overhead. It must be of a terrible aspect." The play was first performed at court, then in public, and in spite of the "weakly manners," had, at least with the public, a great success ; Madame Vestris and Brizard were warmly applauded, and Ducis was thus recompensed for his kindness in not depriving the latter of his part, though the old actor was "falling more and more into ruins," and had lost his memory.[1] At the end of the performance, "the author was called for but without much enthusiasm, the last act having been less successful than the others ; he thought fit however to appear, and even at a moment when no one was thinking about him, for the actor whose business it was to announce the second performance of the play had just informed the public that peace was signed." The preliminaries of the treaty of Versailles with England, recognizing the independence of the thirteen United States, had been signed in fact this very day, Monday, January 20, 1783.

The success of the play nevertheless went on increasing, and the master-critics of the time became more and more indignant at the applause awarded to so many unaccountable strokes of audacity : " But," wrote

---

[1] "Ce qui m'afflige, c'est que l'honnête Brizard tombe de plus en plus en ruines. Quelques personnes m'ont conseillé de donner le rôle à Larive ; mais je me reprocherais d'affliger Brizard, qui a parfaitement saisi toutes mes intentions." To Deleyre, February 21, 1782. Ducis wrote later the long eulogistic epitaph for Brizard's tomb. To Madame Brizard, February, 1791.

La Harpe, "how, it will be asked, has that incredible heap of revolting absurdities, of puerile nonsense . . . managed to obtain a success as great as that of 'Zaïre' and 'Mérope'? Many reasons might be given; the chief one is that our theatre is no longer what it was, a choice assembly of more or less learned amateurs." The rabble has invaded it; "it has been taught to enjoy a pleasure which was not meant for it. . . . All the enlightened men of Paris cry out upon the scandal of such a success. It is even to be noted that this play, so applauded in town, succeeded very badly at court."[1] People seek consolation where they can.

In spite of the success, even Ducis's friends thought he was going too far. He writes: "Monsieur Ducis, I am told, cease for a while to paint such fearful pictures; you may take them up again later; but give us a tender play, in the style of 'Inès,' or of 'Zaïre.'"—No, replied Ducis, after "Léar," you shall have "Macbeth" and "Jean-sans-Terre"; and after "Jean-sans-Terre," "Othello." This was

---

[1] "Mais comment, dira-t-on, cet incroyable amas d'absurdités révoltantes, de niaiseries puériles . . . a-t-il obtenu un succès aussi grand que 'Zaïre' et 'Mérope'? On pourrait en donner bien des raisons, mais la principale c'est que nos spectacles ne sont plus ce qu'ils ont été, une assemblée choisie d'amateurs plus ou moins instruits : c'est le rendez-vous d'une foule désœuvrée et ignorante, depuis que le peuple des petits spectacles n'a eu besoin, pour envahir les grands, que de payer un peu plus cher un plaisir dont on lui a donné le goût, et qui n'était pas fait pour lui. . . . Tout ce qu'il y a d'hommes éclairés dans Paris se récrie sur le scandale d'un tel succès. Il est même à remarquer que cette pièce tant applaudie à la ville a très mal réussi à la cour." "Correspondance adressée au Grand Duc," Letter 181.

Ducis's last Shakespearean adaptation. Talma played the part of the Moor, and was wonderful in it. "People thought they saw, or rather they did see, in M. Talma," says the author, "the living Othello, with all the African energy, all the charm of his love, of his truthfulness, and of his youth. They heard the silence of his terrible despair," that silent way of acting made famous by Garrick in former years and so much admired by Marmontel. Ducis, at the end of his dramatic career, persevered in the methods of his early days. He adapts "Othello" as freely as "Hamlet." The events all take place in Venice, narrative is constantly resorted to, each hero is followed by a confidant, the train-bearer of his thoughts. "Over me," says Hédelmone (Desdemona; Lady Macbeth is called Frédégonde in Ducis's "Macbeth"), "over me you watched from my cradle, dear Hermance, and you, with your milk, sustained my infancy;"[1] in other words, you were my nurse. The heroine thereupon gives an account of this same infancy that the nurse remembered perhaps as well as she did. Lorédan-Cassio makes love to Hédelmone; Pézare-Iago excites the jealousy of the Moor who stabs her; Pézare's treason is discovered, and he is arrested by "those mortals of whom the State salaries the vigilance," usually called policemen.[2]

Ducis had taken particular precautions to render this subject supportable to the public; but they did

---

[1] "Sur moi, dès le berceau, tu veillas, chère Hermance,
   Et c'est toi, de ton lait, qui soutins mon enfance."
[2] "Ces mortels dont l'État gage la vigilance
   Ont de tous ses projets acquis la connaissance."

not prove sufficient, and he had to remodel his play.
No need to say that, following the example of all the
other adapters of "Othello," he had whitened, or at
least yellowed his Moor: "I thought that a yellow,
copper-like complexion, which is, in fact, suitable also
for an African, would have the advantage of not revolting the public, and especially the female eye." He
had softened his Iago as much as possible; they
suffer him in London as he is; but no such example
of rascality could have been tolerated in Paris: "It
is therefore quite intentionally that I have hidden from
my audience that atrocious character, not to revolt
them." Now for the dénouement: there it happened
that Ducis, in spite of all the care he had taken not to
have his Hédelmone smothered, had gone indeed too
far: "I must now speak of my dénouement. Never
was an impression more terrible. The whole assembly
rose with one cry. Several women fainted. It was as
though the dagger with which Othello had stabbed
his love had entered into every heart. But, to the
applause still given to the work, were mingling im-
probations, murmurs, and finally even a sort of
rebellion. I thought for one moment the curtain was
going to drop." Ducis could not refuse some satisfaction to an outburst so spontaneous; he wrote
another ending, leaving stage managers to conclude
as they pleased: "Consequently, to satisfy part of
my audience who found the weight of pity and of
terror excessive and too painful in my dénouement, I
have taken advantage of the plot of my play, which
made this change a very easy matter, to substitute a
happy ending for the one which had offended them."

Nothing, indeed, was easier; Pézare's wiles are discovered in time; Hédelmone, kissing her husband, begs him to "let her tender flame pour joy and peace into his soul":—

"Va, tout est oublié, va, que ma tendre flamme
Remette et le bonheur et la paix en ton âme."

Othello, "too happy not to forgive," pardons Pézare. The "mœurs fluettes" demanded all these concessions in the year of the first performance of "Othello"—1792.

A few months later, Ducis was writing to his friend Vallier: "Why talk to me, Vallier, of composing tragedies? Tragedy walks the streets. If I put my foot out of doors, I have blood up to my ankle." He lived aloof throughout the remainder of his long life, moved by the good and by the evil of which he was a spectator, welcoming his friends in his retreat: "Come, come; palaces may be narrow, but hermitages have a thousand resources;" courageously dating a letter to Paré, Minister of the Interior under the Convention, "the 14th of October of the Christian era, 1793," refusing, under the Empire, a seat in the Senate, a prize from the Academy, the cross of the Legion of Honour,[1] enjoying those simple pleasures which he had formerly described so well: "On this great river of life, amid so many barques that descend

[1] Letter to the Comte de Lacépède, Grand Chancellor of the Legion of Honour, November 27, 1803. Later: "Ma fierté naturelle est assez satisfaite de quelques *non* bien fermes que j'ai prononcés dans ma vie." To M. O'Dogharty de la Tour, November 7, 1806.

---

you," writes Ducis to his nephew, "to lend her your arm." Everything is settled, Julienne will start to-morrow from Versailles, and must be given dinner and bed, "so that she may see she is in my family; and do you, my dear nephew and good friend, kindly arrange everything, so that, by means of the tickets I have placed at your disposal, you may let her see comfortably and perfectly this terrifying tragedy. It cannot but be a keen pleasure for you to see and study in Julienne's face and mind the effects and impressions she receives; you will give me a faithful account of the same."[1] Besides Dante and Shakespeare, Ducis thus found himself imitating Molière.

He died in 1816, aged eighty-three. The success of his singular productions was not an ephemeral one; they outlived him. They had outlived the Revolution, they had been played under the Consulate and the Empire; they were still played under the Restoration; they outlived even the whirlwind of Romanticism; but from that time their popularity decreased, and they have now finally disappeared from the *répertoire*.

VI.

To form an equitable judgment concerning Ducis and his dramatic efforts, the dispositions of the public in his day must be borne in mind. He did what he could, and had to take into account the tastes of the

[1] Versailles, January 13 and 14, 1809. "Lettres de Ducis," ed. P. Albert, Paris, 1879, 8°. What Julienne felt at the sight of the terrifying tragedy is unluckily left for speculation. She subsequently married a baker, and lived very happily with him.

it rapidly, never to ascend it again, it is still a happiness to have found in one's little boat some kind souls who mingle their provisions with yours, and share the feelings of your heart. The sound of the waves is heard, telling us we are passing, and we cast a look on the varied scene of the vanishing shore."[1]

He retained his passion for Shakespeare to the end. A friend coming to see him at Versailles on a cold January morning, found him "in his bedroom, standing on a chair, and absorbed in arranging with some pomp, about the head of the English Æschylus, an enormous bunch of box foliage that had just been brought him." Seeing the surprise of his friend, who was no great admirer of Shakespeare, and according to whom Ducis had "often embellished" his model, he said: "Do you not see that to-morrow is the feast of St. William, the patron saint's day of my Shakespeare." Coming down from his chair, he added: "Dear friend, the ancients used to adorn with flowers the springs whence they had drawn."[2]

He retained his passion; but without understanding the master any better than formerly. He spent his time in retouching his adaptations and, as he thought, perfecting them. He continued with unabated energy both to soften and to overdo his model, in nowise restrained by the sarcasms of Abbé Le Blanc. Talma was his favourite interpreter. Having rearranged a whole act of Hamlet, he wrote to the tragedian: "I have seasoned it as much as I could with grace, pity, and especially terror. I have endeavoured to dip my pen in Dante's inkstand and to place myself in the inmost recesses of the accursed valleys, by the lurid light of Tisiphone's torches, and on the banks of the Phlegethon.

"Friend of mine, when you have fired every imagination, when every one dreams of Talma, what would you say to our producing without uttering a word, and like two villains who act by night, this fifth work of iniquity to crown our horror and our reputation! Your witchcraft alone can render this audacious attempt a possible and perhaps a happy one."[1]

The success of the undertaking equalled Ducis's expectations; his joy being at its height, he took a grave resolve, the importance of which did not escape him as he expatiates on it in several letters. The resolve was to send Julienne, his faithful *servante*, to Paris, that she might witness the play—"Julienne, my cook, who has never seen a tragedy, never been to the theatre, who has seen Talma in this house, who has taken care of him when he came to dine and sleep, and who longs for the pleasure, so new to her, of admiring him in the tragedies composed by her master." She has "a pretty head-dress that belongs to her, and matches a very neat gown, and it will be no shame fo

---

[1] "Sur ce grand fleuve de la vie, parmi tant de barques qui le descendent rapidement pour ne le remonter jamais, c'est encore un bonheur que d'avoir trouvé dans son batelet quelques bonnes âmes qui mêlent leurs provisions avec les vôtres et mettent leur cœur en commun avec vous. On entend le bruit de la vague qui nous dit que nous passons, et l'on jette un regard sur la scène variée du rivage qui s'enfuit." To M. Deleyre; "de notre solitude d'Auteuil," February 3, 1781.

[2] Notice on Ducis, by Campenon, prefacing the "Œuvres posthumes."

[1] Versailles, June 24, 1807.

Nothing, indeed, was easier; Pézare's wiles are discovered in time; Hédelmone, kissing her husband, begs him to "let her tender flame pour joy and peace into his soul":—

> "Va, tout est oublié, va, que ma tendre flamme
> Remette et le bonheur et la paix en ton âme."

Othello, "too happy not to forgive," pardons Pézare. The "mœurs fluettes" demanded all these concessions in the year of the first performance of "Othello"—1792.

A few months later, Ducis was writing to his friend Vallier: "Why talk to me, Vallier, of composing tragedies? Tragedy walks the streets. If I put my foot out of doors, I have blood up to my ankle." He lived aloof throughout the remainder of his long life, moved by the good and by the evil of which he was a spectator, welcoming his friends in his retreat: "Come, come; palaces may be narrow, but hermitages have a thousand resources;" courageously dating a letter to Paré, Minister of the Interior under the Convention, "the 14th of October of the Christian era, 1793," refusing, under the Empire, a seat in the Senate, a prize from the Academy, the cross of the Legion of Honour,[1] enjoying those simple pleasures which he had formerly described so well: "On this great river of life, amid so many barques that descend

---

[1] Letter to the Comte de Lacépède, Grand Chancellor of the Legion of Honour, November 27, 1803. Later: "Ma fierté naturelle est assez satisfaite de quelques *non* bien fermes que j'ai prononcés dans ma vie." To M. O'Dogharty de la Tour, November 7, 1806.

it rapidly, never to ascend it again, it is still a happiness to have found in one's little boat some kind souls who mingle their provisions with yours, and share the feelings of your heart. The sound of the waves is heard, telling us we are passing, and we cast a look on the varied scene of the vanishing shore."[1]

He retained his passion for Shakespeare to the end. A friend coming to see him at Versailles on a cold January morning, found him " in his bedroom, standing on a chair, and absorbed in arranging with some pomp, about the head of the English Æschylus, an enormous bunch of box foliage that had just been brought him." Seeing the surprise of his friend, who was no great admirer of Shakespeare, and according to whom Ducis had " often embellished " his model, he said : " Do you not see that to-morrow is the feast of St. William, the patron saint's day of my Shakespeare." Coming down from his chair, he added : " Dear friend, the ancients used to adorn with flowers the springs whence they had drawn."[2]

He retained his passion ; but without understanding the master any better than formerly. He spent his time in retouching his adaptations and, as he thought,

---

[1] " Sur ce grand fleuve de la vie, parmi tant de barques qui le descendent rapidement pour ne le remonter jamais, c'est encore un bonheur que d'avoir trouvé dans son batelet quelques bonnes âmes qui mêlent leurs provisions avec les vôtres et mettent leur cœur en commun avec vous. On entend le bruit de la vague qui nous dit que nous passons, et l'on jette un regard sur la scène variée du rivage qui s'enfuit." To M. Deleyre ; "de notre solitude d'Auteuil," February 3, 1781.

[2] Notice on Ducis, by Campenon, prefacing the "Œuvres posthumes."

perfecting them. He continued with unabated energy both to soften and to overdo his model, in nowise restrained by the sarcasms of Abbé Le Blanc. Talma was his favourite interpreter. Having rearranged a whole act of Hamlet, he wrote to the tragedian: " I have seasoned it as much as I could with grace, pity, and especially terror. I have endeavoured to dip my pen in Dante's inkstand and to place myself in the inmost recesses of the accursed valleys, by the lurid light of Tisiphone's torches, and on the banks of the Phlegethon.

"Friend of mine, when you have fired every imagination, when every one dreams of Talma, what would you say to our producing without uttering a word, and like two villains who act by night, this fifth work of iniquity to crown our horror and our reputation ! Your witchcraft alone can render this audacious attempt a possible and perhaps a happy one."[1]

The success of the undertaking equalled Ducis's expectations ; his joy being at its height, he took a grave resolve, the importance of which did not escape him as he expatiates on it in several letters. The resolve was to send Julienne, his faithful *servante*, to Paris, that she might witness the play--" Julienne, my cook, who has never seen a tragedy, never been to the theatre, who has seen Talma in this house, who has taken care of him when he came to dine and sleep, and who longs for the pleasure, so new to her, of admiring him in the tragedies composed by her master." She has " a pretty head-dress that belongs to her, and matches a very neat gown, and it will be no shame for

[1] Versailles, June 24, 1807.

you," writes Ducis to his nephew, "to lend her your arm." Everything is settled, Julienne will start to-morrow from Versailles, and must be given dinner and bed, "so that she may see she is in my family; and do you, my dear nephew and good friend, kindly arrange everything, so that, by means of the tickets I have placed at your disposal, you may let her see comfortably and perfectly this terrifying tragedy. It cannot but be a keen pleasure for you to see and study in Julienne's face and mind the effects and impressions she receives; you will give me a faithful account of the same."[1] Besides Dante and Shakespeare, Ducis thus found himself imitating Molière.

He died in 1816, aged eighty-three. The success of his singular productions was not an ephemeral one; they outlived him. They had outlived the Revolution, they had been played under the Consulate and the Empire; they were still played under the Restoration; they outlived even the whirlwind of Romanticism; but from that time their popularity decreased, and they have now finally disappeared from the *répertoire*.

VI.

To form an equitable judgment concerning Ducis and his dramatic efforts, the dispositions of the public in his day must be borne in mind. He did what he could, and had to take into account the tastes of the

---

[1] Versailles, January 13 and 14, 1809. "Lettres de Ducis," ed. P. Albert, Paris, 1879, 8°. What Julienne felt at the sight of the terrifying tragedy is unluckily left for speculation. She subsequently married a baker, and lived very happily with him.

time : "I have to deal," he said, "with a nation that requires a great deal of managing when it has to be led through the blood-stained roads of terror."[1] Had he altered Shakespeare less, he could not have had him played at all ; an Othello wholly black, an Iago wholly perfidious, a Desdemona smothered, would have been hissed. La Harpe, arbiter of taste, showed very clearly, when translating Lillo's "London Merchant," how ticklish the public had remained on the matter of decorum. For a difference of one shade—and how pale a shade !—an author might be applauded or hissed : "I have," he says, "observed as nearly as I could the rules of decorum received on our stage. . . . I have tried to ennoble the character of Milvoud . . . she is not a courtesan as in the English play, she is a widow, who has had an honest estate, but who, fallen into bad fortune through her husband's faults, had resorted to shameful resources."

If, from the works of the arbiter of taste, we pass on to those of a revolutionary theorist like Mercier, we find exactly the same apprehensions and niceties. When either of them indulges in discourses and theories, he is found to be in absolute opposition to the other ; when they come to practical work and write for the stage they cannot but consult the public taste, and then these enemies are discovered unexpectedly to agree. Mercier, who also wrote afterwards a "Timon,"[2] published in 1782 a "Romeo" : "Les Tombeaux de

---

[1] To Garrick, July 6, 1774.
[2] "Timon d'Athènes, en cinq actes et en prose, imitation de Shakespeare," Paris, "an iii.," 8º (with a preface which is a diatribe against Robespierre).

Vérone,"[1] in prose. This great contemner of the classics, of confidants, and of ancient rules, gives Juliet a confidante, Laura ; he has recourse to narratives and monologues and discards action ; he makes use of prose, but a prose full of noble expressions and periphrases, of general terms replacing the word proper. Mercier the revolutionist is seized with terror, his heart wavers, he dares not say : the clock strikes ; he says : " the quivering bronze has struck the twelfth hour."—" L'airain frémissant a sonné la douzième heure."—Juliet, already married, opens the play by a monologue which begins thus : " The twelfth hour has made itself heard. . . . It is the signal. Oh night, deepen your shades, conceal in darkness two unhappy and faithful lovers. . . . The authors of my days, tranquilly sleeping, do not suspect," &c.[2] The play, as in Chastellux's version, has a happy ending. Romeo, in Juliet's sepulchre, is about to pierce himself with his dagger ; the Capulets arrive to kill him ; the Montagus arrive to kill the Capulets ; at that moment Juliet awakes :—

"*Capulet.* My daughter living ! let me embrace her."

These words effect a sudden change. Romeo embraces Juliet ; the Montagus embrace the Capulets, and the curtain falls to the sound of kisses.

[1] Neufchâtel, 1782, 8º.
[2] "La douzième heure s'est fait entendre. . . . C'est le signal. O nuit, épaissis tes ombres, cache dans les ténèbres deux amants malheureux et fidèles. . . . Les auteurs de mes jours, paisiblement endormis ne soupçonnent point que la fille d'un Capulet, amante, épouse d'un Montagu. . . ." Friar Laurence is replaced by " Benvoglio, médecin naturaliste attaché aux deux maisons."

With the Revolution everything is changed in the State, but nothing is changed on the stage. " Frenchmen, my fellow citizens," writes Marie-Joseph Chénier, in 1790, dedicating " to the Nation " his " Charles IX. ou l'École des Rois," " accept the homage of this patriotic tragedy. I dedicate the work of a free man to a nation become free. . . . Women, sensitive and cowering sex, made to be the consolation of a sex that is your support, fear not this austere and tragic picture of political crimes. . . . Fathers of families, let your children come and see these severe sights." Chénier then addressed the king, meaning obviously to forget no one, and he honoured with a versified apostrophe that " head of a trusty nation " who had just returned to Paris, " the abode of his ancestors " :—

> " Monarque des Français, chef d'un peuple fidèle
> Qui va des nations devenir le modèle,
> Lorsqu'au sein de Paris, séjour de tes aïeux,
> Ton favorable aspect vient consoler nos yeux.
> Permets qu'une voix libre," &c.

The stage must, then, be rejuvenated ; there must, it seems, be new dramas for a regenerated people. But, all at once, just after his sounding appeals, Chénier showed by his " Charles IX.," his " Brutus et Cassius ou les Derniers Romains," that in reality nothing at all was changed ; he and his auditors remained just as particular, just as nice as before. Shakespeare, who puts low people on the stage, continued to inspire a feeling of disgust : " With far more ignorance and barbarity," said Marie-Joseph Chénier, " the Englishman Shakespeare has made the

Romans talk in one of the most admired scenes of his
'Julius Cæsar.' Is it possible to hear, without disgust,
Brutus reproach Cassius with feeling an itching in his
hand ? . . . Such words as these are still more revolting :—

> "I had rather be a dog and bay at the moon
> Than such a Roman."

There was no perceptible change ; Palissot and
Clément had expressed themselves in the very same
manner during the thick of the campaign led by
Voltaire against Shakespeare : " If Shakespeare had
not been blinded by the general bad taste then in
vogue, he would have perceived that the Roman people
of Cæsar's and of Cicero's time could never have
expressed themselves like the English populace of the
coarse times in which he lived." [1] People remained
convinced that the Roman populace expressed itself
with nobleness on all occasions, and that it would never
have ventured to use those expressions of anger,
" termes d'emportement," which the Academy had
excluded from its Dictionary, under Louis Quatorze.
The contemporaries of Robespierre trusted the pencil
of David and believed in his grand Romans.

Unity of place is admirably observed in Chénier :
" The scene is at Philippi in Macedonia, *in Brutus's
tent.*" The idea of using prose seems to Marie-Joseph
so inadmissible that it makes him laugh ; he sees in it
" a folly without importance, more diverting than dangerous."

The hold of the " ancien régime " on minds was not

[1] "Journal Français," March, 1777.

yet abolished. More than one among the most influential and independent spirits continued, as formerly, to advocate liberal reforms on all sorts of subjects, but to except tragedy alone. The great romantic of early days, Châteaubriand, who was to contribute so greatly to the impending renovation, devotes, at the beginning of the century, several essays to England and to Shakespeare. "I have traversed," he begins, in a phrase characteristic of his manner, and of the coming changes, "a few regions of the globe, but I confess that I have better observed the desert than mankind." A true romantic speaks here, and Châteaubriand takes the counterpart of the ideas dear to the old French classics, who, like Saint-Evremond, thought that "A true-bred gentleman must live and die in a capital;"[1] dear also to the ancient Greeks who thought with Plato: "Nothing can we learn from the fields and trees; much from towns and the society of men."[2] But as soon as it is a question of tragedy, the tone changes with Châteaubriand, and the ancient régime reappears. Shakespeare is even blacker in his eyes than in Voltaire's; his examples are dangerous both for art and for morals; his works are fit for an audience "composed of judges arriving from Bengal or from the coast of Guinea. . . . Shakespeare should reign eternally with such a people." But a nation who knows the rules of art "cannot return to monsters without risk-

---

[1] "Un honnête homme doit vivre et mourir dans une capitale." To the Earl of Saint-Albans, "Œuvres mêlées," 1708, vol. iii., p. 228.

[2] Τὰ μὲν οὖν χωρία καὶ τὰ δένδρα οὐδέν μ' ἐθέλει διδάσκειν, οἱ δ' ἐν τῷ ἄστει ἄνθρωποι. "Phædrus."

ing its morals. In this respect the liking for Shakespeare is far more dangerous in France than in England. With the English it is only ignorance; with us it is depravity. . . . Bad taste and vice nearly always go together." Shakespeare has, it is true, very unusual " natural talents "; but " with regard to dramatic art," no good can be said of him; to praise him would be equivalent to pretending " that there are no dramatic rules." And this very Châteaubriand, whose " Génie du Christianisme" was to appear the following year, and to second so effectually the romantic renovation, did not hesitate, in order to emphasize his disapprobation of Shakespeare, to compare him to a Gothic cathedral, involving the man and the edifice in the same condemnation: " One beauty in Shakespeare does not excuse his innumerable defects; a Gothic monument may please by its obscurity and by the very difformity of its proportions; but no one dreams of building a palace on such a model."[1] Châteaubriand was writing under the Consulate, when palaces, and even churches, were being built in Greek style. Gothic and barbarous were still, as in Boileau's time, regarded as one and the same thing. " The monument," Boileau had once written to Brossette, respecting a Roman tomb discovered at Lyons, " does not seem to me in very good taste, it has a heaviness which in my opinion borders on the Gothic."[2]

[1] Essay on " l'Angleterre et les Anglais," 1800; on Shakespeare, 1801. Montesquieu had said in the same manner: " Un bâtiment d'ordre gothique est une espèce d'énigme pour l'œil qui le voit, et l'âme est embarrassée comme quand on lui présente un poème obscur." " Encyclopédie," *sub verbo* " Goût " (1757).

[2] May 14, 1704.

Shakespeare's admirers have since accepted Châteaubriand's sentence and have converted it into praise: thus do tastes and judgments sometimes veer round; the same happened with the verdict of Marmontel, who, to show his disdain for Glück, had called him the "Shakespeare of music"[1]—an insult then so great that some Piccinists, maybe, found it excessive—a eulogium so high to-day that many a Glückist deems it exaggerated.

Madame de Stael, so enthusiastic about "northern literature," was not at all blind to Shakespeare's defects; she found in Ossian alone the really characteristic representative of the north: "There exist, it seems to

[1] "Pour qui ne voudrait qu'être remué, Shakespeare serait préférable à Racine : aussi par la même raison qui fait donner à la musique de M. Glück une préférence exclusive sur la musique italienne, a-t-on mis le tragique anglais au dessus de tous nos tragiques ; mais cette nouvelle école de goût n'a pas eu de vogue à Paris." Such was, however, the animosity of Marmontel against Glück that he considered that to call him "le Shakespeare de la musique" was even "un honneur excessif." "Essai sur les Révolutions de la musique," 1777, p. 27. On the quarrel between the Piccinists and Glückists, see Brunel, "Les Philosophes et l'Académie," 1884, p. 290. Fiévée and Palissot published or republished at that time judgments quite as severe as Châteaubriand's: "La tragédie anglaise se compose en général de fous, de folles, de spectres, de meurtes longuement exécutés et de sang. . . . Notre public repousse maintenant de nos théâtres ce qu'on appelle le genre anglais, il a raison. Il faut à une nation délicate des spectacles qui élèvent l'esprit ou qui le réjouissent." Fiévée, "Lettres sur l'Angleterre," 1802, p. 89. The "conjurés" favourable to Shakespeare dream of plunging the nation again into barbarity, "et d'établir le siège de leur Académie à Bedlam." Palissot. "Mémoires pour servir à l'histoire de notre Littérature," Paris, 1803, 2 vols., 8°, vol. i., p. 158.

me, two literatures quite distinct, the one that comes from the south and the one that descends from the north; the one of which Homer is the source, and the one whose source is Ossian." [1]

Shakespeare, meanwhile, was dragging out a career as miserable as ever: Ducis had been really an audacious experimenter. A few celebrated passages from Shakespearean dramas are found occasionally inserted into the tragedies of the day; for instance, in "Épicharis et Néron, ou Conspiration pour la Liberté, tragédie en cinq actes et en vers, par Legouvé, citoyen français; Paris an II." Nero is tormented by the same spectres as Richard III. :—

> "Ne me trompé-je pas ? Je crois voir mes victimes. . . .
> Je les vois, les voila. . . . Du fond des noirs abîmes,
> S'élancent jusqu'à moi des fantômes sanglants ;
> Ils jettent dans mon sein des flambeaux, des serpents . . ."

But generally (Ducis excepted) Shakespeare at that moment furnished chiefly matter for operas, pantomimes, or shows for the circus, such plays as : "Romeo and Juliet, Year Two of the Republic one and indivisible," an opera by Ségur, music by Steibelt, with a happy ending, performed by "le citoyen Chateaufort" (Capulet) and the "citoyenne Scio" (Juliet), with confidants, romantic scenery ("the stage represents an avenue plunged in a darkness that the rays of the moon can hardly pierce"), and an Antonio, "guardian of the ancestral sepulchre," who replaces

---

[1] "De la Littérature considérée dans ses rapports avec les institutions sociales," part i., chap. xi., 1st ed., 1800.

Friar Laurence;—"Hamlet, pantomime tragique en trois actes, mélée de danses," by Louis Henry, "musique de M. le Comte de Gallenberg, chevalier de l'ordre des Deux-Siciles," 1816, with a statue of old Hamlet, that comes to life, like the statue of the Commander in Don Juan;—"Les visions de Macbeth ou les Sorcières d'Écosse, mélodrame à grand spectacle,"[1] with a great deal of magic, "witches rising perpendicularly by the side of a tall pine tree, their feet resting only on the wings of a vulture," a Lady Macbeth who, like Ducis's heroine, is called Frédégonde, and a traitor as black as Iago added to Shakespeare's plot;—"Le More de Venise ou Othello, pantomime entremêlée de dialogues (and dances), représentée sur le théâtre du cirque olympique de MM. Franconi," 1818.

[1] Paris, 1817, composed before 1812. Of the same period, "Shakespeare amoureux," by Alex. Duval, 1804, a *bluette* played by Talma. In his essay on the "Influence de Shakespeare" (Brussels, 1856), M. A. Lacroix mentions an "Imogènes ou la Gageure indiscrète," comedy by Dejaure (a play which I have not seen), music by Kreutzer, 1796, drawn from "Cymbeline." See, on the other hand, in "Corinne" (1807) the description of a performance of "Romeo" in Rome ; Corinne plays the part of Juliet ; "never had any tragedy produced such an effect in Italy." (Bk. vii., chap. iii.)

EPILOGUE

YEARS pass; times change. Between politics and literature the contradiction continues, but is reversed; politics become calmer, literature becomes more turbulent. People were classic under the Terror, they are romantic under the Restoration. Napoleon is at Saint Helena, kings have returned, they are once more " Kings of France," the ancient Court has been reconstituted. Will not halcyon days begin again for ancient tragedy? Not so; its last hour is near; it is about to die, not, however, without a struggle. In its turn it is beleaguered, the day of the independents has come once more. Melpomene still reigns with Louis XVIII.; her star wanes under Charles X. Stendhal, in 1823, finds the quarrel just where Voltaire left it; he takes sides unhesitatingly against received ideas.[1] The redoubts to be carried are exactly the same; he demands: 1st, the faculty of writing in prose; 2nd, the suppression of the unities; 3rd, the right to use the proper word, the most telling expression, and not invariably the noblest and most dignified. He deplores the fact that a number of national subjects should be forbidden to French authors for the mere reason that

---

[1] "Racine et Shakespeare," 1st ed., 1823.

the word "pistol" is not allowed in a tragedy, when the thing had played such a considerable part in the national history. He laments the submissiveness of Legouvé, who having to reproduce the famous saying of Henri IV. on the " poule-au-pot le dimanche " felt bound to make the king speak thus :—

> " Je veux enfin qu'au jour marqué pour le repos,
> L'hôte laborieux des modestes hameaux,
> Sur sa table moins humble ait, par ma bienfaisance,
> Quelques uns de ces mets réservés à l'aisance."

Imagine the lively, outspoken, sharp-witted monarch using such elaborate circumlocutions, speaking of "the hard-working guest of modest hamlets," and not daring to say a peasant, and calling a hen "one of those viands reserved to the well-to-do"! He had to speak thus on the stage in 1806. The destruction of the Bastille had in no wise profited the tragic muse.[1] She continued to express herself as she had in Voltairean days when it took four lines to say such a simple thing as " Phradate gave you an antidote " :—

> " Ces végétaux puissants qu'en Perse on voit éclore,
> Bienfaits nés dans les champs de l'astre qu'elle adore,
> Par les soins de Phradate avec art préparés,
> Firent sortir la mort de vos flancs déchirés." [2]

Shakespeare was now publicly played in English on

---

[1] "La jeunesse," said Stendhal, "si libérale lorsqu'elle parle de charte, de jury, d'élections " becomes " despotique," when it is a question of tragedies. (*Ibid.*)
[2] "Sémiramis," iv., 2.

the boards of a Parisian theatre ; but the attempt was a premature one ; Hamlet and Othello were hissed off the stage. The representations had been organized by Penley, and they began with "Othello" at the Porte-Saint-Martin, on the 31st of July, 1822. Not a word could be heard, violent altercations took place, apples and oranges were thrown at the actors ; "Parlez Français," the audience shouted from all sides.[1] At length the gendarmes interfered and the military took possession of the stage. The comedians persevered, but the event proved that they had appealed "from a tumultuous pit to an infuriated one" ; the "School for Scandal," performed on the 3rd of August, met with a worse reception than even "Othello." Apples and eggs were again used as a means of expressing literary doubts and objections. Miss Gaskell, who played the part of "Lady Smerweld" (Sneerwell) fainted. Her fainting touched many hearts ; but the papers, to prevent a possible reaction, had just republished extracts from Monnet's account of his London experience when his French troupe had met with a similar reception, and one of his actresses had received a burning candle in her bosom : so that no mercy could be shown to Penley and his people. "The

---

[1] Stendhal, "Racine et Shakespeare," 1823. Particular causes and especially the restrictions put upon French representations in London, greatly contributed to increase this animosity : "A Londres les artistes français sont réduits à donner des représentations occultes," "à jouer incognito," that is, to give private representations by subscription. The Paris public wanted the same restrictions to be put upon English players. "Le Miroir," July 31st, Aug. 4th, 1822.

unfortunate artists were obliged to abandon the field of battle, all strewn with projectiles." [1]

They took refuge in the Theatre of the Rue Chantereine, "more like a barn than a theatre," and there gave private performances by subscription. In this "obscure and inelegant nook" the English muses were at length "received with all the consideration due to exiles." The audience was not large but it consisted of "enlightened amateurs" who could this time "peacefully enjoy the pleasure of seeing Desdemona smothered, and Gertrude slaughtered." "Roméo," "Othello," "Hamlet," "Catherine et Pierre," as the papers announced it (obviously Garrick's adaptation of "Taming of the Shrew"), "Le Spectre du Château" (*i.e.*, Addison's "Drummer"), "Richard III." were given in succession; the performances came to an end on the 25th of October. [2]

But the cause of what Stendhal called "romanticisme" was gaining ground; the hour of its triumph was near. Stendhal heralded it: "I raise my voice because I perceive clearly that the death knell of classicism has struck. Courtiers have disappeared, pedants fall or become police censors, classicism fades away."

Five or six years roll by: the new spirit manifests itself; it blows, impetuous and irresistible, over the stage, poetry, arts, music. The national past, foreign literatures, Dante, Ronsard, Shakespeare, Goethe, Byron, are studied with a new ardour. Victor Hugo prepares his manifestoes; Delacroix paints with his

---

[1] Alexandre Dumas, "Mes Mémoires," 1888, vol. iv., p. 277.
[2] "Le Miroir," July to October, 1822.

"inebriated broom," *son balai ivre*, and under his pencil Hamlets, Othellos, Romeos, and Macbeths stand, kneel, pray, dream, and threaten, numberless. The smaller arts, the engraver's, the goldsmith's, transform themselves at the same time : " Célestin Nanteuil," says Théophile Gautier, " stood far above real life, looking down on the ocean of roofs, watching the bluish smoke curl upwards, perceiving from his heights the streets and places like the squares on a checker-board . . . all this, confusedly, through the softening veil of mists, while from his aërial observatory, he saw near him, distinct in every detail, the rose-windows with their stained glass, the pinnacles bristling with croziers, the kings, the patriarchs, the prophets, the saints, the angels of every order, all the monstrous army of demons, or of chimeras, with claws, scales, teeth ; hideously winged, *guivres*, *tarasques*,[1] gargoyles, asses' heads, monkey faces, all the strange bestiary of the Middle Ages."

What language, and what a change ! Will these people who admire *tarasques* and monkeys be afraid of the mouse that stirs, or stirs not, at the beginning of " Hamlet " ? Will they request, like Captain Douin's friends, that " the general terms of the gods of mythology " be used ? Will they have the curtain dropped on Desdemona's death ? They are no longer afraid ; at least, they think so : " The fate of Icarus," writes Gautier again, " now terrified no one. Wings ! wings ! wings ! was the cry on all sides, even should

---

[1] The famous monster of Tarascon, said to have been vanquished by Martha, the sister of Lazarus, who bound it with her girdle ; *Guivres*, heraldic snakes.

we fall into the sea ! To fall from heaven one must have been there ! " All endeavoured to scale the walls of heaven ; the ramparts that protected the ancient unities fell crashing to the ground ; verse, like tragedy, was at length emancipated ; inanimate beings took life ; the " twelve feathers " of the stale alexandrine suddenly became wings ; the poets of the old school were stopped in their game and the racquet fell from their hands : they looked aghast at the familiar "shuttlecock," risen beyond their reach, borne by the winds, a lark in the blue sky :—

> "Le vers qui sur son front,
> Jadis portait toujours douze plumes en rond,
> Et sans cesse sautait sur la double raquette
> Qu'on nomme prosodie et qu'on nomme étiquette,
> Rompt désormais la règle et trompe le ciseau,
> Et s'échappe, volant qui se change en oiseau,
> De la cage césure et fuit vers la ravine,
> Et vole dans les cieux, alouette divine." (*Hugo.*)

It was the end of an epoch and liberty's revenge, a revenge so complete that any liberty seemed good now, whencesoever it came, whithersoever it led. The very word made one start and caused a quiver of enthusiasm. Quinet addressed himself to Herder, 1827 ; Saint-Beuve to Ronsard, 1828 ; Guizot to Shakespeare, 1821 ; and Le Tourneur, rejuvenated, enjoyed a new tide of popularity.

A second attempt was ventured by English comedians. The success was as brilliant as the first failure had been doleful ; for several seasons there were English performances—one at the Odéon in 1827, another at the Favart Theatre in 1828, others later, with Charles

Kemble as Hamlet, Romeo, Othello ; Terry as Lear and Shylock ; Macready as Macbeth ; Kean as Hamlet, Richard III., and Othello; Miss Smithson as Desdemona and Ophelia. All the Paris literary men and artists attended the performances : Hugo, then writing the preface of " Cromwell," [1] was there ; so was Dumas, who felt " bouleversé " by " Hamlet," and understood from that moment, as he expressed it in his immoderate language, " the possibility of building a world " ; so was Berlioz, whose emotion took a quasi-religious turn, and who began to wonder if there was really an eternal life and if in heaven he should meet Shakespeare and his interpreter, the beautiful Henrietta Smithson : " If there is another world, shall we meet ? . . . Shall I ever see Shakespeare ? Will she be able to know me ? Will she comprehend the poetry of my love for her ? " [2] He

[1] Commenced September 30th, finished the following month, 1827. Souriau, " La Préface de Cromwell," 1897, p. 328.

[2] " Il y a aujourd'hui un an que je LA vis pour la dernière fois . . . Oh ! malheureuse, que je t'aimais ! J'écris en frémissant, que je t'aime !

" S'il y a un nouveau monde, nous retrouverons nous ? . . . Verrai-je jamais Shakespeare ? . . . Pourra-t-elle me connaître ? Comprendra-t-elle la poésie de mon amour ? . . . O Juliette, Ophelia, Belvidera, noms que l'enfer répète sans cesse ! . . .

" LA RAISON.—Sois tranquille, imbécile, dans peu d'années il ne sera pas plus question de tes souffrances que de ce que tu appelles le génie de Beethoven, la sensibilité passionnée de Spontini, l'imagination rêveuse de Weber, la puissance colossale de Shakespeare ! . . .

Va, va, Henriette Smithson
et Hector Berlioz
seront réunis dans l oubli de la tombe."

Letter to M. Hiller, 1829, " Correspondance inédite," 1879,

did not have to wait till a future life to realize one of these 'unions; in 1833 he married Ophelia, and immediately a life began for the pair which gave them, alas, no foretaste of the joys of the elect.

The public attended the performances with deep emotion; to assist its understanding of the plays, tiny editions of them had been printed, containing both the French and English text.[1] At times the audience felt a little inclined to laugh, as, for instance, when Hamlet was seen to seat himself on the floor, "a posture so incompatible with tragic dignity," and when Ophelia walked in with "long straws stuck in her hair"; [2] but these disrespectful inclinations were quickly repressed. During the entr'actes, the coulisses and lobbies resounded with discussions; the Press and and the reviews published numerous essays for and against; the "Globe" inserted a series of enthusiastic letters by Charles Magnin, and the "Revue Française" a witty and cutting essay by the Duc de Broglie, who noted the success of the barbarian, the triumph of "Attila - Shakespeare." [3] A proportionate disfavour

---

p. 68. Enthusiasm of Jules Janin for Miss Smithson and for Kean: "Je vois encore Hamlet au cimetière, et le fossoyeur semblable au fossoyeur d'Eugène Delacroix." "Histoire de la littérature dramatique," 1853 ff., vol. vi., p. 331. Berlioz married Miss Smithson in 1833; they separated in 1840.

[1] "Théâtre Anglais, ou collection des pièces anglaises jouées à Paris, publiées avec l'autorisation des directeurs et entièrement conformes à la représentation," but differing greatly from Shakespeare's text. Paris (at Mme. Vergne's), 1827, 12°.

[2] Charles Magnin, Letters to the "Globe," 1827-28, collected and reprinted in "Causeries et Méditations," Paris, 1843, 2 vols., 8°. See the portrait of Miss Smithson by Valmont.

[3] January, 1830, à propos of Vigny's "Othello." "Le Théâtre

MISS SMITHSON AS OPHELIA, LATER MADAME BERLIOZ.
By A. de Valmont.

fell to the lot of the Geoffroys, Duports, and other morose critics who had persisted in declaring Shakespeare unreadable : "What reading for men of the world ! Literary professionals can scarcely bear the length and dulness of it !" But men of the world gave the lie to M. Duport.[1]

The experience of 1827 was decisive. From that moment Shakespeare is admitted into the Pantheon of the literary gods ; French painters, poets, and musicians are of one mind ; Ingres himself, classical Ingres, makes room for him in Homer's cortège.[2] His influence becomes more marked as the romantic movement grows wider. It can be traced in the works of all the literary men of the period from Victor Hugo to Flaubert, from Dumas to Musset. Victor Hugo divides the history of humanity into three periods : periods of the ode, of the epic, and of the drama, represented by Moses, Homer, and Shakespeare ; all the rivers of poetry "flow into the ocean of the drama " ; "everything in modern poetry tends towards the drama," and the drama, according to Hugo, is Shakespeare.[3] Dumas, growing more and more immoderate, goes further still

---

Français s'est rendu faute d'avoir été secouru à propos et ravitaillé en temps opportun. Dans la soirée du 25 octobre dernier, Attila-Shakespeare en a pris possession avec armes et bagages, enseignes déployées, au fracas de mille fanfares. Pauvres poètes de la vieille roche, qu'allez-vous devenir ? "—" Revue Française," No. xiii.

[1] " Essais littéraires sur Shakespeare," Paris, 1828, 2 vols. 8°.

[2] At the Louvre, dated 1827, the figure of the dramatist is however painted so close to the frame that only part of the face is seen.

[3] Preface to " Cromwell."

and calls Shakespeare "the poet who has created most, after God";[1] but does not hesitate, for all his idolatry, to treat rather unceremoniously the productions of this divine being. Belonging, though he does, to the generation which did not fear *guivres* or *tarasques*, Dumas the elder, Dumas the Mousquetaire, dares not confront the mouse in "Hamlet"; and, in the version of the play written by him in collaboration with Paul Meurice in long alexandrine lines, the cowrin, the awful animal is left unmentioned. The two authors end their drama after the manner of Ducis, not after the manner of Shakespeare:—

"*Hamlet*. And I? am I to remain on earth, a disconsolate orphan, breathing this air saturated with misery? . . . Will God stretch forth His arm against me, Father? And what chastisement then awaits me?
Ghost. Thou shalt live."[2]

On this the play ends. The enthusiasm for Shakespeare is none the less durable; it conquers the repre-

---

[1] Preface for the transl. of Shakesp., by Benj. Laroche, 1839.
[2] "*Hamlet*. Et moi, vais-je rester, triste orphelin sur terre,
A respirer cet air imprégné de misère? . . .
Est-ce que Dieu sur moi fera peser son bras,
Père? Et quel châtiment m'attend donc?
Le fantôme.   Tu vivras."

"Hamlet," by Dumas and Meurice, performed December 15, 1847; costumes "copiés sur les tableaux de Lehmann et les croquis d'Eugène Delacroix"; engraving in "L'Illustration," December 25, 1847. The version of the play as given in 1886 (with Mounet-Sully and Mlle. Reichenberg) has been considerably altered to make it more like Shakespeare's. At the beginning, the allusion to the mouse is restored; Hamlet dies at the end. As early as 1842 M. Paul Meurice had given a "Falstaff" at the Odéon.

THE PLAYERS' SCENE IN "HAMLET"
A lithograph by Eugène Delacroix, 1835

sentatives of schools the most opposed. Shakespearean fancy guides the hand of Musset when he becomes a dramatist, and Heine praises him therefore in a book where praise of the French school of poetry does not abound.[1] Lamartine, after Guizot and Hugo, devotes a whole volume to Shakespeare : " Virtue, crime, passion, vices, ridicules, grandeur, pettiness, everything is his domain, the whole keyboard of man's nature lies under his fingers."[2] Flaubert writes to George Sand : " I read nothing now except Shakespeare, whom I have taken up again from one end to the other. It invigorates you and puts air into your lungs as if you were on the top of a high mountain. Everything seems flat by the side of that prodigious *bonhomme*" (1875).

Translations multiply ; complete editions in English are printed in Paris ; every one has become familiar with the " prodigious *bonhomme* " in a thousand ways : through reading, through the performance of his plays in French and English[3] (and even in Italian with Salvini and Rossi, and, at the moment I write, Novelli) ; through adaptations for the stage by Vigny,

---

[1] " De l'Angleterre," 2nd ed., 1881, p. 241.

[2] " Shakespeare et son Œuvre," Paris, 1865, 8°, p. 11.

[3] Various English troupes visited Paris, such as Macready's in 1845, with Miss Helen Faucit (at the " Italiens " ; they played with great applause " Hamlet " at the Tuileries before Louis Philippe) ; Wallack's troupe which had little success ; Daly's American troupe in 1888, at the Vaudeville, with Miss Ada Rehan. She played the " Shrew " ; her playing was admired, but the play was not : " Je ne sais, mais quelque chose se révolte en moi à ces brutalités, elles me navrent et ne m'amusent point. Je ne peux pas rire à la vue de cette femme injuriée, bousculée, frappée même " (Sarcey).

Dorchain, Cressonnois and Samson,[1] Bouchor (for the marionnettes' theatre of the Galerie Vivienne),[2] Haraucourt,[3] Delair,[4] Aicard, &c. ; through commentaries, criticisms, public lectures, drawings, engravings ; through musical works drawn from his plays, the " Roméo et Juliette," and " Béatrice et Benedict " of Berlioz, not to speak of the operas of Gounod, Ambroise Thomas, or Saint-Saëns. No one would think of saying to-day, at a public sitting of the Academy, as Voltaire did addressing his fellow-academicians in the last century : "Some of you, gentlemen, know that there exists a tragedy of Shakespeare's called ' Hamlet.' " Its existence is notorious.

What, then, is the final result of these commotions, revolutions, and literary wars? It is not, as regards the action of Shakespeare, what certain symptoms might have made one fear, nor what numerous angry protestations formerly prophesied. This conqueror, this new

---

[1] "Hamlet" with Sarah Bernhardt as Ophelia (at the Porte-Saint-Martin, 1886).

[2] "La Tempête," "selon nous la plus divine entre les comédies de Shakespeare " (a prose translation, 1888).

[3] Who rivals Dumas in his enthusiasm :—

"O Poète immortel qui pétrissais des âmes,
Frère de Dieu . . .
Du seul baiser des mots tu procréais des hommes.
Quand tu leur disais : marche, ils partaient triomphants,
Roi des âges, et plus vivants que nous ne sommes—
La mort passe sur nous sans toucher tes enfants."

"Shylock," 1889 (Mlle. Réjane as Portia, Albert Lambert as Shylock, at the Odéon).

[4] "La Mégère apprivoisée " at the Français, 1891 (Coquelin as Petrucchio ; a very free adaptation).

"Attila," has enslaved no one; on the contrary he has assisted in a work of emancipation: thereby deserving our gratitude. Revolutions may succeed each other: beneath the various elements of which French minds are formed, a Latin substratum will always remain; French poets may depart from the classic ideal, and have often done so, but even then they keep nearer to it than people of northern climes: thus preserving an originality that is theirs, and for the loss of which no amount of successful imitation could compensate. They may write epigrams on Versailles "where the gods put on such airs in their dried-up basins,"

> "Où les dieux font tant de façons
> Pour vivre à sec dans leurs cuvettes" (*Musset*);

at heart they love Versailles, and if the naiads lack water, springs are made to flow again and the rose-coloured marble of the steps is restored to its former beauty. What was of real import has been done; for a hundred years, scarcely any one had dared walk beyond the alleys of Versailles, and even under pretext of not altering them, they were no longer kept up. Men were wanted bold enough to go further, to pass the limits of the avenues, and walk into the grand and simple landscape seen from the terraces beyond the gardens: for there is room in nature for both one and the other, for parterres and for real country; French gardens there be, and French country too, both very French indeed. It seems as though it was a slight thing to do, and as though one had needed only to dare. No doubt it was, but no one dared until the romantics led the way. "The door was open," it will be said. Assuredly; but not more so than the door of America; and it was, we know, enough for the glory of Columbus that he should have crossed its threshold.

An unexpected consequence has been the result: these struggles, these furious discussions, these stormy representations in which the long-haired romantics ("one cannot be born with wigs," Gautier said), those ferocious reformers "who would have liked to eat an academician," did their worst—these quarrels, instead of blunting the national genius and of wearying it out, not only restored it to, but even increased, its pristine fecundity. France has become, from that moment, the productive nation *par excellence* in dramatic matters. If English novels are everywhere read, French plays are everywhere performed; from Lisbon to St. Petersburg, from Athens to London. French dramatists are now the great purveyors; the theatres of the whole universe are peopled with their heroes. No one disputes France the first rank in this: liberty and competition produce such results; there is no wisdom in always fearing them.

Shakespeare so different, so powerful, so universal, has helped, for his part, to bring about this emancipation. To believe that he has become acclimatized in France, that his genius has penetrated and transformed the French mind, is an error. He is known, the beauty and grandeur of his poetry is felt, this is an undoubted fact and a happy one. There is no reason to demand anything more, and it would besides be asking for an impossibility; all the care in the world will not make fine olive trees grow in Scotland, nor fir trees in

Algeria. It would be a great misfortune if there were to remain upon earth but one genius and but one race, with no more of those contests and contrasts which have ever been such a powerful incentive to progress. What matters, above all, is that the genius of each race should reach its most perfect development; and that cannot come to pass if its nature be thwarted. In its walk through the ages, briars may impede and trammels may arrest its progress; neighbours, rivals, even enemies may prove helpful if they cut those trammels, or merely point them out; but not if they take their rival's place.

There is no danger in the present case of such a substitution; the French national genius, enamoured of straight lines, is too strongly tempered to be metamorphosed. Those who might be inclined to doubt this have only to go and see Shakespeare played at the Théâtre Français or at the Odéon, particularly on a Sunday, for they will then see an average audience which does not form its opinions on formulas learnt in books. They will observe that the public applauds a scene, a tirade, a line, a striking phrase, a tragic episode, but not Shakespeare in his entirety, nor in what is most personal in him. This public listens attentively, admires sometimes, but without being carried away; it is in the presence of a genius too different from its own; the differences arouse a feeling of uneasiness as much as the beauties arouse admiration; the audience is moved and remains in doubt. It will, on the other hand, be passionately interested in Racine's " Iphigénie," or even in a translation of Sophocles' " Œdipus Tyrannus"; there it admires everything, it no longer

cares to discuss, it knows no uncertainty, it is under the
spell. This is exactly the reverse of what takes place in
London. Let the Comédie Française give performances
in England, there the tragic *répertoire* is reduced to a
minimum ; let it go from town to town in the French
provinces, that *répertoire* is the one to draw crowds,
and " the spectators in the cheap places are the most
numerous and the ones who are gripped by their very
heart-strings." This was clearly seen at the time of
the great *tournée* in the provinces in 1893 : " It was
then the tragedians' turn to jeer at their comrades
the comedians. They came loaded with laurels and
bank notes ; it was they who had saved the situation.
In London their *répertoire* had been curtailed ; they
had been kept away from the public as much as
possible." [1]

The innermost substrata of the national nature remain the same. As many people have been killed on
the stage in France since 1830 as in any country in
the world, and yet significant incidents show from time
to time that there is still a difference. " A kind of
rising " at the fatal moment is no longer to be feared,
it is true, as in the days of Ducis ; but yet protestations are sometimes heard. At a performance of
" Macbeth," at the Odéon, lately, when Banquo was
about to be killed, a lady in the stalls exclaimed, " Ah !
I cannot see that," and went out ; she came back
when the deed had been accomplished. The three
unities are no longer imposed on any one, but they

[1] Sarcey, " La Comédie Française en voyage," feuilleton of the
" Temps," August 7, 1893.

remain an ideal to which authors conform with alacrity whenever the subject admits of it ;[1] Augier has shown it on more than one occasion. Stage alexandrines continue to have ardent admirers : "Contrarily to what is generally believed, the public has, riveted in its very soul, a respect and love for verse on the stage—for grand, for heroic verse. The French have tragedy in the blood. It is said that they only enjoy minute descriptions of flat and vulgar reality ; nothing is less true. Throw them fine alexandrines, vibrating and sonorous, and they snatch at them, *ils les gobent;* the word is Parisian slang, but it is the true word."[2] The "Hamlet" of Dumas and Meurice, which is still acted at the Théâtre Français, is entirely written in alexandrines.

Shakespeare has helped to break the old fetters which, grown heavier from generation to generation, and imposed upon every author whatsoever his subject, had at length stopped all movement. He has helped to open the gate of heaven to the "alouette divine" spoken of by Hugo. Upon the importance of his *rôle* in this great crisis different minds may have different opinions ; that he had a *rôle* no one will contest, and that is enough to justify gratitude. This loving tribute is no longer grudged him in France ;

---

[1] "Je vous ferai remarquer que, quoi qu'on pense de ces règles fameuses ... nous voyons que de nos jours même, quand nos auteurs dramatiques veulent obtenir des effets plus saisissants, de ces effets qui ne nous laissent, comme l'on dit, le loisir ni de réfléchir ni de respirer, il commencent par enfermer leurs trois ou leurs cinq actes dans un même décor et par resserrer leur action dans les vingt-quatre heures."—Brunetière, "Les Époques du Théâtre Français."

[2] Sarcey, "Temps" of March 7, 1892.

and it may be accorded the more willingly, in that no one who joins in it is expected to abjure the cult of the ancestors, or to close the door of the temple on those whom France will never weary of hearing called THE JUST.

INDEX

A

Academy, French, addresses Louis XIV., xvi, 113 ff.; 22; its Dictionary, 74, 442; and the "Cid," 92; 152; appealed to on the subject of Shakespeare, 354 ff., 395 ff.; awards special honours to Voltaire, 393; its dictionary to be reformed, 397; Rutledge's appeal to, 400

"Les Accidents," by Collé, 273

Acrobats, English, in Paris, 51

Actors (and actresses), French, on the stage, xiv; English, 127, 192; French, in London, 131, 468; English buried in Westminster, 204, 242; French and English, 293, 295 ff.; rules for, 311; English in Paris, 451, 463. *See* Players

Addison, xviii, 62 ff., 119, 165, 167, 176, 184, 188, 209, 230, 231, 238, 312, 404

"Adélaïde du Guesclin," by Voltaire, 252

Æschylus, 275, 325

"Agrippine," by Cyrano, 79 ff., 248, 249

Aicard, J., 464

Albano, painter, 350

Albert, P., 438

"Albion," by St. Amant, 129

Albon, comte d', xxii, xxiv, xxv, 306, 307, 331, 350

"Alceste," by Quinault, 226

"Alcestes," by Euripides, 245

Alembert, d', 284, 366, with Voltaire against Shakespeare, 376 ff.; as "Bertrand," 388

"All's Well," 278

Allen, cardinal, 7

Amadis, 191

"Amant Loup-Garou" by Collot d'Herbois, 414

Amidor, St. Sorlin's "Visionnaire," 97 ff.

Amyot, 397

Ancients, imitated in France and in England, 33 ff., 65 ff.; excessive imitation of the, 225; and moderns, 330 ff.; Voltaire on the, 245

Ancillon, on the English, 123

Andromeda, 127

"Andromaque," Racine's, 103, 247

"Andronic," by Campistron, 169, 179

"Anglomane, l'," by Saurin, 272, 274, 343, 408

Anglomania, 31, 177, 186, 192, 270 ff., 284 ff.; its counterpart in London, 296; Voltaire on, 380 ff.

Anne of Austria, Queen, xv
"Année Littéraire" of Fréron, 274, 276, 343, 395, 398
"Antony and Cleopatra," Shakespeare's, 39
Apelles, 412
"Apologie for Poetrie," Sidney's, 33
"Appel à toutes les Nations," by Voltaire, 369
"Arcadia," Sidney's, translated into French, 121
Argenson, d', Marc René, 157, 268; René Louis, 267, 268, 269, 270
Argental, count d', 242, 310, 354, 359, 375
Ariosto, 26, 118
Aristophanes, 245
Aristotle, 33, 39, 65, 143, 334, 395
"Arlequin poli par l'amour," by Marivaux, 188
"Armide," by Quinault, xx, 225, 226, 227
Arnaud, on d'Aubignac, 95
Arnaud, abbé, 380
Arnaud, d', *see* Baculard.
"Art Poétique," of Boileau, 105 ff.; of Vauquelin de la Fresnaye, 31, 32
Arthur, king, 127, 151
"Astrée," d'Urfé's, 103, 121, 306
"Athalie," Racine's, 178, 232, 278, 297, 369
"Attila," Corneille's, 245
Aubignac, abbé d', in favour of rules, 98 ff., 226
Aubigny, d', 162
Audran, C., xiii
Auger, 398

Aumont, duc d', 398.
Auvray, on Montchrestien, 48
"Avare," Molière's, xxiii
Aveline, xi, 211
Avril, J. J., 427

B

Babouc, Voltaire's, 242
Bacon, 27, 30, 34, 35, 121, 166, 176
Baculard d'Arnaud, 322 ff., 326
Baillet, 176
"Bajazet," Racine's, 73, 166, 247, 337, 348
Ballads, English, 281
Ballantyne, A., 204
Balzac, 92 ff., 112
Bandello, 39
"Baptiste," by Buchanan, 7
Barbier, J., printer, 8
"Barbier de Séville," by Beaumarchais, 295, 322
Barbin, bookseller, 119
Barclay, Alex., 10, 20
    "   J., 57
Baretti, on Shakespeare and Voltaire, 400, 403
"Barnveldt," by La Harpe, 320
Barry, Madame du, 270
Bartas, du, 5, 18, 27, 28, 36
Basnage, 168
Baudoin, 121
Bayle, 366
Bear-baiting, 37, 137, 144
"Béatrice et Bénédict," by Berlioz, 404
Beauharnais, Fanny de, 318
Beaumarchais, 272, 273, 295, 319, 321, 342
Beaumont (and Fletcher), 173, 175, 176

INDEX

Beeverel, 136 ff, 152
Behn, Mrs., 220, 341, 342
Beljame, on Le Tourneur, 358
Bella, Stephen della, xv
Bellay, J. du, 7, 18, 30
Bellerose, player, 131
Bellin, 281
Belloy, du, 120, 295, 297, 358, 367, 374
Belsunce, Madame de, 271
Belyard, Simon, 45
Bembo, 26
Bénétrix, 28
Bengesco, 245, 267, 369
Bérain, 227
"Bérénice," by Racine, 161, by Thomas Corneille, 226
Bergerac, Cyrano de, 66; supposed imitator of Shakespeare, 79 ff.; 248
Berlioz, on Shakespeare, 455
Bernard, J., on England, 8
Bernhardt, Sarah, 464
Berthelot, 365
"Beverley" Saurin's, 320, 406, Napoléon on, 321
Beza, 38
Bible, English, 7
"Bienséances," 102, 247, 273, 406, 411 ff., 424 ff., 434
Bignon, Jérome, 143
Bilaine, 175
Billard, C., 45
Binet, C., 13 ff.
Blaeu, J., 1, 120
Blair, 297
Bocage, Fiquet du, 224
Bocage, Madame du, 281
Boccaccio, 119
Bochetel, J., 12
Boileau, 46, 84, 98, 111; on Italian and Spanish literature, 119; on Cromwell, 124; 183, 188, 229 237, 245, 296, 310, 325, 425, 444
Boismorand, Chéron de, 184
Boisrobert, abbé de, 123
Boissy, de, 31, 185 ff., 269
Bolingbroke, 204, 207, 255
Bonaparte, Napoléon, 309; on "Beverley" 321; and Ducis, 415; Lucien and Joseph, 272
Bonnefon, J., 176
Bonnet, abbé, 275, 296
Bonrepaus, de, 136
Bosse, Abraham, xii, xiii, xvii, 53, 85
Bossuet on Corneille, Lully and the stage, 111; 245, 284
Boucher, xxiii
Bouchor, 464
Boufflers, Duchesse de, 398
Bouillon, Duchesse de, xvii, 132
Bounin, G., 46, 52, 78, 79
Bourdeille, F. de, 17
"Bourgeois" comedy, 342
Bourgogne, Hôtel de, 36 ff., 51 ff., 69 ff., 85
Boursault, 48
Boyer, A., xviii, 131, 169, 170, 177, 230
Boyle, Roger, earl of Orrery, 46, 164, 168
Brancas, marquis de, on "Romeo," 430
Brantôme, visits England, 16 ff.; 29, 36
Brasey, Moreau de, 136 ff., 165, 170
Briot, Pierre, 166
Brissot, 276
"Britannicus," Racine's, 104, 247

British Museum, 145, 148
Brizard, actor, frontispiece, xi, xxvi, 389, 392, 431
Broglie, comte de, 122, 204, duc de, on Shakespeare, 456
Brossette, 444
Browne, player, 52
Browne, Sir T., 166
Brunel, 445
Brunetière, 469
"Brutus" Voltaire's, 248, 249, 250, 251, 255
Bryan, Sir F., 4, 60
Buchanan, 6, 7, 30, 33, 60, 132
Buckingham, duke of, 162
Budée, 6, 30
Buffon, 270, 374
Bunyan, 143
Burnet, 166
Butini, 412
Butler, Samuel, 183
Byron, 452

C

Calas, 296
"Caliste," by Colardeau, 326
Cambridge, 9
Cambry, 281
Camden, 30, 281
Campenon, 415, 436
Campistron, 169, 179
Canaletto, xxvi, 377
Capilupi, 26
Carlisle, Countess of, 123
Carlos, don, son of Philip II., 169
Carmail, comte de, 87
Caroline, queen, 214, 215
Carré, Jérome, *alias* Voltaire, 369
Cassivelaunus, 175

"Castle of Otranto," Walpole's, 369, 373
Castro, Guillem de, 117
"Catherine and Petruccio," Garrick's, 301, 452
"Catilina," by Crébillon, 236; by Tronchin, 368
"Catiline," by Ben Jonson, 162
"Cato," Addison's, xviii, 165, 170, 171, 184, 230, 312
"Caton d'Utique," by Deschamps, 230, 231
Catuelan, comte de, 357
Cauchon, bishop, 102
Cavalier poets, in France, 130
Cecil, lord high Treasurer, 120
"Centenaires de Corneille," les deux, by Cubières, 353
Centlivre, Mrs., 334, 335, 342
Cérisoles, battle of, 17, 28
Cervantes, 29, 131
Chabannes, Rochon de, 447
Chalon, de, 117
Chamberlayne, Ed., 120, 144, 147
Champmeslé, actress, 315
Chantelouve, F. de, 45, 48 ff.
Chapelain, in favour of prose and blank verse, 77; 84, 105
Chapelle, J. de la, 106
Chapman, G., 45
Chapoton, 250, 264
Chappelain, Geneviève, 121
Chappuzeau, 120, 136 ff., 163 ff., 311
Charles II. Stuart, 5, 130 ff, 151
Charles VII. of France, 4
„ VIII. „ 4
„ IX. „ 58
„ X. „ 449
"Charles IX.," by M. J. Chénier, 441

Charnois, de, 419
Charron, Pierre, 397
Chartier, Alain, 4, 20
Chastellux, chevalier, then marquis de, 305, 379, 404, 407; his "Roméo," 408; 440; countess de, 306
Châteaubriand, on Mrs. Siddons, 426, on Shakespeare, 443
Châteaufort, actor, 446
Châteauvieux (Côme de la Gambe called), 39
Chaucer, 3, 119, 175, 183, 277, 405
Chaufepié, G. de, 366
Chautron, Ch., French player, 52
Chénier, M. J., 441 ff.
Chesterfield, 214, 284, on French and English plays, 299, 333, 335, 424
Chevrette, "Roméo" performed at the château de la, 408 ff.
Childebrand, 107
Choiseul, Duc de, 275; duchesse de, 370
Choruses in plays, 47 ff.
Chrétien, Florent, 6
Cibber, 334, 340
Cicero, 442
"Cid" le, by Corneille, 73, 92, 111, 112, 117, 368, 376
"Cinna," Corneille's, 247
Clairon, Mlle., xx, 239, 241, 292, 296; tries to reform theatrical dress, 315 ff.
Clarendon, earl of, 167
"Clarissa," Richardson's, 268, on the French stage, 317, 318
Claveret, Jean, 101
Clément, N., 170, 173, 176

Clément, P., 182, 186, 237, 400
Cleveland, the poet, 176
"Clitandre," Corneille's, 96, 118
Clopton, Hugh de, 1
Cochin, C. N., xxii, 288, 289
Coffee-houses, French and English, xvii, 148 ff., 191
Colardeau, 326, 349
Colbert, 175
Coligny, Odet de, 25
Collé, 237, 244, 252, 256, 260, 272, 273, 288; and Garrick, 289 ff; and Ducis, 420; 426
Collier, Jeremy, 167, 168, 169, 176
"Colligni" tragédie de, by Matthieu, 45, 50
Collins, J. Churton, 204
Columbus, 466
"Comédie sans Comédie," by Quinault, 226
Comedies, English, laden with incidents, 218; French larmoyant, 237 ff.; 317 ff.; French, adapted, 334, English too coarse, 341, Shakespeare's, adapted, 413 ff.
"Comedy of Errors," 39
Cominges, comte de, 122, 132, 152
Commonwealth, 123 ff.
"Comte de Cominges" le, by Baculard, 325
"Comte d'Essex," le, by La Calprenède, 78
Confidants, 45, in Voltaire, 391; in Ducis 419 ff.; in Mercier, 440
Congreve, 192, 200, 212
Conquest, the, its literary consequences, 31

Constant, baron de, 370
Conti (Natalis Comes), 9
Conti, Prince de, 273
Cooking, in England, 9, 126
Coote, H. C., 57
Coquelin, 464
"Corinne," by Madame de Stael, 316, 426, 447
"Coriolan," le véritable, by Chapoton, 250, 264
Corneille, J. B., painter, xvi
" P., xiv, 73, and rules, 92 ff. ; 98, 103, 111, knows Spanish, 117, and Italian, 117 ; 119, 137, 170, 178, 225, 226, 244, 245, 249, 269, 274, 302, 333, 335, 336, 340, 353, 354, 360, 365, 368, 369, 373, 374, 376, 383, 387, 395, 405
Corneille, T., 137, 226
"Cornélie," by Garnier, 34 ; by Président Hénault, 267
Costar, 132
Cotgrave, Randle, 21 ff., 174
Coulisse, use and abuse of the, 231, 251
Coulon, 129
Coustou, xxii, 302
Cowley, Abr., 130, 176, 177
Coyer, abbé, 275, 281
Coypel, xv, xviii, 159
Craggs, James, 204
Crashaw, 175
Crébillon, the elder, 235 ff., 244, 312, 322
Cressonnois, 464
Cromwell, O., 124, 132
"Cromwell" by Crébillon, 236 ; by Victor Hugo, 140, 143, 232, 319, 455, 459
Cubières-Palmezeaux, le chevalier de, xxiv, 276, 318, 319, 341, and Shakespeare, 342 ff. ; 359
"Cymbeline," 447

D

Daly, his troupe, 463
Dancing, English, 127
Daniel, Samuel, 175
Dante, 117, 437, 438, 426, 452
Davenant, 152, 232
David, painter, 311, 442
Declamation, theatrical, 312, 316 ff.
Deffand, Madame du, 297, 298, 316, 329, 370, 398
Defoe, 184, 267
Delacroix, Eugène, xxviii, 452, 456, 460, 461
Delair, 464
Deleyre, 431, 436
Delille, abbé, 302, on Shakespeare, 322 ; 326
Denham, Sir John, 176, 183
Denis, Madame, xxvi, 241, 305, 389
Denon, Vivant, xxiv
Descartes, on poetry, 108
Descazeaux-Desgranges, 244
Deschamps, E., 3
" F., 231
Desfontaines, abbé, 182, 319
Desforges, Choudard, 318, 406
Desmarets, see St. Sorlin
Desportes, Philip, 18
Destouches, Néricault, 188, 232, 238 ff., 267
Dialogues, Franco-English, 177
Dictionary-ries, of the French Academy, xvi, expurgated, 115 ; discussions on the, 153 ff. ; 181 ; to be reformed, 397 ; 442 ;

Anglo-French, 20 ff., 174, 177; historical, on Shakespeare, 215, 366
Diderot, on Richardson, 268; 287, 316, on the "serious" genre, 319; 320, 333, 342, 357, 359, 365, 366, on Shakespeare, 368, on Ducis, 420 ff., 424, 430
"Dissipateur," Le, by Destouches, 241
Dogs, French, in the Tower, 17
Dolivar, xx
Dondey-Dupré, 277
"Don Japhet d'Arménie," Scarron's, 219
Donne, John, 176
"Don Quixote," 119
"Don Sebastian," Dryden's 192
Dorat, xxiii
Dorchain, 464
Dorez, L., 13
Doucet, C., 380
Douin, captain, 411 ff., 453
Dramas, English, bloody, 56; Chappuzeau on, 152, 154, compared with French ones, 62 ff., 158; French, influenced by Italy, Spain, and the Ancients, 32 ff.; classical, in England, 35, 65 ff.; in France, 36 ff; on same subjects as Shakespeare's, 39 ff.; French and English national, 44 ff., 265 ff., 295, 318; Shakespearean, by Mercier, 439 ff., in English on the French stage, 51 ff., 451, 454 ff.; French, a new genre, 318 ff., 344 ff.; Spanish, 73
"Dramaturgy" Lessing's, 399
Drant, Thomas, 59

Drayton, 175
Dresses, in Louis XIV. style, 107 ff.; for tragic actors, 311 ff.
Drinking, in England, 10, 125
"Drummer" of Addison, 238 performed in Paris, 452
Dryden, 62, 161, 164, 162, preferred to Shakespeare, 177; 183, 192, 232, 334, 340, 414
Du Bail, 43
Du Bos, 143, 179, 250, 311 ff.
Duchemin, actor, 315
Du Chesne, 118
Ducis, xxvii, 296, 358, 359, 398, his adaptations of and veneration for Shakespeare, his character and literary ideal, 414 ff.; does not know English, 427; his success, 432; 446, 460, 468
Duclos, actress, 315
Dumas, Alexandre, père, 452, 455, 459, 464, 469
Dumas, Alexandre, fils, 185
"Dunciade," Palissot's, 343
Duport, P., 459
Durand-Lapie, on St. Amant, 124
Duras, Maréchal de, 374, 376
Duval, Alexandre, 447

E

"Écossaise," l', by Voltaire, 185 246, 256, 317
"Écossoise," l', "ou le désastre," by Montchrestien, 48
"Édouard," by La Calprenède, 78
"Édouard III.," by Gresset, 264
Edward VI., 9
Effen, van, 168

Eisen, xxii, 313
Élisée, Father, 379
Elizabeth, queen, 6; praised by J. Grévin, 12; by Ronsard, 14 ff.; by Brantôme, 17, the great shepheardesse, 18; her translations, 19; her dramatic tastes, 35; put on the stage, 45, 124
Ellys, I., 197
"Encyclopédie," 2, 244, 315; on Shakespeare, 366
"Engagement téméraire," l', by J. J. Rousseau, 409
England, early visitors to, 7 ff.; land of plenty, 152; land of revolutions, 166; described in the seventeenth century, 123 ff., in the eighteenth, 181 ff.
English language, 9; learnt by merchants, 23; Panurge's, 23; generally ignored under Louis XIV., 116 ff., ignored by guidebook makers, and by ambassadors, 122, by the "Journal des Savants," 122; a patois, according to Saint-Amant, 126; grows anyhow, 152 ff.; works in, translated into French, 120 ff, 199, 267, 271 ff., 184; in French libraries, 173 ff., 270 ff.; difficulty of pronouncing, 270; popular in Paris salons, 270 ff.; learnt by Prévost, 191, deserves to be learnt, 200, known by Voltaire, 200, 383; learnt in France, 267, Patu writes in, 280; misspelt, 279. *See* Literature
English, the, their qualities and defects, 10 ff., their ferocity, 11, 123, 140, 192; their militia, 118; immoderate, 143; commit suicide, 125, 143; freethinkers among them, 147; think profoundly, 169, 184 ff., 187 ff., 271 ff.; their manners compared to French ones, 185 ff., 288; their genius according to Voltaire, 209; enthusiastically received in Paris, 284 ff.
"Épicharis et Néron," by Legouvé, 446
Épinay, Madame d', 255, 305, 408, 409
„ Mr. d', 408, 409
"Éryphile," Voltaire's, 250, 251, 252, 260 ff.
Estandoux, C. d', 416
Estienne, H., 26
„ R., 6
Ette, Mlle. d', 408
"Eugénie," by Beaumarchais, 272, 273, 295, 321, 343
Euripides, 126, 177, 245, 268, 373
Evelyn, John, 164
Expilly, abbé, 196, 275, 280

F

Faber, J., 197
Faguet, E., 65
Fairfax, 124
"Fair Penitent," Rowe's, 326
"Fairies," the, by Garrick, 301
Falkener, 207, 242
Falstaff, 57, 219, 414
"Falstaff," by Meurice, 460
Farquhar, G., 192
Fashions, French and English, 11, 274, 329, 354

Fauchet, Claude, 31, 32
Faucit, Miss Helen, 463
"Fausses Infidélités," Les, by Barthe, 414
"Femmes Savantes," Les, by Molière, 287
Fénelon, 119, 131, 153, 154, 181
Festeau, P., 137, 143
Fielding, 220, 267, 334
Fiévée, 445
Figg, James, 195, 197
Fisher, W., 193
Flaubert, 459; on Shakespeare, 463
Fletcher, John, 174, 175, 176
Fleury, Mlle., as Ophelia, xxvii, 421
"Florizel and Perdita," Garrick's, 301
Fontainebleau, plays performed at, xvi., 55 ff., 343 ff.
Fontaine-Malherbe, 357
Fontenelle, 185
Fops, 148
Fouquet, financier, 173 ff.
„ painter, 69
Fournier, P., sculptor, xxii
France, sorrow at leaving, 13. See Drama, Fashions, French, Literature, Shakespeare, Theatre, Verses
Francis I. of France, 5, 18, 19, 266
"François II.," by President Hénault, 265 ff.
"François à Londres," Le, by de Boissy, 31, 185, 186
Francomania in London, 19
Franklin, B., 388
French language used in London, 19 ff., 30 ff., 298, refined, 22;
Ronsard on the, 25 ff., its "précellence," 27; its universality, 119 ff., 298, 405; pruned by the Academy, 152 ff.; 230; Voltaire on the, 397; proposed emancipation of the, 450
French, the, their ideal in art and life, in the seventeenth century, 107 ff.; their manners and tastes in the eighteenth, 310; how influenced by Shakespeare, 466 ff.
Fréron, E. C., 274, 276, 279, 317
Fréron, fils, 343
Fresne, Trichet du, 174
"Frivolité," La, by de Boissy, 269
Furnivall, F. J., 170

G

"Gabinie," by Brueys, 179
Gaguin, R., 4
Gainsborough, xxiii
Galiani, abbé, 270
Gallenberg, comte de, 447
Games in England, 10, 12 ff., 143 ff.
"Gamester," E. Moore's, 320
"Gammer Gurton," 366
Garat, 287, 293
Garguille, Gaultier, xv
Garnier, Robert, 34 ff., 36, 39, 66
Garrick, xxii, xxvii, 273 ff., 279 ff., 288 ff., his portrait, 289; at Collé's house, 291; opinion of Marmontel on, 292, of Madame Necker, 293, of Beaumarchais, 295, would like to play in Paris, 293; a power in France, 294, appealed to by French actors, 295 ff., puts a

play of de Belloy's on the stage, 297; adores but remodels Shakespeare, 300, 333, 334, builds a temple to him, 301; as Beverley, 320; 359; and the Jubilee, 362 ff.; and the grave-diggers, 384; on Voltaire, 399; 411; and Ducis, 416, as Hamlet, 417, 433

Gascoigne, G., 20

Gaskell, Miss, actress, 451

Gautier, Théophile, on the romantic period, 453 ff., 466

"Génie du Christianisme," by Châteaubriand, 444

Geoffroy, critic, 459

George, St., kills the Dragon at Southwark, 137

Gerland, 45

Germanicus, 79

Ghosts in plays, 48 ff., 49, 257, 322 ff., 339, 349

Gibbon, on French tragedies, 284; 294; writes an essay in French, 298; sees Voltaire on the stage, 300; on Shakespeare, 300

"Gil Blas," by Lesage, 297

Gille, of the fair, xxv, 370 ff.

Gladiators, English, 144

Gléon, marquise de, 305, 408, studies Shakespeare, 411

Globe theatre, 37

Glück, and Shakespeare, 445

Goethe, 452

Goldoni, xx, 317

Goldsmith, 278

Gomicourt, Damiens de, 274

"Gorboduc," by Sackville and Norton, 16, 33, 35, 217, 366, 383 ff., 387

Gossec, 414

Gothic, the, and Shakespeare, 444, in favour during the 1830 period, 453

Gothism, 36, 87

Goujet, abbé, 216

Goulard, Simon, 27

Gounod, 464

Gower, J., 175

Gower, lord Ronald, xxii

Gozzi, count, 276

Gozzoli, Benozzo, xiii, 67, 69

Grafton, duke of, 196

Grammars, Anglo-French, 20 ff., 140 ff.

Gramont, 111, 131

„ comtesse de, 144

"Grand Cyrus," Scudéry's, 270

Gravelot, xx, xxi, xxiv, xxvi, 253, 261, 327, 329

Greene, Robert, 30, 40, 52, 316

Greenwich described, 203, 205

Gresset, 264

Greville, Fulke, lord Brooke, 46

Grévin, Jacques, 12 ff., 16, 29, 36, 40, 46, 51, 66, 213

Grimm, baron de, 296, 357, 363, 398, 424, 430

Grisettes, 282

Gros-Guillaume, xiv

Grosart, Dr., 21

Grosley, 196, 199, 280, 295, 302

Guarini, 119

Gucht, van der, xxiii, 323, 329

Guernier, du, 171

Guiard, Madame, 427

Guide-books, for England, 8 ff., 129, 136 ff., 275, 280 ff.

Guilbert, abbé, on plays, xii

Guillaume, fool of Henri IV., 56

"Guillaume Tell," Lemierre's, 407

Guilleragues, de, on Greece, 118
Guilpin, 18
Guise, duc de, 28
"Guisiade," la, by P. Matthieu, 47
Guizot, 399, 454
"Gulliver," 182, 184, 187, 188
"Guysien," le, by Bélyard, 45

H

Hall, J., 120
Hambleton, xxiii
"Hamlet," Shakespeare's, xxiii, xxvii, xxviii, 79, 97, 183, 192, 208 ff., 216, 217, 250, 252, 256, 259, 301, 320, 327, 329, 339, 340, 369, 370, 373, 375, 384, 424, 453, 455, 464, in Paris, 452; before Louis - Philippe, 463; Ducis', 415 ff., 429, 437; Louis Henry's, 447; Dumas and Meurice's, 460 ff., 469
Hanotaux, G., 57
Haraucourt, 464
Hardy, Alex., xiv, 40 ff., 66, 69 ff.
Harrison, W., 9, 138
Harvey, lady, 132
Hatin, 168
Hayman, xxiii, xxvi, 329
Heine, 105, 463
"Hélène" (de Surgères). Ronsard's Sonnets to, 58
Hénault, President, 265 ff., 288
Henri II. of France, 45
„ III. „ 45
„ IV. „ xii, 5, 29, 49, 55 ff., 343, 450
"Henriade," Voltaire's, 204, 358, 374
Henry VIII., 16 ff., 19, 28, 31, 78

"Henry V.," Shakespeare's, 247
"Henry VI.," Shakespeare's, 45, 183, 266
Herbert, G., 176
Herder, 454
Héroard, 55
Herod, king, 43
Heylin, 175
Heywood, Jasper, 34
"Hilas et Silvie," by R. de Chabannes, 414
Hobbes, 152
Hogarth, xxiii, xxvi, 326, 329, 323
Holbach, baron d', 359
Holland, lord, 123
Holyband, see St. Lien
Homer, 4, 119, 177, 268, 277, 380, 400, 446, 459
Hondius, J., xi
Hooper, John, 24
Horace, translated by B. Jonson, by Queen Elizabeth, by Drant, 35, 59; 65, 177
"Horace," Corneille's, 315, 336
Howe, general, 391
Howell, J., 22, 119
Huber, xx
Huc, Father, 129
Hugo, Victor, 92, 222, 232, 263, 319, 325, 343, 452, 455, on Shakespeare, 459, 469
Humanity, xxiv, 318 ff., 330 ff., 368, 423
Hume, 278, in Paris, 287; on Shakespeare, 299

I

"Ibrahim," Scudéry's, 84
"Ile de la Raison," l', Marivaux's, 186

"Illusion Comique," l', Corneille's, 118
"Imogenes," Dejaure's, 447
Independents, literary, 66 ff., 83, derided by St. Sorlin, 97 ff.
"Indian Emperor," Dryden's, 164
Ingleby, Dr., 170
Ingres, and Shakespeare, 459
"Iphigénie," Racine's, 103, 467
"Irène," Voltaire's, 391 ff.
Italians, imitated in France, 4, 18 ff.; their pronunciation of English, 9; their language and literature studied by: Madame de Sévigné, 116, Corneille, 117, Racine, 118, Boileau, 119; play in Paris, 158

J

James IV. of Scotland, 45
„ V. „ 5
James VI. of Scotland, I. of England, 18, 28, 58
Janin, J., 456
Jaquet, *alias* Grenoble, xii
Jascuy, S., 14
Jaucourt, chevalier de, 2, 366
"Jean-sans-terre," by Ducis, 415
"Jephtes," by Buchanan, 6
Joan of Arc, on the stage, 44 ff., 101 ff.
Jodelle, 36, 48 ff., 66, 137
Johnson, Charles, 338
Johnson, Dr. S., 366, 369
Jonson, Ben, 10; his dramatic ideal, 34, 48, 51, in Paris, 57 ff.; on Shakespeare, 95; St. Amant on, 126; 162, 174, 175, 278
Jordan, 212

"Journal Anglais" on English literature and Shakespeare, 277
"Journal Littéraire" of the Hague, on English literature, 183 ff.
"Journal des Savants," 167, 175; mentions Shakespeare, 177; 181, 182, 276
"Journal de Trévoux," 167, 276; on La Place and Shakespeare, 224
Jove, Paul, 31
Julienne, cook of Ducis, at "Hamlet," 437 ff.
"Julius Cæsar," Shakespeare's, 39, 207, 219, 246, 247, 250, 251, 442. *See* "Mort de César"
Julleville, P. de, 35
Junker, 399

K

Kean, plays in Paris, 455, 456
Kemble, Ch., in Paris, 455
"King Lear," Shakespeare's, 280, 293, 301, adapted by Ducis, 415, 426 ff., 430
Kyd, Thomas, 35

L

La Boullaye le Gouz, 129
La Bruyère, 106, 116
La Calprenède, 65, 78
Lacépède, comte de, 435
La Chapelle, J. de, 106
La Chaussée, 237 ff., 317, 344
La Chesnaye des Bois, 268
La Condamine, 196
La Coste, 282
Lacroix, A., 2, 447
La Fontaine, xvii, 84, 125, 132 ff., 139, 151, 169, 183, 225, 388

INDEX

La Fosse, 168, 169, 220, 252, 338
Lagrenée *fils*, painter, 419
La Guernie, 277
La Harpe, 295, 318, 320, 344, 354, 366, 375, 376, 380, 387, 399, 400, 404, 405, 413, 432, 439
Lamartine, 272
La Motraye, de, 137
La Motte-Houdard, 231, 232, 245, 367
Lancelot, Claude, 118
Languages, German, 32, Italian 27, Spanish 27, 29, various, in England, 30, foreign, 25 ff.; *see* English, French, Latin
Languet, Hubert, 60
La Place, translator of Shakespeare, 220, 271, 272, 297, 301, 357, 423
La Porte, abbé de, 186
Largillière, xix, 201
Larmoyant comedies, 237 ff.
La Roche, de, 182
La Rochelle, Née de, 318
Larrey, 165, 166
Larroumet, G., 111
La Serre, Puget de, 40 ff., 69 ff. 78
La Taille, J. de, 33
Latin, in England, 26, 30 ; verses in, by Addison, 118 ; substratum in French minds, 465
La Tour, de Serre de, 280, 281, 282
Launcelot of the Lake, 111
Lauraguais, comte de, 255, 256
"Laure," by Rotrou, 81 ff.
Laurent, M., 70
La Valette, cardinal de, 87

La Vallière, Duchesse de, 287
"Lear," *see* "King Lear"
Le Blanc, abbé, on Shakespeare, 219 ff.; 237, 260, 270, his sham war against Shakespeare, 330 ff.; 437
Le Clerc, 166, 168
Lee, Sidney, xxii, 79
Legouvé, citizen, 446
Lehman, painter, 460
Leicester, earl of, praised by Ronsard, 14
Le Kain, 242, 296, 302, tries to reform dress and delivery on stage, 316 ; 375
Lemierre, 407
Le Nôtre, 152, 409
Le Pautre, xvi
Le Pays, 136 ff., 164
Le Prieur, xxii, xxiv, xxv
Le Roy, 344
Léry, Jean de, 25
Lesage, G. L., 136 ff., 147 ff., 153
Lescure, 281
Lespinasse, Mlle. de, 287
Lessing, 399
Leti, Gregorio, 165
Le Tourneur, xxv, 277, translates Shakespeare, 354 ff., criticised by Voltaire, 357 ff, by Beljame, 358 ; successive instalments of his work, 397 ff. ; corrected by Guizot, 454
"Lettres d'un François," by Abbé Le Blanc, 219, 270, 337 ff.
"Lettres Philosophiques," by Voltaire, 179, 180, 183, 186, 200 ff., 216, 383
Ligne, Princesse de, 398
Lillo, 237, 320, 439
Linacre, 6

Lingée, Ch., xxv
Linguet, 276
Lion, H., 251
Lionne, Hugues de, 111
Literature, English, long unknown in France, 18 ff., 60 ff. ; tableau of, by Du Bartas, 27 ; French, known in England, 18 ff. ; English, opinion of Chappuzeau on, 152 ; French knowledge of, in the eighteenth century, 181 ff, 267 ; French influence on, 296
Livry, Marquis de, 157
Locke, 166, 167
Lodge, Thomas, 18
London, compared to Paris, 9 ; 12 ; gaieties under Charles II., 111
"London Merchant," by Lillo, 237, 320, 439
Lorris, G. de, 20
Louis XII., 5
Louis XIII., at the play, xv, 53 ff. ; 93, 264
Louis XIV., 5, his times, 61 ff., receives the Academy's Dictionary, 113 ; 225, 266, 306, 360, 384
Louis XVI., 270, 350, 358 ff., 429, 441
Louis XVIII., 449
Louis-Philippe, 463
Love, in plays, Boileau on, 106, Bossuet id., 111, Napoléon, id., 321
"Love's Contrivance," by Mrs. Centlivre, 334, 335
Lovelace, Richard, 130
"Lucrèce Borgia," by Victor Hugo, 263
Lulli, 111, 112

"Lutrin," le, by Boileau, 119
Lydgate, 175
Lyly, the Euphuist, 366
Lyndesay, Sir David, 5, 13 ff.

M

Mac Ardell, J., 417
"Macbeth," Shakespeare's, xxiii, 96, 118, 216, 226, 247, 280, 291, 292, with dances, 161 ; 346, 447 ; at the Odéon, 468 ; Ducis's, 415, 426, 433
"Machabées," les, by La Motte, 231
Macready, actor, in Paris, 455
Magdalene, Queen, 5
Magnin, Ch., on Shakespeare, 455 ff.
Mahélot, L., xiv, xv, 70 ff., 96.
Maintenon, Madame de, 144, 170
Mairet, J. de, xiv, 62, 84 ff.
Maizeaux, des, 162
Major, John, 5
Malebranche, 184
Malherbe, 84, 115
Man, in seventeenth century literature, 107 ff. ; 433
"Manie des drames sombres," la, by Cubières, 342 ff.
"Manlius Capitolinus," by La Fosse, 169, 179, 252, 338
Manners, French, on the eve of the Revolution, 429
Marais, Mat., 199, 249
"Marc Antoine," by Garnier, 34
Marcel, H., 220
"Marchand de Londres" of Clément, 237
Mareschal, 121
"Mariage de Figaro," le, by Beaumarchais, 322
"Mariamne," Voltaire's, 248

Marie-Antoinette, queen, 350, 367, 376, 379, 392
Marie (de Guise) queen, 5
Mariette, J., engraver, xvi, xvii
Marigny, 117
"Marius," by President Hénault, 267
Marivaux, 186 ff, 256
Marlowe, 34, 45, 52
Marly, gardens of, xix, 209, 211, 221
Marmontel, 241, 255, on Garrick, 292; 305, on Shakespeare, 367; 376, 404, on French manners, 430; 453, on Glück and Shakespeare, 445
Marot, C., 5, 16, 18
Mary, queen, sister of Henry VIII., 5
Mary, queen, daughter of Henry VIII., 9
Mary Stuart, queen, 5, 14, 17, 18, the subject of plays, 45, 48
Mascarille, 148
Mask, at court, 16
Masson, F., 309, 321
Matthieu, P., 47
Mauger, 137
Maugiron, Louis de, 36
Mayenne, duc de, 84
Mazarin, cardinal, xvii, 92, 132
"Médecin malgré lui," 407
"Médée," by Corneille, 98
Médicis, C. de, 58 ; M. de, 78
"Mégère apprivoisée," la, by Delaire, 464
"Mélite," by Corneille, scenery for, 96
Ménage, on languages, 116 ; 176
"Merchant of Venice," adapted, 413

Mercier, S., xvii, xxvi, xxvii, visits Crébillon, 235 ff.; 274, 276, 315, 359, 367 ff., 392, 399, caricature of, 401 ; in favour of literary reforms, 403 ; his dramas, 439 ff.
"Mercure de France," 182, 260, 276
Merlin, enchanter, 127
"Mérope," Voltaire's, 251, 342, 432
"Merry Wives," 216, adapted by La Place, 413 ; by Collot d'Herbois, 414
Messange, Mallement de, 154
Messengers in tragedies, 47 ff., 50
Metastasio, 279
Meurice, P., 460, 469
Meurier, G., 23
"Midsummer Night's Dream," 186, 201
Miège, 137, 148, 175, 177
Milton, 119, 132, 174, 176, 177, 183, 184, 281, 373, 403, 404
"Mirame," by St. Sorlin and Richelieu, xv, 91
"Miroir," le, 451, 452
"Misanthrope," le, by Molière, 161, 330
"Miser," Shadwell's, 335
"Misfortunes of Arthur," 34, 35
Misson, xvii, 136 ff., 148, 157, 163, 196, 305
"Mock Astrologer," the, by Dryden, 168
"Moïse," by St. Amant, 124
Molé, actor, 296, 420, 421
Molière, xiv, xv, xviii, xxiii, 91, and rules, 104 ; 148, 157, his play-house, 159 ; adapted, 161, 340 ; 178, 183, 186, 225, 326,

329, 330, 333, 334, 335, 348, 349, 353, 360, 374, 387, 407, 438
Mondory, actor, 112
Monnet, C., 271, 273, 275, 298, 451
Montagu, Elizabeth, 369, 380, defends Shakespeare, 399
Montaigne, 6, 18, 33, 36, 397
Montchrestien, 36, 45, 48, 51
Montesquieu, 179, on Shakespeare, 214, 215; 275, on gothic art, 444
"Montgomery," by Gerland, 45
Montluc, 36
Montmorency, constable of, 4
Monval, 137
Moore, E., 320
More, Hannah, 369
More, Sir Thomas, 19 ff., 27, 30, 132; the subject of plays, 78
"More de Venise," le, by Butini, 412
"More de Venise," le, at the Franconi circus, 447
Moreau le jeune, 358, 392, 393
Morel-Fatio, on Spain, 29
Morellet, 275, 296, 300, 301, 315
Moreri, 215
"Mort de César," la, by Grévin, 40, 213
"Mort de César," la, by Voltaire, 250, 267
Morville, comte de, 204
Moses, 268, 459
Motraye, see La Motraye
Motteux, 131
Mouhy, de, 220, 232, 292
Mounet-Sully, 460
Moureau, printer, 388
Muller, engraver, xxvi

Muralt, L. B. de, 136 ff., 163 ff., 170, 182, 183
Murder on the stage, 102; Boileau's opinion concerning, 106; in English plays, 128; 264, 434, 468
Musset, A. de, 459, and Shakespeare, 463, 465
Mylords, their misfortunes, 11 ff.; fight with cabdrivers, 195, 274
Mysteries, xiii, 44, 50, 63, 66, 69

N

"Nanine," Voltaire's, 317
Nantes, edict of, 112
Nanteuil, Célestin, 453
Napoléon I., 276, 449, *see* Bonaparte
Napoléon, Stéphanie, 350
Nash, T., 18, 60, 121
Naturalism, in plays, 347, 375
Nature, to be followed according to Boileau, 105; and country life, 305 ff.; opinion of Voltaire, 305, of Madame Victoire, 306, of Bonaparte, 309, of R. L. Gérardin, 310, of J. J. Rousseau, 310; in Shakespeare, 360; in Châteaubriand, 443
Navarre, Marguerite de, 18, 19
Navy, English, 10
Necker, Jacques, 359; Madame, 293 ff., 398, 399
Neufchâteau, F. de, 317
Newcastle, Duchess of, 163, 214
Newspapers, literary, 167 ff., 181 ff., 275 ff.
Newton, 270
Niceron, 182
Nicole, P., 111

"Night Thoughts," Young's, 272, 330, 349
Noailles, Marshal de, 295
Nolhac, P. de, 58
Northumberland, beheaded, 11
Norton, Th., 16
"Nouvelle Héloïse," Rousseau's, 273
Novelli, 463
Novels, their increased importance, 223; English, popular in France, 272; French and English, 297, 466; *see* Fielding, Richardson
Noverre, 274
Nucius, Nicander, 31

O

O'Dogharty de la Tour, 435
"Œdipe," La Motte-Houdard's, 232
"Œdipe," Voltaire's, 208, 245, 246
"Œdipus," Sophocles', 256 ff., 467
Ogier, F., 74 ff.
Oldfield, Mrs., xix, 191, 193, 204
Oldham, 177
Ollivier, painter, 273
Opera, under Louis XIV., 225, 229
Orléans, duke of, 288, 319
"Orphan," Otway's, 192
"Orphelin de la Chine," Voltaire's, 315, 369
Orville, d', 281
Ossian, 272, 445, 446
"Othello," Shakespeare's, 82, 183, 208, 213, 216, 217, 250, 276, 329, adapted by Douin, 411, by Butini, 412, by Ducis, 415, 432 ff., by Vigny, 456; at the cirque Franconi, 447; in English on the French stage, 451, 452
Otway, 168, 192, 220, 297, 334
Oxford, 9, 129, 152

P

Palissot, 343, 392, 400, 445
Palladio, xvi, 91, 98, 99
Palsgrave, 20 ff.
"Pamela," Richardson's, 237, 268; on the French stage, 317
"Pandoste," by Puget de la Serre, xiii, xiv, 39, 69 ff.
"Pandosto," Greene's, 43, 121
Paradin, on England, 8 ff.
"Paradise Lost," 184
Paré, minister under the Convention, 435
Parfaict, Frères, 169
Parks, "à l'anglaise," 306 ff.
Parliament, 9, is bizarre, 140; 166
Parterres, French, transformed English fashion, 408, 409
Pasquier, E., 22, on the English language, 31, 32
"Passion," the, at Valenciennes, 63, 69
Patin, Gui, 140
Patu, 271, 279, 296, 301, 302
Paul I. of Russia, 344
Pavillon, 151, 191
Payen, his travels, 122, 136 ff
"Pèlerinage de la vie humaine," 18
Pelissary, Madame de, 152
Pelletier-Volmeranges, 318
Pellissier, 28
Pembroke, countess of, translates Garnier, 35
Penley, actor, 451

Pepys, 177
"Père de Famille," by Diderot, 343, 423
Percy, and Maugras, 271, 316
Perlin, 8 ff., 32, 124, 138
Perrault, Ch., xv, 84, 88, 229, 321
Perrin, T. B., 278
Pétau, 185
Petitot, 238
Petrarch, 4, 16, 26, 118, 373
Peyron, 277
"Phèdre," Racine's, 104, 247
Philidor, 318
Philip II., 169
"Philosophe sans le savoir," le, Sedaine's, 320, 343
Pibrac, 19, 21
Piccini, 445
Piccolomini, Æ. S., 130
Pichot, A., 377
Pigalle, xxv, 363, 365
Pindar, 177
Piron, 244, 373
Pitel, French actor, 131
"Plaideurs," les, of Racine, 103
"Plain Dealer," Wycherley's, 161, 334
Plato, 108, 137, on town life, 443
Plautus, 73
Players, English, in Paris, 50 ff., at Fontainebleau, 55, 343; in Germany, 51, their delivery, 57; French, in Germany, 52; Spanish, in Paris, 52; English, 154, how dressed, 158; Italian, are "gestueux," 158. *See* actors
Plays, English, are sanguinary, 217, compared to French, 231. *See* comedy, tragedy
Poinsinet, 318, 342
"Polyeucte," Corneille's, 73

Pompadour, Madame de, 247, 270
Pope, A., 183, 184, 200, 207, 212, 267, 281, 296, on Shakespeare, 299, 302; 325, 404
Pope, T., a player, 52
Port-Royal, doctrine of, concerning the stage, 111
"Pour et Contre," of Prévost, 199
Powell, W., actor, 300
"Précellence du langage françois," by H. Estienne, 26
Précieux style, 43 ff., 79 ff.
"Prétendue Veuve," la, by Descazeaux-Desgranges, 241
Préville, actor, 273, 295, 321, 398
Prévost, abbé, xviii, 179, 186, on England and Shakespeare, 188 ff., 216; 212, 218, 220, 267, 272, 279
Printers, French, 7 ff., 20; English, 8
Prior, Mat., 154, 181, 183, 188
Prose, in tragedies, 77, 101 ff, 246, 367, 375, 403
Protestants, French or English, 7; 131
"Provoked Wife," Vanbrugh's, 169
"Psyché," Corneille's, 335
"Pucelle d'Orléans," la, by d'Aubignac, 101 ff., 226
Puget, *see* La Serre
Pujas, A., xxv, 355
Pynson, R., 8, 20

Q

Quakers, xvii, 141 ff., 147, 207, 212, 214
Quérard, 177
Quinault, xx, 82 ff., 226, 227
Quinet, E., 454

R

Rabelais, 18, 23, 36, 131
Racine, J., xiv, xxvii, 46, 48, 65, 73, and rules 103 ff.; 111, knows Italian; 118, learns Spanish, 118; 119, 131, 132, 157, 161, 170, 176, 178, 183, 218, 229, 247, 279, 309, 333, 335, 337, 346, 354, 360, 369, 373, 374, Voltaire in favour of, against Shakespeare, 375 ff., 379; 387, 405, 445, 467, "the Just" 470
Racine, J. B., 203
„ L., 184, 203
"Racine et Shakespeare," by Stendhal, 449 ff.
Raleigh, Sir W., 18, 167; his son in Paris, 59
Rapin-Thoyras, 166
Rathery, 2, 175
"Ravissement de Proserpine," le, by Claveret, 101
Reeve, Clara, 220
Regnard, 348
Regnault, dramatist, 48
Regnault, F., printer, 7
„ L., translates Greene, 43, 121
Rehan, Miss Ada, 463
Reichenberg, Mdlle., 460
Rembrandt, 350
Renaissance, the, 24 ff., 33, and the drama, 65 ff.
Restoration, the, in England, 130 ff., in France, 449 ff.
Revolution, the French, and the stage, 441 ff.
"Rhadamiste," Crébillon's, 312
Riccoboni, Louis, 217 ff., 329
„ Madame, xxvii, 271, 273, 298, 329, 365, on "Romeo," 409 ff.
"Richard III." Shakespeare's, 50, 183, 247, 280, 325, in Paris, 452; 446; adapted by de Rozoi, 413
Richardson, S., 237, 267, 268, 272, 302, 317
Richelieu, cardinal de, xv, 22, 57, 84, 98, 143
Richmond, Duke of, son of Henry VIII., 5
Rigal, 39
Rigaud, engraver, xix, 205
"Rivales," les, of Quinault, 82
Rivarol, 120, on English literature and Shakespeare, 405
Robespierre, 439
"Robinson Crusoe," 181, 184
Rochambeau, 404
Rohan, duc de, 8
"Roman Father," Whitehead's, 336
Romantics, the, of 1830, 212, 220, Châteaubriand and the, 443, gain ground and win the day, 452, 453 ff.; want to eat Academicians, 466
"Romeo," Shakespeare's, 81, 279, 301, 424, 447, performed in Paris, 452; a French, 39; Cubières', 353; Chastellux's, 379, 408 ff.; Suard's, 411; Ducis's, 415, 423 ff., 430; Mercier's, 439; Ségur's, 446; Berlioz's, 464
"Romulus," by La Motte, 231
Ronsard, in England, 13 ff., said to know English, 14; 15 ff., 18, wants to visit South America, 25; 29, on the French lan-

guage, 25 ff.; 36, 39, 46, 48, 58, 84, 115, 132, 405, 452, 454
Roseli, 220
Rosemond, historian, 165
Rossi, actor, 463
Rotrou, xiv, 39, 81 ff.
Roubillac, his statue of Shakespeare, xxii, 302
Rousseau, J. J., 3, 237, 242, 268, 275, tearful, 302; 310, 318, plays in one of his plays, 409
"Rover," the, by Mrs. Behn, 341
Rowe, N., 182, 336
Rozoi, de, 408, 413
Ruault, 277
Ruelles, 87
Rules, dramatic, 33 ff., 39 ff., 50 ff., 59; accepted in France, rejected in England, 65 ff.; Lope de Vega on, 73, rejected by French independents, 74 ff.; in Italy, 77; in France, 84 ff.; St. Sorlin in favour of, 97 ff., D'Aubignac on, 98 ff.; Racine's followers and, 178; 183, 184, 188, 218, 222, 223, 238, 245, 246, 248, 266, 297, 311, 319, 333, 334, 353, 367, neglected by Shakespeare, 384; 391, 398, 405, introduced into Shakespeare's plays by adapters, 411 ff., 419 ff.
Rupert, Prince, 108
Rutledge, James, 298, on Voltaire and Shakespeare, 400
Rutter, J., 117
"Ruy Blas," Victor Hugo's, 263
Rycaut, Sir P., 166

S

Sabbioneta, theatre at, xvi
Sackville, 5, 16, 57 ff., 181, 217
St. Albans, earl of, 443
St. Amant, on English manners and literature, 124 ff.; 151, 200, 270
St. Apollinia, a mystery play, 69
St. Barthélemi, massacre of the, 45, on the stage, 50
St. Evremond, 104, 135 ff., writes on the French and English stage, 161 ff.; 169, 183, 443
St. Foix, 256
St. Gelais, Melin de, 16, 18
St. Germain, foire, 88, 381
St. Hyacinthe, 185
St. Igny, xvii
St. Jean, engraver, xviii
St. Julien, madame de, 391
St. Lien (*alias* Holyband) 20 ff.
St. Marc, poet, 396
St. Maur, Dupré de, 184
St. Réal, 169
St. Saens, 464
St. Sorlin, Desmarets de, xv, 91, and rules, 97 ff.; 346
Ste. Beuve, 454
Sallengre, A. H., 132, 168
Salisbury, countess of, 78
Salvini, Italian actor, 463
Samson, dramatist, 464
Sand, George, 463
Sarcey, 153, 463, 468, 469
Saulnier *fils*, 277
Saurin, 272, 274, 319, 320, 343, 406, 408
Savage, 177
Savalette, has "Romeo" performed at La Chevrette, 408

Savoie, Louise de, 18
Saxe, maréchal de, 195
Scaliger, 22, 33
Scamozzi, xvi
Scarron, 9, 51, 183, 219, 271
Scenery, for mysteries, xiii, 63; for sixteenth century, plays, xiii, 63, 66; for "Pandoste" ("Winter's Tale") xiii, xiv, 69 ff., at the Hôtel de Bourgogne, xiv, 85, in Richelieu's Palace, xv, 89; in London, 69, 73; "simultaneous," 70 ff.; for plays of Corneille and Racine, 73; embellished, 88, for "Mélite" 96; 225, 231, 249, 251, 255, 261 lugubrious, 326, 339, 353, 431; copied from Delacroix, 460
"Scènes Anglaises," by Destouches, 232
Scheemakers, sculptor, xxii
Schélandre, his castle of Saumazène, 36; 51, 66, his "Tyr," 74; 230, 238
Schmidt, G. F., xix, 189
"School for Scandal," 451
Scio, citoyenne, actress, 446
Scotland, auxiliaries from, in the French service, 3; her wonders, 129
Scudéry, 84, 92
Sedaine, 318, 320, 342, 358, on Shakespeare, 398
Schais, J., English player, 51
"Sejanus," by Ben Jonson, 58, 59, 89 ff., 162
Selden, 30
"Selimus," 46
"Sémiramis," Voltaire's, xxi, 252 ff., 375, 450

Seneca, in English, 34; 79, 80, 126
"Sensibility," in the eighteenth century, 302 ff., 331
"Serious genre," the, opinion of Diderot on, 319, of Beaumarchais, 321 ff.; 342
Sévigné, marquise de, 84, knows Italian, 116; 166
S'Gravesande, 168
Shadwell, 224, 334, 335
Shaftesbury, 167, 168
Shakespeare, his statues, xxii, 302 ff., and Stratford, 1, 2, and the "Encyclopédie," 2; state of French literature in his days, 18 ff., "wanted arte," 34, French dramas on same subjects as his own, 39 ff.; in Germany, 52; friend of Jonson, 59, 62, life by S. Lee, 79, wrongly said to imitate Cyrano, 79, casual resemblances with French dramas, 80 ff.; 88; opinion of Jonson on, 95; his independence, 115; 126, 130, his art, 138, remodelled at the Restoration, 161; his historical plays praised by Muralt, 164, and Moreau de Brasey, 165, and President Hénault, 265 ff., how far known under Louis XIV., 170 ff.; copies of in French libraries, 170 ff.; opinion of Clément, 173, first printed judgment on, 175, first printed mention, 176; peculiar spellings of his name, 176, 182, 265, 269, 274, 413; mentioned by Boyer and by the "Journal des Savants," 177; by the "Spec-

tator," 178 ; judgment of the "Journal de la Haye," 183, of Prévost, 192 ff., 216, of Voltaire, 207 ff. ; compared with Addison, 209, with Grévin, 213, better known owing to Voltaire, 214 ff., opinion of Chesterfield and Montesquieu on, 214, of Louis Riccoboni, 217, of Louis Racine, 218, of abbé Le Blanc, 219 ; his style, 219 ; early French translations, 220, by La Place, 220 ff. ; the "Journal de Trévoux" and F. du Bocage, on, 224 ; his "dramatis personæ," 247 ; imitated by Voltaire, 249, the Shakespeare question in France, 269, his works in the library of ladies, 270 ; Shakespeare and Corneille, 276 ; opinion of the "Journal Encyclopédique," 276, of the "Journal Anglais," 278 ; his sonnets translated, 278 ; extracts from, 278 ; Patu on, 279 ; his plays remodelled in London, 282 ; Garrick interprets, 288 ff. ; French and English critics on, after 1750, 298 ff. ; opinion of Hume and Pope, 299, of Gildon, Gibbon, Morellet, Garrick, 300 ff. ; temple to, 301 ; a model of "sombre," 322 ff.; opinion of Delille, 322 ; 326, 329 ; war à propos of ; sham war, le Blanc, 330 ff. ; Cubières, 341 ff. ; Garrick's remodellings, 334, Shakespeare and Racine, 337 ; mixes tragedy and comedy, 338 ; his battles and ghosts, 339 ; translated by Le Tourneur, 354 ff. ; real war and its causes, 357 ff., his partisans, 359, 361 ff., his jubilee, 362 ff., opinion of the Encyclopædists, of Diderot, Suard, and Marmontel, 2, 366, 367, of Voltaire ; Gille-Shakespeare, 370 ff., Voltaire on the jubilee, 380 ; Shakespeare has sparks of genius, 384. Voltaire's second campaign, 388 ff. ; opinion of Sedaine, 398, of the "Année Littéraire," 398 ; the quarrel after Voltaire's death, 399 ff. ; defended by Elizab. Montagu, by Rutledge and Bareti, 399, 400 ; judgment of Mercier, 403, of Rivarol, 405 ; admitted to the French play-house, 405 ff., studied by the Marquise de Gléon, 411 ; adapted by Chastellux, 408, by Douin, 411, by Butini, 412, La Place, 413, Collot d'Herbois, 414, De Rozoi, 413, Rochon de Chabannes, 414, Ducis, 415 ff. ; opinion of M. J. Chénier, 441, of Châteaubriand, 443, a gothic cathedral, 444, and Glück, 445 ; adapted during the French Revolution, 446, performed in English in Paris, and hissed, 450 ff., and applauded, 454 ff. ; Berlioz, Dumas, Hugo, the Duc de Broglie, Ch. Magnin, Lamartine, Flaubert on Shakespeare, 455 ff. ; text of, printed in Paris, 456 ; recent adapters, 463 ff. ; Sunday performances, 467

INDEX

"Shakespeare amoureux," by Duval, 447
"Shakesperiana," Thimm's, 407
"Shylock," by Haraucourt, 464
Siddons, Mrs., 282, 317, as lady Macbeth, 426
Sidney, Sir Philip, xiii, friend of Du Bartas, 27, 33, 57 ff., 69, 121, 175
"Siège de Calais," by De Belloy, 295, 367
Silhouette, translates Pope, 184
"Silvanire" of Mairet, 88
Simond, L., 426
"Sir Politick Wouldbe," by St. Evremond, 162
Sirven, 296
Skelton, 4, 18
"Skialetheia," by Guilpin, 18
Smith, Richard, 57
„ Sir Thomas, 6
„ Miss L. T., 170
Smithson, miss (Madame Berlioz), xxviii, 455, 456, 457
Socrates, 108
"Soltane," la, by Bounin, 46, 52, 78, 80
Sombre, the, in literature, 322 ff., 329, 424 ff.
Sophocles, 177, 208, 218, 245, 268, 467
"Sophonisbe," by Mairet, 88
Sorbières, 130, 136 ff., on English drama, 163 ff., 144, 157, 214
Soulié, Eudore, 51
Souriau, 455
Soury, J., 306
Spaniards, 28 ff.
Spanish, known, under Louis XIV., 116 ff.

"Spectateur François," le, of Marivaux, 186
"Spectator," 167, mentions Shakespeare, 178 ; 184
Spelman, 174
Spenser, Ed., 18, 175, 278
Sports, 203, 274, see Games
Staël, Madame de, 316, 445
Stage, men of quality on the, xviii, xx, 153 ff., 253, 255, freed, 256 ; English, 252 ; see murder, tragedy, comedy, plays, scenery, theatre
Stair, earl of, 204
Starkey, 31
Steele, 238
Stendhal, 317, 449 ff., 451 ff.
Sterne, 281 ff., 284 ff., in France, 362, on French tragedies, 406
Stillingfleet, 166
Stratford-on-Avon, 1, 2, 137, 362
Suard, 276, 362, 365, 398, 411
Suckling, 176
Suicide, in England, 125, 203 ff., 345 ; on the stage, 320 ; Napoléon and suicide, 321 ; Hamlet on, 373
"Sultana," the, by Ch. Johnson, 337
"Supplément du Génie," le, by Le Blanc, 337 ff.
Surrey, earl of, 6
Swift, 181, 184, 200, 267, 337
"Sylvanire," la, by d'Urfé
Sylvester, J., 19, 21

T

"Tableau de Paris" of Mercier, 274, 403
Taine, 143, 278
"Tale of a Tub," 181

Talma, 316, his acting, 317, as Othello, 433, as Hamlet, 437, 447
Talon, Omer, 143
"Tambour Nocturne," le, by Destouches, 188, 238
"Taming of the Shrew," 278, 301, 463
"Tancrède," by Voltaire, 247, 305
Tardieu, A. P., 201
"Tartufe," 349
Tasso, 118, 119
"Tattler," 184
Taverns, English, 10, 283
"Télémaque," Fénelon's, 119
"Tempest," the, 177, 216, 232, 358, 414
Temple, Sir W., 120, 166, 176
Tencin, Madame de, 284, 299
Terence, 73, 177
Terry, actor, in Paris, 455
Texte, J., on Rousseau, 2 ; 176
"Théâtre anglois" of La Place, 220
Theatre, English, modifies the French, 319 ff. ; mutual borrowings, 330 ff., Voltaire's opinion concerning the English, 383 ff. ; French, its present fame, 466
Theatres, in Southwark, xi, in London, 37 ff., St. Amant on the English, 126 ff., English, seventeenth century, 154 ff. ; 191 ff. ; English eighteenth century, 282 ; in Paris, xiv, xv, 36 ff., 66, embellished, 88, 89 ; in Italy, xvi, 98, 99 ; built by Voltaire, xvi, 241
Theobald, Lewis, xxiv, 329

Thiériot, 209, 213
Thimm, 407
Thomas, Ambroise, 464
"Thomas Morus," by Puget de la Serre, 78
Thou, de (Thuanus), 30
Tickell, 119
Tillotson, 168
"Timocrate," by T. Corneille, 226
"Timon," Shakespeare's, 241 ; Mercier's, 439
Titus Livius, 169
"Toison d'or," la, by P. Corneille, 226
Toland, 168
"Tombeaux de Vérone," les, Mercier's, 439
"Tom Jones," 269, 297, on the French stage, 317, 318
"Tom Jones à Londres," by Desforges, 407
Tonson, J., 170, 182
"Tottel's Miscellany," 16
Tourneux, M., 398, 424
Tourval, 22, 120
Tragedy-ies, classical, in France and in England, 34 ff. ; murders in French, 251 ff. ; its rules, 311, and drama, 317 ff. ; domestic, 319 ; French adapted in England, 334 ff. ; and comedy mixed, 338 ; Mercier on, 367 ff. ; popularity of, in France, 406
Travellers, English in France, 5 ; French in Italy, in England, 7, 8, 11 ff., 123 ff., 131 ff., 138 ff., 275, 280 ff.
"Triomphe de Sophocle," le, by Palissot, 392

INDEX

Tronchin, 368, 398
Tunbridge Wells, described, 191
Turgot, 359
"Tyr et Sidon," by Schélandre, 74, 238

U

Ughes, Thomas, 34
Ugolino, 424, 425
Unities, 33 ff., 101 ff., 112 ff.; *see* Rules
Urfé, d', 77, 103, 230, 306
"Utopia," More's, 30

V

Valmont, A. de, 457
Vanel, 165
"Vathek," 96
Vauquelin de la Fresnaye, 31, 33, 46
Vauxhall, English, 377, 380; French, 380, 381
Vega, Lope de, 73, 208, 245, 334
"Venice Preserved," 168, 179, 192, 220, 252, 297, 338
Vergne, Madame, 456
"Vérité dans le Vin," la, by Collé, 291
Versailles, gardens of, 465
Verses, French alexandrine, 163, 246, 346, 454, 469; blank, 77, 163, 221, 230, Voltaire on, 247, of fourteen syllables, 78, opinion of Boileau, 105 ff., of Descartes, 108
Vesel, C. de, 6
Vestris, Madame, as Irène, 393, as lady Macbeth, 426, 431
Vicenza, theatre at, xvi, 98, 99
"Victim," the, by Ch. Johnson, 338

Victoire, Madame, 306
Vigny, A. de, 456, 463
Villegagnon, 25, 132
Villeray, Le Coq de, 213
Villette, Marquise de, 389
Villevieille, Marquis de, 387
Virgil, 117, 119, 400
Visé, Donneau de, 104
"Visionnaires," les, by St. Sorlin, 97 ff., 346, 347
Visionnaires, quarrel of the, 111 ff.
Visscher, Claes Jan, xi, 37
Voiture, 123
Voltaire, portraits of, xix, xxi, xxv, xxvi, 201, 285, 363, 385; 47, 96, 143, 179, 180, 183; in England, 200 ff.; 216, 217, his tearful plays, 237, 342; and Mlle. Clairon, xx, 239; fond of the stage, 241 ff.; his activity, 244; on dramatic art, 246; his tragedies, his literary reforms, 247 ff.; his knowledge of English, 267; on travelling, 275; his "Appel à toutes les Nations," 276; as a tragic actor, 286 ff.; on De Belloy, 295, on Garrick, 301, in tears, 305; 310, 312, 315, on La Chaussée, 317; against tragedies in prose, 318; on Canada, 329; on sombre dramas, 343; on Le Tourneur's translation, 354 ff.; leads the war against Shakespeare, 357 ff.; statue of, by Pigalle, 363, 365; skirmishes with Elizabeth Montagu, and Walpole, 369 ff.; first Letter to the Academy, 376 ff.; portrait of, shortly before his

death, 385; his success, 387; second campaign, 388 ff., crowned at the French Comedy, 389 ff.; his second Letter, 395 ff.; proposes a reform of the Dictionary, and dies, 397; various replies to the letters of, 399 ff.; on patriotism, 403; Ducis and, 415; 443, 464
"Voyage philosophique," by La Coste, 282 ff.

W

Wallack, his troupe, 463
Waller, 130, 133 ff., 136, 176, 183
Walpole, H., 270, 284, 295, 297, skirmishes with Voltaire, 369 ff., 373
Ward, sculptor, xxii
Warton, T., 279
Warwick, 28

Whitehead, 279, 334, 335 ff.
William the Conqueror, 31
William III., 175
Wilson, B., painter, 417
"Winter's Tale," xii, xiii, 39 ff., 69 ff., 216
Women, English, their beauty, 10, 139, too many blondes, 139, love bloodshed, 144, manners of, 151
Wotton, W., 181
Wyatt, Sir T., 4, 18, 30, 60, 181
Wycherley, 161, 224, 329, 334

Y

Yart, abbé, 225, 272
Young, his cave, xxiv; 272, 330, 349, 351

Z

"Zaïre," Voltaire's, 240, 241, 250, 251, 374, 432

COPENHAGEN, *February*, 1899.

www.ingramcontent.com/pod-product-compliance
Lightning Source LLC
Chambersburg PA
CBHW031948290426
44108CB00011B/725